D0724448

San Francisco

www.timeout.com/san-francisco

Time Out Digital Ltd
4th Floor
125 Shaftesbury Avenue
London WC2H 8AD
United Kingdom
Tel: +44 (0)20 7813 3000
Fax: +44 (0)20 7813 6001
Email: guides@timeout.com
www.timeout.com

Published by Time Out Digital Ltd, a wholly owned subsidiary
of Time Out Group Ltd. Time Out and the Time Out logo are
trademarks of Time Out Group Ltd.

© **Time Out Group Ltd 2016**
Previous editions 1996, 1998, 2000, 2002, 2004, 2006, 2008, 2011.

10 9 8 7 6 5 4 3 2 1

This edition first published in Great Britain in 2016 by Ebury Publishing.
20 Vauxhall Bridge Road, London SW1V 2SA

Ebury Publishing is part of the Penguin Random House group of companies
whose addresses can be found at global.penguinrandomhouse.com

Distributed in the US and Latin America by Publishers Group West
(1-510-809-3700)

For further distribution details, see www.timeout.com.

ISBN: 978-1-84670-362-1

A CIP catalogue record for this book is available from the British Library.

Printed and bound in China by Leo Paper Products Ltd.

Penguin Random House is committed to a sustainable future for our
business, our readers and our planet. This book is made from Forest
Stewardship Council® certified paper.

MIX
Paper from
responsible sources
FSC® C018179

Contents

264

94

119

249

285

Essential Information 270

Maps 306

Time Out San Francisco

Editorial
Editor Bonnie Wach
Listings Editor Adam Brinklow
Proofreader Nicholas Royle

Editorial Director Sarah Guy
Group Finance Manager Margaret Wright
North American Guides Editor Lisa Ritchie

Design
Art Editor Christie Webster
Group Commercial Senior Designer Jason Tansley

Picture Desk
Picture Editor Jael Marschner
Deputy Picture Editor Ben Rowe
Picture Researcher Lizzy Owen

Advertising
Managing Director St John Betteridge
Advertising Sales Mathew Jongsma at
The Advertorialists

Marketing
Senior Publishing Brand Manager Luthfa Begum
Head of Circulation Dan Collins

Production
Production Controller Katie Mulhern-Bhudia

Time Out Group
Founder Tony Elliott
Executive Chairman Julio Bruno
Chief Executive Officer Noel Penzer
Publisher Alex Batho

Contributors
San Francisco's Top 20 Bonnie Wach. **San Francisco Today** Bonnie Wach. **Itineraries** Bonnie Wach. **Diary** Bonnie Wach and contributors to *Time Out San Francisco*. **Explore** Bonnie Wach and contributors to *Time Out San Francisco* (*Taking Modern to the Max* Adam Brinklow). **Children** Bonnie Wach. **Film** Bonnie Wach and contributors to *Time Out San Francisco* (*Essential San Francisco Films* Joshua Rothkopf). **Gay & Lesbian** Adam Brinklow. **Nightlife** Laura Mason. **Performing Arts** Adam Brinklow. **Escapes & Excursions** Bonnie Wach and contributors to *Time Out San Francisco*. **History** Michael Ansaldo. **Architecture** Matt Markovich. **Hotels** Bonnie Wach and contributors to *Time Out San Francisco*.

Maps JS Graphics Ltd (john@jsgraphics.co.uk)

Cover and pull-out map photography © Masterfile

Back Cover Photography Clockwise from top left: Barry J Holmes; Andrew Zarivny/Shutterstock.com; San Francisco Travel Association/Scott Chernis; Joseph Sohm/Shutterstock.com; blvdone/Shutterstock.com

Photography pages 4 Anthony Hall/Shutterstock.com; 5 (top), 11, 94 f11photo/Shutterstock.com; 5 (bottom right), 272, 274, 275, 285 Hans Kwiotek; 7 blvdone/Shutterstock.com; 10/11 Stuart Monk/Shutterstock.com; 12 (bottom) Cesar Rubio; 13 (left), 28/29, 66/67 Joseph Sohm/Shutterstock.com; 13 (right) meunierd/Shutterstock.com; 14 (top) Asta Karalis; 14/15 © Kyle Jeffers; 15 Brocken Inaglory/Wikimedia Commons; 17 (top), 100 (bottom) Stacey Lewis; 17 (bottom left), 136, 137 Ed Anderson; 17 (bottom right) Dylan + Jeni; 18/19 Stelian Popa/Shutterstock.com; 21 victorgrigas/Wikimedia Commons; 22/23, 26 (top), 40/41, 100 (top), 192, 199 San Francisco Travel Association/ Scott Chernis; 24, 55, 72, 73 Barry J Holmes; 24/25 Jorg Hackemann/Shutterstock.com; 25 (left), 244 Wollertz/ Shutterstock.com; 25 (right) Sociopath987/Shutterstock.com; 26 (bottom), 254, 259 Wikimedia Commons; 27 (top left) Michael KC Wong; 27 (top right), 68, 69 Courtesy of The Contemporary Jewish Museum/Bruce Damonte; 27 (bottom left) Asif Islam/Shutterstock.com; 31 (top), 86 San Francisco Travel Association/Can Balcioglu; 32 Larry Ye/ Shutterstock.com; 33 quinn.anya/Wikimedia Commons; 34 Al83tito/Wikimedia Commons; 35 (top) Jere/Wikimedia Commons; 35 (bottom) Kobby Dagan/Shutterstock.com; 36/37 (bottom), 301 Courtesy of the Fine Arts Museums of San Francisco; 38 (bottom) Tev Lee Photography; 39 © Tim Griffith ; 42 Gayle Laird; 44 © Eugene Borodin; 45 Courtesy of Café Claude; 48 Pius Lee/Shutterstock.com; 52 Binksternet/Wikimedia Commons; 56, 57 Eric Wolfinger; 63 Oscity/ Shutterstock.com; 79 (left) Lauri Levenfeld/Zoom Photography; 79 (right), 165 (bottom) Aubrie Pick; 80, 81 Bonjwing Photography Saison; 82 21st Amendment Brewery; 83 (left) MIR and Snøhetta; 83 (right) Steelblue; 84/85 Capture Light/Shutterstock.com; 88 (left) Rob Hyndman; 90 © Robert Harding Picture Library Ltd/Alamy; 92/93 Supercarwaar/ Wikimedia Commons; 94/95 Alejandro De La Cruz/Wikimedia Commons; 105 MKawanophotography; 106 © Danita Delimont/Alamy; 108, 142, 143, 306/307 Elan Fleisher; 111 (top) Another Believer/Wikimedia Commons; 111 (bottom) Dominic Simpson/Wikimedia Commons; 112 Günter Waibel; 114, 115 (left and bottom right) Mariko Reed; 115 (top right) James Slim Dang; 125 Molly DeCoudreaux Photography; 129 Gamma Nine Photography; 130/131 Tupungato/Shutterstock.com; 135 Kelly Ishikawa; 147 ChameleonsEye/Shutterstock.com; 148 nito/Shutterstock. com; 154, 162 Matt Markovich; 154/155, 198 Luciano Mortula/Shutterstock.com; 165 (top) Tyler Gourley; 165 (middle) © Erin Kunkel; 166 Kelly Puleio; 170, 171 David Martinez; 174 Michael O'Neal; 184 (top) Kathryn Whitney/ California Academy of Sciences; 184 (bottom) Tim Griffith/California Academy of Sciences; 186 (left and top right) Jack Ma Studio; 186 (bottom right) Winnie Chien; 190/191, 227 Cory Weaver/San Francisco Opera; 193 (top left) Pacifica Arts, Inc.; 197 Wei Shi; 200 Gundolf Pfotenhauer; 201 Snap Stills/REX Shutterstock; 202 © Barak Shrama; 203 San Francisco Travel Association; 204, 205 Plateaueatplau/Wikimedia Commons; 206 © Dania Maxwell; 212 Meghan K Duffey; 213 Patrick Tiu/sf.infusionlounge.com; 214, 215 Natasha I Gillett; 216 (middle and bottom) © Dan Dion; 224 Richard Barnes; 226 photo.ua/Shutterstock.com; 229 David Allen; 230 Bruce Damonte; 232, 233 David Wilson; 239 Frank Schulenburg/Wikimedia Commons; 252/253 Dorothea Lange/Everett Historical/Shutterstock.com; 257 Everett Historical/Shutterstock.com; 260 Michael Ochs Archives/Getty Images; 262 LPS.1/Wikimedia Commons; 266 Carol M. Highsmith/Buyenlarge/Getty Images; 273 Patricia Parinejad; 288, 289 Joie de Vivre Hotels

The following images were supplied by the featured establishments: 5 (bottom left), 30, 31 (bottom), 38 (top), 51, 58, 64, 65, 66, 74, 75, 76, 77, 84, 88 (right), 99, 104, 118, 119, 122, 134, 140, 152, 160, 161, 169, 176, 177, 178, 183, 193 (bottom left and right), 195, 207, 208, 210, 211, 216 (top), 218/219, 223, 258, 270/271, 278, 279, 281, 282, 286, 287.

About the Guide

GETTING AROUND

Each sightseeing chapter contains a street map of the area marked with the locations of sights and museums (❶), restaurants and cafés (❶), bars (❶) and shops (❶). There are also street maps of San Francisco at the back of the book, along with an overview map of the city. In addition, there is a detachable fold-out street map.

THE ESSENTIALS

For practical information, including visas, disabled access, emergency numbers, lost property, websites and local transport, see the Essential Information section. It begins on page 270.

THE LISTINGS

Addresses, phone numbers, websites, transport information, hours and prices are all included in our listings, as are selected other facilities. All were checked and correct at press time. However, business owners can alter their arrangements at any time, and fluctuating economic conditions can cause prices to change rapidly.

The very best venues in the city, the must-sees and must-dos in every category, have been marked with a red star (★). In the sightseeing chapters, we've also marked venues with free admission with a FREE symbol.

PHONE NUMBERS

The area codes for San Francisco are 415 and 628. Even if you're dialling from within the area you're calling, you'll need to use the area code, always preceded by 1. From outside the US, dial your country's international access code (00 from the UK) or a plus symbol, followed by the number as listed in the guide; here, the initial '1' serves as the US country code. So, to reach the Asian Art Museum, dial + 1-415 581 3500.

FEEDBACK

We welcome feedback on this guide, both on the venues we've included and on any other locations that you'd like to see featured in future editions. Please email us at guides@timeout.com.

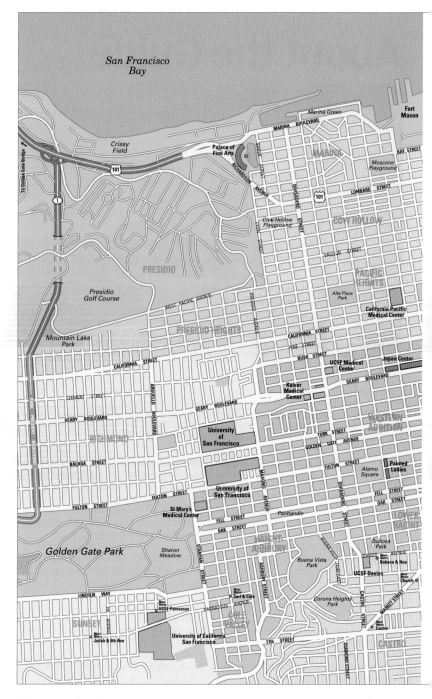

San Francisco
Bay

Fort
Mason

Marina Green

Crissy
Field

Palace of
Fine Arts

MARINA

BAY STREET

Moscone
Playground

LOMBARD STREET

Cow Hollow
Playground

COW HOLLOW

VALLEJO STREET

PRESIDIO

PACIFIC
HEIGHTS

Alta Plaza
Park

Presidio
Golf Course

WEST PACIFIC AVENUE

California Pacific
Medical Center

Mountain Lake
Park

PRESIDIO HEIGHTS

CALIFORNIA STREET

PINE STREET

BUSH STREET

CALIFORNIA STREET

UCSF Medical
Center

Japan Center

GEARY BOULEVARD

CLEMENT STREET

Kaiser
Medical
Center

GEARY BOULEVARD

RICHMOND

University
of
San Francisco

WESTERN
ADDITION

TURK STREET

GOLDEN GATE AVENUE

BALBOA STREET

FULTON STREET

Alamo
Square

Painted
Ladies

University of
San Francisco

FELL STREET

FULTON STREET

St Mary's
Medical Center

Panhandle

OAK STREET

LOWER
HAIGHT

OAK STREET

Golden Gate Park

Sharon
Meadow

HAIGHT-
ASHBURY

Buena Vista
Park

Duboce
Park

Duboce & Noe

UCSF Davies

LINCOLN WAY

Corona Heights
Park

Castro & Cole

UCSF Parnassus

PARNASSUS AVENUE

COLE
VALLEY

SUNSET

Judah & 9th Ave

University of California
San Francisco

17th STREET

CASTRO

0   ¼   ½ mile
0   1 km
© Copyright Time Out Group 2016

Aquatic
Park

San Francisco
Bay

Pier
39

FISHERMAN'S
WHARF

JEFFERSON   STREET   THE   EMBARCADERO

NORTH POINT STREET

BAY   STREET

Russian
Hill Park

San Francisco
Art Institute

NORTH
BEACH

Lombard Street

COLUMBUS

Coit Tower

BATTERY   STREET

RUSSIAN
HILL

Washington
Square

THE   EMBARCADERO

VALLEJO   AVENUE

LARKIN   STREET

POLK   STREET

HYDE   STREET

LEAVENWORTH   STREET

FRANKLIN   STREET

BROADWAY

VALLEJO   STREET

BROADWAY

EMBARCADERO

PACIFIC   AVENUE

Jackson
Square

Transamerica
Pyramid

Ferry Building

JACKSON   STREET

Portsmouth
Square

FINANCIAL
DISTRICT

101

Lafayette
Park

NOB
HILL

CHINATOWN

SANSOME   STREET

BATTERY   STREET

Metro
BART
Embarcadero

STEUART   STREET

Metro
O. Folsom

PACIFIC
HEIGHTS

Huntington
Park

PINE   STREET

KEARNY   STREET

BEALE   STREET

Bay Bridge

St Francis Memorial
Hospital

BUSH   STREET

FREMONT   STREET

SUTTER   STREET

UNION
SQUARE

1st   STREET

THE   EMBARCADERO

TAYLOR   STREET

GEARY   STREET

2nd   STREET

Metro
BART
Montgomery

VAN   NESS   AVENUE

GEARY   STREET

TENDERLOIN

SFMOMA

3rd   STREET

HOWARD   STREET

Metro
Brannan

St Mary's
Cathedral

LARKIN   STREET

POLK   STREET

LEAVENWORTH   STREET

Yerba
Buena
Gardens

FOLSOM   STREET

Jefferson
Square

i

Metro
BART
Powell

HARRISON   STREET

SOMA

BRYANT   STREET

FRANKLIN   STREET

GOLDEN   GATE   AVENUE

Asian Art
Museum

5th   STREET

South
Park

SOUTH
BEACH

Metro
2nd & King

City Hall

CIVIC
CENTER

Metro
BART
Civic Center

4th   STREET

BRANNAN   STREET

KING   ST

AT & T
Park

China
Basin

CalTrain
Depot

Metro
4th & King

HAYES
VALLEY

Metro
Van Ness

80

6th   STREET

3rd   ST

Metro
Mission Rock

MARKET   STREET

HOWARD   STREET

FOLSOM   STREET

BRYANT   STREET

BRANNAN   STREET

UCSF Mission Bay

101

14th   STREET

16th   STREET

UPPER
MARKET

GUERRERO   STREET

SOUTH   VAN   NESS   AVENUE

16th   STREET

Franklin
Square

POTRERO   AVENUE

16th   STREET

Jackson
Park

280

Metro
Mariposa

Central
Basin

Mission
Dolores

16th   STREET

Mission Dolores
BART

17th   STREET

MISSION

3rd   ST

POTRERO   HILL

Metro
26th St

Dolores
Park

101

San Francisco's Top 20

From iconic sights to culinary lights, we count down the essentials.

1 Golden Gate Bridge
(page 127)

The most photographed bridge in the world, the city's twin-towered icon was once dubbed by late columnist Herb Caen as the 'car-strangled spanner'. Regardless of traffic, there's nothing so glorious as driving – or walking – across the Golden Gate at sunset, as the city skyline dances on the waves and the fog creeps over the hills.

2 Cable cars
(page 48)

Cliché though it may be, riding on the cable cars that Andrew Hallidie built to scale San Francisco's steepest slopes is still a thrill. Hang off the running boards, Doris Day-style, as the conductor clangs the bell, and see if you don't get a little lump in your throat.

3 Alcatraz
(page 107)

The island prison in the middle of the Bay draws more than 16 million visitors each year to its haunting cell blocks, where inmates such as Al Capone, George 'Machine Gun' Kelly and Robert 'The Birdman' Stroud did time. 'The Rock' has been chronicled in numerous films, but there's nothing like hearing first-hand (via audio tour) from former inmates and guards what living there was really like.

5

4 Ferry Building Marketplace
(page 61)

The historic clock tower that presides over the Port of San Francisco not only lures the city's produce-obsessed on farmers' market days, but all week long for locavore restaurants and artisan food vendors selling olive oil, goat's cheese, bread, chocolate, oysters, coffee, ice-cream and other delights.

5 Golden Gate Park
(page 181)

The city's collective backyard, Golden Gate Park was transformed in the late 19th century from a barren sand dune into a lush greenbelt that spreads out over three miles of landscaped gardens, forests and meadows. Wander past botanical and Japanese gardens, windmills, a herd of bison, a Victorian

6

conservatory, earthquake relics and two of the city's most acclaimed museums, the de Young and the California Academy of Sciences.

6 War Memorial Opera House
(page 226)

The opera house opened in 1932 with a sold-out performance of Puccini's *Tosca* at the height of America's Great Depression and has been a huge hit ever since. Home to both the San Francisco Opera and Ballet, its graceful gilded halls continue to host envelope-pushing productions, and with the recent opening of the intimate Center for the Opera, the repertoire promises to expand further.

7 AT&T Park
(page 77)

Even if you know nothing about home runs and fly balls, you should include a game at AT&T Park on your agenda. Set on the docks of San Francisco Bay, the park affords fantastic views of

the waterfront, with kayakers and paddle-boarders chasing each other to retrieve 'splash hits' over the right-field fence. And what other ballpark offers flatbreads topped with organic veggies from its own garden in the outfield?

8 Cocktails in SoMa
(pages 73-76)

San Francisco's mixologists were at the forefront of the craft cocktail movement, championing fresh-squeezed, herb-infused and hand-muddled drinks long before it was trendy. In SoMa, Bar Agricole's cocktail list of spirits, vermouths, bitters and syrups is carefully curated down to the ice cubes tailored to each drink.

9 De Young Museum
(page 184)

Built in 1894, the city's premier fine arts museum underwent a complete overhaul in 2005 that brought it firmly

12

15

into the 21st century. Its provocative perforated-copper skin and futuristic tower are designed to develop a patina with age, but still pale next to the vast collections of painting, sculpture, craft and textiles within – some 27,000 works from Africa, Oceania and the Americas dating from the 17th to the 20th centuries.

10 Mission Dolores
(page 157)

The oldest building in San Francisco, humble adobe Mission Dolores is the sixth of 21 California missions founded by Spanish padres in 1776, when the rest of America was in the midst of declaring its independence. Stroll out to the garden cemetery to visit the graves of the city's founding fathers, as well as the mass burial site of 5,000 converted Ohlone natives who perished from disease and poor living conditions.

11 Coit Tower
(page 101)

Brave the steep climb up to this iconic Telegraph Hill monument – a gift to the city from eccentric local character Lillie Hitchcock Coit – for a sweeping panorama. The views aren't the only attraction, though. Inside, the 1930s

murals depicting censorship, oppressed workers and economic disparities confirm San Francisco as a place where left-leaning politics thrive.

12 Mission District dining
(pages 158-165)

The über-hip Mission District has become a breeding ground for artisanal foods and creative gastronomy. Wend your way through house-made pastas and pizza at Flour + Water, shattering croissants at Tartine Bakery, pink grapefruit and tarragon ice-cream at Humphry Slocombe, and date-stamped espresso at Sightglass Coffee.

11

13 Exploratorium
(page 59)

Stretching the length of three football fields along the Embarcadero waterfront, this science nerds' mecca features more than 600 interactive exhibits to challenge your powers of perception and the laws of physics. Take a break on the second-floor Bay Observatory, where you get a spectacular perspective on the geography and ecology of San Francisco Bay.

14 Alamo Square
(page 132)

The line of colourful Victorian homes that front the city skyline on Alamo Square is known as Postcard Row, featured in dozens of TV shows, commercials and films through the years. Explore a little beyond the block of Painted Ladies to discover some of the city's oldest and most architecturally interesting houses – mansions that were miraculously spared by the ravages of the 1906 earthquake and fire.

15 SFJAZZ Center
(page 223)

One step into this sleek concert hall and you'll understand why jazz heavyweights around the world are clamouring to play here, and why it's one of the hottest tickets in town. Opened in 2013, it offers pitch-perfect acoustics and unobstructed sightlines from every seat in the house – plus, you can sip a cocktail while savouring the music.

16 California Academy of Sciences
(page 182)

The Academy combines a natural history museum, aquarium, planetarium and scientific research programme under one 'living' roof – an undulating canopy made up of thousands of native plants. The state-of-the-art 'green' design includes a four-storey rainforest with free-flitting butterflies and birds, the world's deepest living coral reef display, and a café offering dozens of sustainable (and tasty) dining options.

17 Ocean Beach
(page 180)

Though the famous fog can sometimes make San Francisco's coastline a down-parka experience, more often than not temperatures are T-shirt perfect for strolling along uncrowded Ocean Beach. Afterwards, stop by the historic

19 Union Square shopping
(pages 49-51)

The divas of fashion take up residence around Union Square, especially along the upscale alley of Maiden Lane. Once a degenerate red-light district of the Barbary Coast, the side street now houses Chanel, Marc Jacobs, Hermès, Prada and many other top designers.

Beach Chalet, where you can gaze out at the waves while quaffing a house-brewed IPA.

18 City Lights
(page 100)

Founded in 1953, this bookshop and temple to the Beat Generation was the nation's first all-paperback bookstore. Step inside and you can practically hear it howl with progressive politics, fiction, music, philosophy and all manner of poetry and literary voices (Allen Ginsberg's earth-shaking *Howl* was in fact first published here in 1955).

20 State Bird Provisions/ The Progress
(page 137)

Chefs Stuart Brioza and Nicole Krasinski helped transform the struggling Fillmore District with State Bird Provisions, their wildly imaginative take on American dim sum. Then in 2015, they opened next-door sister restaurant the Progress, and turned the notion of family-style dining on its over-sauced ear. Together they make two of the most exciting dining options this food-savvy city has to offer.

San Francisco
Today

Thanks to a tech-fuelled 21st-century Gold Rush, the city is gleaming.

TEXT: BONNIE WACH

The only thing that's truly predictable about San Francisco is that things here are never predictable. A few years back, a triumphant comeback from the bleak economic recession of the mid-noughties seemed inconceivable. Yet the city not only recovered, it went roaring straight into another Gold Rush, defying even its own most optimistic predictions.

Web 2.0 is in now full swing, with techies pouring into town and signing leases on scads of new condo and loft developments, often before the paint in the new units has had a chance to dry. With San Francisco's population at a current all-time high (nearly 850,000), there's just not enough housing to go around, forcing rents and home prices to skyrocket and the working classes to flee to more hospitable climes in Oakland and beyond.

de Young | Legion of Honor

FINE ARTS MUSEUMS OF SAN FRANCISCO

Stunning Views and Exceptional Exhibitions

© Fine Arts Museums of San Francisco

de Young

The de Young features art from all over the world and boasts 360-degree views of San Francisco.

Oscar de la Renta
MARCH 12–MAY 30, 2016

Ed Ruscha and the Great American West
JULY 16–OCTOBER 9, 2016

For more information visit **deyoungmuseum.org**

Photograph by Steve Whittaker © Fine Arts Museums of San Francisco

Legion of Honor

The Legion of Honor overlooks the Golden Gate Bridge and features a collection that spans 4,000 years of ancient and European art.

Sublime Beauty: Raphael's "Portrait of a Lady with a Unicorn"
JANUARY 9–APRIL 10, 2016

Pierre Bonnard: Painting Arcadia
FEBRUARY 6–MAY 15, 2016

For more information visit **legionofhonor.org**

Clarion Alley.

HOME TWEET HOME

The influx of tech into the city is being led by mega companies like Google, Salesforce and Twitter, the latter having moved into swanky new headquarters in the derelict mid-Market Street district in exchange for generous tax breaks. Their residence, however, has also jumpstarted much-welcomed redevelopment and upgrades in the area around Civic Center and the Tenderloin.

Meanwhile, the building frenzy South of Market Street that began with South Beach and China Basin in the early 2000s continues at breakneck speed. Just across Lefty O'Doul drawbridge, the 303-acre swathe of the new Mission Bay development includes a massive research campus and hospital for the University of California, blocks of biotech office space, more than 6,500 condos and lofts, trendy restaurants and bars, retail outlets, markets, a public library and a new Metro line. Within the next several years, Mission Bay will likely add to that an enormous arena for the Golden State Warriors basketball team, and a waterfront park, brewery and shopping/dining complex next to AT&T baseball park. Another area

that has been transformed by rapid gentrification is the Mission District, once a working-class barrio filled with taquerias, dollar stores, strolling mariachis and dive bars. These days, millennials with stock options line up at bus stops to board luxury commuter coaches, and sip craft cocktails at trendy restaurants and bars. The new monied denizens are willing to pay top dollar for their Victorian apartments, fuelling evictions, driving up rents, and further escalating the separation of the haves from the have-nots – in 2015, a one-bedroom apartment in the Mission was renting for upwards of $3,500 a month, while Facebook founder Mark Zuckerberg was widely reported to have paid $10 million for a modest manse overlooking the Mission on Liberty Hill.

Not surprisingly, not all of these changes have gone over well with longtime residents. Corporate shuttles have sparked numerous protests by enraged Muni riders demanding that private companies pay to use public bus stops. And along mural-covered Clarion Alley, activist artists are using their brushes to protest income inequality, corporate takeovers, evictions and all manner of social ills.

Bay Bridge.

SKY-HIGH ASPIRATIONS

Perhaps the most telltale sign of the upbeat economy is the rapidly changing skyline. The Transamerica Pyramid, once the definitive exclamation point in a city fairly devoid of skyscrapers, is rapidly being eclipsed by a series of larger, imposing structures that were begun during the last big boom in the 1990s. The obelisk-like tower of One Rincon Hill next to the Bay Bridge looms some 641 feet above the Bay. When completed in 2018, Salesforce Tower, adjacent to the Transbay Transit Center complex currently under construction south of Mission Street, will rise 1,070 feet behind a quarter-mile-long terminal and a 5.4-acre rooftop park. The so-called 'Grand Central Terminal of the West' will occupy more than a million square feet and be covered by a unique undulating, perforated white-metal skin.

GOING FOR GREEN

The almighty dollar is not the only green making headlines in San Francisco these days. The city's long-held reputation as a bastion for the eco-conscious and conscientious is being reaffirmed in compostable spades. The ongoing drought has taken its toll on lawns and extra glasses of water at restaurants, but San Franciscans remain committed to conservation, leading the state in reducing water consumption even without mandatory rationing. And while climate change is still being hotly debated in Washington, California Governor Jerry Brown has committed to drastically cutting greenhouse gas emissions by 40 percent by 2030, and 80 percent below 1990 levels by 2050. The state is already on track to exceed those goals, hitting 1990 levels by 2020.

San Francisco's Zero Waste programme sets the bar even higher, vowing to make San Francisco waste-free – with nothing incinerated or sent to landfill – by the year 2020. To achieve that target, civic leaders have implemented a number of radical green initiatives over the years, including banning

VISITORS WELCOME

San Francisco has always been a top tourist destination, but the numbers have been climbing in recent years to historic highs. In 2014, more than 18 million visitors left their hearts and wallets in the city, an increase of 6.5 per cent over the previous year. Perhaps even more impressive, they spent $10.67 billion in the City by the Bay, a 13.7 per cent jump over 2013.

Among the biggest beneficiaries have been the city's restaurants. In this town of fanatical foodies, the latest celeb chef openings and of-the-moment dining trends are discussed and debated as hotly as politics. According to personal finance site Mint.com, San Franciscans outspent diners in other large US cities by a large margin in 2014, dropping $347 million at spots around town. Tourists, meanwhile, voted eating out as their top activity when visiting the city. Certainly, they have plenty of options to choose from: with more than 4,000 restaurants packed inside 49 square miles, San Francisco leads the nation in eateries per capita.

ART CITY

The arts have also benefited from the prosperous economy. South of Market Street, the Museum of Modern Art reopens in 2016 with a $600 million new addition by Oslo-based architecture firm Snøhetta that shows off its expanded collection like never before. SFMOMA joins the recently redesigned Museum of the African Diaspora and the über-modern Contemporary Jewish Museum in the expanding Yerba Buena arts district.

Further down on the Embarcadero, the *Bay Lights* sculpture by artist Leo Villareal that spans the Bay Bridge with 25,000 pulsing, sparkling LED lights, went dark in 2015. Happily, public outcry brought it back to life as a permanent installation in 2016, giving art lovers another great reason to stroll the grand waterfront promenade. The resurrection is somewhat ironic, given that when it was first proposed, installing the world's largest LED light sculpture on one of the world's busiest bridges seemed like a logistical impossibility. Never say never to San Franciscans. In a city where earthquakes, fires, economic booms and busts are as common as fog in July, it remains – as President William Howard Taft once said – the 'city that knows how'.

plastic bags and the use of styrofoam in restaurants, prohibiting the sale of plastic water bottles on public property, and of course mandatory recycling and composting.

'Sustainable', 'local', and 'organic' have long been buzz words in Bay Area restaurants, and used oil from deep-fryers now powers many of the city's buses, with the fleet on course to become 100 per cent emission-free by 2020. The boom of bike lanes – and the riders who use them – are also contributing to the reduction of emissions. The powerful SF Bicycle Coalition has spearheaded the Connecting the City campaign, expanding the streets with more than 50 miles of bike lanes and pathways by 2017.

Add to all this bans on smoking just about, well, everywhere, and a growing majority of buildings (including the newest airport terminal and AT&T Park) achieving environmental LEED certification, and the Bay Area has become, as one newspaper editorial put it, 'the world's last, best hope against climate change'.

Itineraries

Make the most of even the shortest SF stay with our two-day tour of the city.

Clockwise from right: **Blue Bottle Coffee; a rolling SF landmark; Fisherman's Wharf**.

9AM

11AM

Day 1

9AM Jumpstart your day with a Gibraltar at artisan roasters Blue Bottle Coffee in SoMa (p73). Then head to Union Square (p44), the city's high-end shopping enclave, and browse the boutiques along chic Maiden Lane. If you're thinking about hitting a show later, make a detour to the TIX kiosk on the west side of the square for discounted same-day theatre tickets. Then pop into the grand lobby of the historic Westin St Francis Hotel, where folks have been meeting under the grandfather clock for more than a century.

11AM From here, stroll to a cable car stop along Powell Street to ride on the world's first moving national historical landmark. To learn more about the history of the cable car, hop off at Mason Street and visit the Cable Car Museum (p86), where you can view Andrew Hallidie's original trolley and watch the giant turbines turning the cables under the street.

1PM From the cable car terminus near Fisherman's Wharf, walk down to Hyde Street Pier (p107) to see the historic ships that once plied the Pacific Coast. If you're feeling peckish, you can pick up a crab cocktail from a sidewalk vendor on Taylor and Jefferson streets. Afterwards, dip into Ghirardelli Square (p109), home of San Francisco's original chocolate maker, for a sweet pick-me-up. If you prefer something stronger, stop by the Buena Vista Café (p109) for a frothy Irish coffee. The bar was the first to serve the boozy hot beverage in America.

4PM Next, amble along Beach Street to Columbus Avenue and into North Beach, aka Little Italy (pp96-104). In the 1850s, the iconic neighbourhood was the heart of the city's notorious Barbary

Coast; a century later, it became the epicentre of the beat movement. Get a taste for its first incarnation at the 19th-century Comstock Saloon (p98), where you can sample a martinez, the 1850s predecessor to the martini. Then fast forward to City Lights (p100), the bookstore that launched the literary careers of Kerouac, Ginsberg and many other 1950s beat writers.

7PM North Beach abounds in both old- and new-school Italian restaurants. Tosca Café (p98) straddles both worlds, its acclaimed restaurant adding to the venerable bar that has stood here for nearly a century.

9PM Cap your evening with an espresso and pastry at one of the cafés around Columbus Avenue. Caffe Trieste and Caffe Puccini (both p101) are two longtime Italian favourites, both offering sidewalk seating with great people-watching.

8AM

Left: **Ferry Building**. Bottom: **Filbert Street Steps**.

Then double-back along the Embarcadero to test your skills of perception at the Exploratorium (p59), the city's renowned hands-on science museum.

2PM From here, head west to Sansome Street and climb the Filbert Street Steps through enchanted gardens to the top of Telegraph Hill and Coit Tower (p101). After you've soaked up the panoramic views of the city, spend time in the lobby admiring the restored 1930s frescoes before descending along the Greenwich Steps to the Embarcadero.

5PM If all that hill climbing has made you thirsty, catch a vintage F line streetcar to 4th and Market Streets in the SoMa District and take the elevator to the fifth floor of the Hotel Zelos to enjoy a hand-muddled craft cocktail from the sunken rooftop terrace of Dirty Habit (p74).

Day 2

8AM Get up early for the freshest picks at the farmers' market at the Ferry Building Marketplace (p61), which is also home to numerous gourmet purveyors and several top restaurants. After you've had your fill of organic produce and artisan-made edibles, walk it off on a stroll down the Embarcadero waterfront promenade.

11AM Start by heading south past Claes Oldenburg and Coosje van Bruggen's monumental *Cupid's Span* sculpture to AT&T Park (p77), the spectacular waterfront home of the San Francisco Giants baseball team (tours are offered daily except when there's an afternoon game). Grab a bite at fan favourite gastropub Public House (p79) near the statue of baseball legend Willie Mays.

7PM When you're ready for dinner, you'll fine no shortage of options in SoMa. Among the most popular are Marlowe (p78), where patrons pack in for chef Jennifer Puccio's creative American menu (don't miss the burgers or brussels sprouts chips), and Mourad (p73), where chef Mourad Lahlou dazzles with inventively interpreted Moroccan cuisine.

10PM Catch a show or dance off the calories in the clubs along 11th Street. Slim's (p219) is the spot for up-and-coming rockers, roots and blues. Or move your feet to a mash-up of musical genres at DNA Lounge (p220).

2PM

SAN FRANCISCO FOR FREE

Some of the best things in the city are literally priceless.

CASHLESS CULTURE

Many major museums waive admission fees on certain days of the month, including the de Young, the Contemporary Jewish Museum (both gratis on the first Tuesday of every month) and the Asian Art Museum (first Sunday of each month). In addition, smaller institutions such as the Cable Car Museum and the Musée Mécanique are always free.

WRITE IT OFF

Word nerds gather every October for Litquake (www.litquake.org), a (mostly) free two-week celebration of all things bookish, featuring readings, performances, panel discussions, author meet-and-greets and more. The event culminates with the annual LitCrawl bacchanalia, when thousands roam through the Mission District stopping along the way for drinks and readings at dozens of bars, galleries, stores and cafés.

ENJOY THE VIEWS

While it will cost you upwards of $7 to drive over the Golden Gate Bridge, walking (or biking) across the famous red-orange span will cost you nada, and give you time to take in the awe-inspiring panorama of the Bay and the city skyline. San Francisco's countless viewpoints include Coit Tower and hundreds of tucked-away elevated spots (see p106 **Secret Stairways to Heaven**).

TICKET-FREE TOURS

More than 200 volunteers from the public library lead free, daily City Guides walking tours (www.sfcityguides.org) around San Francisco, covering everything from Russian Hill stairways to Alfred Hitchcock film locations. Why do they do it without earning a dime? Guides are local history buffs who live to share their knowledge and wax lyrical about the city.

Diary

*Our year-round
guide to the city's best
festivals and events.*

Events in a city as extroverted and dramatic as San Francisco are bound to be colourful, over the top, and at times downright strange. But whether it's a family street festival or Saint Stupid revellers throwing socks at the stock exchange, you're sure to find something to entertain you in all seasons. Spring and summer are peppered with weekly neighbourhood fairs and parades, the only drawback being the accompanying street closures and driving detours. When autumn and winter roll around, most events move indoors, but the activity barely lets up.

For more festivals and events, check out the Arts & Entertainment section. Before you set out or plan a trip around an event, it's wise to call or check online first as dates, times and locations are subject to change. Find our picks of the latest happenings at www.timeout.com/san-francisco.

Cinco de Mayo.

Spring

St Patrick's Day Parade
From 2nd & Market Streets to Civic Center.
Date Sat before 17 Mar.
Everyone gets smiling Irish eyes in time for St Patrick's Day. The parade heads from 2nd and Market Streets to the Civic Center.

St Stupid's Day Parade
Transamerica Pyramid, 600 Montgomery Street, between Washington & Clay Streets, Financial District (www.saintstupid.com). Bus 1, 10, 12, 30, 41, 45, 91/cable car California. **Date** 1 Apr.
This silly only-in-SF costumed procession brings members of the First Church of the Last Laugh through the Financial District every April Fool's Day, stopping off at various 'Stations of the Stupid' (aka noted financial institutions) to pay tribute to the gods of commerce. It concludes with everyone throwing their socks on the steps of the old Pacific Stock Exchange.

Cherry Blossom Festival
Japan Center, Geary Boulevard, between Fillmore & Laguna Streets, Japantown (1-415 563 2313, www.nccbf.org). Bus 2, 3, 22, 31, 38. **Date** Apr.
A joyous whirlwind engulfs Japantown for two weekends in April. The Cherry Blossom Festival is a splendid celebration of Japanese cuisine, traditional arts and crafts, dance and martial arts. The Grand Parade on the final Sunday of the festival starts at Civic Center and goes up Polk to Post ending in Japantown.

Cinco de Mayo
Valencia Street between 21st & 24th Streets, Mission (www.sfcincodemayo.com). BART 16th Street/Metro to Church or Castro/bus 22.
Date wknd before 5 May.
San Francisco's Latino residents and their friends celebrate General Ignacio Zaragoza's defeat of the French army at Puebla in 1862 with this lively weekend of parades, music, dance and fireworks.

AIDS Candlelight Memorial March & Vigil
Castro & Market Streets, Castro (1-415 331 1500, www.candlelightmemorial.org). Metro to Castro/streetcar F/bus 24, 33, 35, 37. **Date** 3rd Sun in May.

IN THE KNOW LAUGHTER FESTS

January's **Sketchfest** (www.sfsketchfest. com) draws top names in comedy for performances, screenings, tribute nights and re-enactments all over town. The free **Comedy Day in the Park** (www.comedyday. org) in September features veteran and up-and-coming stand-up comics busting a gut at Sharon Meadow in Golden Gate Park.

The city pays its respects with a solemn 8pm procession from the Castro along Market Street, ending on the steps of the Main Library. There, crowds gather for speeches, an awards ceremony, celebrations and remembrances.

Bay to Breakers Foot Race
From Howard & Main Streets, SoMa, to Ocean Beach, Golden Gate Park (1-415 231 3130, www. zapposbaytobreakers.com). **Date** 3rd Sun in May.
To raise spirits during the rebuilding process after the 1906 earthquake and fire, William Randolph Hearst's *San Francisco Examiner* started this event in 1912. In 1986, the race set the Guinness World Record for the largest footrace with more than 110,000 participants (most of them seriously inebriated). The event has been watered down in recent years: alcohol and rolling floats (which often housed rolling bars) have been banned. Still, weekend warriors dressed as salmon, tutu-wearing jog-walkers and even a few serious runners find ways to make it fun, running, walking or dancing from the foot of Howard Street (bay), a distance of about 7.5 miles to Ocean Beach (breakers).

Carnaval
Harrison Street, between 16th & 23rd Streets, Mission (1-415 206 0577, www.carnavalsf.com). BART to 16th or 24th Streets/bus 12, 22, 27, 33, 67. **Date** late May.
Organisers call it 'California's largest annual multicultural festival'. Locals call it the best place to eyeball a dazzling parade of skimpily costumed samba dancers gyrating to Latin music. The street food at this Rio-style event is pretty hot, too.

Summer

Union Street Festival
Union Street, between Gough & Steiner Streets, Cow Hollow (1-800 310 6563, www.unionstreet festival.com). Bus 41, 45, 47, 49, 90. **Date** early June.
This weekend-long street fair draws big crowds each June, with its artists' stands, food stalls, bands and assorted other entertainments. Don't miss the annual waiters' race, when the city's best servers race up and down a hill trying not to spill a tray of wine glasses.

Haight Ashbury Street Fair
Haight Street, between Masonic Avenue & Stanyan Street, Haight-Ashbury (www.haight ashburystreetfair.org). Metro to Carl & Cole/ bus 6, 7, 33, 43, 66. **Date** early June.
It's the Summer of Love all over again, with more than 200 booths of greasy food, hippie craftwork and enough roach-clips, skins, bongs and hash pipes to fill out a Cheech and Chong script. Live music comes courtesy of local acts.
▶ *For more on the Summer of Love, see p147.*

North Beach Festival
Grant Avenue, Green Street, Stockton Street & Washington Square, North Beach (1-415 989 2220, www.sresproductions.com/events/north-beach-festival). Bus 10, 12, 30, 39, 41, 45, 91/ cable car Powell-Mason. **Date** June.
Whip out the beret and bang out a rhythm on the bongos, daddio – it's San Francisco's oldest street

party, held in the birthplace of the beatniks. The North Beach Festival celebrates the neighbourhood's Italian heritage, too, and is heavy on art and crafts, including a chalk-art street painting competition. You'll also find live music, wine and, inevitably, plenty of top-notch Italian food.

Summer Solstice

Around the city. **Date** 21 June.

San Francisco's pagans meet on the year's longest day to drum, dance and celebrate. At sunset, pound along with a drum circle in Justin Herman Plaza at the Embarcadero or join the Ocean Beach bonfires.

San Francisco Pride Parade

Market Street, between Embarcadero & 8th Street, Downtown (1-415 864 3733, www.sfpride.org). **Date** last Sun in June.

This San Francisco institution is every bit as campy as you'd expect. Local politicians cruising for the rainbow vote share the route with drag queens, leather daddies and Dykes on Bikes. The wildest, friendliest parade you'll ever witness, it's the culmination of the weekend Pride Celebration, which includes a festival at Civic Center from noon until 6pm on Saturday.

▶ *For more on SF Pride, see p203.*

Left: **Bay to Breakers Foot Race**.
Below: **North Beach Festival**.

PUBLIC HOLIDAYS

New Year's Day
1 Jan

Martin Luther King, Jr Day
3rd Mon in Jan

Presidents' Day
3rd Mon in Feb

Memorial Day
Last Mon in May

Independence Day
4 July

Labor Day
1st Mon in Sept

Columbus Day
2nd Mon in Oct

Veterans Day
11 Nov

Thanksgiving Day
4th Thur in Nov

Christmas Day
25 Dec

Above: **San Francisco Pride Parade**.
Right: **Castro Street Fair**.

Fourth of July Waterfront Festival

Between Aquatic Park & Pier 39, Fisherman's Wharf (San Francisco Visitor Information Center, 1-415 981 1280). Streetcar F/bus 39, 47/cable car Powell-Hyde or Powell-Mason. **Date** July 4.
You'll find plenty of live entertainment and food stalls on the waterfront during the day, but be sure to stay for the spectacular fireworks display that gets under way after dark around 9pm (note: summer fog often makes viewing fireworks more of a theoretical event).

San Francisco Marathon

Around the city (1-888 958 6668, www. thesfmarathon.com). **Date** usually 1st Sun in Aug.
The younger and more athletic cousin of Bay to Breakers Foot Race (*see p30*) has grown every year since its inception in 1977. The course starts at the Ferry Building and then heads round the entire city, through the Mission, Haight, Fisherman's Wharf, across the Golden Gate Bridge and back, before finishing where it started.

Outside Lands Festival

Golden Gate Park (www.sfoutsidelands.com). Streetcar N/bus 5, 7, 21. **Date** early Aug.
The city's biggest rock festival takes over Golden Gate Park every August in an epic celebration of music, food, wine, beer, art and comedy. Big names such as Mumford & Sons, D'Angelo, the Black Keys and Elton John grace six stages for three days. In recent years, the food and beverage offerings have almost eclipsed the music, including an entire stage devoted to GastroMagic and an area called Beer Lands. It's not cheap – tickets run upwards of $135 per day.

Autumn

Ghirardelli Square Chocolate Festival

Ghirardelli Square, between North Point, Beach, Larkin & Polk Streets, Fisherman's Wharf (1-415 775 5500, www.ghirardellisq.com). Streetcar F/bus 19, 28, 30, 47, 90, 91/cable car Powell-Hyde or Powell-Mason. **Date** early Sept. **Map** p312 J2.
Keep reminding yourself that doctors say a little chocolate is good for you, as you sample chocolate-covered strawberries, decadent mousses, brownies, and all manner of over-the-top indulgences. If you need another excuse, proceeds go to charity.

Folsom Street Fair

Folsom Street, between 7th & 12th Streets, SoMa (1-415 777 3247, www.folsomstreetfair.org). Bus 12, 14, 19, 47. **Date** last Sun in Sept.
The Queen Mother of all leather street fairs, the Folsom Street Fair is a veritable gawkfest for visitors. Don your studded jockstrap (and nothing else) and be prepared for masks, whips, chains and fetish gear of all stripes. Needless to say, this might not be suitable for the whole family.

Hardly Strictly Bluegrass Festival

Golden Gate Park (www.hardlystrictlybluegrass. com). Metro N/bus 5, 7, 21. **Date** first wknd in Oct.
This three-day music festival draws more than 750,000 people with a top-flight, eclectic lineup of

artists to rival the New Orleans Jazz Fest. Started in 2001, it's entirely free, thanks to the late founder, Warren Hellman. While the assortment of top names in bluegrass, folk, rock, and roots who perform each year varies, the festival invariably concludes with Emmylou Harris, Steve Earle and Robert Earl Keen.

ArtSpan Open Studios

SOMArts Gallery, 934 Brannan Street, SoMa & various other venues (1-415 861 9838, www. artspan.org). **Date** Oct.

Throughout October, more than 900 artists' studios open up to the public, with a different neighbourhood showing off its work every weekend. You'll find a free map detailing participating venues and the Directory of San Francisco Artists at SOMAarts Gallery, which also hosts the opening exhibition.

Castro Street Fair

Market & Castro Streets, from 16th to 19th Streets, Castro (1-800 853 5950, www.castrostreetfair.org). Metro K, L, M to Castro/streetcar F/bus 24, 33, 35, 37. **Date** early Oct.

A taste of the softer side of gay life in San Francisco, this one-day fair – started in 1974 by the late Harvey Milk – features food, crafts and community activists' stalls, along with plenty of rainbow merchandise.

Fleet Week

Fisherman's Wharf & Piers 30-32, Embarcadero (1-415 306 0911, www.fleetweeksf.org). Streetcar F/bus 19, 39, 44, 47/cable car Powell-Hyde or Powell-Mason. **Date** Oct.

Since the early 1980s, the US Navy's acrobatic Blue Angels have rattled nerves and torn up the skies over San Francisco on Columbus Day weekend. The fleet sails into San Francisco Bay on Saturday morning; a spectacular air show and free battleship tours follow.

Halloween

Market Street, from 15th to Castro Streets; Castro Street, from Market to 19th Streets, Castro. Metro to Castro/streetcar F/bus 24, 33, 35, 37. **Date** 31 Oct.

City Hall has effectively shut down the riotous festivities that used to take place in the Castro over Halloween, but you'll still find drag queens, pagans and Hillary Clinton lookalikes strutting their stuff in the neighbourhood. It's always entertaining.

Día de los Muertos

24th & Bryant Streets, Mission (1-415 826 8009, www.dayofthedeadsf.org). Bus 27, 33, 48. **Date** 2 Nov.

Marchers gather at 24th and Bryant Streets to celebrate the Mexican Day of the Dead. After a traditional blessing, the music starts and the procession begins: Aztec dancers, children in papier-mâché skull masks and women clutching bouquets of wilted flowers. Things wind up in Garfield Square, where people leave candles at a huge community altar. Dress code: dark but showy. If you really want to blend in, paint your face a ghoulish white and bring a noisemaker. *Photo p34.*

Holiday Lighting Festivities

Union Square, between Geary, Powell, Post & Stockton Streets, Downtown; Ghirardelli Square,

Above: **Día de los Muertos**. *See p33.*
Right: **Chinese New Year**.

900 North Point Street, at Polk Street, Fisherman's Wharf (www.gosanfrancisco.about.com). **Date** late Nov.

The lights go on all over town as the holidays approach, including at the above locations. At Union Square, a 67ft living white-fir Christmas tree is decorated with 2,000 lights, 400 ornaments and 500 bows. A 22ft wooden menorah is also lit as part of Hanukkah celebrations.

Winter

New Year's Eve
Embarcadero waterfront near Pier 14.
Date 31 Dec.

For many years, San Franciscans have been gathering at Union Square or Ocean Beach to ring in the New Year. In recent years, the city fathers have sponsored free midnight fireworks along the Embarcadero, usually preceded by a cavalcade of bands performing in tents.

Martin Luther King Jr Birthday Celebration
Around Yerba Buena Gardens (1-415 691 6212, www.sfmlkday.org). **Date** Mon after 15 Jan.

Festivities celebrating Dr King's birthday include a film festival, speeches, live music and poetry, and a parade from 4th Street and Townsend Avenue to Yerba Buena Center for the Arts.

Tet Festival
Around Civic Center & the Tenderloin (1-415 351 1038, www.vietccsf.org). **Date** Jan-Feb.

San Francisco has a large population of Vietnamese-Americans who, along with Cambodian, Latino and African-American families, transform the city centre into a multicultural carnival during this annual celebration of spring and the lunar new year.

San Francisco Tribal, Folk & Textile Arts Show
Fort Mason Center, Marina Boulevard, at Laguna Street, Marina (www.caskeylees.com). Bus 22, 28. **Date** early Feb.

Upwards of 100 folk and ethnic-art dealers sell all manner of pottery, baskets, textiles and jewellery.
▶ *For more on Fort Mason, the site of various theatres and festivals, see p123.*

SF Beer Week
Around the Bay Area (www.sfbeerweek.org). **Date** early Feb.

The San Francisco Brewers Guild launched this celebration of craft beer back in 2009 and since then it has grown into an epic week-long suds fest with more than 600 events hosted by breweries, restaurants, bars and retailers all around the Bay Area. The week kicks off with a gala event at Fort Mason, where aficionados sample beers, meet brewers and geek out over equipment and all things hoppy.

Noise Pop

Around the city (www.noisepop.com). **Date** late Feb. This 12-day citywide series of indie music, arts and film is your best bet for seeing emerging artists. The event started in 1993, and bands that have graced the stage include the White Stripes, Death Cab for Cutie, The Shins, and the Flaming Lips.

Chinese New Year

Market Street, at 2nd Street, & around Chinatown (1-415 680 6297, www.chineseparade.com). BART & Metro or Bart to Montgomery/bus Market Street routes. **Date** Feb. **Map** p313 N5.
The start of the lunar new year offers the city's best parade that doesn't involve public nudity. The Miss Chinatown USA pageant, drumming, martial arts competitions, mountains of food, firecrackers, and a huge procession of dancing dragons, lions, acrobats and stilt-walkers are highlights. It's also the occasion of the enormously popular annual Chinese New Year Treasure Hunt (www.sftreasurehunts.com), which gets nearly 1,600 people scurrying round Chinatown trying to solve clues for prizes and bragging rights.

HOLY MARY!
Check out these only-in-SF spring events.

DOGFEST
Mid Apr, www.mckinleyschool.org/dogfest
Every dog has its day – especially in a city where (very pampered) pooches outnumber kids. At this annual contest and costume parade in the Castro's Duboce Park, doggies stroll the catwalk wearing crowns, tuxedos and tutus. Canines compete in categories such as Best Body Part, Best Trick, Best Bark and, of course, Best Costume. Proceeds benefit a local elementary school.

BRING YOUR OWN BIG WHEEL RACE
Easter Sunday, www.bringyourown bigwheel.com
This event wouldn't seem like anything out of the ordinary were it not for the fact that the racers are full-grown adults and they're careening down one of the steepest and crookedest streets in San Francisco on trikes with their knees up to their jawlines. The race's original Lombard Street location was dropped for Vermont Street (between 20th and 22nd Streets), on the backside of Potrero Hill, when a video of the event went viral bringing in thousands the following year. As you might guess, the prize is not crossing the finish line first but getting there in spectacular style (and in one piece).

HUNKY JESUS CONTEST
Easter Sunday, www.thesisters.org
The other side of the SF Easter spectrum is brought to you by the Sisters of Perpetual Indulgence, a charitable/activist street performance group of cross-dressers who don nuns' habits and white faces as a form of protest against gender roles and organised religion. Their wildly popular Hunky Jesus Contest sees loincloth-wearing Jesus lookalikes vying in a beauty contest. In 2014, the group also started a Foxy Mary pageant.

San Francisco's Best

Check off the essentials with our list of handpicked highlights.

Wave Organ.

Legion of Honor.

Transamerica Pyramid p52
The spiky spire is a distinctive feature of the city's skyline.

Cable cars p48
The mobile landmarks still climb halfway to the stars.

PUBLIC ART
Mission murals p162
Eye-popping large-scale works with a social message.

Wave Organ p123
Acoustic sound sculpture set in the Bay.

CHILDREN
California Academy of Sciences p182
Aquarium, planetarium and natural history museum.

Exploratorium p59
A cool hands-on institution, perfect for science geeks of all ages.

Urban Putt p194
Steampunk indoor minigolf course in an old mortuary.

Musée Mécanique p107
A collection of vintage arcade games that proves there was fun before video.

Alcatraz p107
Formidable defunct island prison in the middle of the Bay.

Sutro Baths p185
Resplendent ruins of a 19th-century Victorian bathhouse.

OUTDOORS
Golden Gate Park p181
The city's beautiful backyard.

The Presidio p125
Magnificent army base-turned-national park.

Crissy Field p125
Stroll the waterfront promenade of a reclaimed wetland.

ICONS
Golden Gate Bridge p127
The engineering marvel is shorthand for San Francisco.

Eating & drinking

INSTITUTIONS
Tadich Grill p54
SF's oldest restaurant and still one of the best.

Swan Oyster Depot p88
Belly up for Dungeness crab and local seafood.

Sam's Grill p54
Serving San Francisco specialities since 1867.

Waterbar.

Tartine Bakery p164
Heavenly bread and pastries.

BLOWOUTS
Saison p79
A multi-course farm-to-fork extravaganza.

Michael Mina p54
French-influenced food made with Japanese ingredients, from kitchen royalty.

Gary Danko p109
This culinary superstar delivers five-star California-French cuisine.

HOTSPOTS
State Bird Provisions p137
American dim sum and the trickiest reservation in town.

Flour + Water p161
This temple to pasta and pizza is worth the inevitable wait.

Quince p56
Northern California cuisine hits new heights.

COFFEE
Blue Bottle Coffee p73
The king of artisanal coffee roasters.

Philz Coffee p163
Custom blends, filter-dripped to individual perfection.

FISH & SEAFOOD
Bar Crudo p132
Top-notch raw bar with an excellent beer list.

Waterbar p80
Seasonal, sustainable seafood served bayside.

MODERN MELTING POT
Burma Superstar p186
Flavourful Burmese cuisine.

Aziza p186
Moroccan food with inventive NorCal twists.

The House p98
East meets west at this house of Asian fusion.

BARS
Burritt Room & Tavern p49
Clandestine cocktails in the shadow of Sam Spade.

Rickhouse p54
A haven for whisky lovers.

Bix p57
Martinis served in Jazz Age opulence.

Paxton Gate.

Magnolia Brewing Company/ Smokestack p176
House-made cask beer and barbecue in a converted can factory.

Shopping

FOOD & DRINK
Ferry Building Marketplace p61
A vast emporium highlighting the Bay Area's bounty.

Liguria Bakery p104
The city's best focaccia, and nothing else.

Dandelion Chocolate p167
Bittersweet bars and sipping cocoa at this bean-to-bar chocolate factory.

GIFTS & SOUVENIRS
Park Life p187
Prints, housewares and clever San Francisco-themed T-shirts.

Paxton Gate p168
Taxidermied mice, scarab beetles and odd ephemera.

Schein & Schein p104
Antique maps and other printed travel treasures.

BOOKS & MUSIC
City Lights p100
The historic bookshop that launched the beat movement.

Green Apple Books p187
A wall-to-wall bastion for used and hard-to-find books.

Amoeba Music p146
Volumes of vinyl and DVDs, plus free on-site concerts.

LOCAL DESIGNERS
Margaret O'Leary p50
Exquisitely handcrafted knits.

Dema p167
Modern interpretations of vintage classics from designer Dema Grim.

Rickshaw Bagworks p177
Dogpatch's hip made-to-order messenger bag manufactory.

DEPARTMENT STORES & MALLS
Gump's p50
San Francisco's original fancy-accoutrements store.

Neiman Marcus p50
Even if you can't afford the designer goods, come to ogle the opulent rotunda.

Westfield San Francisco Centre p51
Shop five levels of luxury labels, plus branches of Bloomingdale's and Nordstrom.

Nightlife

CLUBS
DNA Lounge p220
Goth kids meet mash-up mavens at this venerable SoMa dance club.

Mighty p214
Light up the night on this massive dance floor and backyard patio.

Mezzanine p214
Multi-level club featuring local, national and international DJs.

MUSIC
Independent p219
This no-frills venue has a stellar sound system and eclectic acts.

The Fillmore p218
Legendary stage where the San Francisco Sound was born.

SFJAZZ Center p223
State-of-the-art venue for rising stars and giants of jazz.

Arts

THEATRE
American Conservatory Theater (ACT) p231
San Francisco's acclaimed resident repertory theatre.

Beach Blanket Babylon p231
Campy musical send-ups and humongous hats.

FILM
Castro Theatre p198
Glorious art deco movie palace.

Sundance Kabuki p197
Robert Redford's multiplex for indie films.

CLASSICAL & DANCE
Louise M Davies Symphony Hall p224
See the award-winning SF Symphony under the baton of Michael Tilson Thomas.

War Memorial Opera House p225
Historic home of the San Francisco Opera and Ballet.

SFJAZZ Center

Explore

Downtown

San Francisco's downtown area may be the hub that saves the city from being seen simply as a series of villages. With its myriad cultural attractions and stellar shopping, it lends the city a cosmopolitanism that exceeds its modest size. It's compact enough to navigate easily on foot, and if you don't want to climb those daunting hills, there are always the famous cable cars.

The centre of the action is Union Square, a handsome public space ringed with shops and hotels. East of here, the Financial District, one of the few places where you can see Northern Californians in business attire, extends to the Embarcadero promenade and waterfront. To the west, the Theater District gives way to the Tenderloin, the longtime seedy underbelly of the city, now rapidly evolving with restaurants, galleries and non-profits thanks to a big infusion of tech money. Beyond it, the Beaux Arts Civic Center is home to City Hall and cultural heavyweights that include the War Memorial Opera House, Louise M Davies Symphony Hall and the Asian Art Museum.

EXPLORE

Exploratorium.

Don't Miss

1 Ferry Building Marketplace Cruise through this massive foodie destination (p61).

2 Tadich Grill Taste the Barbary Coast (p54).

3 Exploratorium The ultimate science geeks' playground (p59).

4 Rickhouse A cosy place to hit the bottle (p54).

5 Asian Art Museum A millennia-spanning collection in a beautifully restored landmark (p64).

Café Claude.

UNION SQUARE & AROUND

The best place to begin an exploration of Union Square is at the corner of Post and Stockton Streets, where a timeline of its history is etched in granite. In 1839, Jean Vioget laid out a park in the location when designing Yerba Buena, the city that would become San Francisco. In 1850, Colonel John Geary (who would give his name to Geary Street, south of the square) deeded the land to the city for use as a public space.

The square's name harks back to its use in 1861 as a pro-Union rallying point on the eve of the Civil War. The 97-foot Corinthian column that rises from the middle of the square was designed by Robert Aitken to commemorate Admiral Dewey's 1898 victory at Manila during the Spanish-American War.

In 1941, the square was rebuilt according to a design by Timothy Pflueger, known for his art deco buildings and movie palaces. Pflueger's

vision can still be seen in the early Francis Ford Coppola film *The Conversation*. In 1997, a competition was held to create a new Union Square. After much wrangling, April Phillips and Michael Fotheringham's open, inviting design was unveiled in 2002. Once a major hangout for San Francisco's homeless population, it's now a lively gathering place where shoppers and lunch-breakers sprawl on strips of lawn or rest their feet on one of the many benches.

At the southwest corner, the **TIX Bay Area kiosk** offers half-price tickets for shows and events throughout the city. Across the square is a branch of the **Emporio Rulli café**, with sandwiches, strong espressos and frosty-mugged beers. Across Powell Street at no.335, the still-glamorous **Westin St Francis Hotel** is where silent-era film star Fatty Arbuckle's lethal libido ignited Hollywood's first sex scandal in 1921, when a starlet ended up dead in his hotel room.

The stretch of **Powell Street** that links Union Square to Market Street is among the city's busiest thoroughfares. Watching the cable cars clatter past, as the cables that pull them hum beneath your feet, is a quintessential San Francisco experience. At the foot of Powell, huge queues wait to catch a cable car at the roundabout, where conductors manually rotate the cars on a giant turntable for the return journey up the hill.

San Francisco's central grand boulevard, **Market Street** cuts a diagonal swathe through downtown at the bottom of Powell Street. While the thoroughfare's glory days may be past, a revitalisation fuelled by tech giants Twitter, Zendesk and others is restoring some of the

IN THE KNOW NOIR BAR

The byzantine plot of Dashiell Hammett's *The Maltese Falcon* begins with the murder of Sam Spade's partner, Miles Archer, in Burritt Street, an alley north of Union Square. The street opposite is named after the author, who, like his fictional alter ego, frequented **John's Grill** (63 Ellis Street, between Market & Powell Streets, 1-415 986 0069, www.johnsgrill.com).

glamour to the long-neglected strip, especially to the downtrodden section near Civic Center.

The streets north of Market Street and east of Union Square are home to several handsome little alleyways missed by many visitors, but treasured by locals for their relative peace and quiet. Adjoining the square, **Maiden Lane** (*see p50* **In the Know**), once the notoriously sleazy red-light district, is now lined with designer boutiques – Marc Jacobs, Chanel and Prada among them – and one-off stores. Further north sit two more notable alleys. **Belden Place**, a small street between Kearny and Montgomery Streets, is the main artery of downtown's unofficial French Quarter, offering dining both fine and casual, plus the most enthusiastic Bastille Day celebrations in the city.

Restaurants & Cafés

Bourbon Steak

335 Powell Street, between Geary & Post Streets (1-415 397 3003, www.bourbonsteaksf.com). BART & Metro to Powell/cable car Powell-Hyde or Powell-Mason. **Open** 5.30-10pm Mon-Thur, Sun; 5.30-10.30pm Fri, Sat. **Main courses** $34-$110. **Map** p46 D3 ❶ **Steakhouse**

NYC meets SF at this outpost of celeb chef Michael Mina's steak- and whisky-themed powerhouse. Decadent is the only way to describe the steaks, and that's not because of the portion size or price – though both are hefty – it's how the beef is cooked. Mina's steaks are slowly poached in butter for an hour in thermal circulators that are precise to within a tenth of a degree, then seared for a minute on each side on a wood-fired grill. The result? Super tender,

perfectly cooked steaks worth their weight in…butter. For those feeling less carnivorous, there are seafood options, including a sumptuous lobster pot pie.

Café Claude

7 Claude Lane, between Sutter & Bush Streets (1-415 392 3505, www.cafeclaude.com). BART & Metro to Montgomery/bus 2, 3, 30, 38, 45 & Market Street routes/cable car Powell-Hyde or Powell-Mason. **Open** 11.30am-10.30pm Mon-Sat; 5.30-10.30pm Sun. **Main courses** $21-$28. **Map** p46 D4 ❷ **French**

Café Claude is a perfect reincarnation of a Parisian boîte set in a petite alleyway with outdoor seating. The illusion is reinforced with live jazz and French café music, classic dishes such as niçoise salad, steak tartare, trout almondine and duck confit, and just the right amount of *l'attitude*.

Colibrí Mexican Bistro

438 Geary Street, between Taylor & Mason Streets (1-415 440 2737, www.colibrimexicanbistro.com). BART & Metro to Powell/bus 2, 3, 30, 38, 45 & Market Street routes/cable car Powell-Hyde or Powell-Mason. **Open** 11.30am-10pm Mon; 11.30am-11pm Tue-Thur; 11.30am-midnight Fri; 10.30am-midnight Sat; 10.30am-10pm Sun. **Main courses** $18-$22. **Map** p47 E3 ❸ **Mexican**

In the heart of the Theater District, this unpretentious restaurant serves fresh central Mexican fare culled from family recipes passed down to owners Eduardo and Sylvia Rallo. The extensive list of *antojitos* (appetisers) includes fantastic fresh made-to-order guacamole with handmade tortillas. Also on the menu are an excellent tortilla soup,

EXPLORE

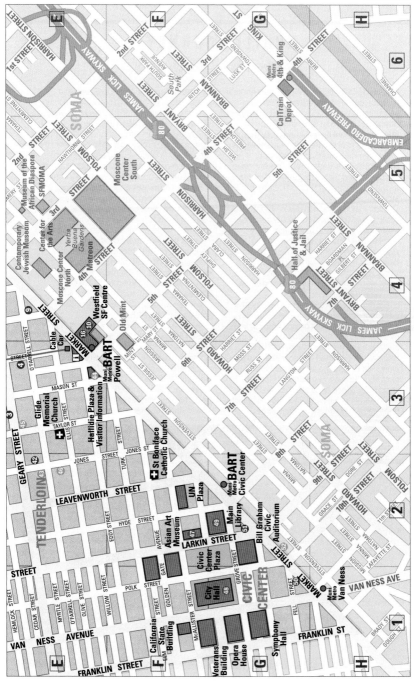

EXPLORE

UPHILL JOURNEYS

Ride on a piece of rolling history.

Installed in 1873 by wily Scotsman Andrew Hallidie, cable cars were an ingenious solution to San Francisco's eternal problem: how to get up those damn hills. Nob Hill and Russian Hill in particular were tempting morsels of real estate, yet for many years they remained mostly undeveloped. Horse-drawn carriages could barely make the climb, and Victorian gentlefolk were unwilling to exhaust themselves by slogging up on foot.

Enter Hallidie and his idea of introducing cable-drawn transport to the city streets, a method he had first used hauling ore carts in California's gold mines. When, to everyone's amazement, his first cars worked flawlessly, imitators sprang up overnight. Soon, more than 100 miles of tracks criss-crossed the city, operated by seven cable car companies.

It didn't last. Earthquakes, fires and the advent of automobiles and electric trolleys spelled doom for most of the cable car lines; by 1947, the city had proposed tearing up the last lines and replacing them with buses. Happily, the outraged citizenry stopped the plan. Since then, the government has declared the system a National Historic Landmark. Three lines survive: the Powell-Mason and Powell-Hyde lines, both of which depart from Powell and Market Street turnaround and run to North Beach and Fisherman's Wharf; and the California line, which runs along California Street between Market Street and Van Ness Avenue.

First-timers are often surprised to learn that cable cars have no engine or other means of propulsion. They use a 'grip', a steel clamp that grabs on to a subterranean cable, running under the streets at a constant 9.5mph. The cables never stop moving: you can hear them humming even when there are no cable cars in sight. Every car has two operators: a gripman, who works the cranks and levers that grab on to and release the underground cable; and a conductor, who takes fares and somehow manages to cram 90-plus passengers, many of them hanging off the running boards, on to a single vehicle. Visit the **Cable Car Museum** (*see p86*) to inspect the system's immense winding turbines, as well as Hallidie's original 1873 car.

While the cable cars are a legendary part of San Francisco history, so is the hassle of waiting for one at Powell Street turnaround. So don't. Instead, walk up Powell a few blocks and board the car at O'Farrell or Union Square. Or, if you aren't going anywhere in particular, take the rarely crowded California line. The views aren't as good as on the Powell lines, but it's still a cable car.

tamarind-sautéed prawns served with corn cakes, and a hugely flavourful chicken mole poblano made with chilli, nuts and chocolate that will have you raving almost before you put down your fork.

Kuleto's & Bar Norcini

Villa Florence Hotel, 221 Powell Street, at O'Farrell Street (1-415 397 7720, www.kuletos.com). BART & Metro to Powell/bus 2, 3, 30, 38, 45 & Market Street routes/cable car Powell-Hyde or Powell-Mason. **Open** 7-10.30am, 11.30am-10.30pm Mon-Thur; 7-10.30am, 11.30am-11pm Fri; 8-10.30am, 11.30am-11pm Sat; 8-10.30am, 11.30am-10.30pm Sun. **Main courses** $21-$38. **Map** p47 E3 **❹**
Italian & pizza
This sophisticated spot for authentic, seasonal and expertly executed Italian food has been atop diners' and critics' lists for more than 30 years. Up front, Bar Norcini features house-baked pastries in the morning, pizzas and paninis at lunch, and a wine bar with housemade salumi, artisan cheeses, grappas and 40 wines by the glass every evening.

Scala's Bistro

Sir Francis Drake Hotel, 432 Powell Street, between Post & Sutter Streets (1-415 395 8555, www. scalasbistro.com). BART & Metro to Powell/bus 2, 3, 30, 38, 45 & Market Street routes/cable car Powell-Hyde or Powell-Mason. **Open** 7-10.30am, 11.30am-3pm, 5.15-11pm Mon-Fri; 8am-2pm, 5.15-11pm Sat, Sun. **Main courses** $32-$35. **Map** p46 D3 **❺** California
Yes, it's based in a hotel, but this bustling bistro is frequented not only by guests but also locals attracted by robust, reasonably priced Cal-Mediterranean food. Reliable choices range from the daily risotto to fresh-made pasta, crafted with a constantly changing array of seasonal produce. Meal-size salads are perennially popular, especially the fritto misto, made with fennel, onion, asparagus, calamari, mushrooms and anchovy-roasted garlic aioli.

Bars

★ Burritt Room & Tavern

417 Stockton Street, between Bush & Sutter Streets (1-415 400 0561, www.charliepalmer.com/burritt-room-and-tavern). Bus 2, 3, 4, 30, 45, 76/cable car Powell-Hyde or Powell-Mason. **Open** 5pm-midnight Mon-Thur, Sun; 5pm-2am Fri, Sat. **Map** p46 D4 **❻**
Slip through the monochrome lobby of the Mystic Hotel, ascend a narrow staircase, and you'll find Burritt Room, a 1920s-style lounge with plush velvet couches and vintage chandeliers. With a prime location in Union Square, the spot draws date-night couples and tourists on romantic getaways to its curtained booths and dark, intimate corners. Sip classic cocktails like Vieux Carré or house creations like the complex Death March, a mix of mescal, maraschino liqueur, pineapple and nutmeg bitters. Under the direction of owner and celeb chef Charlie Palmer,

the restaurant's modern American menu, heavy on steaks and chops, is on a par with the cocktails. The Burritt's decidedly noir feel does justice to its namesake Burritt Street, which played a lethal role in Dashiell Hammett's *The Maltese Falcon*.

Slide

430 Mason Street, between Geary & Post Streets (1-415 421 1916, www.slidesf.com). BART & Metro to Powell. **Open** 9pm-3am Wed-Sun. **Map** p46 D3 **❼**
This posh basement bar was once home to Coffee Dan's, a notorious speakeasy that patrons accessed by riding down a 15-foot slide. Featured in the 1927 Al Jolson movie, *The Jazz Singer*, it was also a gambling den and cabaret that hosted the likes of Artie Shaw. As the current name suggests, guests once again enter the bar via a long slide that launches them into an elegant interior with plush booths, bottle service (for a hefty premium), a striking back-lit honey-onyx bar, acres of mahogany panelling, and a DJ booth housed in a grand piano. Despite the establishment's unbeatable provenance, the current crowd is heavily suburban. At the very least, it's worth sliding in to sample some of the many martinis or champagne cocktails.

Shops & Services

Archive

317 Sutter Street, between Grant Avenue & Stockton Street (1-415 391 5550, www.archivesf. com). BART & Metro to Montgomery. **Open** 10.30am-6.30pm Mon-Sat. **Map** p46 D4 **❽** Fashion
This is not the store for guys who live in jeans and T-shirts. It's a men's boutique for adventurous dressers and fashion followers (more *L'Uomo* than *GQ*) with disposable income to spend. In the modernist, white-walled shop the racks are draped with more than 30 labels from around the world, many of whom are small-production and exclusive to the Archive in the Bay Area, including Japanese line Devoa and Barcelona-based French/German designer Boris Bidjan Saberi. But the real standouts are the luxe leather jackets and hoodies.

EXPLORE

IN THE KNOW BRAZEN MAIDEN

Today, Maiden Lane is one of downtown's most refined shopping strips, but its origins are a lot less classy. Known in the Barbary Coast days as Morton Street, it was home to the city's sleaziest brothels, where hookers enticed customers by standing naked to the waist behind small barred windows that fronted 'cribs' – tiny rooms where they performed all manner of depraved acts.

Barneys New York

77 O'Farrell Street, at Stockton Street (1-415 268 3500, www.barneys.com). BART & Metro to Powell/bus 2, 3, 5, 6, 9, 14, 21, 27, 30, 31, 38, 45, 71, 76, 91 & Market Street routes/cable car Powell-Hyde or Powell-Mason. **Open** 10am-7pm Mon-Wed, Fri, Sat; 10am-8pm Thur; noon-7pm Sun. **Map** p47 E4 ❾ **Department store**

The hip Manhattan-born department store arrived in San Francisco in 2007 in a low-key manner in keeping with its tasteful style, and quickly made its presence known among local followers of fashion with its spare modernist decor and laid-back sell. An iron spiral staircase leads the way to the women's shoe salon, where you'll find heels, booties and flats from Alaïa, Chloé, Miu Miu and the house line, among others. Designer and contemporary collections are arranged on labelled racks positioned on the diamond-checked floors. Another winding staircase leads up to the top floor men's salon, where shirts of every shade are shelved in orderly rows.

Bloomingdale's

Westfield San Francisco Centre, 845 Market Street, between 4th & 5th Streets (1-415 856 5300, www.bloomingdales.com). BART & Metro to Powell/bus 5, 6, 9, 14, 21, 27, 30, 38, 45, 71, 91 & Market Street routes/cable car Powell-Hyde or Powell-Mason. **Open** 10am-9pm Mon-Sat; 11am-8pm Sun. **Map** p47 E4 ❿ **Department store**

Filling the retail gap between Macy's and Neiman Marcus, the Little Brown Bag's temple to luxury wares fills the cavernous space that once housed the stodgy Emporium department store. Of note here are the lavish fragrance section and the sparkling array of fine china and glassware to be found on the ground floor.

Diana Slavin

3 Claude Lane, between Sutter & Bush Streets (1-415 677 9939, www.dianaslavin.com). BART & Metro to Montgomery/bus 2, 3, 5, 6, 9, 10, 12, 21, 30, 38, 45, 71, 91/cable car Powell-Hyde or Powell-Mason. **Open** 11am-6pm Tue-Fri; noon-5pm Sat. **Map** p46 D4 ⓫ **Fashion**

In this tucked-away studio and boutique, Slavin designs and displays her trademark women's

clothing – menswear-inspired styles in rich, subtle colours and lush fabrics. Vintage Vuarnet shades and Maison Margiela shoes complete the look.

★ Gump's

135 Post Street, between Grant Avenue & Kearny Street (1-415 982 1616, www.gumps.com). BART & Metro to Montgomery/bus 2, 3, 5, 6, 9, 12, 14, 21, 30, 38, 45, 71, 76, 91 & Market Street routes/cable car Powell-Hyde or Powell-Mason. **Open** 10am-6pm Mon-Sat; noon-5pm Sun. **Map** p46 D4 ⓬ **Gifts & souvenirs**

Established in 1861 by the Gump brothers in the wake of San Francisco's newly minted Gold Rush millionaires, Gump's is the place where moneyed San Franciscans buy their wedding presents, china and a variety of baubles, from black pearls to custom green peridot necklaces. It's a thoroughly elegant shopping experience for those who think a silver service for less than 12 is simply out of the question.

Margaret O'Leary

1 Claude Lane, between Sutter & Bush Streets (1-415 391 1010, www.margaretoleary.com). BART & Metro to Montgomery/bus 2, 3, 5, 6, 9, 10, 12, 30, 31, 38, 45, 71, 91/cable car Powell-Hyde or Powell-Mason. **Open** 10am-5pm Tue-Sat. **Map** p46 D4 ⓭ **Fashion**

Irish-born O'Leary is one of San Francisco's design treasures. Her exquisite hand-loomed sweaters, dresses and tunics are very familiar to buyers at Neiman Marcus and Saks, but her namesake boutiques feature the full line – knitwear and sportswear made with eco-friendly yarns and fabrics, ultra-feminine and accented with perfect details.

Other location 2400 Fillmore Street, at Washington Street, Pacific Heights (1-415 771 9982).

Neiman Marcus

150 Stockton Street, at Geary Street (1-415 362 3900, www.neimanmarcus.com). BART & Metro to Powell/bus 2, 3, 5, 6, 9, 14, 21, 27, 30, 31, 38, 45, 71, 76, 91 & Market Street routes/cable car Powell-Hyde or Powell-Mason. **Open** 10am-7pm Mon-Wed, Fri, Sat; 10am-8pm Thur; noon-6pm Sun. **Map** p46 D4 ⓮ **Department store**

Somewhat affectionately referred to as 'Needless Markup', Neiman Marcus occupies one of the city's most impressive buildings. First-timers often stop in their tracks to gape at the opulent rotunda. The structure is topped by an elaborate stained-glass dome, which was salvaged from San Francisco's famous (and since demolished) City of Paris department store. As you ascend to the two levels above, floor-to-ceiling windows offer views of Union Square. Escalators to each floor reveal a central shopping corridor with the season's latest offerings, and designer shops line either side. Luxe labels include Prada, Chanel, Gucci, Oscar de la Renta, Stella McCartney and many more.

Saks Fifth Avenue

384 Post Street, at Powell Street (1-415 986 4300, www.saksfifthavenue.com). BART & Metro to Powell/bus 2, 3, 5, 21, 27, 30, 31, 38, 45, 76, 91 & Market Street routes/cable car Powell-Hyde or Powell-Mason. **Open** 10am-7pm Mon-Wed; 10am-8pm Thur-Sat; noon-7pm Sun. **Map** p46 D3
⑮**Department store**

This outpost of the upscale department store chain has been open since 1952, and it remains one of the top destinations in the city for designer labels. The women's shoe department is a major draw, sprawling over the entire bottom floor and packed with lofty labels (Christian Louboutin, Prada, Gucci, Jimmy Choo and the like). The store is laid out in a lattice formation of ascending escalators: each floor bears a handful of designers, with cliques of chic mannequins wearing the season's latest arrivals. The most extravagant of the floors is the evening-gown salon, where frocks of every silhouette are grouped by hue and towering floral arrangements adorn mirrored tables. The multi-level Saks Fifth Avenue men's store is a couple of blocks east at 220 Post Street, offering a wide array of shoes, suiting, shirting and accessories.

Westfield San Francisco Centre

865 Market Street, at 5th Street (1-415 495 5656, www.westfield.com/sanfrancisco). BART & Metro to Powell/bus 5, 6, 9, 14, 21, 27, 30, 38, 45, 71, 91 & Market Street routes/cable car Powell-Hyde or Powell-Mason. **Open** 10am-8.30pm Mon-Sat; 10am-7pm Sun. **Map** p47 E3/4 ⑯ **Mall**

Spiral escalators wind slowly up this vast mall, enticing shoppers with mid-priced chain stores such as J Crew, Nine West and Abercrombie & Fitch. Department store Nordstrom resides on top like a society matron; express elevators whizz you straight there. On the east side, further draws include upscale merchants (including Kate Spade, Bloomingdale's and Tiffany & Co), and a nine-theatre cineplex. You won't go hungry, either, with a sprawling gourmet food court on the basement level and more upscale eateries such as Lark Creek Steak and chef Martin Yan's MY China on the 4th floor under the dome.

Wilkes Bashford

375 Sutter Street, between Grant Avenue & Stockton Street (1-415 986-4380, www.wilkes bashford.com).Bus 2, 3, 8AX, 8BX, 8X, 30, 45, 76X, 91/cable car Powell-Hyde, cable car Powell-Mason. **Open** 10am-6pm Mon-Sat. **Map** p46 D4 ⑰ **Department store**

San Francisco's iconic clothier is designed to feel like an opulent seven-storey townhouse rather than a sterile department store, decked out with limestone and marble detailing, reclaimed eucalyptus wood from the Presidio and a wrought-iron staircase. Founded in 1966 by bon vivant haberdasher Wilkes Bashford, the store was one of the first US retailers to sell European designers. Today, Wilkes carries dozens of high-end fashion labels, including Andrew Gn, Ermenegildo Zegna, Jean Paul Gaultier, Oscar de la Renta and Loro Piana. Each floor has a different theme – suiting in the library; women's shoes on the terrace – and each is linked to the others by a

EXPLORE

Wilkes Bashford.

EXPLORE

IN THE KNOW ARTY PARTY

First Thursday, a monthly open house hosted by the San Francisco Art Dealers Association, is like happy hour for art lovers. Some 50 galleries around the city stay open late, and you can partake in free wine and nibbles as you hop between spaces. A map and list of participating galleries is available at www.firstthursdayart.com.

curving staircase lined with vintage photos (mostly of Bashford glad-handing various celebrities), news clippings and old advertisements. The penthouse is where you'll find the made-to-measure lounge, complete with fireplace, leather club chairs and a bar.

THE FINANCIAL DISTRICT

Bounded by Market, Kearny and Jackson Streets, and the Embarcadero to the east, the Financial District has been the business and banking hub of San Francisco, and the West at large, since the 1849 Gold Rush. Its northern edge is overlooked by the **Transamerica Pyramid** (600 Montgomery Street, between Washington & Clay Streets). Built on the site of the Montgomery Block, a four-storey office building that formerly housed writers, artists and radicals including Rudyard Kipling and Mark Twain, the structure provoked public outrage when William Pereira's

design was unveiled. However, since its completion in 1972, the 853-foot building has become an iconic spike that defines the city's skyline. The pyramid sits on giant rollers that allow it to rock safely in the event of an earthquake. It sounds a little wacky, but it works: the building came out unscathed by the 6.9-magnitude Loma Prieta earthquake in 1989.

On the pyramid's east side, tiny **Redwood Park** is a cool refuge that lunching workers share with majestic trees and bronze sculptures of frogs that are frozen mid-leap in the pond. Across from the Transamerica, in front of the **California Pacific Bank**, a plaque marks another classic piece of vanished Americana: the Western Headquarters of Russell, Majors & Waddell, founders and operators of the Pony Express (1860-61), whose riders tore across the West at breakneck speeds delivering messages over the 1,665 miles from St Joseph, Missouri, to Sacramento, California. The fastest run on record took seven days and 17 hours, with riders averaging 10.6mph over some of the world's most rugged and dangerous terrain and carrying packages of real import – not least among them, President Abraham Lincoln's first inaugural address. Further south, on nearby Commercial Street, in the city's former mint, the modest **Pacific Heritage Museum** holds an art collection that's small but worth a peek.

Continuing south from the Transamerica, the area's history as the financial heart of the American West reveals itself further in its

Pacific Coast Stock Exchange.

architecture. The **Omni Hotel** (500 California Street, at Montgomery Street) was built in 1926 as a bank and wears its origins proudly; just up the road is the small but nonetheless enjoyable **Wells Fargo History Museum**. However, both are dwarfed by the nearby Bank of America Center, now officially known as **555 California Street**, which towers over the Financial District. The skyscraper is 74 feet shorter than the Transamerica, but feels more massive thanks to its great girth and its carnelian granite zigzag frame. At its entrance, the 200-ton black granite sculpture by Masayuki Nagare titled *Pacific Heritage* is appropriately known locally as 'The Banker's Heart'.

A block east of Bank of America sits the **Merchants Exchange** (465 California Street, between Sansome & Montgomery Streets, 1-415 591 1833). The building is no longer used by share traders, but its historic spaces illustrate the important role it once played in the financial life of the city. The lavish trading hall, designed by Julia Morgan, is now the lobby of the California Bank & Trust offices and home to an impressive collection of William Coulter seascapes.

There's further financial heritage close by at the **Union Bank of California's Museum of the Money of the American West** (400 California Street, at Sansome Street, 1-415 705 7142, 9am-4.30pm Mon-Fri). The museum's modest Wild West collection may be dwarfed by the bank's doors and imposing columns, but it includes some fascinating artefacts. Among them is a hyper-rare three-dollar bill signed by the founder of Mormonism, Joseph Smith, and a pair of duelling pistols used in a fatal 1859 encounter between a former Chief Justice of the California Supreme Court and a US Senator. The museum also reveals a little about William Chapman Ralston, the bank's founder, a major figure in the development of the city and the man responsible for the lavish Palace Hotel (*see p285* **Ralston's Palace**).

FREE Pacific Coast Stock Exchange

155 Sansome Street, at Pine Street. Bus 1, 10, 12, 15, 41/cable car California. **Map** p46 C5 ⓲
The Exchange was modernised in 1928 by deco architect Timothy Pflueger, who believed art should be an integral part of architecture. He commissioned sculptor Ralph Stackpole to create the two granite statues outside, which represent Agriculture and Industry (the twin sources of wealth), while above the entrance is a figure called Progress of Man with arms outstretched. The stock exchange trading floor closed in 2002 and the building now houses an Equinox gym. The main attraction, however, is Diego Rivera's 1931 mural *Allegory of California*, can still be viewed on the tenth floor of the neighbouring City Club (tours are available by appointment only, www.cityclubsf.com). It is richly ironic that Rivera,

a committed communist, should have been allowed to create such a magnificent work within the heart of capitalism; Stackpole, an old friend of the artist, had recommended him for the job. The mural shows Bay Area industries, including aviation and oil, with Califia (the fictional warrior queen for whom the state is named) in the centre and the emphasis firmly on workers rather than bosses, highlighting Rivera's socialist penchant for sticking it to the authorities.

FREE Pacific Heritage Museum

608 Commercial Street, at Montgomery Street (1-415 399 1124, www.lokstuff.com/UCB). Bus 1, 10, 12, 15, 41/cable car California. **Open** 10am-4pm Tue-Sat. **Admission** free. **Map** p46 C4 ⓳
Formerly the city's mint, this structure is now an EastWest Bank, and also contains this museum. Emphasising San Francisco's connections with the Pacific Rim, the museum features changing exhibits of contemporary artists from countries such as China, Taiwan, Japan and Thailand. Much of what is displayed here is on loan from private collections and is rarely seen elsewhere.

FREE Wells Fargo History Museum

420 Montgomery Street, at California Street (1-415 396 2619, www.wellsfargohistory.com). Bus 1, 10, 30, 41/cable car California. **Open** 9am-5pm Mon-Fri. **Admission** free. **Map** p46 C4 ⓴
Wells Fargo is California's oldest bank, and this collection of Gold Rush memorabilia provides a nice overview of banking in California. You'll find gold nuggets, an old telegraph machine and a Concord stagecoach, built in 1867, plus historical photos.

Restaurants & Cafés

Alfred's Steakhouse

659 Merchant Street, between Kearny & Montgomery Streets (1-415 781 7058, www. alfredssteakhouse.com). Bus 1, 8AX, 8BX, 10,

IN THE KNOW
COMMEMORATING THE QUAKE

A uniquely San Franciscan ritual is played out every year at the intersection of Market, Kearny and Geary Streets. At 5.12am on 18 April, the survivors of the 1906 earthquake (at time of writing, one remains), their descendants and civic leaders gather around the ornate lion-headed Lotta's Fountain (named after the popular vaudevillian Lotta Crabtree, who donated it to the city), just as they did more than a century ago when families separated by the huge quake used the fountain as a meeting point.

EXPLORE

12, 30, 41. **Open** 5-9.30pm Tue, Wed, Fri, Sat; 11.30am-2pm, 5-9.30pm Thur. **Main courses** $19.50-$61.50. **Map** p46 C4 ㉑ **Steakhouse**

One of the city's oldest restaurants, Alfred's feels like a time capsule, with old-school leather booths, crystal chandeliers and hefty martinis served from huge shakers. But it still ranks among the city's best steakhouses, with the loyal fan base to back it up. The chief attractions are giant Chicago ribeyes, tender T-bones and a porterhouse that covers the plate, but the rack of lamb and fish dishes are also top drawer. Along with the superlative martinis, the bar stocks more than 100 single malts.

Michael Mina

252 California Street, between Battery & Front Streets (1-415 397 9222, www.michaelmina.net). BART & Metro to Embarcadero/streetcar & bus all Market Street routes. **Open** 11.30am-2pm, 5.30pm-10pm Mon-Thur, Sun; 11.30am-2pm, 5.30pm-10.30pm Fri, Sat. **Main courses** (lunch) $26-$45. **Prix fixe** (dinner, three courses) $105. **Map** p46 C5 ㉒ **American**

Famed chef Michael Mina created a stir when he uprooted his Union Square restaurant and relocated back to the spot in the Financial District where he got his start (the former Aqua). He hasn't lost a step since. His menu, as executed by Ron Siegel, has scrapped the signature three-way preparations in favour of French-influenced food made with Japanese ingredients. Less frou frou than its predecessor, it's still dining on a grand scale (and at a grand price), but one taste of the ahi tuna tartare or butter-poached Maine lobster and you'll whip out your credit card without a second thought. For an extra-special splurge, consider opting for the seasonal tasting menu ($170).

Plouf

40 Belden Place, between Bush & Pine Streets (1-415 986 6491, www.ploufsf.com). BART & Metro to Montgomery/bus 1, 2, 3, 15, 30, 38, 45 & Market Street routes/cable car California. **Open** 11.30am-3pm, 5.30-10pm Mon-Thur; 11am-3pm, 5.30-11pm Fri; 5.30-11pm Sat. **Main courses** $18.50-$25. **Map** p46 D4 ㉓ **French**

This charming, always-packed restaurant is named after the 'sound a stone makes when it drops into a French stream'. No dining experience here is complete without a bucket of steamed mussels, but the ever-changing roster of fish is also excellent. At lunch, join the throngs at sidewalk tables in the alley for a little bit of Paris.

Sam's Grill

374 Bush Street, between Kearny & Montgomery Streets (1-415 421 0594, www.samsgrillsf.com). BART & Metro to Montgomery/bus 1, 2, 3, 15, 30, 38 45 & Market Street routes/cable car California. **Open** 11am-9pm Mon-Fri. **Main courses** $18-$28. **Map** p46 D4 ㉔ **American**

Sam's has been satisfying San Franciscan appetites since 1867, when the original owner, Michael Molan Moraghan, was known as the 'Oyster King'. Current proprietor Peter Quartaroli has kept seafood and local tradition in the forefront since taking over in 2014, with favourites such as Hangtown Fry (oysters and eggs), sand dabs doré, petrale sole meunière, and Dungeness crab cakes served in a charming, wood-panelled dining room punctuated by white tablecloths. If you're not into seafood, the burgers at lunch are a must.

★ Tadich Grill

240 California Street, between Battery & Front streets (1-415 391 1849, www.tadichgrill.com). BART & Metro to Embarcadero/streetcar & bus all Market Street routes. **Open** 11am-9.30pm Mon-Sat. **Main courses** $16-$50. **Map** p46 C5 ㉕ **Fish & seafood**

Established in 1849, Tadich is the city's oldest restaurant, and still one of its most popular. Power-lunching politicians, techies and tourists alike belly up to the classic mahogany horseshoe bar and tuck into old-school San Francisco dishes such as crab Louis, shrimp à la Newburg, Hangtown Fry and giant bowls of San Francisco cioppino (Italian shellfish stew) accompanied by a big hunk of sourdough bread. If you prefer more private seating, let one of the white-coated waiters usher you into a wooden booth (with service bell). No reservations are accepted and there's invariably a line out the door, but it's worth it to experience a bit of Barbary Coast San Francisco.

Bars

Hidden Vine

408 Merchant Street, between Battery & Sansome Streets (1-415 674 3567, www.thehiddenvine.com) BART & Metro to Montgomery/bus 5, 6, 9, 21, 31, 38. **Open** 4-10pm Mon; 4pm-midnight Tue-Sat. **Map** p46 B5 ㉖

A discreet doorway on an inconspicuous alley leads to this charming mood-lit brick-walled wine bar staffed by knowledgeable people who don't understand the meaning of the word pretentious. There are literally hundreds of bottle selections from around the world (a different region is featured every month, with special emphasis on California cabernets), as well as more than 40 selections by the glass and several tasting flights. Grab a glass, a plate of flatbreads or pulled-pork sliders and head out back to the sweet little bocce ball court sandwiched between brick walls in the courtyard.

Rickhouse

246 Kearny Street, at Bush Street (1-415 398 2827, www.rickhousebar.com). BART & Metro to Montgomery/bus 5, 6, 9, 21, 31, 38. **Open** 5pm-2am Mon, Sat; 3pm-2am Tue-Fri. **Map** p46 D4 ㉗

Rickhouse.

This candlelit, two-level saloon is panelled in reclaimed barrel-wood, lending the impression that you're sipping whiskey from its source. Grab a seat at the bar before the tall wall of booze (accessed by a rolling library ladder) and watch the 1920s-attired bartenders expertly stirring, shaking and spritzing cocktails. The 15 speciality drinks are categorised under terms familiar to whiskey drinkers: the Family Estate, Cask Strength, Special Reserve and the like. Though you'll find other spirits in the mix as well, the majority of the cocktails showcase whiskey and bourbon. Try the Bone Park, a cocktail blending scotch whisky, Mandarine Napoléon liqueur, Cardamaro and mole bitters.

Shops & Services

Manika Jewelry

645 Market Street, between Annie & New Montgomery Streets (1-415 399 1990, www. manikajewelry.com). BART & Metro to Montgomery. Open 10am-6pm Mon-Sat. Map p46 D4 **❽ Accessories**
Though Manika relocated from Maiden Lane to a tourist-laden stretch of Market Street in 2013, the boutique maintains its commitment to independent artisans. Owner Peter Walsh has cultivated an international coterie of designers, including Nina Basharova and Toby Pomeroy, alongside locals including Sarah Graham, Rebecca Overmann and Sarah Swell. You'll find party-ready cocktail rings sparkling with tourmaline and diamonds, ebony bangles and minimalist gold pendants, all draped across organic wooden blocks in cases.

JACKSON SQUARE

The northern edge of the Financial District is marked by the **Jackson Square Historical District** (bounded by Washington, Kearny and Sansome Streets, and Pacific Avenue). It's the last vestige of San Francisco's notorious Barbary Coast, once a seething mass of low-life bars and 19th-century sex clubs that made modern-day Tijuana seem like an ice-cream social. The few blocks of 1850s-era brick buildings that once stood on the shoreline are now far from the waterfront, and house upmarket antiques shops and lovingly restored offices. Many of their foundations are made from the hulls of ships abandoned by eager gold-seekers that eventually filled in the bay.

Stroll along Jackson Street (between Montgomery & Sansome Streets) and Hotaling Place to see the only neighbourhood left in San Francisco that predates the ubiquitous Victorian style. It was spared during the 1906 quake and the subsequent fire, not least because several of the buildings were liquor warehouses built of stone. By the 1930s, Jackson Square was popular with a number of bohemian artists and writers: John Steinbeck and William Saroyan, among others, used to drink at the now long-vanished Black Cat Café (710 Montgomery Street). For a bit of the maritime history of these few blocks, duck into the **Old Ship Saloon** (298 Pacific Avenue, at Battery Street, 1-415 788 2222). A ship that ran aground on Alcatraz Island, the *Arkansas*, was towed to the corner where the bar now resides

Cotogna.

– the original proprietor simply cut a door in the hull to allow access. Over the past century, the boat has morphed into a fairly conventional bar, but the story holds water: the remains of ships are still regularly unearthed in the area as crews excavate for new constructions.

Restaurants & Cafés

★ Cotogna
490 Pacific Avenue, at Montgomery Street (1-415 775-8508, www.cotognasf.com). BART & Metro to Embarcadero/bus 1, 10, 12, 20, 41. **Open** 11.30am-10.30pm Mon-Thur; 11.30am-11pm Fri-Sat; 5pm-9.30pm Sun. **Main courses** $21-$34. **Map** p46 B4 ㉙ Italian
The more casual next-door neighbour to Michael Tusk's two Michelin-starred Quince, Cotogna is one of the most authentic Italian restaurants in the city. In dish after dish, Tusk manages to find the perfect balance of colour, flavour and texture, creating exquisitely nuanced dishes such as luscious ravioli stuffed with creamy ricotta and golden farm egg, and grilled octopus so tender you'll wonder if he knows a secret fishing spot. The daily changing menu offers antipasti, grilled and spit-roasted meats, house-made pastas and wood-oven pizzas, as well as a good-value three-course prix fixe menu and specials of the day.

Kokkari
200 Jackson Street, at Front Street (1-415 981 0983, www.kokkari.com). BART & Metro to Embarcadero/bus 1, 10, 12, 20, 41. **Open** 11.30am-2.30pm, 5.30pm-10pm Mon-Thur; 11.30am-2.30pm, 5.30pm-11pm Fri; 5pm-11pm Sat; 5pm-10pm Sun. **Main courses** $22-$52. **Map** p46 B5 ㉚ Greek
Calling it 'the food of the gods' may be hyperbolic, but Kokkari's 'Hellenic cuisine' – essentially an inventive and seasonal update of traditional Greek – comes pretty close. Start with *marithes tiganites* (crispy smelt with lemon) or *octapodaki tou uiorgou* (grilled octopus with lemon, oregano and olive oil) and work your way up to the moussaka, a rich, creamy baked casserole of eggplant, lamb ragout and béchamel.

Quince
470 Pacific Avenue, between Montgomery & Sansome Streets (1-415 775 8500, www. quincerestaurant.com). BART & Metro to Embarcadero/bus 1, 10, 12, 20, 41. **Open** 5.30-9.30pm Mon-Thur; 5-9.30pm Fri, Sat. **Tasting menu** $198. **Map** p46 B4 ㉛ American
From the moment you step into this elegant, chandelier-lit dining room, it feels like a special occasion. And the food only elevates the experience. Michael Tusk's eight-course tasting menus (including a vegetarian option and a champagne-and-caviar-focused Salon menu) are exquisitely presented symphonies of Northern California cuisine with Italian and Japanese influences that have earned him two Michelin stars. The daily changing options start with Black River Russian caviar and might include courses such as tagliolini of squid, gaper clam and samphire, and Cinta Senese pork with vine cuttings and chanterelles.

Bars

Bix

56 Gold Street, between Montgomery & Sansome Streets (1-415 433 6300, www.bixrestaurant.com). Bus 9X, 10, 12, 20, 41. **Open** 4.30-10pm Mon-Thur; 11.30am-midnight Fri; 5.30pm-midnight Sat; 5.30-10pm Sun. **Map** p46 B4 ⊛

Bix's tucked-away location and supper-club menu evoke the Jazz Age, an impression bolstered by jacketed bartenders, live jazz and expertly crafted classic cocktails. Named for owner Doug 'Bix' Biederbeck, who was 'very vaguely related' to 1930s jazz cornet legend Bix Beiderbecke, the room effectively combines the glamour of Harlem's Cotton Club with the splendour of a cruise liner dining room – you half expect to spy Rita Hayworth sipping a martini in a booth. Acclaimed chef Bruce Hill's menu adds to the decadent appeal: after your Manhattan, slip into truffled cheese croques, foie gras torchon, lobster spaghetti, or a half-dozen oysters.

THE EMBARCADERO

For decades, San Franciscans old enough to remember the majesty of the original Embarcadero became misty-eyed for the old days when it was a palm-lined thoroughfare rather than a looming double-decker freeway. Then came the devastating 1989 Loma Prieta earthquake, which felled the Embarcadero's ill-considered upper deck, returning it to its former glory. Today, refurbished antique streetcars from around the world – including Zurich, Milan and even a pair of roofless numbers from the English resort town of Blackpool – ply the ribbon of unobstructed road that unfurls along the Bay.

At the foot of Market Street stands the centrepiece: the beautifully restored **Ferry Building**, which divides even-numbered piers (to the south) from odd (to the north). Major renovations to the 1898 landmark were unveiled in 2003; the building now bustles with the unmatched **Ferry Building Marketplace** (*see p61*), where stallholders sell organic produce, artisan breads and chocolate, cheeses and many other gourmet delicacies. Especially on days when the **Ferry Plaza Farmers' Market** (*see p63* **Fresh From the Farm**) is in residence, the 660-foot Grand Nave gets packed with foodies as day-trippers pile out of the back, laden with picnic supplies, to hop on ferries to Sausalito, Tiburon, or the East Bay.

Opposite the Ferry Building is Justin Herman Plaza, where you'll be confronted by Benicia-born artist Robert Arneson's bronze sculpture *Yin and Yang*. Looming behind it is a mysteriously dry series of square pipes that together make up a much-criticised fountain created by French-Canadian artist Armand Vaillancourt. The phalanx of towers behind the plaza at the foot of Sacramento Street comprises the **Embarcadero Center**, a series of office towers that also contains shops and restaurants, and a theatre complex that screens art-house movies.

Walk south from the Ferry Building along the Embarcadero to Howard Street, and you'll see low cement walls where bronze starfish, turtles and

HOW BAZAAR

Find out why Treasure Island lives up to its name.

Bargains are plentiful and rarities beg to be haggled over at the Bay Area's flea markets. Come prepared: bring plenty of cash, as well as sturdy bags. The earlier you arrive the better the buys, although at the end of the day, you just might score an art deco nightstand with Bakelite handles for $5 from that weary peddler who simply doesn't want to pack it up again.

The best of the bunch – showcasing everything from Victorian lace and Depression-era dishware to 1950s Formica kitchen tables and 1970s stacked Superfly boots – is **Alameda Point Antiques Faire**, across the Bay Bridge in Oakland at the former Alameda Point Naval Air Station (6am-3pm, 1st Sun of mth, 1-510 522 7500, www.antiquesbybay.com). Touted as Northern California's largest antiques and collectibles show, with more than 800 dealers, the event takes about half a day to cover and entry costs $5-$15 (it's cheapest after 9am). Quality is high: everything sold here must be at least 20 years old, and no reproductions are permitted.

Treasure Island Flea (1 Avenue of the Palms, 10am-4pm, last weekend of mth, $3 admission, www.treasureislandflea.com), a monthly market located halfway across the Bay Bridge (easily accessible by Muni or car), affords scenic views of the city skyline. The manmade 1937 island formerly served as a naval station and military base. The best time to visit is April through November, when the market is stationed on the Great Lawn and dogs and kids can frolic to live music. Around 350 vendors attend each month, selling vintage clothing and housewares, art, upcycled furniture, jewellery and crafts. Around 20 food trucks and a well-stocked bar make it a prime spot for picnicking.

Also worth a peek is San Francisco's **Alemany Flea Market** (100 Alemany Boulevard, 6am-3pm Sun, 1-415 647 2043), held in the concrete freeway nexus of Highways 101 and 280, at 100 Alemany Boulevard. In the shadow of the I-280 overpass, it isn't fancy, but what it lacks in ambience it makes up for in affordability and eccentricity. The speciality is antiques and artisan works, though that designation is relatively loose. You'll find a wealth of furniture, art, picture frames, sports gear, chinoiserie and costume jewellery among the piles. But it's the weird, one-of-a-kind finds that seal this SF market's oddball appeal.

Treasure Island Flea.

EXPLORE

octopi have been 'washed up' on the shore. Nearby, and easy to miss, is the small sign that marks Herb Caen Way, named after the late and ever-popular *San Francisco Chronicle* columnist. Lovers who come down this way may feel they've walked into their destiny when they spy an immense Cupid's bow in gold, complete with a silver and red arrow. This is Claes Oldenburg and Coosje van Bruggen's *Cupid's Span*, installed in 2002 in a field of native grass.

After taking in the wonderful views of the **Bay Bridge** (if it's nighttime, don't miss the *Bay Lights*, a permanent installation of 25,000 LED lights by artist Leo Villareal), continue south to **Red's Java House** (Pier 30, 1-415 777 5626), a small and quirky dockworkers' snack shack that has been a favourite for coffee and burgers since it opened in 1912.

Between Brannan and Townsend Streets, you'll see a cement marker reading 'Great Seawall'. This is exactly what the Embarcadero was built to be. It is entirely man-made, neatly rounding off the treacherous crags and coves that had been the end of many ships plying the San Francisco waters. Work on the sea wall started in 1878 and continued for nearly five decades, adding another 800 acres to the city and an additional 18 miles of useable dock space. Today, a push to revitalise vacant hangars has brought new stores, restaurants, public spaces and a state-of-the-art cruise ship terminal to the waterfront.

A block inland from the south end of the Embarcadero, **Rincon Center** (at the corner of Mission and Spear Streets) is the former main post office, now containing a number of impressive art pieces and historic murals, and the popular dim sum palace **Yank Sing** (*see p60*).

Alternatively, heading north from the Ferry Building, **Pier 7** juts into the Bay offering lovely views of **Treasure Island**. Built on the shoals of neighbouring Yerba Buena Island, the flat-as-a-pancake isle is entirely man-made from boulders and sand. Originally constructed as a site for 1939's Golden Gate International Exposition, the island was requisitioned by the US Navy in 1942. It served as a troop deployment staging area for many years, until it was returned to the city in 1997. It now functions as a sort of mid-Bay suburb, with little league baseball fields, wine-making warehouses, a monthly vintage flea market (*see p58* **How Bazaar**), and former military housing with spectacular vistas. Recently, long-awaited revitalisation plans have won approval, with builders poised to start in on a grand scheme that will include up to 8,000 homes, three hotels, restaurants, retail, entertainment venues, and a waterfront park. Neighbouring **Yerba Buena Island** – literally, 'Good Herb Island' in reference to an aromatic perennial from the mint family used in medicinal tea by Native Americans – is an important Coast Guard station.

Sights & Museums

★ Exploratorium

Pier 15, The Embarcadero, at Green Street (1-415 528 4444, www.exploratorium.edu). Streetcar F/ bus 2, 6, 14, 21, 31. **Open** 10am-5pm Tue-Sun (6-10pm Thur over-18s only). **Admission** $29; $19-$24 reductions; free under-4s. **Map** p46 A5 ③

Covering the length of three football fields, the Exploratorium features more than 600 interactive exhibits that test the boundaries of physics and human perception. The museum was founded in 1969 by physicist Frank Oppenheimer (brother of J Robert Oppenheimer, the father of the A-bomb), who was dedicated to the idea of getting people to explore, experiment with and test their notions of scientific principles. Every aspect of the Exploratorium is hands-on – from the storage lockers that play tones when you touch them, to the mind-bending parabolic mirror and the numerous optical and sensoral illusion puzzles. Popular mainstays include the Sweeper's Clock, a fascinating movie on a loop in which two street sweepers keep time by pushing around piles of trash; a marble maze you build from hardware store odds and ends; and the Tactile Dome, a crawl-through maze that you navigate in complete darkness (advance reservations highly recommended). The in-house restaurant showcases sustainable seafood and sushi, as well as small regional farms – and (note to parents) there's a full bar featuring artisanal cocktails.

Rincon Center

101 Spear Street, at Mission Street (1-415 243 0473). BART & Metro to Embarcadero/ bus 1, 12, 20, 30, 41 & Market Street routes. **Open** 8.30am-5.30pm daily. **Admission** free. **Map** p46 C6 ③

The lobby (facing Mission Street) of this art deco post office-cum-residential and office tower has intriguing Works Progress Administration (WPA)

EXPLORE

murals. Painted in 1941 by the Russian Social Realist painter Anton Refregier, this luscious historical panorama was hugely controversial at the time of its unveiling, not only because it was the most expensive of the WPA mural projects, but also because it included many dark moments from California's past. The central atrium has a unique all-water sculpture by Doug Hollis, *Rain Column*: 55 gallons of recycled water fall 85 feet into a central pool every minute.

Restaurants & Cafés

Americano

Hotel Vitale, 8 Mission Street, at the Embarcadero (1-415 278 3777, www.americanorestaurant.com). BART & Metro to Embarcadero/streetcar F/bus 2, 14, 31, 41 & Market Street routes. **Open** 6.30-10.30am, 11.30am-2.30pm, 5.30-10pm Mon-Fri; 7.30-11am, 5.30-10pm Sat; 7.30-11am, 4-10pm Sun. **Main courses** $16-$36. **Map** p46 C6 ③ **Italian**
This sleek, understatedly elegant restaurant in the Hotel Vitale offers seasonally fresh, Italian-inspired food, with many ingredients sourced from the Ferry Plaza Farmers' Market across the street. Try panini at lunch, grilled ribeye at dinner, and the restaurant's house-made gelato for dessert. Much attention is also paid to the breakfasts.

Boulevard

1 Mission Street, at Steuart Street (1-415 543 6084, www.boulevardrestaurant.com). BART & Metro to Embarcadero/streetcar F/bus 2, 14, 31, 41 & Market Street routes. **Open** 11.30am-2.15pm, 5.30-10pm Mon-Thur; 11.30am-2pm, 5.30-10.30pm Fri; 5.30-10.30pm Sat; 5.30-10pm Sun. **Main courses** $25-$49. **Map** p46 C6 ③ **American**
Since 1993, this classic-looking restaurant has been one of San Francisco's most consistently reliable: from the service to the cooking, there's seldom a misstep. Always busy, it attracts locals and visitors with its hearty food and waterfront views. Self-taught chef Nancy Oakes specialises in elaborate New American dishes – pork chops, steaks and risottos – although wood-roasted items are another strength.

Slanted Door

1 Ferry Building, at The Embarcadero (1-415 861 8032, www.slanteddoor.com). BART & Metro to Embarcadero/streetcar F/bus 2, 14, 31 & Market

Street routes. **Open** 11am-4.30pm, 5.30-10pm Mon-Sat; 11.30am-4.30pm, 5.30-10.30pm Sun. **Main courses** $20-$48. **Map** p46 A6 ③ **Vietnamese**
The sleek lines and Bay views of Charles Phan's popular Ferry Building restaurant are alluring, but the main attraction remains Phan's incredible, inventive Vietnamese-inspired food. There isn't a bad choice on the menu, although the shaking beef, the spicy short ribs and the shrimp and crab spring rolls are still standouts.

Yank Sing

Rincon Center, 101 Spear Street, at Mission Street (1-415 781 1111, www.yanksing.com). BART & Metro to Montgomery/bus 2, 31, 38, 108 & Market Street routes. **Open** 11am-3pm Mon-Fri; 10am-4pm Sat, Sun. **Dishes** $6-$20. **Map** p46 C6 ③ **Chinese**
The quality of Yank Sing's dim sum explains how it manages to thrive in the corner of a massive office complex. Mostly non-English-speaking waitresses roll out an endless array of dumplings – from steamed shrimp-and-pork siu mai to Shanghai soup dumplings – and the loyal, on-the-go business crowd snaps them up with speed.
Other location 29 Stevenson Street, between 1st & 2nd Streets, SoMa (1-415 541 4949).

Bars

Hard Water

Pier 3, The Embarcadero (1-415 392 3021, www.hardwaterbar.com). BART & Metro to Embarcadero. **Open** 11.30am-midnight Mon-Sat; 11.30am-10pm Sun. **Map** p46 B6 ③
Backed by a glowing wall of booze, the horseshoe-shaped bar is the centrepiece of this intimate whiskey lover's haven, offering a panoramic view of the Bay. New Orleans-style tipples include Cocktail à la Louisiane, which blends Rittenhouse 100 rye, vermouth, Benedictine, absinthe and Peychauds bitters, but true connoisseurs come here for the flights – four or five half-ounce pours of various whiskeys, bourbons and ryes. Start with the Craft Distillers flight, which includes sips from distilleries such as Peach Street, Garrison Brothers, and Old Potrero. Rich snacks and dishes like pork belly cracklings, cornmeal-crusted alligator, and an extensive raw bar stand up nicely to the bold cocktails. Reservations are highly recommended.

Ferry Plaza Wine Merchant

1 Ferry Building, Shop 23 (1-415 391 9400, www. fpwm.com). BART & Metro to Embarcadero. **Open** 11am-8pm Mon; 10am-8pm Tue; 10am-9pm Wed-Fri; 8am-8pm Sat; 10am-7pm Sun. **Map** p46 B6 ④
Part of the vast artisanal marketplace and organic farmers' market at the Ferry Building on the Embarcadero, FPWM is a combo shop/wine-tasting bar offering a huge selection of small-production wines from Napa and Sonoma vintners, as well as from European winemakers – with 15 to 20

IN THE KNOW TV STAR

A couple of blocks inland from the **Exploratorium** (see p59), where Green and Sansome Streets meet, is the former laboratory of boy-genius Philo T Farnsworth. Here, in 1927, Farnsworth invented the current system of television transmission; a small plaque marks the achievement.

EXPLORE

available for tasting every day. Pair your wine with cheese, antipasti, salumi or caviar – or, better yet, grab some freshly baked bread from neighbouring Acme Bakery and cheese from Point Reyes' Cowgirl Creamery, and settle in for power people-watching.

Shops & Services

★ Ferry Building Marketplace

Ferry Building, The Embarcadero, at Market Street. BART & Metro to Embarcadero/bus 2, 6, 9, 14, 21, 31 & Market Street routes (1-415 291 3276, www.ferrybuildingmarketplace.com). **Open** (hours vary for some businesses) 10am-6pm Mon-Fri; 9am-6pm Sat; 11am-5pm Sun. *Farmers' Market* 10am-2pm Tue, Thur; 8am-2pm Sat. **Map** p46 B6 ⓸ **Food & drink**

No mere shopping destination, the Ferry Building Marketplace is a sightseeing attraction in its own right. On market days, 75 regional farmers and artisan food purveyors offer a dizzying array of organic fruit and vegetables, and gourmet goodies from olive oils, meat, cheese and bread to chocolate, jams and flowers. Vendors' white tents spill out into the open air from both the north and south arcades and the city's best artisanal products and gourmet take-out counters, including homegrown brands such as Acme Bread, Cowgirl Creamery, Hog Island Oyster Co and Blue Bottle Coffee, sell from permanent stalls lining the nave.

THE TENDERLOIN

There are two competing stories as to how the Tenderloin got its name. The first is that police who worked the beat here in the 19th century were paid extra for taking on such a tough neighbourhood, and could therefore afford to buy better cuts of meat. The second is similar, but with one key change: the cops got their extra cash not from police chiefs in the form of wages, but from local hoods in the form of bribes. No one is sure which tale is correct, but neither reflects well on an area that's always lived on the wild side.

The Tenderloin is a far cry from the retail mecca of Union Square a few blocks to the east and even from the few blocks that skirt the edge of Nob Hill (known as the Tendernob). The area is home to a spirited community and its reputation shouldn't put people off visiting the local theatres, staying in one of its stylish hotels, or checking out its myriad cool dive bars. That said, there's not much reason to visit the area during the day, when the only street life comes courtesy of the panhandlers and drug addicts who cluster on corners. Depending on where you're planning to walk (Geary Street and points north are usually safe; streets south of it can get a bit sketchy), it may be best to hail a cab at night.

While the city struggles with the question of how best to care for the Tenderloin's dissolute souls (it's been a key issue in every mayoral contest for at least two decades), soup kitchens provide a partial solution. In particular, one pair of churches share a long and compassionate history. **St Boniface Catholic Church** (133 Golden Gate Avenue, at Leavenworth Street) hosts dozens of benefit programmes and has a dining room that serves food to the needy, while the Free Meals programme at **Glide Memorial Church** (330 Ellis Street, at Taylor Street), started back in 1969, offers similar sustenance. Both, of course, also hold services, and the ecstatic gospel singing at Glide (9am, 11am Sun) drags an amazingly diverse congregation to its feet; get there early if you want to attend, as the place is usually packed.

The area is also known as the Tandoor-loin because of the surprising profusion of good and affordable Indian restaurants on or near O'Farrell Street: try **Shalimar**, which offers inexpensive Pakistani and Indian food, or **Naan 'n' Curry** (336 O'Farrell Street, near Mason Street, 1-415 346 1443). Wherever you eat, follow it up with a beer or a cocktail at one of countless bars in the locale, which range from spit 'n' sawdust dives to a handful of fairly swanky spots that have taken advantage of lower rents.

The **Great American Music Hall** (859 O'Farrell Street, between Polk & Larkin Streets; *see p218*), said to be the oldest nightclub in San Francisco and now a beautiful music venue with an interior that evokes Versailles' Hall of Mirrors, is an anchor in the neighbourhood. However, even this grand space is not as virtuous as it looks: it spent a number of its early years as a bordello.

Restaurants & Cafés

$ Shalimar

532 Jones Street, between Geary & O'Farrell Streets (1-415 928 0333, www.shalimarsf.com). BART & Metro to Powell/bus 2, 3, 27, 31, 38/ cable car Powell-Hyde or Powell-Mason. **Open** noon-midnight daily. **Main courses** $7-$10. **No credit cards. Map** p47 E2 ⓸ Indian

In-the-know locals head to the Tenderloin for good, cheap Indian and Pakistani food, and everyone has their own favourites. But Shalimar serves some of the best in the city, despite the nonexistent decor and grubby location. Dishes here are fairly spicy, turned out at speed and at predictably keen prices. **Other location** 1409 Polk Street, at Pine Street, Polk Gulch (1-415 776 4642).

Bars

Bourbon & Branch

501 Jones Street, between Geary & O'Farrell Streets (1-415 346-1735, www.bourbonandbranch.com). Bus 27, 31, 38. **Open** 6pm-2am daily. **Map** p47 E2 ⓸

EXPLORE

Yes, there's a whiff of pretension to this spot, from the 'secret' password at the door to the ban on cell phones. That said, it's worth it. Bourbon & Branch actually houses five bars under its roof, including the grand chandelier-lit main bar and the book-lined library bar. But whiskey lovers will be best served by making a reservation at Wilson & Wilson, the detective-themed bar accessible off Jones Street. There, you'll find dark, candlelit booths, a pressed-tin ceiling and an extensive menu (in the style of case files) that progresses from aperitifs to boozy, spirit-forward drinks. Try the Pinkerton: bourbon, coffee syrup, cranberry-infused angostura-orange bitters and tobacco-bourbon tincture.

Mikkeller Bar

34 Mason Street, between Turk & Eddy Streets (1-415 984-0279, www.mikkellerbar.com). BART & Metro to Civic Center. **Open** noon-midnight Mon-Wed, Sun; noon-2am Thur-Sat. **Map** p47 E3 ㊹
This beer oasis draws hop heads from all over the city. The centrepiece of the brick-walled canteen and bar is an epic 42-tap setup, augmented by a specialised bottle selection. The draft menu comfortably stretches over a wide and generally affordable range of European and domestic suds, featuring about ten of Mikkeller's house brews including IPA, pale ale and lambic. Mikkeller is also one of the few places in the city that serves cask-conditioned ales. To pair, a sturdy food menu features beer-friendly standbys such as charcuterie, cheeses and house-made sausages.

Redwood Room

Clift Hotel, 495 Geary Street, at Taylor Street (1-415 929 2372, www.clifthotel.com). BART & Metro to Powell/bus 2, 3, 4, 27, 38, 76/cable car Powell-Hyde or Powell-Mason. **Open** 5pm-2am Mon-Thur, Sun; 4pm-2am Fri, Sat. **Map** p47 E3 ㊺
No time was wasted in adding a bar to the Clift after the repeal of Prohibition in 1933, and the magnificent result has been a fixture for high-end cocktailing ever since. Although the decor shifted from art deco to postmodern, the bar is neither tacky nor too flamboyant, its towering walls still panelled in redwood thought to have come from a single tree. A DJ spins four nights a week for a sophisticated mix of locals and out-of-towners, and the place has an air of clandestine affairs and under-the-table friskiness. Fun fact: the portraits hanging around the room move ever so slightly, haunted house-style.

Tradition

441 Jones Street, between Ellis & O'Farrell Streets (1-415 474-2284, www.tradbar.com). BART & Metro to Powell. **Open** 6pm-2am Mon-Sat. **Map** p47 E2 ㊻
At odds with its gritty location, Tradition is one of the most beautiful bars in San Francisco, with a panelled grandeur that evokes a 19th-century train station. An elaborate wood-and-glass bar hangs

from the tall ceiling, dwarfing the half-dozen braces-clad bartenders hustling to dispense drinks to the throngs. The bar has three levels. The main space on the ground floor gets packed at weekends, while the quieter mezzanine provides a view of the action below. Sitting between the two are a series of slightly elevated 'snugs' – couples and groups of up to eight people can reserve one of these semi-enclosed booths, which have table service and an extended menu. As suggested by the vintage posters from various decades on the walls, the cocktail programme takes you through the history of American tippling with drinks from each era, spanning everything from Prohibition old-fashioneds to tiki-bar mai tais, made with quality spirits and fresh fruit.

CIVIC CENTER

Southwest of the Tenderloin and north of Market Street, San Francisco's Civic Center is a complex of imposing government buildings and stately performance halls centred on the **Civic Center Plaza**. By day, it's populated by a diverse cross-section of society, from vagrants to smartly turned-out dignitaries. At night, the worker bees are replaced by culture vultures, here to take in a concert, ballet, lecture or opera at one of the area's several venues.

Facing the plaza, and dominating the area, is the 1915 Beaux Arts **City Hall**, stunning both inside and out. Across the four lanes of traffic on Van Ness Avenue is a trio of grand edifices. The multistorey curved-glass façade of the **Louise M Davies Symphony Hall** (201 Van Ness Avenue, at Hayes Street; *see p224*) would be unforgettable even without the reclining Henry Moore bronzes in front, while just north of Grove Street sits the **War Memorial Opera House** (301 Van Ness Avenue, at Grove Street; *see p225*), also designed by architect Arthur Brown.

The last of the triumvirate is the **Veterans Building**. On its main floor sits the tiny San Francisco Arts Commission Gallery, which specialises in politically or sociologically driven art. The bottom floor houses the beautiful Herbst Theatre (due to reopen following renovation by publication of this guide), which holds a distinction in San Francisco history as being the site where the UN Charter was drafted and signed on 26 June 1945.

In the southeast corner of Civic Center Plaza is the **Bill Graham Civic Auditorium** (99 Grove Street, at Polk Street; *see p217*), named after the concert promoter who almost single-handedly created the San Francisco Sound of the 1960s. The 7,000-capacity hall now stages gigs by big names. Nearby is the **Main Library**, a six-storey building mixing Beaux Arts elements with modernism; in 2003 it replaced the old library, which is now home to the world-class **Asian Art Museum**.

FRESH FROM THE FARM

Farmers' markets are a grown-in-San Francisco staple.

It's been decades since California cuisine exploded on to the dining scene, but the idea of freshly picked, seasonal, local and sustainably farmed ingredients has continued to root itself in the San Francisco consciousness. There is now a weekly farmers' market in practically every neighbourhood in the Bay Area, and at local restaurants the term 'farm-to-table' is as common as 'pass the salt'. City markets have also evolved far beyond generic produce stands, with most offering prepared foods and gourmet goods, live entertainment and educational resources for weekend gardeners and backyard farmers. The Big Three – at the Ferry Building, on Alemany Boulevard, and in Civic Center's United Nations Plaza – each draw vastly different crowds, who shop for everything from Asian greens and hard-to-find mushrooms to speciality peppers, organic meats, orchids and handmade cheeses.

The first farmers' market in California, **Alemany Farmers Market** (100 Alemany Boulevard, at Tompkins Avenue, 1-415 647 9423, www.sfgsa.org, 6am-3pm Sat) in the decidedly untouristy Bernal Heights neighbourhood, offers an amazing variety of affordable regional produce, giving rise to its moniker as the 'people's market'. Established as a Victory Garden during World War II to support regional family farms, it has vendors spanning several generations. The market sells every sort of fruit and vegetable imaginable, from crookneck squash and parsnips to hot chilli peppers, pluots and pomegranates, plus prepared foods from a variety of ethnic purveyors.

The **Ferry Building Marketplace** (see p61) has evolved into a must-see destination for discerning foodies, with the tri-weekly **Ferry Plaza Farmers' Market** (www.cuesa.org, 10am-2pm Tue, Thur; 8am-2pm Sat) featuring more than 75 producers and scores of vendors selling everything from locally made jam, cheeses, breads and baked goods to prepared snacks.

The nonprofit farmer-operated **Heart of the City Farmers Market** (Market Street, between 7th & 8th Streets, 1-415 558 9455, hotcfarmersmarket.org, 7am-5.30pm Wed, 7am-5pm Sun), established in 1981 to bring fresh produce to low-income, senior and ethnic communities in the surrounding neighbourhoods, in Civic Center's United Nations Plaza (see p62) is where you'll find your baby bok choy, lemongrass, Vietnamese herbs, and other Asian ingredients.

EXPLORE

Ferry Plaza Farmers' Market.

On the edge of the Civic Center is the **United Nations Plaza**. A farmers' market operates here on Wednesdays and Sundays (*see p63* **Fresh From the Farm**), with gourmet food truck coalition Off the Grid (*see p129* **Cooking With Gas**) moving in on Thursday afternoons. The action takes place under the approving gaze of a mounted statue of Simón Bolívar, the great liberator of Central America.

Sights & Museums

★ Asian Art Museum

200 Larkin Street, at Fulton Street (1-415 581 3500, www.asianart.org). BART & Metro to Civic Center/streetcar F/bus 5, 19, 21, 47, 49 & Market Street routes. **Open** 10am-5pm Tue, Wed, Fri-Sun; 10am-9pm Thur. **Admission** $15; $10 reductions; free under-12s; free 1st Sun of mth. **Map** p47 F2 ❹

This popular museum has one of the world's most comprehensive collections of Asian art, spanning 6,000 years and more than 18,000 objects on display. Artefacts range from Japanese Buddhas and sacred texts to items from the Ming Dynasty. The café is a great place to enjoy American- and Asian-inspired dishes, and the gift shop is stocked with high-quality stationery, decorative items and a handsome selection of coffee-table books. The institution resides in the former home of the San Francisco Public Library, which was beautifully redesigned in 2003 by Gae Aulenti, the architect responsible for the heralded Musée d'Orsay conversion in Paris.

FREE City Hall

1 Dr Carlton B Goodlett Place (Polk Street), between McAllister & Grove Streets (1-415 554 4933, tours 1-415 554 6139). BART & Metro to Civic Center/streetcar F/bus 19, 21, 47, 49 & Market Street routes. **Open** 8am-8pm daily. *Tours* 10am, noon, 2pm Mon-Fri. **Admission** free. **Map** p47 G1 ❹

Built in 1915 to designs by Arthur Brown and John Bakewell, City Hall is the epitome of the Beaux Arts style visible across the whole Civic Center. The building features a five-storey colonnade, limestone and granite masonry and a gold-topped dome – modelled on the one at St Peter's in Rome – higher than the one on the nation's Capitol. After the edifice was damaged in the 1989 earthquake, city planners spent $300 million protecting it against future shocks and restoring it to its original grandeur. Its 600 rooms have seen plenty of history: Bay Area native son Joe DiMaggio got hitched to Marilyn Monroe on the third floor in 1954, while on a more sombre note, it was here that Dan White assassinated Mayor George Moscone and City Supervisor Harvey Milk in 1978. Today, the building houses the legislative and executive branches of both city and county government. Free tours offering behind-the-scenes views of the Board of Supervisors' chambers (panelled in hand-carved Manchurian oak) are available Monday to Friday.

FREE San Francisco Main Library

100 Larkin Street, between Grove & Fulton Streets (library 1-415 557 4400, history room 1-415 557 4567, www.sfpl.org). BART & Metro to Civic Center/bus 5, 21, 47, 49 & Market Street routes. **Open** *Library* 10am-6pm Mon, Sat; 9am-8pm Tue-Thur; noon-6pm Fri; noon-5pm Sun. *History Room* 10am-6pm Tue-Thur, Sat; noon-6pm Fri; noon-5pm Sun. *Tours* noon 1st Tue of mth. **Admission** free. **Map** p47 G2 ❹

Built in 1996 by the architectural firm Pei Cobb Freed & Partners, San Francisco's public library is beautifully designed. On the top floor, the San Francisco History Room offers changing exhibitions, a large photo archive and knowledgeable, approachable staff. The small shop on the main floor has bargains on local titles. Readings by big-name and up-and-coming authors are held regularly.

Restaurants & Cafés

Alta, CA

1420 Market Street, at 10th Street (1-415 590 2585, www.altaca.co). BART & Metro to Civic Center/Streetcar F/bus 5, 21, 47, 49 & Market Street routes. **Open** 11.30am-2am Mon-Fri; 5pm-2am Sat, Sun. **Main courses** $16-$25. **Map** p47 G1 ❺ **Eclectic**

The first upscale restaurant to debut in the burgeoning tech mecca along mid-Market Street, Alta is the brainchild of wunderkind chef/author Daniel Patterson, who also owns the two Michelin-starred Coi in North Beach. Alta is more down to earth, with a menu, as executed by chef David Goody, that marries Eastern Europe (house-made pastrami, bialys, eggplant pierogi, beef stroganoff) with more lofty farm-to-table fare, such as pork and squid salad, Fort Bragg king salmon with artichokes, and braised duck leg. The cool, salvaged decor, big central bar and open kitchen add to the relaxed vibe. It's a great spot for a pre-theatre bite.

$ Ananda Fuara

1298 Market Street, at Larkin & 9th streets (1-415 621-1994, www.anandafuara.com) BART & Metro to Civic Center/bus 5, 21, 47, 49 & Market Street routes. **Open** 11am-3pm Mon, Sun; 11am-8pm Tue-Sat. **Main courses** $8.75-$10. **Map** p47 G2 ➄ Vegetarian

A longtime staple on the vegetarian scene, Ananda Fuara is run by followers of Indian guru/musician/athlete Sri Chinmoy, offering vegetarian and vegan cuisine served in a bright cafeteria-style atmosphere by a sari-wearing waitstaff. The samosas, curry wraps and falafel are all pretty tasty, but the order of the day for most is the 'neatloaf' sandwich, a

vegetarian interpretation of meatloaf made from grains, eggs, ricotta cheese, tofu and spices, baked and topped with a tomatoey sauce.

Bars

Dirty Water

Suite 180, 1355 Market Street, between 9th & 10th Streets (1-415 792 5101, www.dirtywatersf. com). BART & Metro to Civic Center/Streetcar F/ bus 5, 21, 47, 49 & Market Street routes. **Open** 11am-1am Mon-Sat; 11am-10pm Sun. **Map** p47 G2 ➅

Sharing a building with Twitter's new SF headquarters, Dirty Water is a bar, restaurant and brewery made for young technorati, offering a truly dizzying array of craft cocktails, house-brewed and tap beers, wines by the glass and small-batch liquors. The name refers to a pre-Prohibition moniker for whisky, and anyone looking for that particular spirit won't be disappointed: the scotch menu alone would make a Highlander weep. Of note among the myriad cocktails is 140 Characters, a homage to Twitter combining Zu vodka, Ancho Reyes, lime and egg whites. The food menu focuses on 'American Primal' dishes such as Axis deer tartar, Monterey abalone and bone broth stew, as well as an extensive selection of cheeses and charcuterie.

EXPLORE

Dirty Water.

SoMa & South Beach

Following devastation in the 1906 fire, the streets south of Market Street became an industrial wasteland, and stayed that way for much of the 20th century. With the dotcom boom of the 1990s came rapid regeneration: warehouses were converted into high-end loft apartments, bars and restaurants opened to serve the new locals, and South of Market took off. The dotcom implosion of the early 2000s saw vacancy signs everywhere, but with Web 2.0 in full swing and the transformation of a dilapidated dockside area into Mission Bay, SoMa has risen once again.

In South Beach, the primary draw remains the San Francisco Giants baseball team, fresh off their third World Series win. Their stadium, AT&T Park, draws huge crowds for its 80-plus home games each spring and summer, packing the surrounding watering holes and eateries.

Bar Agricole.

Don't Miss

1 SFMOMA A modern-art gem is getting even better with expansion (p72).

2 Bar Agricole The cocktails are as seasonal and well-crafted as the food (p73).

3 Blue Bottle Coffee Nirvana for coffee nerds and casual caffeine seekers alike (p73).

4 Marlowe The burger here is legendary (p78).

5 AT&T Park Take in the game *and* the Bay (p77).

EXPLORE

Contemporary Jewish Museum.

YERBA BUENA GARDENS & AROUND

Bounded by Mission, 3rd, Folsom and 4th Streets, the Yerba Buena Gardens complex was renovated as part of a city-funded project in the 1980s and '90s. Attractions and businesses are housed in a series of structures that is half above ground and half below it. Within the Gardens is an urban park with sculpture walks, shady trees and the Martin Luther King Jr Memorial & Waterfall, constructed in 1993 in memory of the assassinated civil rights leader. A selection of Dr King's quotes is inscribed beneath the waterfall in various languages. On one side of the block sits the **Yerba Buena Center for the Arts**, an architectural beauty in itself. Filling the other half of the block (4th Street, from Howard to Mission Streets) is the **Metreon** (www. shoppingmetreon.com), a futuristic, four-storey mall where 16 cinema screens (including a giant-screen IMAX) are backed up by shops, eateries and a large Target store.

Across 3rd Street from Yerba Buena Gardens sits the **San Francisco Museum of Modern Art**, set to reopen in spring 2016 after a major expansion (*see p83* **Taking Modern to the Max**). Next door is the St Regis Museum Tower, a luxury hotel that also houses the **Museum of the African Diaspora** (*see p72*). The **Moscone Center** (747 Howard Street, between 3rd & 4th

Streets), named after assassinated mayor George Moscone, is a similarly imposing building. Most of it is of little interest to casual visitors, but the **Rooftop at Yerba Buena Gardens**, ingeniously covering the top of the Moscone Center on the south side of Howard Street, houses the **Children's Creativity Museum** (*see p194*), a delightful carousel and-carved by Charles Looff in 1906, an ice-skating rink, a bowling alley, and an ultra-cool interactive sculpture by Chico Macmurtrie. Sit on the middle pink bench and your weight moves the metal figure up and down on top of its globe (attempt this only before lunch).

Contrasting with all this modernity is the high-ceilinged **St Patrick's Church** (756 Mission Street, between 3rd & 4th Streets, 1-415 421 3730, www.stpatricksf.org). Built in 1851, the church ministered to the growing Irish population brought to the city by the Gold Rush. It was destroyed by the 1906 earthquake but subsequently restored to its original state; it now hosts both services and concerts. Nearby is the architecturally startling **Contemporary Jewish Museum** and the **California Historical Society**.

Several blocks southwest of Yerba Buena, **Folsom Street** savours its kinky reputation during the annual **Folsom Street Fair** (*see p32*) in September, but the **Cake Gallery** (290 9th Street, at Folsom Street, 1-415 861 2253,

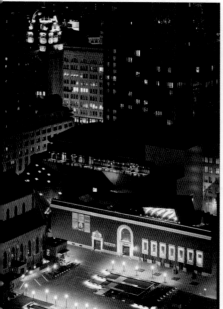

www.thecakegallerysf.com) is a year-round thrill: with a nod to the legendary Magnolia Thunderpussy, it's the only bakery in the city that sells pornographic cakes. Nearby are many good restaurants catering to the young and hip, and the **Brain Wash Café** (1122 Folsom Street, between 7th & 8th Streets, www.brainwash.com), a spot about which weary travellers have fantasised for generations: a combo bar/music venue/restaurant/laundromat, where you can sip some suds and wash your duds.

Sights & Museums

California Historical Society

678 Mission Street, between 3rd & New Montgomery Streets (1-415 357 1848, www.calhist. org). BART & Metro to Montgomery/bus 9, 9X, 10, 14, 30, 45, 71. **Open** 11am-8pm Tue; 11am-5pm Wed-Sun. **Admission** $5. **No credit cards** (except bookstore purchases). **Map** p70 C3 ❶
The state's official history group has focused its efforts on assembling this impressive collection of Californiana. The vaults hold half a million photographs and thousands of books, magazines and paintings, as well as an extensive Gold Rush collection; selections are presented as changing displays on the state's history. The delightful gift shop and bookstore is a joint venture between CHS and Heyday Publishing, offering books about California and local crafts.

Contemporary Jewish Museum

736 Mission Street, between 3rd & 4th Streets (1-415 655 7800, www.thecjm.org). BART & Metro to Montgomery/bus 9, 9X, 10, 14, 30, 45, 71. **Open** 11am-5pm Mon, Tue, Fri-Sun; 11am-8pm Thur. **Admission** $12; $10 reductions; $5 Thur after 5pm; free 1st Tue of mth. **Map** p70 C3 ❷
Across from Yerba Buena Gardens, the museum is devoted to linking the art of the Jewish community with the community at large. One of the best reasons to visit is the building itself, carved out of a 1907 Willis Polk power substation. New York architect Daniel Libeskind married the old brick façade to a sci-fi-looking blue-steel cube. Inside, there are soaring skylights that shed light on exhibits about Jewish culture, history, art and ideas. The café serves traditional dishes such as latkes and bagels with lox.

IN THE KNOW BALLPARK PERKS

As befits this foodie city, snacks at **AT&T Park** (*see p77*) go far beyond ordinary ballpark franks, with stands offering everything from Neapolitan pizza and fresh sushi to grilled crab and ahi tuna sandwiches. If the game drags, kids can ride slides inside an 80-foot Coke bottle and admire the gargantuan baseball-mitt sculpture out behind centre field.

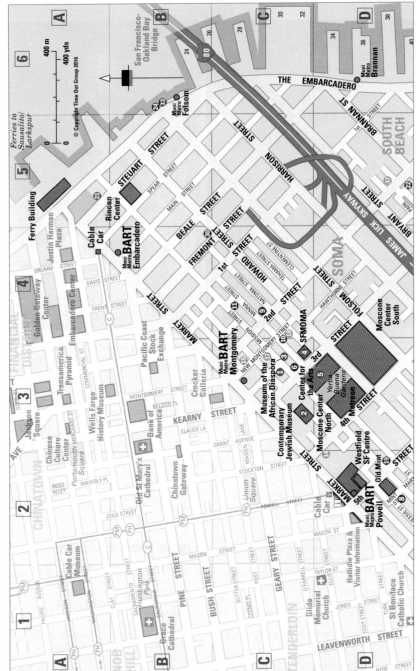

SoMa & South Beach

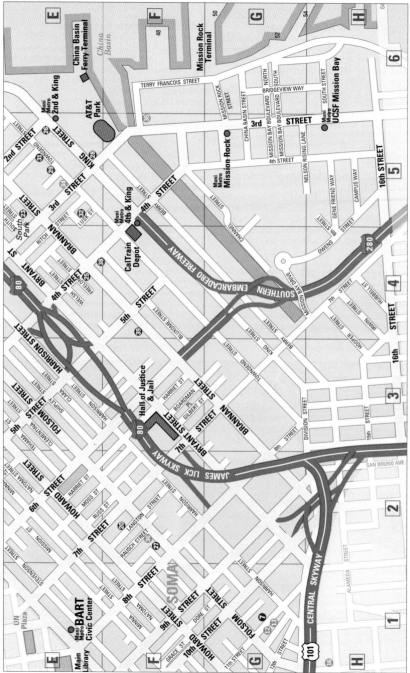

EXPLORE

Museum of the African Diaspora

685 Mission Street, at 3rd Street (1-415 358 7200, www.moadsf.org). BART & Metro to Montgomery/ bus 9, 9X, 10, 14, 30, 45, 71. **Open** 11am-6pm Wed-Sat; noon-5pm Sun. **Admission** $10; $5 reductions; free under-12s. **Map** p70 C3 ❸

Located on the first three floors of the St Regis Museum Tower, MoAD is the world's first museum dedicated to exploring the international impact of the diaspora of African peoples across the globe. Rotating exhibitions highlight the art and culture of the continent, with multimedia exhibits and moving first-person accounts.

★ San Francisco Museum of Modern Art (SFMOMA)

151 3rd Street, between Mission & Howard Streets (1-415 357 4000, www.sfmoma.org). BART & Metro to Montgomery/bus 9, 9X, 10, 14, 30, 45, 71. **Open** Call or see website for information. **Admission** Call or see website for information. **Map** p70 C3 ❹

The second-largest US museum devoted to modern art, SFMOMA reopens in spring 2016 after a major expansion. The permanent collection houses some 30,000 paintings, sculptures, works on paper, photographs and media arts, and includes works by such varied artists as René Magritte, Jeff Koons and Piet Mondrian. Now that gallery space has increased by 50%, some pieces are on display for the first time. *See p83* **Taking Modern to the Max**.

Yerba Buena Center for the Arts

701 Mission Street, at 3rd Street (1-415 978 2787, www.ybca.org). BART & Metro to Montgomery/bus 9, 9X, 10, 14, 30, 45, 71. **Open** noon-6pm Wed, Sun; noon-8pm Thur-Sat. **Admission** $10; $8 reductions. Free 1st Tue of mth. **Map** p70 C3 ❺

Yerba Buena Center stands opposite SFMOMA and is somewhat in its shadow, yet it seems unintimidated, tugging at the modern art scene's shirttails with a scrappy itinerary and great attitude. Housed in Fumihiko Maki's futuristic-looking building, it contains four galleries for changing shows and a 96-seat theatre. The focus is on the contemporary and the challenging (installation and video art, outsider art); exhibitions have included work by such diverse names as Henry Darger, Fred Tomaselli, Anna Halprin and Kumi Yamashita.

▶ *For performing arts at Yerba Buena, see p225.*

Restaurants & Cafés

Ame

689 Mission Street, at 3rd Street (1-415 284 4040, www.amerestaurant.com). BART & Metro to Montgomery/bus 12, 14, 30, 45 & Market Street routes. **Open** 6-9.30pm Mon-Thur; 5.30-10pm Fri, Sat; 5.30-9.30pm Sun. **Main courses** $38-$44. **Map** p70 C3 ❻ **American creative**

Hiro Sone and Lissa Doumani's East-meets-West cuisine and impeccable preparations have earned them a Michelin star eight years running. Housed

Blue Bottle Coffee.

in a stylish and intimate dining room in the St Regis Hotel, the restaurant emphasises raw (sashimi, crudo, poke, carpaccio) and modern American cuisine (grilled Snake River Farm pork chop with chorizo-corn ragout; NY strip steak with summer beans in miso red wine sauce). The bar features limited-edition sakés and small-batch wines.

★ Bar Agricole

355 11th Street, between Folsom & Harrison Streets (1-415 355 9400, www.baragricole.com). Bus 9, 12, 27, 47. **Open** 6-10pm Mon-Thur, Sun; 5.30pm-11pm Fri, Sat. **Main courses** $28-$49. **Map** p71 G1 ❼ **American**

With an artisanal cocktail list that's as extensive as the food menu, you'll be hard-pressed to choose between another Monkey's Gland or a second order of the sheep's milk ricotta dumplings with fiddlehead ferns. Go for both – and while you're at it, try the albacore confit with tomatillos or any of the other exquisitely seasonal, impeccably fresh plates, as you sip your slavishly crafted cocktail (even the ice is tailor-made for each drink). Undoubtedly the biggest thing to hit the hopping 11th Street corridor in recent years, Bar Agricole feels at once earthy and ethereal, with walls covered with old barrel staves and light fixtures made from hundreds of glass tubes that look like windswept waves. Belly up to the bar (getting a sit-down reservation can be challenging) or try to snag a table for brunch on the sunny, enclosed front patio.

★ $ Blue Bottle Coffee

66 Mint Street, at Jessie Street (1-415 495 3394, www.bluebottlecoffee.net). BART & Metro to Powell/streetcar F/bus 5, 14, 27 & Market Street routes. **Open** 7am-7pm daily. **Sandwiches** $12. **Map** p70 D2 ❽ **Café**

Grounds zero for the city's coffee-obsessed, Blue Bottle's loyal fans temper caffeine highs with breakfast and lunch snacks (frittatas, soups, salads and sandwiches). The main draw is still single-origin small-batch and ridiculously fresh coffee (nothing is more than 48 hours out of the roaster), and the fascinatingly complicated coffee-making equipment. A five-light siphon bar is the first of its kind in the United States; the beakers and flasks that drip Kyoto-style iced-coffee are something out of a mad scientist's lab. Order a Gibraltar (you have to ask; it's not on the menu) – the perfect blend of espresso and foam, served in a short glass.

▶ *For more on SF's coffee culture, see p174.*

Jersey

145 Second Street, between Minna & Natoma Streets (1-415 912 1502, www.jerseysf.com). BART & Metro to Montgomery/streetcar F/bus 14 & Market Street routes. **Open** 11am-10pm Mon-Thur; 11am-11pm Fri, Sat. **Main courses** $17-$28. **Map** p70 C4 ❾ **Italian**

East Coast transplants rejoiced when the Rosenthal brothers opened this paean to the Garden State in 2015. New Jersey-style pizza tops the hit list – there are a dozen options starting with Trenton Tomato Pie, a thick-crust pizza topped with crushed tomatoes, sliced mozzarella and parmesan. Non-pizza options include fried softshell crab with grilled peach relish, and meatballs on sourdough. There's also a breakfast pizza with smoked salmon, garlic, and scrambled eggs. Looking for a greasy dollar slice? Fuhgeddaboudit.

Mourad

140 New Montgomery, at Minna Street (1-415 660 2500, www.mouradsf.com). BART & Metro to Montgomery/streetcar F/bus Market Street routes. **Open** 11.30am-2pm, 5.30-10pm Mon-Fri; 5.30-10pm Sat, Sun. **Main courses** $19-$60. **Tasting menu** $120. **Map** p70 C3 ❿ **Moroccan**

Chef Mourad Lahlou won the hearts of San Franciscans and Michelin inspectors with modern interpretations of dishes from his Moroccan childhood at Aziza in the Outer Richmond. With Mourad, a gorgeous 21st-century Moroccan/NorCal restaurant set in the historic art deco PacBell building, he's stepped it up a notch. Nineteen-foot-high windows and enormous circular chandeliers soar above the glamorous dining room. The menu features Moroccan-influenced à la carte offerings such as charmoula-seasoned lamb with fennel, dates and pistachio, as well as a family-style menu that includes a succulent whole roast chicken, and an epic ten-course tasting menu.

EXPLORE

Dirty Habit.

EXPLORE

Salt House

545 Mission Street, between 1st & 2nd Streets (1-415 543 8900, www.salthousesf.com). BART & Metro to Montgomery/bus 10, 12, 14 & Market Street routes. **Open** 11.30am-2pm, 5.30-10pm Mon-Wed; 11.30am-2pm, 5.30-11pm Thur, Fri; 5.30-10pm Sat; 5.30-9pm Sun. **Main courses** $24-$39. **Map** p70 C4 ⓫ **American**

Built into a loft-style space in a small brick building that's quickly being overshadowed by new skyscrapers, this downtown hotspot (from the people behind Town Hall) offers inventive contemporary American cuisine that changes seasonally. Standouts include roasted lamb loin and dry-aged ribeye grilled to perfection. At lunch, don't miss the Cuban pork sandwich and house-made chips.

Bars

Bergerac

316 11th Street, between Folsom & Harrison Streets (1-415 255 9440, www.bergeracsf.com). Bus 9, 12, 27, 47. **Open** 5pm-2am Tue-Sat. **Map** p71 G1 ⓬

Get funky at this self-proclaimed 'party mixology' bar furnished with mismatched sofas, chandeliers and old-fashioned globes. A prime weekend destination for hipsters and tech workers, the design is deliberately disorienting, modelled after Villa Nellcôte, the Côte d'Azur mansion where the Rolling Stones partied and recorded in 1971. Easy-to-gulp original cocktails feature unusual ingredients such as mole bitters, tobacco tincture and maraschino liqueur infused with Indian curry spices. Meanwhile, throwback drinks (Grasshoppers, daiquiris), beer-and-shot combos (rye plus lager, or the popular cinnamon Fireball liqueur served with cider) and 'social' drinks meant for four to seven people can jumpstart idling conversation. Soak up the boozy excess with nibbles including truffle fries, Asian-style tacos and charcuterie. Those looking to amp up their night can hop upstairs to sister bar Audio Discotech, a DJ nightclub pimped out with premium audio equipment and bottle-service booths.

Butter

354 11th Street, between Folsom & Harrison Streets (1-415 863 5964, www.smoothasbutter. com). Bus 9, 12, 27, 47. **Open** 6pm-2am Wed-Sat; 8pm-2am Sun. **Map** p71 G1 ⓭

Butter combines chill-room vibe (complete with DJ) with trailer-trash kitsch and food. After years on the scene, it still packs people in, and its magic-formula trio – a can of Pabst Blue Ribbon, a corn dog and a Twinkie – may just prove to be the elixir of life.

Dirty Habit

Hotel Zelos, 12 4th Street, between Market & Mission Streets (1-415 348 1555, www. dirtyhabitsf.com). BART & Metro to Powell/ streetcar F/bus 5, 14, 27 & Market Street routes. **Open** 5-11pm Mon-Sat. **Map** p70 D2 ⓮

This swanky SoMa rooftop bar and restaurant (on the fifth floor of Hotel Zelos) feels downright cosy – especially when you're nursing a tumbler of bourbon beside the fire pit. Bar manager Brian Means is a brown spirits enthusiast, offering more than 300 rare varieties from around the world. Creative seasonal drinks are served in vintage cocktail glasses and incorporate tea, spices and fresh herbs. And though the Habit's patrons are largely a suit-and-stiletto set – some sipping 'communal' cocktails designed for sharing – the bar doesn't take itself too seriously. The beer selection ranges from PBR to La Chouffe, and beer-and-shot pairings come in tongue-in-cheek combinations like the Red-Headed Stepchild: a Heretic Red IPA and a Pierre Ferrand 1840 cognac. On the food front, chef David Bazirgan's menu veers to Mediterranean with sharing plates such as foie gras torchon and Aquavit-cured salmon that pair perfectly with the cocktails.

House of Shields

39 New Montgomery Street, at Stevenson Street (www.thehouseofshields.com). BART & Metro to Montgomery/bus 9X, 12, 30, 45, 76 & Market Street routes. **Open** 2pm-2am Mon-Fri; 3pm-2am Sat, Sun. **Map** p70 C3 ⑮
One of the oldest and most storied bars in San Francisco, House of Shields was started by one Eddie Shields in 1908 and is said to house a subterranean network of tunnels once frequented by surreptitious tipplers during the dark days of Prohibition. Its carved, redwood bar was originally intended for the Palace Hotel across the street, but was moved here after it wouldn't accommodate the Maxfield Parrish painting in the hotel's Pied Piper bar. Purchased by local chef/restaurateur Dennis Leary (no, not that one), it's been lovingly restored to its former glory, including the original mosaic floors. And – odd observation though this may be – the gents' must have the biggest urinals in the world.

Nihon Whisky Lounge

1779 Folsom Street, at 14th Street (1-415 552 4400, www.dajanigroup.net/establishments/ nihon-whisky-lounge). BART to 16th Street/ streetcar F/bus 14. **Open** 5.30pm-1.30am Tue-Sat. **Map** p71 H1 ⑯
It may be in an out-of-the-way location, but at this swanky, sceney sushi-and-whisky destination, you can accompany Japanese small plates, maki and sashimi with tipples from a 500-plus single malt selection – the largest on the West Coast, according to the bar. Spirits are available by the glass, by the flight or by the bottle. The place will even stow unfinished bottles in a private locker until your next visit.

Novela

662 Mission Street, at Annie Street (1-415 896 6500, www.novelasf.com). BART & Metro to Montgomery/bus 10, 12, 14 & Market Street routes. **Open** 4pm-1am Mon-Wed; 4pm-2am Thur, Fri; 7pm-2am Sat; 7pm-1am Sun. **Map** p70 C3 ⑰

EXPLORE

This literary-themed bar combines two of life's great pleasures: booze and books. Wall-spanning shelves of colour-coordinated classic tomes punctuate the strikingly modern black-and-white interior. The design foreshadows a seasonal cocktail menu that nods to beloved literary characters such as Romeo and Juliet, Mary Poppins, Ichabod Crane and others. The Emma Woodhouse, for instance, a bright and refined mix of gin, peach liqueur, Aperol, dry vermouth, Peychaud bitters and maraschino liqueur, pays homage to Jane Austen's heroine. Another novel touch is the bar's punch programme. Crafted in bulk using the labour-intensive traditional method, it's available on tap in six strong and delicious seasonal flavours, organised by the main liquor. Choose your poison (gin, pisco, tequila, rum, corn whiskey, or the house recipe made of three different types of whiskey) and order it by the cup, the flight or the pitcher.

Trou Normand

140 New Montgomery Street, at Natoma Street (1-415 975 0876, www.trounormandsf.com). BART & Metro to Montgomery/bus 10, 12, 14 & Market Street routes. **Open** 11.30am-midnight Mon-Fri; 10.30am-midnight Sat, Sun. **Map** p70 C4 ⑱

Located in SoMa's majestic PacBell building, Trou Normand brings a certain *je ne sais quoi* to the after-work happy-hour scene, with tall windows, a curved marble bar and handsome leather booths.

A courtyard at the back whisks you away from the urban surroundings to a tree-lined patio outfitted with long tables, heat lamps and a glass canopy. Equal parts restaurant and bar, it's modelled on a contemporary French café. The spot is known for its cocktails, house-made cordials and bitters, and many drinks incorporate cognacs and armagnacs the bar team has selected by the barrel from France. Enjoy these drinks with a simple but thoughtful daily menu comprised of house-cured meats (more than 40 types of salumi and charcuterie), simply prepared seasonal vegetables, and meaty mains that include one of the city's best pork chops.

Shops & Services

Good Vibrations

899 Mission Street, at 5th Street (1-415 513 1635, www.goodvibes.com). BART & Metro to Powell/ bus 14, 27 & Market Street routes. **Open** 10am-9pm Mon-Thur, Sun; 10am-11pm Fri, Sat. **Map** p70 D2 ⑲ **Sex shop**

Bright, clean and inviting are not adjectives synonymous with sex shops, but the latest SF location of the Good Vibes mini-empire is as uniformly immaculate as its predecessors. (The Polk Street store, however, is the only one to tout a Vibrator Museum.) Catering to both men and women, offerings range from bachelorette party novelties to the truly hardcore. Staff pride themselves on providing non-judgmental information on sex toys of every imaginable kind.

Trou Normand.

Other locations 189 Kearny Street, Financial District (1-415 653 1364); 603 Valencia Street, Mission (1-415 503-9522); 1620 Polk Street, Polk Gulch (1-415 345 0400).

Seventh Son Tattoo

65 Langton Street, between Folsom & Howard Streets (1-415 551 7766, www.seventhsontattoo. com). Metro to Civic Center/streetcar F/bus 14, 19. **Open** noon-7pm Mon-Sat. **Map** p71 F2 ⓴ **Tattoos** Tucked away in a quiet alley, Luke Stewart's bright, pristine studio is a peaceful place to get inked. Seventh Son is a good bet if you want to decorate your bod with a particularly intricate and vibrant splash of colour. The range of artists' specialities here includes traditional Japanese and biomechanical art – which entails a detailed, sci-fi take on muscles and bones.

SOUTH PARK & SOUTH BEACH

If any one area in San Francisco embodies the dotcom rollercoaster ride, it's this one. In the '90s, finding a clear space in the green oval of South Park, the original 'Multimedia Gulch', took more time and moxie than snagging one of the coveted parking spaces. Techies would duck out to grab a burrito and end up never returning to the office: they'd been poached by a rival offering an extra 20k a year. Then, for a while after the dotcom bust, it returned to being a serene oasis of green. Today,

it's back to a pleasant buzz, with cafés and restaurants feeding the new wave of digerati.

Back in the 1800s, South Park was San Francisco's first gated community, until it suffered from a string of misfortunes. Getting burned to the ground early in the 20th century may have been careless, but it was pure bad luck that the invention of the cable car caused the local millionaires to abscond to Nob Hill. The building of the Bay Bridge separated the haves and the have-nots even further. After World War II, the area fell into neglect until a tornado of young men fuelled by and fluent in Java arrived in the 1990s.

Establishments that represent the new tenor of South Park include the **American Grilled Cheese Kitchen** (*see p78*) and **Caffe Centro** (102 South Park Avenue, 1-415 882 1500, www. caffecentro.com), which serves soups, salads and sandwiches to lunching workers.

A few blocks southeast, **AT&T Park** (24 Willie Mays Plaza, at 3rd & King Streets, 1-415 972 2000, www.sfgiants.com) is home to the San Francisco Giants baseball team. Instantly hailed as a classic when it opened in 2000, the waterside ballpark is a wonderful place to catch a game, with a design that shelters fans from blustery breezes. There isn't a bad seat in the park – upper decks enjoy unobstructed views of the entire field and the Bay.

Close by stands an intriguing architectural gem: the **Francis 'Lefty' O'Doul Bridge** (3rd

Street, near Berry Street), the only working drawbridge in the city. A charming antique, it was designed by JB Strauss, better known for designing the Golden Gate Bridge. Born in San Francisco, 'Lefty' started out as a pitcher but made his name as a hitter in New York and Philadelphia, before eventually returning home to manage the minor league San Francisco Seals. The restaurant and bar he opened just steps from downtown's Union Square in 1958, **Lefty O'Doul's** (333 Geary Street, at Powell Street, 1-415 982 8900, www.leftyodouls.biz), remains in business to this day.

Just across the bridge, **Mission Bay** is a burgeoning 303-acre swathe of new development anchored on the massive research campus and hospital of the University of California, San Francisco. Since it first broke ground in the early noughties, construction on the old Southern Pacific railyards, decrepit warehouses and shipyards and mouldering docks has been escalating at breakneck speed. Some 6,500 condos and lofts have been – or are currently being – built alongside biotech office space, trendy restaurants and bars, retail and market centres, greenways, a public library and a new Metro line. Within the next several years, an enormous arena for hometown NBA basketball team, the Golden State Warriors, and a waterfront park, brewery and shopping/dining complex next to AT&T Park is likely to take shape.

Sights & Museums

FREE San Francisco Railway Museum

77 Steuart Street, between Market & Embarcadero (1-415 974 1948, www.streetcar.org). BART & Metro to Embarcadero/bus Market Street routes. **Open** 10am-6pm daily. **Admission** free. **Map** p70 A5 ❷

San Francisco proudly preserves its rail transportation heritage, from its famous cable cars to the fleet of vintage streetcars running along Market Street. The small Railway Museum is a homage to the technological innovations of the last century, with displays that chronicle the city's early transit history. Among the highlights are vintage rail photographs and a full-sized replica of the motorman's platform of a 1911 streetcar emerging from the Twin Peaks Tunnel. The front of the museum is a shop offering rail-themed souvenirs.

Restaurants & Cafés

$ American Grilled Cheese Kitchen

1 South Park Street, at 2nd Street (1-415 243 0107, www.theamericansf.com). Metro to 2nd & King/bus 10, 12, 30, 45, 91. **Open** 8am-5pm Mon-Fri; 10am-5pm Sat, Sun (until 7pm on Giants game days). **Main courses** $7-$12. **Map** p70 D5 ❷ American

If your idea of a perfect meal is melted cheese oozing from between two slices of grilled sourdough bread and a bowl of smoky roasted-tomato soup, then your life is now complete. On a corner of hip South Park, the American offers a brief, but satisfying menu of gourmet grilled-cheese sandwiches (think sharp cheddar, gruyère, fontina, havarti), augmented by items like applewood smoked bacon and roasted wild mushrooms. Seasonal soups, salads and housemade desserts round out the lunch menu. The place also serves egg and cheese combos for breakfast, and, in a nice mash-up of low- and highbrow, afternoon wine and grilled-cheese pairings.

$ Butler & the Chef

155 South Park Street, at 3rd Street (1-415 896 2075, www.butlerandthechef.com). Metro to 2nd & King/bus 10, 12, 30, 45, 91. **Open** 8am-3pm Tue-Sat; 10am-3pm Sun. **Sandwiches** $14-$15. **Map** p71 E5 ❷ Café

This *très* French little café is always crowded with locals who queue for the fresh-made breakfast pastries and wonderful breads. Tuck into pain au chocolat or sip a Pernod while chatting with Pierre, the amiable owner.

Epic Steak

369 The Embarcadero, at Folsom Street (1-415 369-9955, www.epicsteak.com). **Open** 11.30am-2.30pm, 5.30-9.30pm Mon-Thur; 11.30am-2.30pm, 5.30-10pm Fri; 11am-2.30pm, 5.30-10pm Sat; 11am-2.30pm, 5.30-9.30pm Sun. **Main courses** $33-$180. **Map** p70 B6 ❷ Steakhouse

The first destination restaurant to be built on the Embarcadero waterfront in decades, Epic Steak and its adjoining seafood-focused sibling, Waterbar, co-opted a pristine piece of real estate with spectacular views of the Bay Bridge for their haute surf and turf. Out of the wood-fired oven come daily-procured selections of dry aged ribeye, côte de beouf, porterhouse, prime rib and filet mignon, which you can augment with your choice of béarnaise, madeira, chimichurri or horseradish. Accompany your steak with sides such as spätzle gratin, sautéed spinach and fried green tomatoes.

★ Marlowe

500 Brannan Street, at 4th Street (1-415 777-1413, www.marlowesf.com). Bus 2, 3, 8AX, 8BX, 8X, 30, 38, 45, 76X, 81X, 91. **Open** 11.30am-10pm Mon-Wed; 11.30am-11pm Thur, Fri; 5.30-11pm Sat; 10am-10pm Sun. **Main courses** $16-$30. **Map** p71 E4 ❷ American

If you haven't tried the brussels sprout chips, burger and poulet vert at Marlowe, you may be the only one in town. The cosy South of Market hotspot relocated to larger digs, giving fans many more opportunities to experience chef Jennifer Puccio's winning menu of inventive American food. Toasted pistachios with bourbon, maple and smoked salt, and those crispy, addictive brussels sprout chips (fried with meyer lemon and sea salt) are appetiser highlights. Among the mains, don't miss pork chops with nettle pesto risotto, poulet vert (chicken marinated overnight in a mash of basil, parsley, tarragon and other herbs), and the near-mythical Marlowe burger – a combo of beef and lamb, with caramelised onions, cheddar, bacon and horseradish aioli.

MoMo's

760 Second Street, at King Street (1-415 227 8660, www.sfmomos.com). Metro to 2nd & King/bus 15, 30, 45, 80X. **Open** 11.30am-10pm Mon-Fri; 11am-10pm Sat; 11am-9pm Sun (varies on Giants game days). **Main courses** $13-$35. **Map** p71 E5 ㉖ **American**

Across the street from AT&T Park, MoMo's front patio gets jam-packed before and after (and sometimes during) Giants games. The menu is a mix of bar and grill classics and SF fare: pulled pork sliders, fried calamari, linguini and clams, Dungeness crab cioppino and terrific burgers. Five dollar martinis and draught beers make happy hour hop on weekdays, and weekend brunch is lively – especially on sunny days. Note that the kitchen closes about an hour before the bar.

$ Pinkie's Bakery

1196 Folsom Street, between Rodgers & 8th Streets (1-415 556 4900, www.pinkiesbakerysf.com). Metro Civic Center/bus 6, 7, 9, 14. **Open** 8am-3pm Mon-Wed; 8am-4pm Thur, Fri; 9am-3pm Sat, Sun. **Pastries** $4. **Map** p71 F2 ㉗ **Café**

Pinkie's Bakery, an adjunct to Citizen Band restaurant in the South of Market district, took the city by storm a few years ago with its cream cheese-stuffed cookie sandwiches, bacon and cheese brioche, lemon bars, cupcakes and decadent speciality cakes. Just looking at the devil's food cake filled with bittersweet chocolate mousse and frosted with chocolate ganache and Maldon sea salt will put ten pounds on you (totally worth it, though). Don't miss doughnuts on Saturdays.

Public House

24 Willie Mays Plaza, corner of King & 3rd Streets (1-415 644 0240, www.publichousesf.com). Metro to 2nd & King/bus 10, 30, 45, 47, 91. **Open** 4-10pm Mon-Thur, Sun; 4-11pm Fri, Sat. **Main courses** $13-$21. **Map** p71 E5 ㉘ **American**

Traci Des Jardins of Jardinière and the Commissary (*see p128*) oversees the menu at this sports pub and grill at AT&T ballpark, with giant TVs in every room, a huge selection of draught beers and cask ales, and good comfort food, including chops, steak, ribs, burgers, and mac and cheese.

Saison

178 Townsend Street, between 3rd & Stanford Streets (1-415 828 7990, www.saisonsf.com). Metro to 2nd & King/bus 10, 12, 30, 45, 47, 91. **Open** 5.30-9.30pm Tue-Sat. **Prix fixe** approx $248-$348. **Map** p71 E5 ㉙ **American creative**

There's something at once disconcerting and reassuring about a three-star Michelin restaurant that crafts arguably the most exquisite and intricate farm-to-table cuisine in the city and accompanies it with a soundtrack that veers from Phil Collins to Tom Petty. That hard-to-peg sensibility follows through to the wear-anything ambience of the 18-seat restaurant that serves a nightly changing 15- to 20-course prix fixe meal with a bill that

Marlowe.

EXPLORE

might give even Google stockholders pause (prices vary according to tasting menu and market prices). Committed diners settle in for a three-hour-plus, intensely personal fine-dining extravaganza from chef Joshua Skenes that begins with herbal tea, and unfolds with anything and everything hand-foraged and fire-kissed – from sea urchin atop liquid toast to uni-turnip custard and squash blossom stuffed with carrot puree and fennel pollen. It's a wild and exciting dance of textures, colours and flavours that for many is worth breaking the bank over.

Town Hall

342 Howard Street, at Fremont Street (1-415 908 3900, www.townhallsf.com). BART & Metro to Embarcadero/bus 5, 9, 14, 38, 41, 71, 108. **Open** 11.30am-2.30pm, 5.30-10pm Mon-Thur; 11.30am-2.30pm, 5.30-11pm Fri; 5.30-11pm Sat; 5.30-10pm Sun. **Main courses** $27-$40. **Map** p70 B4 ⑩ **American**

Chefs Mitchell and Steven Rosenthal and legendary front-of-house man Doug Washington cultivate a chummy loyal crowd for their American and southern classics at this little slice of NOLA by the bay. Highlights might include cornmeal-fried oysters, beer-marinated pork chop, or buttermilk-fried chicken with baked beans. The bar is known for its speciality cocktails, including an excellent sazerac.

Tres

130 Townsend Street, at Stanford Street (1-415 227 0500, www.tressf.com). Metro to 2nd & King/ bus 10, 12, 30, 45, 47, 91. **Open** 11.30am-9.30pm Mon-Thur; 11.30am-10.30pm Fri; 11am-10.30pm Sat; 11am-9.30pm Sun. **Main courses** $12-$24. **Map** p71 E5 ㉛ **Mexican**

Tequila expert Julio Bermejo teamed up with impresario Eric Rubin, chef Joseph Manzare and rocker Sammy Hagar to create this homage to the Mexican state of Jalisco, home to the town that gave the potent spirit its name. The cavernous brick and timber space has an ample bar to dispense flights of artisan, pure-agave tequilas, or mix them in signature cocktails, while the kitchen turns out gourmet regional Mexican cuisine. With a location across from AT&T Park, this place hops on game days.

Twenty Five Lusk

25 Lusk Street, off Townsend Street between 4th & Ritch Streets (1-415 495 5875, www.25lusk.com). Metro to 2nd & King/bus 10, 12, 30, 45, 47, 91. **Open** 5.30-10pm Mon-Thur; 5.30-11pm Fri, Sat; 5pm-9pm Sun. **Map** p71 E5 ㉜ **American**

Not since the giddy days of the first dotcom boom has San Francisco seen anything this glamorous South of Market. The name refers to the address – tucked down an obscure alley in a 1917 meat-processing warehouse. Inside, the huge bi-level space, designed by architect Cass Calder Smith, combines original brick and exposed timbers with glass and polished metal. A slick bar and lounge with steel ski-lodge

Saison. See p79.

fireplaces occupies the downstairs; upstairs diners view the kitchen through glass panels, where chef Matthew Dolan crafts intricately composed plates of local, seasonal ingredients – the likes of grilled steelhead with fennel, black garlic, Dungeness crab and lobster beignet. For dessert, the redcurrant soufflé with espresso chocolate sauce is a winner.

Waterbar

399 The Embarcadero, at Harrison Street (1-415 284 9922, www.waterbarsf.com). BART & Metro to Embarcadero/streetcar F/bus 2, 14, 31, 41 & Market Street routes. **Open** 11.30am-9.30pm Mon, Sun; 11.30am-10pm Tue-Sat. **Main courses** $37-$40. **Map** p70 B6 ㉝ **Fish & seafood**

The seafood-focused sister restaurant to Epic Steak, Waterbar takes full advantage of its Embarcadero waterfront location with panoramic views of the Bay from both inside and the outdoor patio. A pair of 19-foot-high circular aquariums, filled with all manner of fish and marine creatures, anchors the main floor. A horseshoe-shaped raw bar under a glass caviar-inspired chandelier is dramatic seating for the sustainably harvested fare, which includes a full oyster menu and seasonal selections such as

EXPLORE

wood-oven-roasted Alaskan halibut with fresh pole beans and mussels en papillote.

Bars

Alchemist

679 3rd Street, at Townsend Street (1-415 746 9968, www.alchemistsf.com). Metro to 2nd & King/ bus 10, 12, 30, 45, 47, 91. **Open** 5pm-1.30am Mon-Fri; 7pm-1.30am Sat. **Map** p71 E5 ³⁴

This loft-like speakeasy is where the SoMa start-up crowd unwinds after-hours. Expect button-down and blazer-clad business types in the evening and a preponderance of Mission plaid as the night wears on. The space is sleek yet unintimidating; dudes in hoodies lounge on tufted leather sofas and coworkers sip scotch-infused cocktails while facing off at the shuffleboard table. Climb the stairs to the second-level lounge to scope out the scene from above.

Anchor Brewing Company Beer Garden

3rd Street & Terry A Francois Boulevard (no phone, www.theyardsf.com). Metro to 2nd & King/bus 10, 12, 30, 45, 47, 91. **Open** 11am-9pm daily (varies on Giants game days). **Map** p71 F5 ³⁵

If you're a fan of beer and baseball, this outdoor drinking venue is for you. Part of the Yard at Mission Rock, a semi-permanent pop-up of shipping containers that purvey food, drink and SF-made souvenirs across from the ballpark, the beer garden shouldn't be confused with the actual Anchor Brewery (*see p173*). You may not be able to see brewing in action here, but you can belly up to the bar for a pour from one of the 16 taps and follow up your drinking escapades with a bite from one of the stellar food trucks parked on-site (the french-fry-filled California burritos with Korean-style pork from Senor Sisig are legendary).

City Beer Store

1168 Folsom Street, between 8th & Rausch Streets (1-415 503 1033, www.citybeerstore.com). Bus 9X, 12, 19, 27, 47. **Open** noon-10pm daily. **Map** p71 F2 ³⁶

This modest storefront and beer-tasting bar consists of four tables and floor-to-ceiling refrigerators packed with hundreds of bottled beers and 15 rotating beers on draught. Sample something on tap while you nosh on a small plate of regional cheeses, fava bean hummus, or candied bacon caramel corn, and banter with the other beerophiles. When it's time to head out, the owners encourage patrons to mix and match a six-pack to take home.

21st Amendment

563 2nd Street, at De Boom Street (1-415 369 0900, www.21st-amendment.com). Metro to 2nd & King/bus 9X, 10, 12, 30, 45, 76. **Open** 11.30am-midnight Mon-Sat; 10am-midnight Sun. **Map** p70 D5 ㊲

Named in honour of the constitutional diktat repealing Prohibition, this convivial brewpub gets packed with Giants fans looking to load up on good, nicely priced booze (a mix of house-label and guest beers) before getting hit by the exorbitant beer prices inside the stadium. The place also serves decent pub grub.

Shops & Services

K&L Wine Merchants

638 4th Street, between Bluxome & Brannan Streets (1-415 896 1734, www.klwines.com). Metro 2nd & King/bus 12, 15, 30, 45, 76. **Open** 10am-7pm Mon-Fri; 9am-6pm Sat; 11am-6pm Sun. **Map** p71 E4 ㊳ **Food & drink**

The SF branch of California-focused K&L is a modest warehouse, filled with carefully selected wines and spirits. Most of the staff claim specialisations in particular regions and/or varietals.

★ San Francisco Flower Mart

640 Brannan Street, between 5th & 6th Streets (1-415 392 7944, www.sanfranciscoflowermart. com). Bus 8AX, 8BX, 8X, 12, 14X, 19, 27, 30, 45, 47, 91. **Open** 10am-3pm Mon-Sat. **Map** p71 F4 ㊴ **Market**

Badge-holding florists arrive before dawn to scoop up the best botanicals at wholesale prices, but the warehouse-like market opens to the public at 10am, when you can ogle (and inhale the scent of) hundreds of blooms from local growers under one roof. The overflowing tubs include roses, orchids, tulips, ranunculus, lilies and dozens of exotic flowers you've never heard of. The stems can be purchased singly or arranged in bouquets, and prices vary from booth to booth. Many of the vendors here grow locally, which means the blooms last longer than the grocery store variety, and the prices are typically cheaper as well. Wear a jacket – the building is kept cool to preserve the plants' freshness.

21st Amendment.

TAKING MODERN TO THE MAX
A striking addition has doubled SFMOMA's attractions.

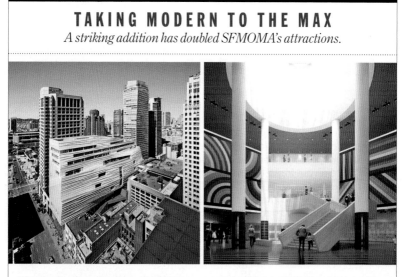

When the **San Francisco Museum of Modern Art** (see p72) moved from its fourth-floor Civic Center digs into a dramatic new home designed by Swiss architect Mario Botta in 1995, the West Coast's first museum of modern and contemporary art finally had a building befitting the quality and size of its collection of more than 26,000 works.

Fourteen years later, GAP clothing-empire founders Doris and Donald Fisher decided to donate their entire collection of 1,100 paintings, sculptures and photographs to their beloved hometown museum. Amassed over decades, the extraordinary cache includes seminal works by leading 20th- and 21st-century artists such as Alexander Calder, Chuck Close, Andy Warhol and Richard Diebenkorn.

By this time, Botta's striking red-brick building, with its huge, circular skylight and spectacular catwalk accessible from the top-floor galleries, was looking a little, well, cramped. It was time to grow.

In spring 2016, SFMOMA completes a three-year, $600-million metamorphosis that has more than doubled its size via a 235,000-square-foot addition rising behind and above the original structure. Designed by Snøhetta, the Oslo-based architecture firm behind NYC's National September 11 Memorial Museum, the new building is covered in an innovative glass fibre-reinforced concrete (no two of its uniquely shaped panels quite alike), the rippling surface of

which is meant to resemble the waters of the San Francisco Bay.

Inside, the new and improved SFMOMA has space to show off its full collection like never before. The new John and Lisa Pritzker Center for Photography, for example, is the largest photography exhibition space in the US, containing some 17,000 photos from the likes of Ansel Adams and Edward Weston.

On the third floor, you'll find a 3,000-square-foot gallery dedicated to dozens of sculptor Alexander Calder's famed hanging mobiles. The animated nature of the Calder mobiles all but demands they be seen on their own, but step outside and you'll encounter Calder's larger, stationary 'stabile' sculptures on a 5,600-square-foot terrace framed by a 'living wall' covered in 16,000 types of native plants.

Up on the seventh floor, curators have consolidated the collection's best contemporary artists of the last 20 to 30 years on a terrace with a breathtaking city view; inside is the museum's first dedicated space for new media works. Meanwhile, on the fourth floor they're busy redefining what art is with a 200-seat theatre for performance art, theatre, dance and elaborate 'human installation' pieces.

Undoubtedly the biggest spotlight stealer, however, is Richard Serra's 13-foot-high steel sculpture *Sequence*, on display free to the public behind 23-foot glass walls in the ground-floor gallery.

EXPLORE

Nob Hill & Chinatown

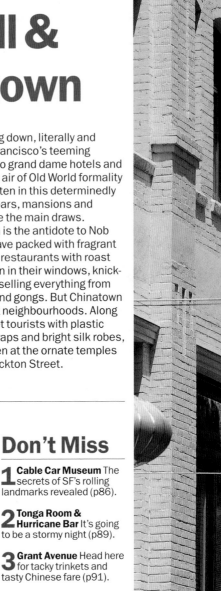

Sitting on a perch looking down, literally and figuratively, over San Francisco's teeming masses, Nob Hill is home to grand dame hotels and the social elite, exuding an air of Old World formality and elegance all but forgotten in this determinedly casual city. Historic hotel bars, mansions and stately Grace Cathedral are the main draws.

Down the hill, Chinatown is the antidote to Nob Hill's stiff reserve, an enclave packed with fragrant herbalists, hole-in-the-wall restaurants with roast ducks hanging upside down in their windows, knick-knack shops and markets selling everything from live fish and chickens to wind gongs. But Chinatown itself feels like two distinct neighbourhoods. Along Grant Avenue, stores target tourists with plastic Buddhas, Chinese finger traps and bright silk robes, while little English is spoken at the ornate temples and food stalls around Stockton Street.

Tonga Room & Hurricane Bar.

Don't Miss

1 Cable Car Museum The secrets of SF's rolling landmarks revealed (p86).

2 Tonga Room & Hurricane Bar It's going to be a stormy night (p89).

3 Grant Avenue Head here for tacky trinkets and tasty Chinese fare (p91).

4 Chinatown Kite Shop The sky's the limit at this well-stocked store (p93).

5 Golden Gate Bakery Sample moon cakes and other authentic treats (p93).

Grace Cathedral.

NOB HILL

A short but incredibly steep walk up from Union Square, the summit of Nob Hill stands 338 feet above the Bay. Both the houses and their residents retain an appropriately haughty grandeur. After the cable car started running up the hill in the 1870s, the area began to attract wealthy folk, among them the 'Big Four' railroad tycoons: Charles Crocker, Mark Hopkins, Leland Stanford and Collis P Huntington. Their grand mansions perished in the fire that followed the 1906 earthquake – in fact, only the 1886 mansion belonging to millionaire silver baron James C Flood survived. Later remodelled by Willis Polk, the brownstone is now the site of the private **Pacific-Union Club** (1000 California Street,

at Mason Street). Next to it, at the corner of California and Taylor Streets, is the public **Huntington Park**, with a fountain modelled on Rome's Fontana delle Tartarughe. Across the park, **Grace Cathedral** is a Gothic landmark.

Elegant hotels surround the park and the club. The **Fairmont San Francisco** (950 Mason Street, at California Street; *see p282*) has a plush marble lobby and the fabulously tacky **Tonga Room**, complete with regularly scheduled monsoons. The quieter **Scarlet Huntington** (1075 California Street, at Taylor Street; *see p282*) is known as a royals' hideaway, but you don't have to stay there to use its luxurious Nob Hill Spa (1-415 345 2888). Nearby, the **Top of the Mark** bar (*see p89*), on the 19th floor of the **Mark Hopkins Inter-Continental Hotel**, has terrific views over the city. Moving down the hill, the free **Cable Car Museum** displays antique cable cars and the mighty turbines that power the cables beneath the city's streets.

On the other side of the hill, along the corridor that runs between it and Russian Hill, **Polk Gulch** was the city's original gay neighbourhood until the 1970s (the first Gay Pride parade was held here in 1972). These days, gay bars, bathhouses and sex clubs have given way to more mainstream entertainment, the likes of indie-rock haven **Hemlock Tavern** (*see p220*) and classic cocktail lounge **Hi-Lo Club** (*see p88*).

Sights & Museums

★ FREE **Cable Car Museum**
1201 Mason Street, at Washington Street (1-415 474 1887, www.cablecarmuseum.org). Bus 1, 9, 12, 30, 45/cable car Powell-Hyde or Powell-Mason.

IN THE KNOW HOBNOBBING ON THE HILL

Though some lowlanders may playfully disagree, the name Nob Hill did not come about from removing the 'S' before Nob. The neighbourhood's designation goes back to the Gold Rush days, when the lofty denizens of the district were referred to as 'nabobs', a Hindu word for a person of conspicuous wealth and high standing. Having amassed their fortunes in gold, silver and railroads, the city's nabobs (eventually shortened to nobs) sought more refined air, building their stately mansions atop what was previously known as California Hill – and even installing their own cable car line.

EXPLORE

Open *Oct-Mar* 10am-5pm daily. *Apr-Sept* 10am-6pm daily. **Admission** free. **Map** p87 C2 ❶
It's worth interrupting your cable car ride to see how these marvels of engineering manage to scale San Francisco's steep slopes. The museum at Mason and Washington Streets houses a trove of cable car history, including the original car Andrew Hallidie built in 1873. Inside, watch giant wheels turn the underground cables that power the cars at a steady 9.5 miles per hour, and view the cable-winding machinery. Vintage cable cars and associated artefacts, the history of their traditions (such as the annual bell-ringing competition) and dozens of old photographs round out the collection.

FREE Grace Cathedral

1100 California Street, at Taylor Street (1-415 749 6300, www.gracecathedral.org). Bus 1, 2, 3, 4, 27/ cable car California. **Open** 8am-6pm Mon-Wed, Fri-Sun; 7am-6pm Thur. **Tours** 10am Wed-Sat. **Admission** free. *Tours* $25. **Map** p87 C2 ❷
Begun in 1928, this Episcopalian cathedral was once the site of a private mansion. The ruins of the property were donated to the church after the 1906 fire and turned into an architectural extravaganza by the standards of most US cathedrals, with a façade modelled on Paris's Notre Dame. There's a fine rose window, a magnificent organ and gilded bronze portals made from casts of the Gates of Paradise in Florence's Baptistery. Murals depict the founding of the United Nations and the burning of Grace's predecessor; the AIDS Interfaith Chapel has an altarpiece by Keith Haring. Two massive labyrinths, based on the 13th-century labyrinth at Chartres, allow visitors to wander in a contemplative manner.

Restaurants & Cafés

Harris'

2100 Van Ness Avenue, at Pacific Avenue (1-415 673 1888, www.harrisrestaurant.com). Bus 47, 49, 90. **Open** 5.30-9.15pm Mon-Fri; 5-9.45pm Sat; 5-9.15pm Sun. **Main courses** $32-$195. **Map** p87 A2 ❸ **Steakhouse**
One of San Francisco's steakhouse veterans, Harris' offers classy old-style dining, with big steaks, big martinis, and big bills at meal's end. Sink into your booth, start with a strong cocktail, then proceed with a textbook Caesar salad (put together at your table), a prime piece of carefully aged steak (from Harris' own ranch) and a baked potato with all the trimmings. Hefty desserts follow.

Parallel 37

600 Stockton Street, between Pine & California Streets (1-415 773 6168, www.ritzcarlton.com).

EXPLORE

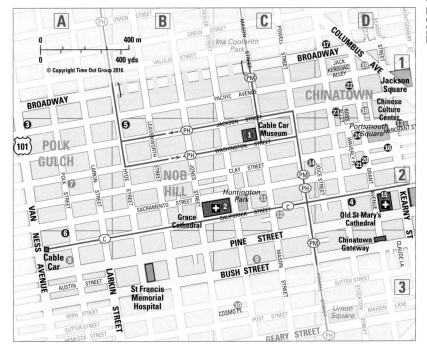

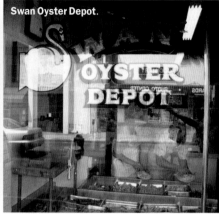

Swan Oyster Depot.

EXPLORE

Bus 1, 2, 3, 4, 27/cable car California. **Open** 6.30-
11am Mon; 6.30-11am, 6-9.30pm Tue-Fri; 6.30-
11.30am, 6-9.30pm Sat; 6.30am-11.30am Sun. **Prix-
fixe dinner** $65-$155. **Map** p87 D2 ④ **California**
Named for the line of latitude that runs through San
Francisco, the sleek, contemporary dining room at
the Ritz-Carlton lives up to its lofty location on the
upper slope of Nob Hill, as does Michael Rotondo's
menu, filled with 'wow' factor dishes such as Maine
lobster with pea tendrils and kumquat, roasted ter-
rine of guinea hen, and 32-day dry-aged ribeye. The
multi-course Chef's Tasting Menu ($155) takes din-
ner to an even higher level.

Seven Hills

*1550 Hyde Street, between Pacific & Jackson Streets
(1-415 775 1550, www.sevenhillssf.com). Bus 10,
12, 27/cable car Powell-Hyde.* **Open** 5.30-9.30pm
Tue-Thur; 5-10pm Fri, Sat; 5-9.30pm Sun. **Main
courses** $16-$35. **Map** p87 B2 ⑤ **Italian**
Candlelit and atmospheric to the max, Seven Hills is
an intimate gem of an Italian restaurant, featuring
expertly prepared farm-to-table Roman cuisine by
chef Anthony Florian. Authentic regional dishes
such as house-made ravioli uovo (egg yolk, ricotta
and brown butter) and tagliolini with truffles and
lobster mushrooms are the stars of the succinct
menu, which also offers a family-style option with
four courses for up to ten guests for $65.

★ Swan Oyster Depot

*1517 Polk Street, between California & Sacramento
Streets (1-415 673 1101). Bus 1, 2, 3, 12, 19, 47,
49, 90/cable car California.* **Open** 8am-5.30pm
Mon-Sat. **Main courses** $13-$45. **No credit
cards. Map** p87 A2 ⑥ **Fish & seafood**
Don't miss this institution just east of Nob Hill in
Polk Gulch: half fish market, half counter-service
hole in the wall, it has been delighting locals since
1912. The best time to visit is between November

and June, when the local Dungeness crab is in season. But at any time of year, the selections at Swan
are straight-from-the-water fresh. Specialities include clam chowder and an obscenely large variety
of oysters, best downed with a pint of locally brewed
Anchor Steam beer.

Bars

Amelie

*1754 Polk Street, at Washington Street (1-415 292
6916, www.ameliewinebar.com). Bus 12, 19, 27,
47, 49/cable car Powell-Hyde.* **Open** 5pm-2am
Mon-Sat. **Map** p87 A2 ⑦
Cosy, candlelit and oh so French, this Polk Gulch
boîte will educate you in the ways of viognier and
mourvèdre as it seduces you with tantalisingly titled
flights such as Sade 'Smooth Operator' and Marilyn
Manson 'Tainted Love'. Stylish decor (vintage theatre seats, wine-bottle light fixtures, red lacquered
bar) and well-priced customised flights ($10 for
three pours during the 5-7pm happy hour) create a
lively scene most nights. On the food side, cheeses,
charcuterie and other small bites give way to more
substantial offerings such as steamed mussels, croque monsieur, duck leg confit, and Gratin de Raviole
du Royans – a southern French speciality of tiny
pasta pockets stuffed with herbs, comté and cottage
cheese.

Hi-Lo Club

*1423 Polk Street, between California & Pine Streets
(www.hilosf.com). Bus 1, 2, 3, 19, 27, 47, 49, 90.*
Open 4pm-2am Mon-Sat. **Map** p87 A3 ⑧
This old-timey cocktail bar offers a welcome reprieve
from the typical collegiate-tinged watering holes
along Polk Street. It's charming without feeling precious, busy yet not overcrowded. Distressed concrete
walls, flickering candles and pressed tin ceilings lend
the impression of romantic decay, and single-bulb

light fixtures evoking Parisian lampposts arch over each table. Around 10pm, gussied-up singles start arriving in groups. Should you hit it off, the booths (built from old cable car benches) make cosy nooks for getting acquainted.

Hopwater Distribution

850 Bush Street, between Mason & Taylor Streets (www.hopwaterdistribution.com). Bart & Metro to Powell/bus 2, 3, 27, 30, 38, 45, 91. **Open** 5-11pm Mon-Wed, Sun; 5pm-1am Thur-Sat. **Map** p87 C3 ⑨
This Cali-focused beer mecca strikes an ideal middle ground between a sports bar and a cocktail lounge: design savvy, but not pretentious; popular, but low pressure. (Bonus: you won't be shelling out for $12 drinks.) You'll find 31 California beers and ciders on tap, ranging from IPAs to stouts and hard-to-find sour ales. The long wraparound bar on the main floor is well situated for casual mingling, while the booths upstairs are open seating.

Le Colonial

20 Cosmo Place, between Jones & Taylor Streets (1-415 931 3600, www.lecolonialsf.com). Bus 2, 3, 4, 27, 38, 76. **Open** 5.30-10pm Mon-Wed, Sun; 5.30-11pm Thur-Sat. **Map** p87 C3 ⑩
Designed to approximate Vietnam c1920, when the country was still a French colony, this elegant hideaway has a sizeable dining room, while the stylish upstairs lounge serves tropical drinks, exotic teas and a menu highlighting Vietnamese fusion cuisine. The comfortable couches invite cocktailing and more in a lush environment of palm trees, rattan furniture and shuttered windows.

★ Tonga Room & Hurricane Bar

Fairmont, 950 Mason Street, between California & Sacramento Streets (1-415 772 5278, www.fairmont.com). Bus 1, 8, 30, 45/cable car California, Powell-Hyde or Powell-Mason. **Open** 5-11.30pm Wed, Thur, Sun; 5pm-12.30am Fri, Sat. **Map** p87 C2 ⑪
Despite the all-you-can-eat happy-hour dim sum, the sarong-clad waitresses and the enormous exotic cocktails (the Lava and Scorpion Bowls come with straws for four), the real attraction at this long-lived tiki bar is the spectacle of house musicians performing covers of cheesy pop songs while afloat on a raft on the Tonga's 'lagoon'. There's even an indoor thunderstorm every 20 minutes, complete with rain.

Top of the Mark

Inter-Continental Hotel Mark Hopkins, 1 Nob Hill, at California & Mason Streets (1-415 392 3434, www.topofthemark.com). **Open** 4.30-11pm Mon-Thur; 4.30pm-12.30am Fri, Sat; 10am-1pm, 5-11.30pm Sun. **Admission** $10 after 8pm Fri, Sat. **Map** p87 C2 ⑫
Originally opened in 1939, the Top of the Mark is a stately, storied bar named for its location at the summit of the Inter-Continental Mark Hopkins Hotel. It was once a tradition for US Navy officers to belly up for a send-off drink before shipping out during World War II. (The northwest corner, dubbed the 'Weepers' Corner', is where their girlfriends would watch the ships depart the bay.) The vibe has changed significantly since then – Solange Knowles dropped in to DJ the bar's 75th anniversary party – but the sweeping view remains, encompassing the Financial District, Bay Bridge, Chinatown, North Beach and Golden Gate Bridge. Though the menu offers more than 100 variations on the martini, you're best sticking with classics. Bands play live music several nights a week; check the online calendar.

CHINATOWN

The 1849 Gold Rush and its promise of untold prosperity drew shiploads of Cantonese to California. The excitement didn't last, but many immigrants decided to stay, finding work on the railroads or the farms of the San Joaquin Valley. Californians both feared and loathed the Chinese, and were enthusiastic about the federal Chinese Exclusion Act of 1882, which halted the immigration of almost anyone of Chinese origin. Only officially repealed in 1943, the act also effectively made existing Chinese immigrants permanent aliens, with no hope of gaining citizenship. However, famine and unrest across China gave the immigrants little incentive to return home, and their understandable need for a strong community led to a 20-block enclave in central San Francisco. Chinatown soon developed a reputation for vice; curious Caucasians were lured here round the clock by cheap hookers, well-stocked opium dens and all-hours gambling.

After the 1906 earthquake and fire devastated the district, the city fathers tried to clean up the neighbourhood and, crucially, appropriate what had become prime real estate. However, not only did the illicit activity continue, the Chinese held fast and rebuilt their community.

The crowded streets and dark alleys of Chinatown – bordered today by **Bush Street** to the south, **Broadway** to the north, and **Powell** and **Kearny Streets** from west to east – evoke an earlier era. There are nearly 100 restaurants, some serving exotic specialities. Elsewhere, herbalists prepare natural remedies and laundry flutters from windows above the streets. Many wealthier Chinese immigrants have spread out over the city, with mini-Chinatowns in the Richmond and Sunset districts, but some 10,000 Chinese and Chinese-Americans still live in Chinatown proper, making it one of the largest Asian populations outside Asia itself.

Today, Chinatown also feels like two distinct neighbourhoods. A few blocks from Union Square, at Grant Avenue and Bush Street, the

EXPLORE

EXPLORE

SQUARE ROOTS

Portsmouth Square is the historic heart of Chinatown – and the whole city.

Even some longtime residents are unaware that Portsmouth Square can lay claim to being the true birthplace of San Francisco, if not California. It was in this unassuming plaza (on the corner of Clay and Kearny Streets) that Captain John B Montgomery first hoisted the US flag in the state. Montgomery captured the city – then known as Yerba Buena – from Mexico on 9 July 1846, and the plaza is named in honour of his ship, the USS *Portsmouth*.

Just two years later, newspaper boss Sam Brannan stood on this same spot and announced that gold had been discovered at Sutter's Mill, sparking the Gold Rush and his own meteoric rise to fame and riches. In addition to founding San Francisco's first newspaper, Brannan owned a number of stores that sold goods and supplies to the throngs of hopeful prospectors. If records are to be believed, just one of Brannan's stores in Sutter's Fort cleared $150,000 a month in 1849. The state's first millionaire, Brannan was also a senator, founder of the Society of California Pioneers, and builder of the first

Cliff House (for the current structure, *see p186*). In the years following the Gold Rush, however, Brannan lost much of his fortune in a divorce settlement. He moved south to San Diego where he became a brewer and, later, a land speculator along the Mexican border. He was eventually reduced to selling pencils door to door and did not leave enough cash to pay his funeral expenses.

By the 1850s, Chinese immigrants had settled in Portsmouth Square. Robert Louis Stevenson frequented the park when he lived nearby at 608 Bush Street in 1879; a monument to the author is shaped like the galleon *Hispaniola* from his novel *Treasure Island*. Flanking the square at 743 Washington Street, the Bank of Canton is one of the most photographed structures in Chinatown. The pagoda-like structure was built in 1909 for the Chinese American Telephone Exchange, where for four decades, multilingual phone operators routed calls throughout Chinatown by memory alone. Today, elderly residents congregate in the square to practice t'ai chi and play cards.

dragon-topped **Chinatown Gate** heralds the southern entrance. A gift from Taiwan in 1970, the green-tiled portal is made to a traditional design, and comes complete with a quotation from Confucius that urges passers-by to work for the common good.

Grant Avenue is Chinatown's main thoroughfare and arguably the oldest street in the city. In the 1870s and '80s, when it was called Dupont Street (it was renamed in honour of President Ulysses Grant after the 1906 earthquake), it was controlled by tongs. These days, however, the main activities are commercial: almost as far as the eye can see, souvenir shops sell T-shirts, toys, ceramics and jewellery, the genuine mixed with the junk. Still, a day in Chinatown would not be complete without an hour or two spent browsing for fun and tacky trinkets.

Although most buildings on Grant have been built in undistinguished American styles, a few structures stand out. The **Ying On Labor Association** building (nos.745-747) is a gaudy study in chinoiserie; across the street, the **Sai Gai Yat Bo Company** building (no.736) features ornate balconies and a pagoda-style roof. Slightly more kitsch – check the circular gold entrance – is the **Li Po** dive bar (no.916, *see p92*), named after the great drunken poet of the T'ang Dynasty. Even the street lamps are sculpted in the likeness of golden dragons, created during the tourist boom of the 1920s at the behest of the Chinese Chamber of Commerce. The shops are a mixed bunch, but one popular stop is the **Ten Ren Tea Company** (no.949, 1-415 362 0656, www.tenren. com), which offers free samples to help its patrons choose. On the corner of Grant and California Streets, meanwhile, is the Roman Catholic **Old St Mary's Cathedral**, a sturdy 1854 edifice made of granite imported from China.

You'll see very few tourists among the throngs of customers that pack the markets of **Stockton Street**. Whether selling medicines or turtles (many of the markets here are 'live', with fish and animals on display in tanks and cages), the enterprises on Stockton cater to locals, who conduct their business in a range of dialects. In much the same way, the restaurants have a more authentic feel than those on Grant; for many, Stockton Street constitutes the 'real' Chinatown.

One of the oldest religious structures in San Francisco, the **Kong Chow Temple**, stands on Stockton Street (no.855, between Sacramento & Clay Streets). Established in the 1850s, it was moved to its present home on the fourth floor of the Chinatown Post Office in 1977. Divination sticks, red satin banners and flowers flank a fabulous altar from which a statue of the god Kuan Ti has a keen view of the Bay. Nearby, the façade of the photogenic **Chinese Consolidated Benevolent Association**

Building (no.843) features stone lions, ceramic carp and coloured tiles.

A true taste of old Chinatown can be found in the alleys a half-block east of Stockton Street, sprouting off Jackson and Washington Streets. In cosy **Ross Alley**, you can watch cookies being made by hand at the **Golden Gate Fortune Cookie Factory** (no.56, 1-415 781 3956), or have a trim at **Jun Yu's Barber Shop** (no.32), which, since opening in 1966, has reputedly sheared celebrities including Michael Douglas and Clint Eastwood. Sweet **Waverly Place**, just to the south, was the scene of a famous 1879 battle between two tongs (local organised crime gangs that ran gambling and prostitution) over the ownership of a prostitute – at least four men are believed to have been hacked to death by cleavers during the skirmish. These days, it's best visited for the historic **Tin How Temple** (no.125). Another kind of history was made in adjacent **Spofford Street**, where between 1904 and 1910 Sun Yat-sen launched a revolution against the Manchu Dynasty from the **Ghee Kung Tong Building** (no.36).

An intriguing landmark stands just south of here, at 920 Sacramento Street. Named after Donaldina Cameron, the New Zealander who devoted her life to saving San Francisco's Chinese girls from prostitution and slavery, **Cameron House** provides help to low-income Asian immigrants and residents. However, it's also just about the only place in the city where you can still see traces of the great 1906 fire: misshapen 'clinker' bricks, melted by the intense heat, protrude from the walls.

Sights & Museums

FREE Chinese Culture Center
3rd floor, Hilton Hotel, 750 Kearny Street, at Washington Street (1-415 986 1822, www.c-c-c. org). Bus 1, 9X, 12, 20, 41/cable car California. **Open** 9.30am-6pm Tue-Fri; 10am-4pm Sat. **Admission** free. **Map** p87 D2 ⑬
Linked to Portsmouth Square by a footbridge and located on the third floor of a Hilton hotel, the centre hosts a variety of events, including Asian-themed art exhibitions and performances, as well as workshops and walking tours.

FREE Chinese Historical Society of America Museum
965 Clay Street, between Stockton & Powell Streets (1-415 391 1188, www.chsa.org). Bus 1, 9, 12, 30, 45/cable car Powell-Hyde or Powell-Mason. **Open** noon-5pm Tue-Fri; 11am-4pm Sat. **Admission** free. **Map** p87 C2 ⑭
Founded in 1963, CHSA is the oldest and largest organisation in the country dedicated to the documentation, study and presentation of Chinese American history. In 2001, it moved into the historic

Chinese YWCA building, designed by renowned local architect Julia Morgan. Since then, the museum has expanded its exhibits and public programming, with displays in English and Chinese that follow California's Chinese population from the frontier years to the Gold Rush, through the building of the railroads and the Barbary Coast.

FREE Old St Mary's Cathedral

660 California Street, at Grant Avenue (1-415 288 3800, www.oldsaintmarys.org). Bus 1, 9X, 30, 45/cable car California. **Open** 7am-4.30pm Mon-Fri; 10am-6pm Sat; 7.30am-3pm Sun. **Map** p87 D2 ⑮
Much early missionary work, and the city's first English lessons for Chinese immigrants, took place under this 19th-century building's foreboding clock tower: 'Son, observe the time and fly from evil,' it warns. Free Tuesday lunchtime concerts (www.noontimeconcerts.org) are staged in the cathedral's dainty yet glorious interior.

Restaurants & Cafés

San Francisco's best Chinese food is probably found in the Richmond District (see p185), but there are still worthwhile options in Chinatown. The Chinese crowd at **Dol Ho** (808 Pacific Avenue, at Stockton Street, 1-415 392 2828) speaks volumes about the cuisine's authenticity, and though the **House of Nanking** (919 Kearny Street, at Jackson Street, 1-415 421 1429) is touristy, its dishes never disappoint.

R&G Lounge

631 Kearny Street, between Clay & Sacramento Streets (1-415 982 7877, www.rnglounge.com). Bus 1, 10, 12, 30, 41, 45, 91. **Open** 11am-9.30pm daily. **Main courses** $15-$50. **Map** p87 D2 ⑯ **Chinese**
Always busy and often chaotic, R&G has two levels for dining, neither of them much to look at. However, the Hong Kong-style food is authentic, emphasising seafood that's taken mainly from the in-house tanks. People come from miles around to try the deep-fried salt and pepper crab and barbecue pork.

Yuet Lee

1300 Stockton Street, at Broadway (1-415 982 6020). Bus 10, 12, 20, 30, 39, 41, 45, 91/cable car Powell-Mason. **Open** 11am-midnight Mon-Thur, Sun; 11am-3am Fri, Sat. **Main courses** $9.50-$20.50. **Map** p87 D1 ⑰ **Chinese**
Terrific seafood and the opportunity to indulge in some small-hours dining attract sundry Chinese folk to this tiny, bright-green eaterie. The roasted squab with fresh coriander and lemon, sautéed clams with black bean sauce, and 'eight precious noodle soup', made with eight kinds of meat, are all worth trying. Bear in mind, though, that the lighting is glaringly unflattering and the service matter-of-fact.

Bars

Li Po

916 Grant Avenue, between Jackson & Washington Streets (1-415 982 0072). Bus 1, 30, 45. **Open** 2pm-2am daily. **Map** p87 D1 ⑱
A fun spot for a pick-me-up when you're done with the junk shops on Grant Avenue, Li Po is basically a dive, but the cave façade and giant, tattered Chinese lantern inside give it irresistible kitschy charm. This watering hole will take you back to Barbary Coast-era San Francisco with no risk of being shanghaied by anything except the potent cocktails.

Mr Bing's

201 Columbus Avenue, at Pacific Avenue (1-415 362 1545). Bus 1, 10, 12, 30, 41, 45, 91. **Open** 11am-2am Tue-Sun. **Map** p87 D1 ⑲
Some call nearby Li Po and Buddha Lounge dive bars, but there's nothing divey about a $9 Mai Tai or a beer shaped like Buddha. This tiny, old-school spot (on the border of North Beach) is just far enough from Grant Avenue to cut back on tourist interlopers. Sidle up to the horseshoe bar and order a beer, a shot or – if you're feeling celebratory – a $5 martini. You're not here for the mixology or the craft beers (there's nothing on tap, anyway). You're here for the unpretentious atmosphere and the bang-for-your-buck value. Word to the wise: unless you can drink like a Russian or lie like a politician, do not take the bartender up on his offer of a game of Liar's Dice.

Grant Avenue. *See p91.*

Shops & Services

★ Chinatown Kite Shop

717 Grant Avenue, between Commercial & Sacramento Streets (1-415 989 5182, www. chinatownkite.com). Bus 1, 10, 12, 30, 41, 45, 91/ cable car California. **Open** 10am-8pm daily. **Map** p87 D2 ⑳ **Gifts & souvenirs**

This excellent, long-standing kite shop is stocked with hundreds of different kites in every imaginable shape and colour. It's perfectly situated for you to get kitted out before heading down to Marina Green.

Clarion Music Center

816 Sacramento Street, at Waverly Place (1-415 391 1317, www.clarionmusic.com). Bus 1, 30, 45, 91/cable car California. **Open** 11am-6pm Mon-Fri; 9am-5pm Sat. **Map** p87 D2 ㉑ **Books & music**

Didgeridoos and African drums are just the starting point at this local institution. Head into truly exotic waters with affordable H'mong jaw harps, say, or an impressively costly deluxe pipa.

★ $ Golden Gate Bakery

1029 Grant Avenue, between Jackson Street & Pacific Avenue (1-415 781 2627, www. goldengatebakery.com). Bus 1, 30, 45. **Open** 8am-8pm daily. **Map** p87 D1 ㉒ **Food & drink**

Every September during the Autumn Moon Festival, the lines form round the block for Golden Gate's famous moon cakes, filled with things like pineapple, coconut, lotus seed, red-bean paste and sugared melon. A 40-year-old Chinatown institution, the bakery is also the place for other Chinese baked specialities, including egg custard tarts, coconut macaroons, sweet rice cakes and vanilla cream buns.

New Sam Bo Trading Co

51 Ross Alley, between Jackson & Washington Streets (1-415 398 3828). Bus 1, 10, 12, 30, 41, 45, 91/cable car Powell-Hyde or Powell-Mason. **Open** 10am-6pm daily. **Map** p87 D1 ㉓ **Gifts & souvenirs**

The best things in Chinatown are found down the area's side streets, and this tiny shop of Buddhist and Taoist religious items is a prime example. New Sam Bo sells Buddhas, ceremonial candles and incense, along with intriguing paper goods that are to be burned in honour of ancestors or to request a favour of the gods.

Red Blossom Tea Company

831 Grant Avenue, between Clay & Washington Streets (1-415 395 0868, www.redblossomtea.com). Bus 1, 10, 12, 30, 41, 91/cable car California. **Open** 10am-6.30pm Mon-Sat; 10am-6pm Sun. **Map** p87 D2 ㉔ **Food & drink**

Red Blossom has been in the tea business for more than two decades – and it shows. The selection tops 100 – black and green? Pshaw! Get into pu-erh and white. But that's not all; you can also get advice on the art of proper brewing.

EXPLORE

North Beach & Around

EXPLORE

Among the city's many notable neighbourhoods, North Beach is one of the best known, a popular destination for tourists, beloved by locals and an integral part of the old Barbary Coast. Grant Avenue, which runs through its centre, is San Francisco's oldest street. Along with the North Point docks, the century-old ethnic enclave of Little Italy, and its neighbour, Chinatown, are reminders that San Francisco once served as the gateway to the west. With the legendary City Lights bookstore and a variety of cafés, the area also retains its links to the beat movement of the 1950s.

To the north of North Beach is the tourist trap of Fisherman's Wharf. Looking down on it are the residents of Russian Hill, one of the city's wealthiest, and nicest, neighbourhoods. Bisected by tiny alleyways and pretty pocket gardens, it draws tourists for its unique feature: zigzagging Lombard Street.

Don't Miss

1 Alcatraz Do some time on this notorious island prison (p107).

2 City Lights The lit hub that nurtured Kerouac, Ginsberg et al (p100).

3 Coit Tower Brave the climb for the wonderful murals and lofty views (p101).

4 Caffe Trieste The ultimate Beat Generation café (p101).

5 Molinari Delicatessen If it was good enough for Joe DiMaggio... (p100)

Alcatraz.

North Beach

North Beach, north and east of Columbus Avenue, was the place that turned San Francisco into the counterculture capital of the US. Established in the early 20th century by the city's Italian community, it came to attract leagues of writers and artists, drawn not only by the European aura but also the low rents. The Beat Generation reigned here in the 1950s, and later their trailblazing path of individualism and artistic endeavour carried into the early 1960s, when nightclubs such as the Purple Onion and the Hungry i showcased an array of boundary-pushing comedians such as Woody Allen and Lenny Bruce. Later, punk venues solidified the indelible stamp of hipness. Today, North Beach has avoided falling victim to homogeny. The mellow streets, with their famously lambent light on sunny days, are still home to elderly Italians playing *bocce*, reading Neapolitan newspapers and nibbling *biscotti* at sidewalk cafés. But time hasn't stood still here. Amid the long-standing strip clubs and vintage cafés sit shops offering handmade goods, top-notch restaurants serving all manner of classic, contemporary and international cuisine, and a slew of lively bars and nightclubs.

COLUMBUS AVENUE & AROUND

Much of North Beach's history and many of its treasures lie along **Columbus Avenue**, especially close to the three-way junction of Columbus, Broadway and Grant Avenue.

To get up to speed on the beats and their legacy, check out the **Beat Museum** (540 Broadway, at Columbus Avenue; *see right*) before heading over to a landmark of the movement, **City Lights** bookstore (261 Columbus Avenue, at Broadway; *see p100*). Still presided over by the original owner, nonagenarian poet Lawrence Ferlinghetti, City Lights has grown to occupy an entire building. Ferlinghetti founded it with the then-radical concept of selling only paperbacks, believing that the best books should be available to as many people as possible, in an economical form. To this day, City Lights stocks house-published books alongside world literature, political writing, poetry and small-circulation periodicals.

Step across Jack Kerouac Alley to **Vesuvio** (255 Columbus Avenue, at Broadway; *see p100*), which welcomes mad poets and tourists in equal measure, much as it did when Kerouac and crew drank here in the 1950s. **Tosca Café** (242 Columbus Avenue, between Broadway Street & Pacific Avenue) was another favourite watering hole of the beats; a facelift and restaurant addition have given it new life,

but it still serves up its Armagnac-infused house cappuccinos to a scratchy operatic soundtrack.

The copper-sheathed **Columbus Tower** at the corner of Columbus and Kearny Streets, purchased by film director Francis Ford Coppola following the resounding success of *The Godfather*, houses his American Zoetrope Studios, as well as office space for a number of independent film producers. On the ground floor is charming **Café Zoetrope** (916 Kearny Street, at Jackson Street, 1-415 291 1700, www.cafecoppola.com), which also sells wines from the director's own Napa Valley vineyard. Further up Columbus, **Molinari Delicatessen** (373 Columbus Avenue, at Vallejo Street; *see p100*), one of San Francisco's most beloved institutions, is the place to pick up a sopressata sandwich on a hard roll and take it up the road to Washington Square for an impromptu picnic.

East of here, **Broadway** is lined with brash nightclubs, several featuring strippers and sexy floorshows. History was made at the **Condor Club** (560 Broadway, at Columbus, 1-415 781 8222, www.condorsf.com) in 1964 when a buxom waitress named Carol Doda went topless onstage for the first time in US history. Just down the street, the **Hungry i** (546 Broadway, at Columbus Avenue), once a nightclub that launched the careers of luminaries such as Barbra Streisand and Woody Allen, is now a strip club.

Sights & Museums

Beat Museum

540 Broadway, at Romolo Place (1-415 399 9626, www.kerouac.com). Bus 9X, 12, 20, 30, 41, 45. **Open** *10am-7pm daily.* **Admission** *$8; $5 reductions.* **Map** *p97 D4* ❶

The Beat Museum houses an impressive archive of letters, magazines, pictures, first editions and arte-facts – including 100 editions of *On the Road* translated into dozens of languages, and a signed copy of Allen Ginsberg's seminal poem, *Howl* – that explore the lives of beat figures such as Jack Kerouac, Lawrence Ferlinghetti, Ginsberg and Neal Cassady. The gift shop and bookstore are free to peruse. The museum also offers Beat Generation walking tours through WalkSF Tours.

▶ *For more on the beats, see p260.*

Restaurants & Cafés

Henry's Hunan

924 Sansome Street, between Broadway & Vallejo Streets (1-415 956 7727, www.henryshunan.com). Bus 19, 27, 47. **Open** *11.30am-9pm Mon-Thur; 11.30am-9.30pm Fri, Sat.* **Main courses** *$8-$12.* **Map** *p97 D5* ❷ **Chinese**

Henry and Diana Chung started this local chain of Chinese restaurants in 1974, introducing the spicy,

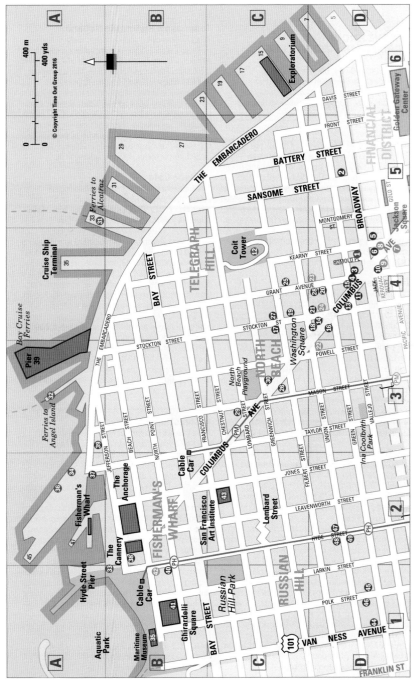

EXPLORE

smoky dishes of their native Hunan province to San Francisco. It's been a love affair ever since, with locals flocking to their downtown and neighbourhood locations for the Marty's Special (hot and spicy smoked ham and chicken with vegetables in black bean sauce), cold noodle salad (shredded chicken, cucumbers and peanut sauce), deep-fried onion cakes, hot and sour soup, and Diana's legendary meat pie – ground pork in garlicky chilli sauce topped with shredded lettuce sandwiched between circles of flaky fried bread. **Other locations** throughout the city.

The House
1230 Grant Avenue, between Columbus Avenue & Vallejo Street (1-415 986 8612, www.thehse.com). Bus 10, 12, 30, 39, 41, 45, 91. **Open** 11.30am-2.30pm, 5.30-10pm Mon-Thur; 11.30am-2.30pm, 5.30-11pm Fri; 11.30am-2.30pm, 5-11pm Sat; 5-10pm Sun. **Main courses** $10-$26. **Map** p97 D4 ❸ **Asian fusion**
This no-frills (though often ear-shatteringly loud) Chinese fusion dining room works wonders with fresh, seasonal produce and East-meets-West preparations. The Chinese chicken salad with sesame soy is typical of the menu: light, tangy and big enough to be a meal on its own. The menu changes often, resisting trends while remaining decidedly sophisticated.

★ Il Casaro
348 Columbus Avenue, between Grant Avenue & Vallejo Street (1-415 677 9455, www.ilcaaro sf.com). Bus 41, 8X, 8BX, 10, 12, 30, 34, 41, 91. **Open** 11am-11pm Mon-Thur, Sun; 11am-midnight Fri, Sat. **Pizzas** $13-$17. **Map** p97 D4 ❹ **Italian & Pizza**
A recent entry on the Neapolitan pizza scene with a location smack in the centre of Little Italy, Il Casaro is rapidly developing a devoted following. The brief menu focuses on pizzas from the coal-fired oven that are made before your eyes by the pizzaiolo, and emerge in minutes achingly thin, light and bubbling to chewy perfection. The prosciutto pizza, made with San Daniele prosciutto, arugula, tomatoes, mozzarella, and raspa dura (a shaved Italian cheese) is a marvel of flavour. Sharing star billing is the mozzarella bar, featuring appetiser plates of buffalo, fior di latte and burrata cheese, and antipasti such as panuozzo – a kind of pizza-dough sandwich stuffed with cheese, sausage and broccoli rabe.

Tommaso's Ristorante Italiano
1042 Kearny Street, between Broadway & Pacific Avenue (1-415 398 9696, www.tommasosnorth beach.com). Bus 1, 10, 12, 20, 30, 41, 45, 91. **Open** 5-10.30pm Tue-Sat; 4-9.30pm Sun. **Main courses** $14-$24. **Map** p97 D4 ❺ **Italian & pizza**
Tommaso's is known citywide for its simple Italian food, which has been served family-style in a tiny, boisterous room since 1935. The wood-fired pizzas and calzones deserve their reps and the house red is surprisingly good. No affectations, no frills and no reservations. Join the queue and keep your eyes peeled: you never know who might walk in.

★ Tosca Café
242 Columbus Avenue, between Broadway & Pacific Avenue (1-415 986 9651, www.toscacafesf. com). Bus 10, 12, 41. **Open** 5pm-2am daily. **Main courses** $16-$42. **Map** p97 D4 ❻ **Italian**
Open since 1919, this legendary North Beach spot has drawn a shifting cast of celebrities from Hunter S Thompson and Francis Ford Coppola to Johnny Depp and Sean Penn. In 2013, renowned restaurant duo April Bloomfield and Ken Friedman (of New York's Spotted Pig) took it over and started serving modern, seasonal Italian fare (don't miss the roast chicken for two or the bucatini with tomato, guanciale and chilli). Yet Tosca has maintained much of its original charm with an impressive front bar and a jukebox blaring eclectic tunes. Rising mixology star Joe Cleveland, previously of Coqueta, is behind the perfectly executed craft cocktails. Order a House Cappuccino, and you'll get a hot, Armagnac-and-bourbon-spiked afterdinner drink frothed in the antique espresso machine.

Bars

★ Comstock Saloon
155 Columbus Avenue, at Pacific Avenue (1-415 617 0071, www.comstocksaloon.com). Bus 10, 12, 41. **Open** noon-2am Mon-Fri; 4pm-2am Sat; 4pm-midnight Sun. **Map** p97 D4 ❼
With its original mahogany bar intact, this saloon dates from 1907, but Comstock, which debuted in the space in 2010, is no fusty relic of a bygone age. Under bar manager Johnny Raglin, who was at the vanguard of the SF craft cocktail movement, the place brings fresh twists to classic cocktails, such as the Sazerac, Manhattan, Blood and Sand and Pisco Punch. Or put your fate in the bartender's hands by ordering a 'Barkeep's Whimsy'. Hearty pub food includes dishes like roast chicken, oysters and cheese plates. It's worth stopping by on Friday afternoons, since Comstock has resurrected the old saloon tradition of providing free lunch with the purchase of two cocktails.

Specs
12 William Saroyan Place, off Columbus Avenue (1-415 421 4112). Bus 9X, 12, 20, 30, 41, 45. **Open** 4.30pm-2am Mon-Fri; 5pm-2am Sat, Sun. **No credit cards. Map** p97 D4 ❽

MIX MASTERS

San Francisco's inventive cocktail culture dates back to the Gold Rush.

A hard-drinking town since the 49ers rolled into town seeking gold and whiskey, San Francisco lays claim to the invention of several legendary cocktails. In 1853, Duncan J Nicol, aka 'Pisco John', crafted a concoction of fresh pineapple, gum syrup, distilled water, lime juice, and the potent Peruvian brandy pisco at a bar called the Bank Exchange & Billiard Saloon (where the Transamerica Pyramid now stands). Pisco punch was an instant smash and the Bank Exchange became the preferred watering hole for the city's social scene – Mark Twain purportedly raised a glass of pisco punch here with the real-life Tom Sawyer, a San Francisco fireman. Old San Francisco's Mystery Drink even worked its wiles on Rudyard Kipling, who wrote in his 1889 travelogue, *From Sea to Sea*, that it was 'compounded of the shavings of cherubs' wings, the glory of a tropical dawn, the red clouds of sunset and the fragments of lost epics by dead masters'. Nicol died in 1926, taking his punch recipe to the grave, where it mouldered until cocktail aficionados rediscovered the drink in the early noughties. Today, master mixologists such as Duggan McDonnell of **Cantina** (580 Sutter Street, between Mason & Powell, 1-415 398 0195, www.cantinasf.com) are championing a revival of the classic cocktail. McDonnell is even spearheading a campaign to make pisco punch the city's official cocktail.

Another legendary barman, 'Professor' Jerry Thomas, is credited by many for the martini, or at least its precursor. The oft-disputed tale goes that Thomas came up with the recipe in 1850 when a miner on his way across the Bay to the town of Martinez placed a gold nugget on the bar and demanded Thomas make him something special before the chilly ferry ride. The result – a mix of sweet vermouth, Old Tom gin, bitters and maraschino – was dubbed the 'Martinez'. While the martini went on to James Bond fame and fortune, the Martinez was all but lost in the fog of history, until rediscovered by a few savvy SF bartenders. At the **Comstock Saloon** (*see p98*) Jonny Raglin mixes it up in a 1907 building that once housed the San Francisco Brewing Company, in the heart of the Barbary Coast.

Though undeniably a Dublin invention, it was Jack Koeppler, owner of the **Buena Vista Café** (*see p109*), and a San Francisco newspaper columnist who first brought Irish coffee to the US in 1952, nabbing the recipe from a Dublin bartender and perfecting it at the BV. Today, white-jacketed barmen serve up some 2,000 of these frothy whiskey concoctions daily.

Last but certainly not least, the bragging rights to Hawaii's most iconic cocktail, the mai tai, go to Oakland across the Bay, where restaurateur Victor Bergeron of **Trader Vic's** (9 Anchor Drive, Emeryville, 1-510 653 3400, www.tradervicsemeryville.com) is said to have created the first one in 1944 for some visiting Tahitian friends. The blend of Jamaican rum, lime juice, rock candy syrup and orgeat hit the spot and his friends proclaimed it '*Mai tai roa ae*' ('Out of this world').

EXPLORE

City Lights.

Specs really is the quintessential old-school San Francisco bar: one part North Beach bohemian and one part Wild West saloon, with a dash of weirdness thrown in for good measure. It's tucked away in a false alley (you'll see what we mean), with nearly every inch covered with dusty detritus from around the world. If you're feeling peckish, a basket of saltines and a wedge of cheese can be had for around four bucks.

★ Vesuvio

255 Columbus Avenue, between Broadway & Pacific Avenue (1-415 362 3370, www.vesuvio. com). Bus 9X, 12, 20, 30, 41, 45. **Open** 6am-2am daily. **Map** p97 D4 ⑨

A funky old saloon with a stained-glass façade, Vesuvio preserves the flavour of an earlier era. It's next to the famous City Lights bookshop (*see below*), just across Jack Kerouac Alley (the writer was a regular here), and its walls are covered with beat memorabilia. Sit on the narrow balcony and check out the scene downstairs and on the street.

Shops & Services

★ City Lights

261 Columbus Avenue, between Broadway & Jack Kerouac Alley (1-415 362-8193, www. citylights.com). Bus 8AX, 8BX, 8X, 10, 12, 41. **Open** 10am-midnight daily. **Map** p97 D4 ⑩ **Books & music**

Since 1953, City Lights has been a San Francisco institution. Situated just off the seedy strip of Broadway, the shop feels like (and is) a small piece of history. The beats are the shop's patron saints, and quotes and photos of Burroughs, Kerouac and Ginsberg are displayed throughout the store. (Quotes also gleam underfoot in the adjacent alleyway, like a counterculture yellow brick road.) It's a beautiful space, with arched doorways, vintage art and light filtering in through large east-facing windows. Beat literature and poetry is housed upstairs, while current literature, fiction and nonfiction is shelved on the main floor. Many of the staff picks have progressive political leanings, as you might expect from a shop where posters read 'Eat, sleep, read, provoke', and 'A literary Habitat for Humanity'. It's not just a bookstore – it's a legacy.

★ Molinari Delicatessen

373 Columbus Avenue, at Vallejo Street (1-415 421 2337, www.shop.molinarideli.net). Bus 10, 12, 30, 39, 41, 45, 91. **Open** 9am-6pm Mon-Fri; 9am-5.30pm Sat; 10am-4pm Sun. **Map** p97 D4 ⑪ **Food & drink**

The quintessential San Francisco Italian deli, Molinari's has been in business since 1896, selling its legendary salami and prosciutto sandwiches on hard rolls (try the Joe's Special: mozzarella, just-sliced prosciutto and pesto), house-made gnocchi and meatballs. North Beach native son Joe DiMaggio loved

Molinari's so much, he specified in his will that they cater his wake. It's worth tolerating the huge crowds just to admire the crammed shelves full of anchovies, artichokes, olive oils, pasta and sauces, the cases stuffed with all kinds of cheese, and the salamis, coppa and cured meats hanging from every rafter.

WASHINGTON SQUARE & AROUND

Overlooked by the white stucco Romanesque Church of St Peter and St Paul (where Marilyn Monroe and local hero Joe DiMaggio had their wedding photos taken), **Washington Square** is a sunny green expanse that feels like a miniature town square. An 1879 statue of Benjamin Franklin stands in the park on a granite-encased time capsule – it's scheduled to be reopened in 2079. Flanked by iconic neighbourhood restaurants and cafés, the square is ground zero for revellers during the annual North Beach Festival every June (*see p30*).

Nearby, at **Caffè Roma** (*see below*), coffee is freshly roasted on the premises, while at **Liguria Bakery** (*see p104*), the locals stand in line for foccacia made in-house, baked by members of the same family since 1911.

Walk up Grant Avenue and browse blocks of one-of-a-kind boutiques, antiques and curiosity shops. From luxury lingerie to Asian antiquities, Grant Avenue is entertaining in itself, but perhaps the best place to stop for a bit of history is **Schein & Schein** (no.1435, *see p104*), a miscellany of antique maps and prints, and also home to a fascinating collection of vintage photographs. Just down the street is **Savoy Tivoli** (no.1434, *see p103*), a bar that has been in operation since 1907, and a great place to stop for a drink on the patio.

The district of **Telegraph Hill**, bordered by Grant Avenue and Green, Bay and Sansome Streets, got its name as the site of the West Coast's first telegraph. The landmark **Coit Tower** sits on top. Two nearby hotels neatly sum up the area. The **Hotel Bohème** (444 Columbus Avenue, between Vallejo & Green Streets, *see p284*) celebrates beat heritage with framed snapshots of life in jazzy bohemian North Beach in the 1950s and '60s, while the pensione-like **San Remo Hotel** (2237 Mason Street, at Chestnut Street, *see p284*), a pretty Italianate Victorian, is an ideal base for soaking up the area's Italian ambience.

Sights & Museums

Coit Tower
1 Telegraph Hill, at the end of Telegraph Hill Boulevard (1-415 249 0995). Bus 39. **Open** *May-Oct* 10am-6pm daily. *Nov-Apr* 10am-5pm daily. **Observation deck** $8; $2-$5 reductions. **Map** p97 C4 ⑫

This 210ft concrete turret, built by City Hall architect Arthur Brown in 1933, was a gift to the city from the eccentric Lillie Hitchcock Coit, famed for her love of firemen. Legend has it that as a schoolgirl, Coit happened upon the Knickerbocker #5 Volunteer Fire Company attempting to haul their fire engine up steep Telegraph Hill. As their energy flagged, she grabbed the rope and exhorted the men to pull on. From that day on, she became the mascot of the #5s. Upon her death, she bequeathed $125,000 to the city. A memorial to her beloved Knickerbockers was erected in Washington Square, and Coit Tower was built to fulfil her wish to 'add to the beauty of the city I have always loved'. While most assume that the tower represents the nozzle of a fire hose, the architects always denied it. The spectacular views from the top aren't the tower's only attraction. The base of the tower is ringed with marvellous 1930s WPA murals, recently restored, which were the collaborative effort of more than 25 artists, many of whom studied under Mexican painter Diego Rivera. Many depict California agriculture and industry; some reflect the left-leaning social-realist bent of the artists, at the time considered subversive enough to delay the opening in 1934 so that an errant hammer and sickle could be erased. *Photo p103.*

Restaurants & Cafés

Caffe Puccini
411 Columbus Avenue, at Vallejo Street (1-415 989 7033). Bus 10, 12, 30, 39, 41, 45, 91/cable car Powell-Mason. **Open** 6am-midnight daily. **Main courses** $6-$20. **Map** p97 D4 ⑬ Café
Like the composer after whom the café is named, friendly owner Graziano Lucchese is from Lucca in northern Italy. His welcoming café serves vast sandwiches stuffed with salami, prosciutto and mortadella.

$ Caffè Roma
526 Columbus Avenue, between Green & Union Streets (1-415 296 7942, www.cafferoma.com). Bus 10, 12, 30, 39, 41, 45, 91/cable car Powell-Mason. **Open** 6am-7pm Mon-Thur; 6am-9pm Fri; 6.30am-10pm Sat; 7am-7pm Sun. **Main courses** $7-$12.50. **Map** p97 D4 ⑭ Café
Some say Roma serves the strongest coffee in the city – the café is certainly among the most atmospheric, with beans roasted on the premises in the heart of North Beach by three generations of the Azzollini family. Espressos and other coffees, a range of Italian pastries (don't miss the tiramisu), and a substantial lunch menu of sandwiches, salads and pastas are served in a large, airy space, perfect for sipping, thinking and explaining your latest conspiracy theory.

★ $ Caffe Trieste
601 Vallejo Street, at Grant Avenue (1-415 392 6739, www.caffetrieste.com). Bus 10, 41. **Open** 6.30am-10pm Mon-Thur, Sun; 6.30am-11pm Fri, Sat. **Coffee & pastries** $5-$8. **No credit cards.** **Map** p97 D4 ⑮ Café

EXPLORE

EXPLORE

One of the city's original Italian coffeehouses, Caffe Trieste was one of the seminal gathering spots in North Beach during the 1950s beat movement. A former hangout for Jack Kerouac, Allen Ginsberg and their pals, it's also the spot where Francis Ford Coppola is said to have written the screenplay for *The Godfather*. Trieste still roasts its beans in San Francisco and arguably produces some of the best espresso in town – available packaged for purchase from its shop next door. Inside the café, the dark walls are plastered with photos of opera singers and famous regulars, and on select Saturdays, members of the extended Giotta family continue their long-standing tradition of performing popular Italian songs and operatic arias.

► *For more about SF's coffee culture, see p174* **Grounds Control**.

L'Osteria del Forno

519 Columbus Avenue, at Green Street (1-415 982 1124, www.losteriadelforno.com). Bus 8, 30, 39, 41, 45, 91. **Open** 11.30am-10pm Mon, Wed, Thur, Sun; 11.30am-10.30pm Fri, Sat. **Main courses** $11-$24. **No credit cards. Map** p97 D4 ⑯ Italian

On a street awash with knock-offs, this tiny osteria stands out for its humble authenticity. The room is the size of a postage stamp, but two Italian ladies and their oven deliver big time. The focaccia (and focaccia sandwiches) and thin-crust pizzas are top notch, and the singular roast of the day (pray for the roast pork braised in milk) is a labour of love and tenderness. The menu also features salads, soups and fresh pastas (try the penne baked in bolognese and béchamel sauce). Baskets of warm focaccia keep you going while you wait for main courses. There's a full bar with a nice selection of grappas.

$ Mama's on Washington Square

1701 Stockton Street, at Filbert Street (1-415 362 6421, www.mamas-sf.com). Bus 8, 30, 39, 41, 45/cable car Powell-Mason. **Open** 8am-3pm Tue-Sun. **Main courses** $7-$14. **Map** p97 C4 ⑰ Café

The 'wow' factor here is not necessarily on the menu, but in the festive atmosphere that prevails at this mainstay North Beach brunch spot, run by the Sanchez family for more than 50 years. Even the (sometimes epic) weekend queue is part of the fun. Once seated, you'll be faced with such temptations as a giant made-to-order 'm'omelette', huevos rancheros, or the Monte Cristo, a gargantuan sandwich of ham, turkey, cheddar and gruyere dipped in egg batter and grilled. Service is swift and familiar.

Mario's Bohemian Cigar Store

566 Columbus Avenue, at Union Street (1-415 362 0536). Bus 8BX, 8X, 30, 39, 41, 45, 91/cable car Powell-Mason. **Open** 10am-11pm daily. **Main courses** $7.50-$15. **Map** p97 D4 ⑬ Café

Despite the fact that you can't buy a cigar at Mario's (or smoke one), you shouldn't miss this classic North Beach café, which drips with as much atmosphere as its fabulous oven-baked meatball focaccia sandwiches. Wedged like a slice of pie onto a prominent corner in North Beach overlooking Washington Square Park, it's the perfect perch to sip an Italian soda or a cappuccino and watch the world go by.

Park Tavern

1652 Stockton Street, between Filbert & Union Streets (1-415 989 7300, www.parktavernsf.com). Bus 8BX, 8X, 30, 39, 41, 45, 91. **Open** 5.30-10pm Mon-Thur, Sun; 5.30-11pm Fri, Sat. **Main courses** $25-$36. **Map** p97 C4 ⑲ American

Anna Weinberg and chef Jennifer Puccio are the winning team behind Park Tavern, the second in a successful trio of San Francisco restaurants, each imbued with a pitch-perfect sense of culinary and neighbourhood identity. In the heart of North Beach, with windows overlooking Washington Square Park, the Tavern is a boisterous American brasserie that manages to make its large space intimate. Every single item on the appetisers menu is a must-have – from the addictive lemon chips with burrata to the smoked devilled eggs with bacon and pickled jalapeño. Among the stellar main options is the poulet noir – a whole herb-stuffed chicken served standing up on a cast-iron plate with black truffles, pecans and currants. If you can, save room for the monthly rotating 'birthday' cake.

Sodini's Green Valley Restaurant

510 Green Street, at Grant Avenue (1-415 291 0499). Bus 10, 12, 30, 39, 41, 45, 91. **Open** 5-10pm Mon-Thur; 5-11pm Fri; 10.30am-11pm Sat; 10.30am-10pm Sun. **Main courses** $12-$28. **Map** p97 D4 ⑳ Italian

Sodini's is small and darkly romantic, in a Chianti-bottle-as-candle-holder sort of way. Patrons are jammed close together to enable the servers to squeeze past with platters of sloppy pasta and rib-sticking lasagne. The fact that it's off the beaten track doesn't dampen its popularity: be sure to arrive earlier than you intend to eat and sign the list; you can then drop over to a neighbourhood bar while waiting for a table. Once inside, the wine is cheap and in plentiful supply.

★ Tony's Pizza Napoletana

1570 Stockton Street, at Union Street (1-415 835 9888, www.tonyspizzanapoletana.com). Bus 8BX, 8X, 30, 39, 41,45, 91. **Open** noon-10pm Mon; noon-11pm Wed-Sun. **Pizzas** $11-$41. **Map** p97 D4 ㉑ Pizza

Don't come here looking for New York-style pizza. This is Tony Gemingnani's paean to Napoli, complete with ten different kinds of pizza baked in seven different ovens, ranging in temperature from 550 to 1,000 degrees. Gemingnani has an impeccable pedigree: he's the first American to win the World

Coit Tower. See p101.

Champion Pizza Maker title in Naples, and the sometimes epic wait for a table in this busy corner of North Beach attests to his star power. Heavenly Tomato Pie made with hand-crushed tomato sauce and cooked in a 1,000-degree coal-fired oven, and the award-winning Margherita, with handmade San Felice-flour dough and San Marzano tomatoes (limited to 73 per day), are just the tip of menu. Among the other dizzying choices are Detroit and Sicilian styles, stromboli and calzone.

Bars

Rogue Ales Public House

673 Union Street, at Powell Street (1-415 362 7880, www.rogue.com). Bus 9X, 20, 30, 39, 41, 45. **Open** noon-midnight Mon-Thur, Sun; noon-2am Fri, Sat. **Map** p97 D3 ㉒

Oregon microbrewery Rogue Ale's bold land grab is evidenced by this ale house, devoted to its staggering array of brews. The standard selection of ambers and lagers is supplemented by such gems as chilli-pepper-tinged Chipotle Ale, Smoke Ale (with strong flavours of smokehouse almonds), Coffee Stout, and Iron Chef Morimoto's Black Obi Soba Ale.

Savoy Tivoli

1434 Grant Avenue, between Green & Union Streets (1-415 362 7023). Bus 9X, 12, 20, 30, 39, 41, 45. **Open** 6pm-2am Tue-Thur; 5pm-2am Fri; 3pm-2am Sat. **No credit cards. Map** p97 D4 ㉓

Opened in 1906, this bar tends to get packed on warm, weekend nights due to the patio seating out front, but when things are a bit slower it's a perfect

place to grab a beer and people-watch, or enjoy a few games of pool. On weekends, live jazz – often played by veteran old-timers – recalls the neighbourhood's beat roots.

Tony Nik's

1524 Stockton Street, between Green & Union Streets (1-415 693 0990, www.tonyniks.com). Bus 9X, 12, 20, 30, 39, 41, 45. **Open** 4pm-2am Mon-Fri; 2pm-2am Sat, Sun. **Map** p97 D4 ㉔

This venerable, timeless lounge, which is essentially a long bar with a few extra seats, opened the day after Prohibition was repealed in 1933, and keeps its cool vibe alive thanks to Atomic Age decor and comfortably hip and friendly environs. Cocktails are a serious business here.

Shops & Services

AB Fits

1519 Grant Avenue, between Filbert & Union Streets, North Beach (1-415 982 5726, www.ab fits.com). Bus 10, 12, 30, 39, 41, 45, 91. **Open** 11.30am-6.30pm Tue-Sat; noon-6pm Sun. **Map** p97 C4 ㉕ **Fashion**

The jean-ius of Howard Gee and Christopher Louie is to sell a mix of well-crafted denim lines, both widely known and more rarefied – brands for men and women include Raleigh Denim, Notify, Tellason, Circle of Friends, Frame and Earnest Sewn. Jeans always too long on you? The store offers an alteration service to ensure they'll fit perfectly. You'll also find separates and accessories by designers like Jill Platner, dePalma and Jungmaven.

Graffeo Coffee Roasting Company

735 Columbus Avenue, between Filbert &
Greenwich Streets (1-800 222 6250, 1-415 986
2420, www.graffeo.com). Bus 30, 39, 41, 45, 91/
cable car Powell-Mason. **Open** 9am-6pm Mon-Fri;
9am-5pm Sat. **Map** p97 C3 **㉖ Food & drink**
If you're awake, you'll smell it. This San Francisco
institution stocks fresh coffee from various plantations
around the world, roasting its beans on the premises.

★ Liguria Bakery

1700 Stockton Street, at Filbert Street (1-415 421
3786). Bus 8X, 39, 41, 45. **Open** 8am-1pm Tue-Fri;
7am-1pm Sat. **No credit cards. Map** p97 C4 **㉗**
Food & drink
The tiny Italian bakery does nothing but turn out ten or
so kinds of focaccia – onion, tomato, raisin, rosemary-
garlic, olive – from old-fashioned brick ovens.
Founded on this corner in 1911 by three brothers from
Genoa, it is still run by members of the same family.
Locals line up to get their squares of pillowy bread,
wrapped in butcher paper and tied up with string.
When the shop runs out (usually by midday), it closes.

★ Schein & Schein

1435 Grant Avenue, between Green & Union
Streets (1-415 399 8882, www.scheinandschein.
com). Bus 8X, 30, 39, 41, 45, 91. **Open** 11am-5pm
Mon, Sun; 11am-6pm Tue-Fri; 10am-7pm Sat. **Map**
p97 D4 **㉘ Gifts & souvenirs**
Stepping into Jim and Marti Schein's quiet, sunny
shop feels like entering a time warp. The walls are
adorned with cartography, and maps and prints are
organised in vintage produce and shipping crates
and letterpress-type cabinets. Though the speciality
is antique maps, particularly those of San Francisco
and greater California, you'll also find hotel and travel
brochures; lithographs; scientific, medical, astrologi-
cal and anatomical illustrations; rare atlases; and copper and steel engravings. Though rare maps can run
into the thousands, prints for as little as $5 can be had
from the discount crates near the entryway.

Tattoo City

700 Lombard Street, at Mason Street (1-415
345 9437, www.tattoocitysf.com). Bus 8X, 30, 45/
cable car Powell-Mason. **Open** noon-7pm daily.
Map p97 C3 **㉙ Tattoos**
The third incarnation of ink icon Ed Hardy's original
Mission District parlour, Tattoo City opened in 1999
– and the place still rocks. Though Hardy has retired
from the craft, his son Doug carries on the family
business. Inside, illustrations of classic pin-up girls
and seafaring imagery hint at the dominant house
styles: traditional Americana and Asian.

★ XOX Truffles

754 Columbus Avenue, at Greenwich Street
(1-415 421-4814, www.xoxtruffles.com). Bus 30.
Open 10am-7pm Mon-Sat; 10.30am-6pm Sun.
Map p97 C3 **㉚ Food & drink**

Chef Jean-Marc Gorce has garnered so many accolades (from the likes of the Food Network and the
New York Times) for his rich, dreamy bite-sized
creations, he could use an extra shop window just to
post them all. Instead, he lets the truffles do the talking at his modest storefront in North Beach, turning
out irresistible (and inexpensive) confections, from
cocoa-dusted crème de framboise and Earl Grey to
chilli-tequila and vegan soy truffles. Any of them
make the perfect partner for espresso-sipping and
people-watching on the sidewalks of Little Italy.

FISHERMAN'S WHARF

Fisherman's Wharf dates back to the Gold Rush,
when Italian and Chinese immigrants plied the
Bay for crab and other seafood and sold it right
off their boats. Famous families included the
DiMaggios (kin of late baseball great Joe
DiMaggio) and the Alioto clan (who own an
eponymous restaurant on the wharf, *see p108*).
Alas, there is little evidence of that historic past
today: roughly bounded by Jefferson, North Point
and Kearny Streets and Fort Mason, Fisherman's
Wharf is little more than a conglomeration of
novelty attractions, tacky shops and heavy
pedestrian traffic – in surveys, it routinely ranks
as the No.1 destination for visitors, despite the
fact that its main attractions were built in the
late 1960s and '70s. Still, those with a few hours
to kill can find some inexpensive entertainment
here, along with fresh crab cocktails from
sidewalk vendors (November through May),
and unrivalled views of the Bay.

Schein & Schein.

Along **Jefferson Street**, the wharf's main drag, you'll find such kitschy dockside attractions as the San Francisco branch of **Madame Tussauds** (no.145, 1-866-223-4240, www.madametussauds.com), **Ripley's Believe It Or Not! Museum** (no.175, 1-415 202 9850, www.ripleys.com), and the **Rainforest Café** (no.400, 1-415 440 5610, www.rainforestcafé.com) – if nothing else, a fail-safe diversion for cranky kids. Elsewhere, sidewalk crab stalls and seafood restaurants thrive.

For the only remaining glimpse of Fisherman's Wharf as it once was, turn towards the water off Jefferson and on to Leavenworth Street, then slip into **Fish Alley**. There, you will find real fishing boats and real fishermen. Although it's within shouting distance of Jefferson, it feels like miles away. You can catch another remnant of fishing life at **Frank's Fisherman** (366 Jefferson Street, between Leavenworth Street & Al Scoma Way, 1-415 775 1165, www.franksfisherman.com), which sells everything from silk yachting shirts to antique scrimshaw tusks.

At the eastern end, **Pier 39** is a sprawling prefab array of seafront shops, attractions and arcade games. Luckily, crowds of sea lions barking and belching on nearby pontoons provide a natural respite. Offshore from H Dock on Pier 39, **Forbes Island** (1-415 951 4900, www.forbesisland.com) is 530 tons of manmade, engine-propelled, floating lighthouse and restaurant. Further west, at Pier 45, the USS *Pampanito* (*see p108*) World War II submarine is open to the public for self-guided tours.

A reminder of the area's former industrial life is the **Cannery** (2801 Leavenworth Street, enter on Jefferson or Beach Streets, 1-415 771 3112, www.delmontesquare.com). Built in 1907 as a fruit-canning factory, it's now just another mall. The red-brick **Ghirardelli Square** (at North Point & Larkin Streets) dates from the 19th century and housed a chocolate factory until the 1960s; the namesake chocolate is still sold, but the building itself is now a complex of shops and restaurants. Despite all this, the **Ghirardelli Ice Cream & Chocolate Shop** (*see p109*) on the southern edge of the square is the place to get some of the best hot fudge sundaes on earth. The lovely Mermaid Fountain in the square's central plaza was sculpted by local artist Ruth Asawa. There's more refreshment nearby at the famous **Buena Vista Café** (2765 Hyde Street, *see p109*), where Irish coffee was introduced to the US in 1952.

Head west from here to the shores of **Aquatic Park** (between Hyde Street & Van Ness Avenue) for one of the best strolls in the city, with a panorama of the Golden Gate Bridge, Alcatraz, windsurfers, sailing boats, wildly coloured kites and dogs catching frisbees. Along the **Municipal Pier** (access from the northern end of Van Ness Avenue), fishermen try their luck; at **Hyde Street Pier**, a fleet of carefully restored historic ships is docked permanently and open to the public.

The **Golden Gate Promenade** begins here, continuing for three miles along the shoreline to **Fort Point** (*see p127*). The entire stretch of waterfront from Aquatic Park to Ocean Beach was incorporated into the Golden Gate National

EXPLORE

SECRET STAIRWAYS TO HEAVEN

Step up to some of the best city views.

Often overgrown with foliage and unmarked, San Francisco's network of nearly 400 stairways connecting the city's 42 hills are some of the city's most untravelled and spectacular byways.

Leafy **Macondray Lane** (off Leavenworth Street, between Union and Green Streets), was the inspiration for Armistead Maupin's Barbary Lane in *Tales of the City*. Idiosyncratic houses line one side, through which you can catch tantalising glimpses of the Bay beyond. The signpost for the steps is hard to spot – look for the name imprinted in the concrete of the curb.

The architect-designed steps on **Vallejo Street** (between Jones and Mason Streets) have breathtaking views and flowerbeds full of arum lilies. Try walking east from Jones and Vallejo Streets (uphill) for a block, admiring the collision of architecture at the peak of Nob Hill. Take the stairs to the right of the overlook and, winding past landscaped backyards and friendly cats, descend slowly to Ina Coolbrith Park a block down. Continue down the steps for showstopping views of the Bay Bridge, the piers and Treasure Island.

Tucked between North Beach and the Embarcadero, the glorious **Filbert Street** steps take you from the bottom of Sansome and Filbert streets up to Coit Tower, along the way passing through the lovely, rambling Grace Marchant Gardens with their famous flocks of wild parrots.

The steps along **Broadway** between Taylor and Jones Streets lead to a perch where you can take in vistas of the Bay Bridge with the Transamerica Pyramid and the Financial District spread out below. Over in Twin Peaks, the spectacular panorama from Tank Hill is your reward for climbing the steep **Pemberton Steps**, accessed at the intersection of Corbett and Clay Streets.

Arguably the grandest stairway in the city is on **Lyon Street**, between Green Street and Broadway, a stairway 'street' built in 1916 to connect Cow Hollow with the loftier climes of Pacific Heights. Four sets of stairs, totalling 288 steps, take you past manicured hedges, flower gardens and stately mansions, to an iron gate that marks the entrance to the Presidio. From the top, there are views of Alcatraz, the Palace of Fine Arts and the Golden Gate Bridge.

For more stairways, consult Adah Bakalinsky's exhaustive (and exhausting) guide, *Stairway Walks in San Francisco*.

EXPLORE

Recreation Area in 1972, with the authorities thankfully arresting Fisherman's Wharf-style tourist kitsch spreading any further along one of the most scenic bits of coast in the region.

Sights & Museums

★ Alcatraz

Alcatraz Island, San Francisco Bay (www.nps.gov/alcatraz). Alcatraz Cruises ferry from Pier 33, Embarcadero (1-415 981 7625, www.alcatraz cruises.com). Streetcar F. **Tickets** (incl audio guide) $30-$37; $18.25-$21.75 reductions. **Map** p97 A5 ❶

'Alcatraz' is Spanish for pelican, but to its inmates it was simply known as 'the Rock'. The West Coast's first lighthouse was built here in 1854, but it was soon decided that the island's isolated setting made it perfect for a prison. It became a military jail in the 1870s, but it wasn't until it was converted into a high-security federal penitentiary in 1934 that the name Alcatraz became an international symbol of punishment. Despite being in operation for less than 30 years, Alcatraz remains fixed in the popular imagination as the ultimate penal colony. Today, its ominous prison buildings are no longer used (its last inmates left in 1963), but the craggy outcrop, now a National Park, lures over a million visitors each year. Despite what you might expect, Alcatraz is far from being a tourist trap. The audio tour, which features actual interviews from a variety of former prisoners and guards, is powerful, chilling and evocative, and the buildings retain an eerie and fascinating appeal. Departure times for both the day tours and the far less frequent (and wildly oversubscribed) evening jaunts vary by season: check the website for details. One word of warning: capacity on the tours is limited, so it's best to book ahead.

Angel Island

Angel Island State Park, San Francisco Bay (1-415 435 1915, www.angelisland.org). Blue & Gold ferry from Pier 41, Embarcadero (1-415 705 8200, www.blueandgoldfleet.com). Streetcar F. **Tickets** $16; $9 reductions. **Map** p97 A3 ❷

Richard Henry Dana recounts in his *Two Years Before the Mast* (1840) how he collected a year's supply of wood for his ship *Alert* when it stopped at Angel Island in the winter of 1835-36. Later, the island served as one of America's busiest immigration ports – 'the Ellis Island of the West' for mostly Chinese immigrants. In its darkest chapter, it was as temporary internment camp for Japanese-Americans during World War II. Converted to a California State Park in 1954, Angel Island offers numerous recreation opportunities, including hiking, biking, and camping. Blue & Gold runs a ferry service; times vary with the season, so check online or call before setting out. Boats arrive at the Ayala Cove visitors' centre, where there are maps, bikes to rent, picnic tables and a café (open daily April-Oct, weekends Feb-Mar, Nov).

Views from the island are unrivalled. At its peak, there are 360-degree views of the entire Bay Area – one of the primary reasons the top was sheared off and replaced with a gun bunker as a part of the Bay's coastal defences. Luckily, they replaced the top, but the bunkers are still scattered around the island, their history dating back to before the Civil War.

Hyde Street Pier

Foot of Hyde Street (1-415 561 6662, www. maritime.org). Streetcar F/bus 19, 30, 47, 90/ cable car Powell-Hyde. **Open** 9.30am-5pm daily. **Admission** $5; free under-16s. **No credit cards**. **Map** p97 B1 ❸

Maritime fans, students of history, and children will love the historic vessels permanently docked here. Typical of the ships that would have been common here in the 19th and early 20th centuries, they include the 1886 full-rigged *Balclutha*, built to carry grain from California to Europe; the *CA Thayer*, an 1895 sailing ship that carried timber along the West Coast; the *Alma*, an 1891 scow schooner that hauled cargo throughout the Bay Area; *Hercules*, a 1907 ocean tugboat; and the 1890 commuter ferry *Eureka*.

Along with the San Francisco Maritime Museum, the set-up is the highlight of what is officially designated as the San Francisco Maritime National Historic Park. The park's lovely visitors' centre, at the corner of Jefferson and Hyde Streets (June-Sept 9.30am-7pm daily; Oct-May 9.30am-5pm daily), contains fascinating displays on the area's seafaring history. For more on the park and its various services and attractions, call 1-415 447 5000 or visit www.nps.gov/safr.

★ FREE Musée Mécanique

Pier 45, at the end of Taylor Street (1-415 346 2000, www.museemecanique.org). Streetcar F/ bus 19, 30, 47, 90/cable car Powell-Mason. **Open** 11am-7pm Mon-Fri; 10am-8pm Sat, Sun. **Admission** free. **Map** p97 A2 ❹

Part museum, part old-fashioned arcade, the Musée Mécanique houses a collection of more than 200 coin-operated games and amusements dating back to the 1880s, amassed by late owner Ed Zelinsky. The result is a love letter to the era before video games, as well as to turn-of-the-century San Francisco. Gypsy fortune tellers, giant mechanical-circus dioramas, can-can girl stereoscopes, carnival strength testers, player pianos, and a looming Laffing Sal (a cackling mechanical relic salvaged from the defunct Playland at the Beach amusement park) are among the games that delight kids and adults alike. Along the walls, photos of early San Francisco and earthquake memorabilia set the mood for a time when the city was still something of a western outpost on the edge of the Pacific.

FREE Maritime Museum

900 Beach Street, at Polk Street (1-415 447 5000, www.maritime.org). Streetcar F/bus 19, 30, 47, 90/cable car Powell-Hyde. **Open** 10am-4pm daily. **Admission** free. **Map** p97 B1 ❺

EXPLORE

EXPLORE

Boudin Sourdough Bakery & Café.

The Moderne cruiseliner that houses the museum was recently refurbished and the fantastic Atlantis murals by Hilaire Hiler in the lobby fully restored. The building also contains a vast maritime archival collection of books, paintings, drawings, photographs, charts and maps – the largest maritime collection on the West Coast.

USS Pampanito

Pier 45 (1-415 775 1943, www.maritime.org). Streetcar F/bus 10, 19, 30, 47/cable car Powell-Hyde. **Open** *Mid Oct-late May* 9am-6pm Mon-Thur, Sun; 9am-8pm Fri, Sat. *Late May-mid Oct* 9am-8pm Mon, Tue, Thur-Sun; 9am-6pm Wed. **Admission** $15; $4-$6 reductions; $45 family. **Map** p97 A2 ③

Docked behind the Musée Mécanique, the *Pampanito* is a World War II, Balao-class Fleet submarine with an impressive record: it made six patrols in the Pacific at the height of the war, sinking six Japanese ships and damaging four others. The vessel has been restored to look much as it would have in its prime in 1945. The sub is still seaworthy: in 1995 it sailed under the Golden Gate Bridge for the first time in 50 years.

Restaurants & Cafés

Alioto's

8 Fisherman's Wharf, at Taylor & Jefferson Streets (1-415 673 0183, www.aliotos.com). Streetcar F/ bus 39, 47/cable car Powell-Mason. **Open** 11am-11pm daily. **Main courses** $14-$55. **Map** p97 A2 ③ **Fish & seafood**

Alioto's began as a sidewalk stand serving crab and shrimp cocktails to passers-by. Now more than eight decades later, the crab stand (which still offers fresh-caught Dungeness to throngs of hungry tourists) is part of a hugely popular restaurant owned by members of the same local family. The room offers amazing views of the Bay, and the kitchen manages to turn out decent (if pricey) seafood, as well as fish-centric Sicilian specialities.

Blue Mermaid

Argonaut Hotel, 471 Jefferson Street, at Hyde Street (1-415 771 2222, www.bluemermaidsf.com). Streetcar F/bus 19, 30, 47, 91/cable car Powell-Hyde. **Open** 7am-9pm Mon-Thur, Sun; 7am-10pm Fri, Sat. **Main courses** $19-$29. **Map** p97 B2 ③ **Fish & seafood**

Designed to recall the history of the working wharf (don't miss the excellent on-site museum), this rustic-looking restaurant is set into the corner of the Argonaut Hotel. The menu is perfect for San Francisco's fogged-in days, with hearty chowders spooned up from large cauldrons – the award-winning Dungeness crab and corn are winners. There's also a good children's menu, making it a top choice for families.

Boudin Sourdough Bakery & Café

160 Jefferson Street, between Mason & Taylor Streets (1-415 928 1849, www.boudinbakery.com). Streetcar F/bus 39, 47/cable car Powell-Mason. **Open** 11.30am-10pm Mon-Thur; 9.30am-10pm Fri, Sat; 9.30am-10pm Sun. **Main courses** *Bistro* $15-$40. *Café* $9. **Map** p97 A3 ③ **Café**

Sourdough bread is as synonymous with San Francisco as fog and Twitter. At the flagship Boudin Bakery on Fisherman's Wharf, tangy loaves are still made from a mother dough first cultivated here in 1849. You can watch the bread-making process, sample it at the café, and even buy a few loaves. There's also a bistro with an all-day menu, including sandwiches, salads, Dungeness crab cakes and clam chowder in (you guessed it) a bread bowl. **Other locations** throughout the Bay Area.

Gary Danko

800 North Point Street, at Hyde Street (1-415 749-2060, www.garydanko.com). Bus 47/ cable car Powell-Hyde. **Open** 5.30-10pm daily. **Tasting menus** $81-$117. **Map** p97 B1 ⑩
American creative

Eating here is like dinner and a night at the theatre rolled into one. The superstar chef, winner of numerous culinary awards, is a fanatic about details – from the perfectly spaced white-clothed tables, arrangements of fresh flowers, and amazingly well-informed and attentive staff, to the flawless presentation of signature dishes such as his trademark glazed oysters with lettuce cream, salsify and osetra caviar. Danko's French-California cuisine changes seasonally. It's pricey, but worth ponying up for the five-course tasting menu – a gastronomic spectacular that includes a swoon-inducing cheese cart (wine pairings extra). Reservations are essential.

$ Ghirardelli Soda Fountain & Chocolate Shop

900 North Point Street, at corner of Beach & Larkin Streets (1-415 447 2846, www.ghirardelli. com). Powell/Hyde cable car/bus 47. **Open** 9am-11pm Mon-Thur, Sun; 9am-midnight Fri, Sat.
Ice-cream $8-$11. **Map** p97 B1 ⑪ **Ice-cream**
Domingo Ghirardelli, the granddaddy of San Francisco chocolatiers, opened his factory here in 1852, and despite the touristy crowds that pack in on weekends, this is still the place to head for those classic chocolate squares or a (literally) over-the-top ice-cream confection. The fountain offers such gut-busting creations as the eight-scoop, eight-topping Earthquake. At the back, you can see a demonstration production room where melted chocolate sloshes around in big vats. The shop sells Ghirardelli cocoa products in all forms and flavours: bars, squares, beans, syrups, powder – even boxed inside miniature cable cars.

Bars

★ Buena Vista Café

2765 Hyde Street, at Beach Street (1-415 474 5044, www.thebuenavista.com). Powell/Hyde cable car/bus 47. **Open** 9am-2am Mon-Fri; 8am-2am Sat, Sun. **Map** p97 B1 ⑫
As atmospheric as the clang of the cable car on a foggy night, the chummy wood-panelled Buena Vista has been a local watering hole and hangout

for seafaring folk since 1916, but its claim to fame is that it was the bar that first introduced Irish coffee to America. The recipe was nabbed from a Dublin bartender by a local newspaper columnist in 1952, and today, white-jacketed bartenders serve some 2,000 of these frothy whiskey concoctions daily from the long, mahogany bar. The cosy surroundings, in an old Victorian overlooking Aquatic Park and Fisherman's Wharf, make it an ideal place to unwind. There's also a pub menu that includes burgers and seafood specialities.

RUSSIAN HILL

Russian Hill got its name when several Cyrillic-inscribed gravestones were discovered here during the Gold Rush. Local lore has it that a Russian warship put into the harbour of San Francisco in the early 1840s, and a number of the disease-stricken crew died while ashore. As they belonged to the Orthodox Church, they couldn't be buried in any of the existing Protestant or Catholic cemeteries, so one was created for them in this area. By the late 1800s, the gravestones had disappeared; along with them went any trace of Russian influence.

Today, Russian Hill is a quiet, residential and pricey neighbourhood roughly bordered by Larkin and North Point Streets, Columbus Avenue, Powell Street and Pacific Avenue. Its most notorious landmark is the world's 'crookedest' street (though technically the 'real' crookedest street, with even tighter turns, lies on the back side of Potrero Hill, along Vermont Street). **Lombard Street**, which snakes steeply down from Hyde Street to Leavenworth, packs nine hairpin bends into one brick-paved and perfectly landscaped block. In summer, tourists queue for the thrill of driving down its hazardous 27 per cent gradient at 5mph, to the annoyance of local residents. Arrive early or late to avoid the throng. For further thrills, test your skills behind the wheel on the steepest street in the city: **Filbert Street** between Hyde and Leavenworth descends at a whopping 31.5 per cent gradient. Also up on Russian Hill is the **San Francisco Art Institute**, housed in an attractive 1920s Spanish Revival building on Chestnut Street and containing a wonderful Diego Rivera mural.

Struggle up Vallejo Street to Taylor Street to take in the views from tiny **Ina Coolbrith Park**. Dedicated in 1911, the park honours California's first Poet Laureate. Up from the park, the top of the **Vallejo Street Stairway**, designed by Willis Polk and surrounded on each side by landscaped gardens, is the apex of the neighbourhood. Laura Ingalls Wilder, author of *Little House on the Prairie*, lived here (at 1019 Vallejo). Russian Hill is riven with quaint stairs and alleyways: fun to explore if you don't mind the ups and downs.

EXPLORE

Other landmark addresses in the district include **29 Russell Street**, off Hyde Street, where Jack Kerouac lived with Neal and Carolyn Cassady during his most creative period in the 1950s; and the **Feusier Octagon House**, one of the city's oldest dwellings, at 1067 Green Street, near Leavenworth. The pastel structure is one of only two survivors of the 19th-century octagonal-house craze (the other is in Pacific Heights).

Sights & Museums

FREE San Francisco Art Institute
800 Chestnut Street, between Leavenworth & Jones Streets (1-415 771 7020, www.sfai.edu). Bus 30, 47, 91/cable car Powell-Hyde or Powell-Mason. **Open** *Diego Rivera Gallery* 9am-5pm daily. *Walter McBean Gallery* 11am-6pm Tue-Sat. **Admission** free. **Map** p97 C2 ㊷

This hip and prestigious art school offers the full spectrum of fine arts, including painting, film, photography, sculpture and new media. Its student shows are legendary. Most people visit to see Diego Rivera's mural *The Making of a Fresco*. Recover from all those hills with a rest in the pretty open-air courtyard, or grab a cheap snack in the cafeteria and soak up the views.

Restaurants & Cafés

Helmand Palace
2424 Van Ness Avenue, between Union & Green Streets (1-415 345 0072, www.helmandpalacesf. com). Bus 12, 19, 27, 41, 45, 47, 49, 90. **Open** 5.30-10pm Mon-Thur, Sun; 5.30-11pm Fri, Sat. **Main courses** $12-$23. **Map** p97 D1 ㊹ **Afghan**
The Helmand – the city's only Afghan restaurant – moved from North Beach and added 'Palace' to its name, but it's still as good as it ever was. Influenced by the flavours of India, Asia and the Middle East, the food is deliciously aromatic, with marinades and fragrant spices. Specialities include leek ravioli and lamb *lawand* (leg of lamb sautéed with garlic, onion, tomatoes, mushrooms, yoghurt and spices).

La Folie
2316 Polk Street, between Union & Green Streets (1-415 776 5577, www.lafolie.com). Bus 19, 45, 47/ cable car Powell-Hyde. **Open** 5.30-10.30pm Mon-Sat. **Prix-fixe** $95-$135. **Map** p97 D1 ㊺ **French**
This is one of the city's few truly French restaurants that has never bowed to the whims of fashion. For more than 27 years, chef Roland Passot has enjoyed a passionate following. Opt for the five- or seven-course tasting menus and you'll see why: meticulously prepared updated classics such as frog legs with trumpet mushroom ragout and butter-poached lobster with carrot sauce. The Provençal decor and attentive staff add to the charm of this delightfully haute but not at all haughty establishment. The adjoining Green Room is a good option for intimate dining.

Reverb
2323 Polk Street, between Union & Green Street (1-415 441 2323, www.reverbsf.com). Bus 19, 45, 47/cable car Powell-Hyde. **Open** 5.30-10pm Mon-Fri; 10am-2.30pm, 5.30-10pm Sat; 10am-9pm Sun. **Main courses** $16-$28. **Map** p97 D1 ㊻
American creative
Capitalising on their huge success at haute vegetarian Gather restaurant in Berkeley, partners Eric Fenster and Ari Derfel came west to Russian Hill. Under chef Ryan Shelton, the restaurant has taken an omnivorous comfort-food turn, but still culls the best and freshest selections from local gardens, farms and ranches. The menu strikes a smart balance between vegetarian and meat/fish dishes – from chilled coconut soup with crispy padron peppers to roasted duck breast with caramelised plum and snap peas. Sunday features all-day, all-night brunch.

Zarzuela
2000 Hyde Street, at Union Street (1-415 346 0800). Bus 19, 41, 45/cable car Powell-Hyde. **Open** 5.30-10pm Tue-Sat. **Main courses** $14-$19. **Tapas** $7. **Map** p97 D2 ㊼ **Spanish**
The tapas and paella are always spot-on at cosy Zarzuela, served amid walls of bullfight posters and maps of Spain. Old standbys such as grilled aubergine filled with goat's cheese, sautéed shrimps in garlic and olive oil, and fried potatoes with garlic and sherry vinegar never disappoint.

Shops & Services

Elle-même
1210 Union Street, at Hyde Street (1-415 921 2100, www.elle-meme.com). Bus 19, 41, 45. **Open** noon-6pm Tue-Fri; 11am-5pm Sat, Sun. **Map** p97 D2 ㊽ **Accessories**
Denise Kohne's vintage shop is a homage to throwback glamour. The selection includes costume and fine jewellery spanning the 1880s to 1980s, neatly arranged in tall built-in glass cabinets that line the perimeter of the store. Depending on Kohne's latest estate sale scores, that might mean art deco pendants dotted with gems, serpentine gold bangles, 1920s crystal brooches or gala-ready chandelier earrings.

No.3
1987 Hyde Street, at Union Street (1-415 525-4683, www.shopno3.com). Bus 19, 41, 45. **Open** 2-7pm Thur, Fri; noon-7pm Sat; noon-5pm Sun. **Map** p97 D2 ㊾ **Accessories**
Run by Jenny Chung – owner of Hayes Valley boutique Acrimony (www.shopacrimony.com) – this intimate, 200-square-foot shop sells trendsetting jewellery from around a dozen designers. Rose gold, pave and sterling silver designs by Anna Sheffield, Bliss Lau and Gabriela Artigas glint from the boutique's terrariums and glass globes. The rings are standouts, as are the interchangeable earrings that complement multiple piercings, like Maria Black's Reverse Wings.

WALK THE BEAT GOES ON
Follow in the footsteps of Jack Kerouac and friends.

Our walk starts on Columbus Avenue and Broadway in North Beach, where the literary spirits are tightly packed. First, peek into **Vesuvio** (no.255 Columbus Avenue, *see p100*); the jaunty multicoloured sign has welcomed poets and artists since the place opened in 1948. Neither Dylan Thomas nor Jack Kerouac could resist when they were in town, and nor can the dipsomaniacal poets of today. To the side of Vesuvio is **Jack Kerouac Alley**, renamed by the city in 1988, and the famous **City Lights** bookstore (no.261, *see p100*).

Now cross Columbus heading east along Broadway. **Tosca** (242 Columbus Avenue, *see p98*) can lay proud claim to having ejected Bob Dylan one boisterous evening, and it was at **Specs** (12 William Saroyan Place, *see p98*) that columnist Herb Caen coined the derogatory term 'beatnik' to describe the increasingly large numbers of youths heading to North Beach in search of jazz and poetry. They found the former, at least, just away from City Lights along the righthand side of Broadway: at nos.471-3, the **Jazz Workshop** once hosted the likes of Miles Davis, John Coltrane, Sonny Rollins and Ornette Coleman; it was also here that Lenny Bruce was first arrested for obscenity in 1961.

Head up Montgomery Street for a great view of the Bay Bridge, then cross Broadway. Allen Ginsberg lived at **1010 Montgomery** with Peter Orlovsky, and probably conceived his epochal poem *Howl* here. The site is now an old folks' home. Heading back

along Broadway you will pass the **Green Tortoise Hostel** at no.494. It may not look like much now, but this was once the chic El Matador, where Frank Sinatra and Duke Ellington performed.

Turn right on to Kearny and you're facing more than 100 pretty steps. Locals call them the Kearny Steps, but the official title is the **Macchiarini Steps** – named for a local artisan family that's been making jewellery here since 1948 (at 1544 Grant Avenue, www.macreativedesign.com). From the top, it's downhill again for a break at **Caffe Trieste** (601 Vallejo Street, *see p101*), the coffee house where Francis Ford Coppola is said to have worked on *The Godfather*.

Turn right down Green Street. If it's sunny, turn left and head up to **Washington Square** for a glorious mix of tatty old bohemians, wannabe alternative types and discreet Chinese ladies doing t'ai chi. Otherwise, zigzag across the intersection between Green, Columbus and Stockton. Stick on Green Street, passing **Caffè Sport** at no.574. When this was the Cellar, Kenneth Rexroth and Ruth Weiss read to improvised accompaniment here, a first foray into jazz poetry. Turn right on to Grant Avenue and head past the **Grant & Green Saloon** (no.1371), until you reach the plain old **Saloon** (no.1232). This is San Francisco's oldest bar, open since 1861. There's no smoky jazz, but there is live blues.

EXPLORE

Pacific Heights & the Marina

EXPLORE

If there's one classic San Francisco view – in a city that has a multitude – it's the vista across the Bay from Pacific Heights and the northern waterfront. What sets it apart is the iconic Golden Gate Bridge, yet the wealthy had staked their claim to these hills long before its construction began in 1933.

The area covered in this chapter spans Bush Street to the Bay and from Van Ness Avenue to the Presidio, and it has much to offer beyond the engineering marvel that grabs all the attention. The Pacific Heights mansions overlook some of the most beautiful coastline in the US, while the vast expanses of the Presidio butt up against the well-scrubbed opulence of the Marina.

Crissy Field.

Don't Miss

1 Golden Gate Bridge The views are golden from the iconic crossing (p127).

2 B Patisserie A superior pastry stop in posh Pac Heights (p115).

3 Crissy Field Get a prime panorama from this bayside promenade (p125).

4 Walt Disney Family Museum Meet the man behind the mouse (p128).

5 Greens Heaven for herbivores – and even non-vegetarians (p124).

EXPLORE

Bun Mee.

PACIFIC HEIGHTS

True to its name, **Pacific Heights** peers over the Pacific from on high, its mansions home to the cream of San Francisco's high society for generations. The Casebolt house at 2727 Pierce Street was built in 1866, the Burr mansion at 1772 Vallejo Street in 1878 and the Flood mansion (now a school) at 2222 Broadway was completed in 1901. You need to be a multimillionaire to buy around here, but you can get a taste of the Heights life at the **Hotel Drisco** (*see p287*), housed in a grand building constructed in 1903.

As if anyone needed further proof of the neighbourhood's cup running over, billionaire socialites Gordon and Ann Getty and Oracle billionaire Larry Ellison have houses here, as do many of the 'old' families of San Francisco (the Floods, the Bechtels and others). The eastern edge of the area contains some beautiful Victorian houses. The blue-and-white **Octagon House** (*see p122*) is perhaps the most famous, but there are also rich pickings to the south: the **Haas-Lilienthal House**, for example, which offers visitors a rare chance to see inside a grand old Queen Anne. Nearby is the ornate **Spreckels Mansion**, which spans the entire block between Jackson, Gough, Washington and Octavia Streets.

Built by sugar heir Adolph Spreckels for his young wife Alma (the model for the statue that adorns the top of the Dewey Monument in Union Square), the 'Parthenon of the West' has been used as a location in several films, most notably Steve McQueen's *Bullitt*. It's now home to the novelist Danielle Steel.

Wander west from here, perhaps stopping in **Lafayette Park** (Washington & Gough Streets) to watch pedigree dogs walking their pedigree owners, to the stretch of **Fillmore Street** between Bush and Jackson Streets. This is the main shopping hub of the area, lined with smart shops and restaurants. A few blocks west, elegant antiques shops, ateliers and boutiques sit on **Sacramento Street** between Presidio Avenue and Spruce Street.

It may come as some surprise to learn that it was from this now-highfalutin neighbourhood that poet Allen Ginsberg launched a cultural renaissance in 1955, when he gave the first public reading of *Howl* at the long-vanished Six Gallery (3115 Fillmore Street, at Filbert Street). Northwest of here, past **Alta Plaza Park** (Jackson & Steiner Streets), things grow even more handsome: the stretch of **Broadway** between Divisadero Street and the Presidio holds some of the most regal architecture in the city.

Sights & Museums

Haas-Lilienthal House

2007 Franklin Street, between Washington &
Jackson Streets (1-415 441 3000, www.sfheritage.
org/haas-lilienthal-house). Bus 1, 10, 12, 19,
27, 47, 49, 90. **Open** noon-3pm Wed, Sat;
11am-4pm Sun. **Admission** $8; $5 reductions.
Map p117 H4 ❶
Built in 1886 by Bavarian immigrant William Haas,
this 26-room house has elaborate wooden gables
and a circular tower, clearly delineating the Queen
Anne style. Fully restored and filled with period
furniture, it also contains photos documenting its
history and that of the family that occupied it until
1972. It's maintained by San Francisco Architectural
Heritage, which also organises walking tours.

Restaurants & Cafés

★ $ B Patisserie

2821 California Street, at Divisadero Street
(1-415 440 1700, www.bpatisserie.com). Bus
1, 2, 3, 10, 22, 24. **Open** 8am-6pm Tue-Sun.
Pastries & sandwiches $1.75-$10.50.
Map p117 F5 ❷ **Bakery/café**
Belinda Leong and Michel Suas's cosy, neighbourhood patisserie is one of the best things to happen to
lower Pacific Heights in decades. Leong's signature
kouign amman (a chewy croissant-like bun from
Brittany) tops an exhausting list of viennoiseries
that includes cakes, tarts, macaroons, scones, ver-
rines and millefeuille, as well as tartines (open-faced
sandwiches) served on house-made levain bread.
Leong recently expanded her operation across the
street to B On the Go, offering a more savoury menu
of hot and cold sandwiches and salads.

$ Bun Mee

2015 Fillmore Street, between California &
Pine Streets (1-415 800 7696, www.bunmee.co).
Bus 3, 22. **Open** 11am-8pm Mon-Fri; 11am-
7pm Sat. **Sandwiches** $7-$8.50. **Map** p117 G5
❸ **Vietnamese**
Banh mi sandwich spots in San Francisco are almost
as common as pizza joints in New York, with followers who will argue the merits of their favourite
places just as fiercely. While Bun Mee may not win
over purists, the inventive flavours are deeply satisfying. Variations include grilled lemongrass pork
with shaved onion pickled carrot, daikon, jalapeños,
cucumber and cilantro, spread with garlic mayo on a
French roll; and the Belly Bun, made with Kurobuta
belly, radish relish and hardboiled egg. Whatever
you do, order a side of the sweet potato fries, which
comes with red curry mayo dip.

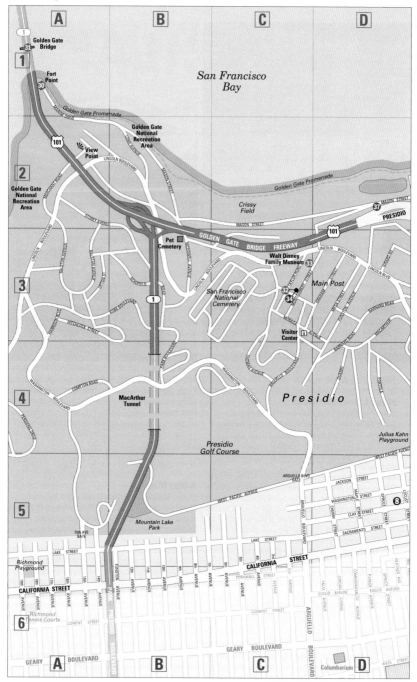

EXPLORE

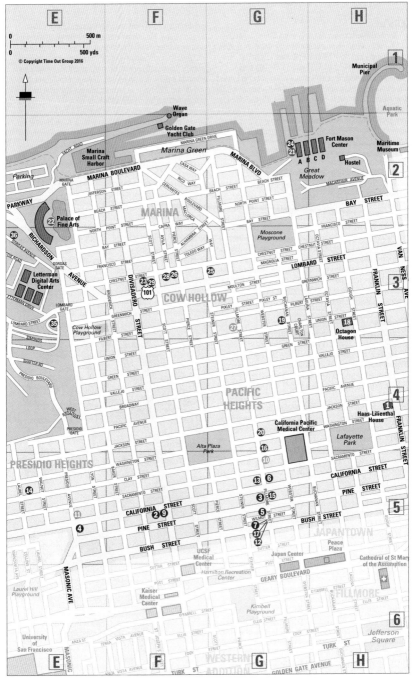

Ella's

500 Presidio Avenue, at California Street (1-415 441 5669, www.ellassanfrancisco.com). Bus 1, 2, 3, 43. **Open** *7am-3pm Mon-Fri; 8.30am-2pm Sat, Sun.* **Main courses** $12-$15. **Map** p117 E5 ❹ **Café**
This stylish, neighbourly corner restaurant is famed for its weekend brunch. The wait for a table can be long, but it's worth it. Standouts include the chicken hash with eggs and toast, and the potato scramble, prepared with a frequently changing list of fresh ingredients. The thick, perfectly crisped French toast is superb.

Florio

1915 Fillmore Street, at Wilmot Street (1-415 775 4300, www.floriosf.com). Bus 1, 2, 3, 22, 24. **Open** *5.30-10pm daily.* **Main courses** $15-$30. **Map** p117 G5 ❺ **Italian/Mediterranean**
A quintessential local bistro, Florio is warm and welcoming, with just the right degree of refinement. Dark wood and white tablecloths set the tone for rustic Italian/Mediterranean cooking, plus a few classic French-influenced dishes that are holdovers from a previous incarnation, including the ever-popular steak-frites with bernaise sauce. Cacciucco (Tuscan seafood stew) is a perennial soul-warming favourite. Service is swift and friendly.

Fresca

2114 Fillmore Street, between California & Sacramento Streets (1-415 447 2668, www.frescasf.com). Bus 1, 2, 3, 10, 22, 24. **Open** *11am-3pm, 5-9pm Mon, Tue; 11-am-3pm Wed-Fri; 11am-4pm, 5-10pm Sat; 11am-4pm, 5-9pm Sun.* **Main courses** $12-$19. **Map** p117 G5 ❻ **Peruvian**
Fresca claims to have San Francisco's only ceviche bar, but the eaterie offers a broader menu than you might expect. Try tangy halibut ceviche or flambéed pisco prawns to start, followed by grilled ribeye with fries and plantains or sweet soy-roasted trout. The space can be very loud and tables are crammed together, but the quality of the Peruvian food makes up for any discomfort.
Other locations 3945 24th Street, between Noe & Sanchez Streets, Noe Valley (1-415 695 0549); 24 West Portal Avenue, between Ulloa & Vicente Streets, Sunset (1-415 759 8087); 737 Irving Street, between 8th & 9th Avenues, Sunset (1-415 759 8087).

★ SPQR

1911 Fillmore Street, between Bush & Wilmot Streets (1-415 771 7779, www.spqrsf.com). Bus 1, 1BX, 2, 3, 22. **Open** *5.30-10.30pm Mon-Fri; 11am-2.30pm, 5.30-10.30pm Sat; 5.30-10pm Sun.* **Main courses** $27-$66. **Map** p117 G5 ❼ **Italian**
The spirits of both Northern California and Italy shine through in this small, lively dining space. SPQR (an acronym for Senatus Populesque Romanus) has hit new heights under chef Matthew Accarrino,

garnering a Michelin star and several James Beard nominations. His menu reflects a philosophy that is at once modern and traditional, with every detail of texture, flavour and presentation bearing a personal stamp. Raves are rightly earned for antipasti such as octopus with kale sprouts, chickpeas, pistachios and preserved lemon, and handmade pastas (the meyer lemon fettuccini in an albalone alfredo will bowl you over). Pair them with owner/sommelier Shelley Lindgren's spectacular Italian wine list and it will be an evening to remember.

Spruce

3640 Sacramento Street, between Locust & Spruce Streets (1-415 931 5100, www.sprucesf.com). Bus 1, 2, 3, 33. **Open** *11.30am-2pm, 5-10pm Mon-Thur; 11.30am-2pm, 5-11pm Sat; 10.30am-2pm, 5-9pm Sun.* **Main courses** $28-$52. **Map** p116 D5 ❽ **American**
In the sleepy but upscale Presidio Heights neighbourhood, this posh, handsome restaurant has managed to set the city abuzz, and the scarcity of reservations shouldn't put you off. Once you're in, you're part of the scene, which has a locals-only feel, comprising a lounge, a takeout area and a formal dining room. Specialities of the fresh, inventive menu include butter-poached lobster and grilled steak, among other extravagances.

dining room. Specialities of the fresh, inventive menu include butter-poached lobster and grilled steak, among other extravagances.

Tataki

2815 California Street, at Divisadero Street (1-415 931 1182, www.tatakisushibar.com). Bus 1, 2, 3, 10, 22, 24. **Open** 11.30am-2pm, 5.30-10pm Mon-Thur; 11.30am-2pm, 5.30-10.30pm Fri; 5-10.30pm Sat; 5-9.30pm Sun. **Sushi** $12-$36. **Map** p117 F5 **❾** **Japanese**

When Raymond Ho and Kin Lui opened this tiny 26-seat eaterie in 2009, it was the first entirely sustainable sushi bar in the US, serving only fish available and caught using environmentally friendly methods. Others have since joined the movement, but Tataki is a standard-bearer – not just for its green credentials, but for its fresh, flavourful and inventive fare. Light, delicate arctic char often substitutes for salmon in signature 'tataki' dishes such as seared and marinated char with capers in yuzu reduction, and in hand-rolls such as the 49er – masago (smelt roe) and avocado topped with char and lemon. Other fish on the extensive sushi and sashimi menus might include Atlantic mackerel, wild Thai snapper, skipjack, pole-caught albacore, and sablefish. The duo has since expanded with two additional restaurants that feature grilled yakitori and kushiyaki skewers and house-made ramen, in addition to sushi. **Other locations** 1740 Church Street, at 29th Street, Noe Valley (1-415 282 1889); 678 Chenery Street, at Diamond Street, Glen Park (1-415 859 9383).

Bars

Palmer's

2298 Fillmore Street, at Clay Street (1-415 732 7777, www.palmerssf.com). Bus 1, 1BX, 2, 3, 22. **Open** 4-10pm Mon-Thur; 4-11pm Fri; noon-2.30pm, 5.30-11pm Sat; noon-2.30pm, 5.30-10pm Sun. **Map** p117 G5 **❿**

This chummy yet upscale cocktail lounge fits its affluent Pacific Heights demographic perfectly – decked out with nostalgic red leather booths, wood panelling, mounted sailfish and deer heads. Alongside the classic and infused cocktails, a comfort-food menu includes iceberg wedge salad, steak tartar, crab cakes, hefty braised lamb shank and a ginormous burger. At the weekend brunch, don't miss the bacon bloody marys.

Spruce.

Swank Cocktail Club

Laurel Inn, 488 Presidio Avenue, at California Street (1-415 346 7431, www.jdvhotels.com/ restaurants/the-laurel-inn/swank-cocktail-club). Bus *1, 2, 3, 4, 43.* **Open** *5-10pm Mon-Thur; 5pm-midnight Fri; 6pm-midnight Sat.* **Map** p117 E5 ⓫

Ever wished you could have a cocktail on the set of *Mad Men*? Swank's midcentury modern decor invites patrons to enjoy period cocktails with a decidedly contemporary attention to top-shelf spirits and ingredients. Spread out on the settee in front of the fireplace and enjoy a selection of small plates from the limited bar menu.

Shops & Services

Crossroads Trading Co

1901 Fillmore Street, at Bush Street (1-415 775 8885, www.crossroadstrading.com). Bus 1BX, 2, 3, 22. **Open** *11am-8pm Mon-Sat; 11am-7pm Sun.* **Map** p117 G5 ⓬ **Fashion**

Crossroads may be a national chain, but the Bay Area is its hub, with four shops in SF and two more in the East Bay. Staff buy with an eye for seasonal trends and the 'recycled' fashion is gently used, with most prices ranging from $10 to $50. Though there are plenty of fast fashion discards from Forever 21 and H&M, you'll also find designer duds in the mix. The denim section, in particular, yields some steals. **Other locations** throughout the city.

Gallery of Jewels

2115 Fillmore Street, between California & Sacramento Streets (1-415 771 5099, www. galleryofjewels.com). Bus 1, 3, 22. **Open** *10.30am-6.30pm Mon-Sat; 11am-6pm Sun.* **Map** p117 G5 ⓭ **Accessories**

Peruse local creations of silver and semi-precious stones, as well as funky beads and antique bracelets. Designs run from classic to contemporary. **Other locations** 427 Post Street, between Mason & Powell Streets (1-415 617 0007); 4089 24th Street, at Castro Street, Noe Valley (1-415 285 0626).

GoodByes

3483 Sacramento Street, between Laurel & Walnut Streets (1-415 674 0151, www.goodbyessf.com).

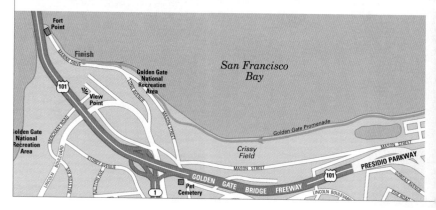

EXPLORE

WALK GOING FOR GOLDEN
Stroll down San Francisco's spectacular northern waterfront.

Part of a contiguous waterfront path that makes up the Bay Trail, the 3.5-mile **Golden Gate Promenade** is San Francisco's most scenic biking, jogging and walking path. Beginning at Aquatic Park, follow the path around the tip of the promontory to **Fort Mason** (*see p123*), the former military base that now houses several small museums and theatres, **Greens Restaurant**, and the

Readers Café Bookstore, where you can pick up old library books at bargain prices.

From here, stroll past the marina until you hit **Marina Green**, a curious and blissful cross-section of sunbathers, volleyball players, rollerbladers, cyclists and wealthy boat owners who have vessels parked at the **St Francis Yacht Club**. To the west is **Crissy Field**, the restored wetlands recreation area

Bus 1, 2, 3, 43. **Open** 10am-6pm Mon-Wed, Fri, Sat; 10am-8pm Thur; 11am-5pm Sun. **Map** p117 E5 ⓮ **Fashion**

For a rich treasure trove of second-hand pickings, take advantage of this consignment boutique's Pacific Heights proximity. Cast-offs from some of the town's most upscale closets might include a barely worn Miu Miu sweater, say, or a classic Chanel suit. There are also men's and sale stores in the same block (3462 & 3464 Sacramento Street; 1-415 346 6388).

International Orange

2044 Fillmore Street, between California & Pine Streets (1-415 563 5000, www.international orange.com). Bus 1, 2, 3, 10, 22, 38. **Open** 11am-9pm Mon-Fri; 9am-7pm Sat, Sun. **Map** p117 G5 ⓯ **Health & beauty**

Be sure you get an appointment: the secret is out about the refined treatments and professional facials here. Try the Red Flower Japan massage, a soothing mix of botanicals that awakens your senses (or, at least, leaves you smelling decent for a good 48 hours).

Nest

2300 Fillmore Street, at Clay Street (1-415 292 6199, www.nestsf.com). Bus 1, 3, 10, 22, 24. **Open** 10.30am-6.30pm Mon-Fri; 10am-6pm Sat; 11am-6pm Sun. **Map** p117 G4 ⓰ **Gifts & souvenirs**

A nest in the magpie sense, this Parisian bohemia-inspired shop stocks a beguiling compilation of tin jack-in-the-boxes, gauzy Chinese lanterns, wood-cuts, glassware, French jewellery and a selection of adorable kids' clothes.

Zinc Details

1905 Fillmore Street, between Bush & Wilmot Streets (1-415 776 2100, www.zincdetails.com). Bus 1, 2, 3, 22, 38. **Open** 10am-6pm Mon-Sat; noon-6pm Sun. **Map** p117 G5 ⓱ **Homewares**

Fun, funky and often fabulous contemporary design by Artemide, Le Klint, Marimekko, Vitra and other European and Japanese makers can be found in this forward-thinking, jam-packed emporium. In addition to furniture and lighting, stock includes more portable items such as rugs, glassware, textiles, art and vases.

---

that once served as an army airfield. Today, it's populated by weekend windsurfers, strollers, joggers, beach-goers, and picnickers who hang out on the grassy expanse that skirts the shoreline.

When you're ready to grab a bite, there are two good stops for refuelling along the route: the **Beach Hut Cafe**, near the **Crissy Field Center**, and the locals' favourite, **Warming Hut**, which offers organic soups, sandwiches and espresso, as well as a terrific book and gift shop. Lying between the two, inside former military buildings, are the **Greater Farallones National Marine Sanctuary Visitor Center**, a small museum with displays on local

marine life that's great for young kids; the **Planet Granite** rock-climbing gym (www.planetgranite.com); and **House of Air** (www.houseofair.com), an enormous indoor trampoline park.

At the western end of the promenade, **Fort Point**, a military fortification built between 1853 and 1861 to protect San Francisco from an attack by sea that never came, was immortalised as Kim Novak's suicide spot in *Vertigo*. The point commands awe-inspiring views of the tremendous underbelly of the **Golden Gate Bridge**. You can view a film about the construction of the bridge daily inside the Fort Point bookstore.

EXPLORE

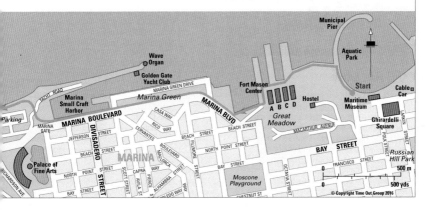

dedicated to an ancient strain of Hinduism that holds all religions to be viable paths to spiritual awareness. Accordingly, each of its six domes represents a different architectural style, with elaborate Moorish arches, a Saracenic crescent, a Russian onion-style dome and a Victorian gingerbread trim.

Sights & Museums

FREE Octagon House

2645 Gough Street, at Union Street (1-415 441 7512, www.nscda-ca.org/octagon-house). Bus 41, 45. **Open** *noon-3pm 2nd & 4th Thur, 2nd Sun of mth.* **Admission** *free.* **Map** *p117 H3* ⑱
The 1861 Octagon House is home to the small Museum of Colonial and Federal Decorative Arts, but is most notable as one of three surviving examples of eight-sided homes in the city. Across the nation, 700 such houses were built in the belief that they improved their occupants' health by letting in more natural light. Once owned by a wealthy dairyman named Charles Gough (back when nearby Cow Hollow still contained cows), the Octagon House stands on the street to which he magnanimously gave his name while on the city's naming commission; he also named an adjacent street 'Octavia' in honour of his sister.

Restaurants & Cafés

Palm House

2032 Union Street, between Buchanan & Webster Streets (1-415 400 4355, www.palmhousesf.com). Bus 22, 41, 45. **Open** *11am-3pm, 5-9pm Mon-Thur; 11am-3pm, 5-10pm Fri; 10.30am-3.30pm, 5-10pm Sat; 10.30am-3.30pm, 5-9pm Sun.* **Main courses** *$$12-$25.* **Map** *p117 G3* ⑲ **Caribbean**
One of the city's most popular brunch spots, Palm House occupies the 1854 dairy that gave Cow Hollow its name. On weekends, crowds line up on the patio, sipping tropical cocktails while they wait. The menu is a mélange of island influences, with such creative mash-ups as biscuits and gravy with house-made jerk sausage, and salmon lomi lomi ceviche. Few can resist the pineapple sugar-cane-glazed bacon.

Shops & Services

★ Freda Salvador

2416 Fillmore Street, at Washington Street (1-415 872 9690, www.fredasalvador.com). Bus 41, 45, 47, 49, 76X, 90. **Open** *11am-7pm Mon-Sat; 11am-6pm Sun.* **Map** *p117 G4* ⑳ **Accessories**
Local co-designers Megan Papay and Cristina Palomo-Nelson make wear-everywhere shoes that can tackle San Francisco's steep terrain without sacrificing style. The duo launched their label in 2012 with a collection of convertible leather ankle boots and snakeskin-print leather loafers that were an instant hit with the Bay Area style cognoscenti.

Octagon House.

COW HOLLOW

From Pacific Heights, it's only a few blocks downhill towards the Bay to Cow Hollow. Once a dairy pasture, the area is still serene, but its grazers are now of the well-heeled, two-legged kind. The activity is centred on **Union Street** between Broderick and Buchanan Streets, a chic and bijou stretch of bars, restaurants and boutiques.

The nearby **Vedanta Temple** (2963 Webster Street, at Filbert Street, www.sfvedanta.org) dates from 1905. Built by the Vedanta Society, it's

Since then, the pair has branched into chunky-heeled booties, multi-strap sandals, and wedge sneakers, all artfully displayed across bookshelves and coffee tables in their Cow Hollow design studio and shop. The space looks like an it-girl's apartment, decked with midcentury modern couches and glamorous depictions of the designers' inspiration, Frida Kahlo, but the cobbler credentials are solid – Paloma-Nelson hails from a family of shoemakers.

THE MARINA & THE WATERFRONT

Built on soft rubble from the 1906 earthquake, the Marina, between the Fort Mason Center and the Presidio, shook harder than any other part of San Francisco in 1989's Loma Prieta quake. But the only reminders of the damage are the renovated pavements and suspiciously new structures among the otherwise staid townhouses.

Conspicuously straight, pastel-painted Marina is one big pick-up joint. By night, its bars fill with twentysomethings sipping cocktails and making eye contact; for decades, even the local **Safeway** (15 Marina Boulevard, at Laguna Street) was a pulling spot – featured in Armistead Maupin's *Tales of the City*. The main commercial drag is **Chestnut Street**, where residents promenade with iced coffees in hand. The stretch between Fillmore and Divisadero Streets is a shrine to self-indulgence, with clothing boutiques and beauty salons seeming to occupy half the shopfronts.

A little more gravitas is provided at the eastern edge of the Marina waterfront. The **Fort Mason Center** started out as a US Army command post in the 1850s, and its reconditioned military buildings retain a forbidding mien; these days they house some fine little museums and exhibitions, plus the **Magic Theatre** (*see p231*). For the 1915 Panama-Pacific Exposition, a mile-long swathe of temporary structures was erected all the way from here to **Fort Point** (*see p127*). This fantastical city-within-a-city was torn down to make way for the houses we see today, but a small part of the fantasy-scape survived in the shape of the **Palace of Fine Arts**.

The vast, sloping lawns of the **Marina Green** (Marina Boulevard, between Scott and Webster Streets) are the locals' favourite place to fly kites, jog or picnic, with dizzying views of the Golden Gate Bridge and the Bay. At the far west side of the green, a path leads past the boat marina to the Dynamo Donuts kiosk, serving artisan treats (don't miss the maple-glazed bacon apple) and Four Barrel Coffee.

From here, head west along the edge of Marina Boulevard and around the harbour. Either continue west to the beautifully revitalised **Crissy Field** and explore a model of wetlands restoration, or follow the signs to the **Golden Gate Yacht Club**, along a kind of expansive promontory. Keep going past the boats and, when you can go no further, you'll get to Peter Richards's amazing **Wave Organ**. Part artwork, part musical instrument, this mostly underwater structure is made up of pipes and benches built from dismantled cemeteries; the tubes make eerie music with the ebb and flow of the Bay.

Sights & Museums

★ FREE Fort Mason Center
Marina Boulevard, at Buchanan Street (1-415 345 7500, www.fortmason.org). **Bus** *22, 28.* **Map** p117 G2 ㉑
This collection of ex-military buildings features various cultural institutions, including the Museo ItaloAmericano (Building C, 1-415 673 2200, www.museoitaloamericano.org) and the airy SFMOMA Artists' Gallery (Building A, 1-415 441 4777, www.sfmoma.org), the latter selling and renting out contemporary works by northern Californians. Both are closed on Mondays and admission is free. Other enterprises here include the Readers Café Bookstore (Building C, 1-415 771 1011, www.readerscafe.org), which sells rejected stock from the public library, as well as LPs and art. Over in Building D is the Magic Theatre (1-415 441 8822, www.magictheatre.org), which stages works by a mix of emerging and established playwrights in its two performance spaces. Before the performance, have dinner at Greens (Building A; *see p124*), one of the city's best vegetarian eateries. An array of changing displays is on view at two bayside pavilions, including art shows, book sales and festivals. On Fridays from early March through October, Fort Mason hosts the Off the Grid food truck gathering with live music (5-10pm, www.offthegridsf.com). Sunday brings the year-round weekly farmers' market (9.30am-1.30pm, www.cafarmersmkts.com).

FREE Palace of Fine Arts
Lyon Street, at Bay Street (1-415 563 6504, www.palaceoffinearts.org). Bus 28, 30, 43, 91. **Map** p117 E2 ㉒
Architect Bernard Maybeck's pièce de résistance, the Palace is a neoclassical domed rotunda supported

---

IN THE KNOW SAFE CROSSING

Debate about erecting a suicide barrier on the Golden Gate Bridge has raged for years (it's estimated that around 1,700 people have died after plunging the 250 feet or more into the water below). But in 2014 the Bridge District finally approved plans for a $76 million net extending 20 feet below and 20 feet from the side of the span. It's expected to be completed sometime in 2018.

EXPLORE

by a curved colonnade topped with friezes and statues of weeping women, and flanked by a pond populated by ducks, swans and lily pads. Initially designed as a temporary structure, the original building was demolished in 1964, leaving only the shell of the rotunda intact, then reconstructed at ten times the original cost. The Palace has been repeatedly saved by generations of San Franciscans – most recently with a splendid $21 million restoration.

Restaurants & Cafés

★ A16

2355 Chestnut Street, between Divisadero & Scott Streets (1-415 771 2216, www.a16sf.com). Bus 28, 30, 43, 76. **Open** 5.30-10pm Mon, Tue; 11.30am-2.30pm, 5.30-10pm Wed, Thur; 11.30am-2.30pm, 5.30-11pm Fri; 11.30am-2.30pm, 5-11pm Sat; 11.30am-2.30pm, 5-10pm Sun. **Main courses** $13-$36. **Map** p117 F3 ㉓ **Italian**
This warm and casual eatery has been a go-to spot for Neapolitan pizza and southern Italian cuisine for over a decade. Focusing on the Campania region, chef Rocky Maselli crafts fresh pasta dishes such as ricotta gnocchi with lamb sugo, house-cured antipasti, and thin-crust pizzas that include vongole (topped with clams and cherry tomatoes). Co-owner and wine director Shelley Lindgren guides diners through one of the city's most exciting wine lists, featuring around 40 by the half-glass, glass and carafe.

★ Greens

Fort Mason, 2 Marina Blvd, Building A (1-415 771 6222, www.greensrestaurant.com). Bus 24, 30. **Open** 11.45am-2.30pm Tue-Fri; 11am-2.30pm, 5.30-9pm Sat; 10.30am-2pm, 5.30-9pm Sun. **Main courses** $19-$26; four-course prix-fixe $56 Sat. **Map** p117 G2 ㉔ **Vegetarian**
A pioneer of farm-to-table vegetarian cuisine for more than three decades, Greens almost singlehandedly exploded the stereotype of vegetarian cooking as variations on alfalfa sprouts and tofu. The restaurant has a prime waterfront location, with the Golden Gate Bridge as backdrop, and chef Annie Somerville's wildly inventive menu continues to win carnivore hearts and minds. Dishes such as warm cauliflower salad with crisp capers and pine nuts, coconut risotto cakes in red curry, or wild mushroom and caramelised onion gratin with fromage blanc custard, could have you swearing off meat altogether. If you can't get a dinner reservation, go for brunch, when the kitchen dreams up some of its most imaginative offerings, such as spiced carrot cake pancakes, or Merguez poached eggs with vegetable ragout, grilled polenta and goat cheese.

Isa

3324 Steiner Street, between Chestnut & Lombard Streets (1-415 567 9588, www. isarestaurant.com). Bus 22, 28, 30, 43, 45, 91. **Open** 5.30-9.30pm Mon-Thur; 5.30-10pm Fri;

5-10pm Sat; 5-9pm Sun. **Main courses** $18-$26. **Map** p117 G3 ㉕ **California**
Cosy and with a secluded back patio, Isa is winningly free of Marina affectations. Expect interesting fare such as roast mussels with shallots and white wine, or hanger steak with tarragon mustard and roast garlic potatoes from the Cal-French small-plates menu.

Tipsy Pig

2231 Chestnut Street, between Avila & Pierce Streets (1-415 292-2300, www.thetipsypigsf.com). Bus 28, 30, 43, 76. **Open** 5-10pm Mon-Fri; 11am-2.45pm, 5-10pm Fri-Sun (bar open until 2am daily). **Main courses** $10-$18. **Map** p117 F3 ㉖ **American**
This popular 'gastrotavern' strikes a happy balance between the boisterous Marina singles who pack the bar, and the neighbourhood regulars and families who dine on upscale comfort food in the cosy library or on the heated deck out back. Don't-miss signature dishes include BBQ sliders (mini beer-braised pulled pork sandwiches), chicken pot pie, a sublime burger on a house-made bun, and the near-legendary smoked-bacon mac and cheese. Accompany superior pub grub with an artisanal cocktail or one of 40 or so premium and craft beer selections.

Bars

Mauna Loa

3009 Fillmore Street, between Filbert & Union Streets (1-415 563 5137). Bus 22, 28, 41, 43, 45, 76. **Open** 2pm-2am Mon-Fri; noon-2am Sat, Sun. **No credit cards. Map** p117 G3 ㉗
This wood-panelled 1939 watering hole is perhaps the only bar in the Marina that could be considered divey; the crowd, at least, is far more down to earth than you'll find in the area. A pool table, foosball and Pop-A-Shot entertain patrons, but the place can be a crush on weekends.

Shops & Services

Books Inc

2251 Chestnut Street, at Avila Street (1-415 931 3633, www.booksinc.net). Bus 2, 4, 8, 10, 18, 24, 44. **Open** 9am-10pm Mon-Sat; 9am-9pm Sun. **Map** p117 F3 ㉘ **Books & music**
This lively lit hub offers a huge selection of fiction and non-fiction and a wide array of authors' readings, discussions and other events.
Other locations 601 Van Ness Avenue, at Golden Gate Avenue, Civic Center (1-415 776 1111); 3515 California Street, at Locust Street, Presidio Heights (1-415 221 3666); 2275 Market Street, between 16th & Sanchez Streets, Castro (1-415 864 6777).

Kara's Cupcakes

3249 Scott Street, between Chestnut & Lombard Streets (1-415 563 2252, www.karascupcakes. com). Bus 28, 30, 43, 76. **Open** 10am-8pm

Greens.

Mon-Thur, Sun; 10am-10pm Fri, Sat. **Map** p117 F3
29 Food & drink
For owner Kara Haspel Lind, opening a bakery was
an act of rebellion – her father is a dentist. While the
cupcake craze may have tipped into overkill, we love
these designer versions of the kids' treat, elevated
with a light, fluffy cake and a dense dollop of but-
tercream. The shop cycles through 17 flavours –
some gluten-free and all available by custom order
– including fleur de sel, passion fruit, and chocolate
raspberry. Each season also brings a new 'charity'
cupcake, the proceeds of which benefit a hand-
picked non-profit organisation.

THE PRESIDIO

The Presidio is sometimes called 'the prettiest
piece of real estate in America'; it's certainly
among the most valuable. At the northern tip of
the city, overlooking the Bay, the Pacific and the
Golden Gate Bridge, the location could hardly be
more stunning, but for centuries it endured a
workaday existence as a military base, closed to
the public. Now completely demilitarised and
amazingly revitalised, it has become a national
park, complete with 11 miles of hiking trails,
14 miles of bicycle routes and three miles of
beaches, and with the more recent addition of
residential housing and several fine restaurants.

The tip of the San Francisco Peninsula was
first established as a military outpost in 1776,
when a group led by Captain Juan Bautista de
Anza planted the Spanish flag here to protect the
newly discovered San Francisco Bay. The site was
claimed as a garrison first for Spain (*presidio* is
Spanish for fortress) and then for Mexico, but the
US took it over, along with the rest of California,
in 1848. The military embarked on a huge
landscaping project that converted hundreds of
acres of windswept, sandy moors into a tree-lined
garden. However, by 1994 they'd had enough.
After 220 years, the US Army handed the Presidio
over to the Park Service, claiming it could no
longer afford the upkeep. The dramatic
changeover, from army base to national park,
followed soon after.

Among the businesses based here, George
Lucas's Industrial Light & Magic film company
spent $350 million to transform the 24-acre plot
at the former Letterman Hospital into the
Letterman Digital Arts Center. The state-of-
the-art complex of offices and studios features
whitewashed buildings that blend into their
bucolic surroundings, criss-crossed by paths and
grassy expanses. The public can visit the lobby
of Building B during business hours to view a
gallery of Lucas film memorabilia that includes
props and costumes from the *Star Wars* film
series. Both the Letterman complex and nearby
park also now boast a variety of dining options.
Upscale **Presidio Social Club** (*see p128*),
housed in beautifully restored barracks, serves
gourmet versions of San Franciscan and
American classics. **Arguello** (50 Moraga
Avenue, 1-415 561 3650, www.arguellosf.com)
offers modern Mexican cuisine inside the historic
Presidio Officers' Club.

Given the sheer size of the park, not to mention
its inevitably hilly nature, it's worth considering
hiring a bike from one of the rental firms at
Fisherman's Wharf. While getting lost in this
curious environment can be a pleasure, maps are
available at several information points: the Crissy
Field Center on Mason Boulevard (enter the
Presidio at Marina Boulevard, in its northeast
corner, and carry on down the road for around
half a mile); the Visitor Center in the old Officers'
Club at the Main Post (*see p127*), close to the
centre of the park and easily accessible from any
entrance; and at the Battery East Overlook close
to the Golden Gate Bridge.

The grassy area and bucolic wetlands area on
the northern Presidio shoreline has a military
past as an army airfield. Since its return to the city
it has been restored to its original state, planted
with more than 100,000 native plants: a pristine
tidal marshland home for hundreds of migrating
bird species. The shoreline promenade now lures
walkers and joggers, daredevil kiteboarders, and
windsurfers who challenge the notorious waters.
For more on Crissy Field and this stretch of the
Bay Trail, *see p120* **Walk**.

EXPLORE

SHORE THINGS

Soak up the scenery, if not the sun, at these urban beaches.

Unlike Southern California, the majority of beaches in and around San Francisco aren't great for swimming. But between cavorting families, picnicking couples, idle promenaders and – on one or two beaches – clothes-free pick-up artists, the locals aren't short of activities.

Most visitors start with the **East Beach**, close to the Marina in the Presidio. During the week, it can be very pleasant, with dog-walkers, joggers and cyclists (including many tourists bound for the Golden Gate Bridge, *see p127*) passing the time of day along the edge. However, on weekends, it gets a little busier, and space is at a premium. Many people head further west to **Crissy Field**, where there's a lagoon popular with kiddies, and a lovely (if unofficial) beach that's part of the protected shoreline along Golden Gate Promenade.

Running for almost a mile along the craggy western Presidio shoreline, **Baker Beach** is a better bet. It's accessible, for one thing, and offers both great views and easy access to

the city's most popular nudist beach, the north end of the same stretch. In 1905 the US Army decided to use Baker as the hiding place for a huge 95,000-pound cannon. The naval invasion it was built to repel never came, but a replica of the original has been installed for the curious.

Hidden between Baker Beach and Lincoln Park, in the exclusive Seacliff neighbourhood, you'll find the exquisitely sheltered James Phelan Beach. Better known as **China Beach** (Seacliff Avenue, off 26th Avenue), it gets its nickname from the Chinese fishermen who camped here in the 19th century. With parking, a sundeck, showers and changing rooms, it's the favourite beach of many locals.

Extending from Cliff House (*see p186*) south towards the city limits, **Ocean Beach** (Great Highway, between Balboa Street & Sloat Boulevard) is San Francisco's biggest beach: a three-mile sandy strip along the Pacific, popular with surfers. Widening into dunes and plateaux at the end of the Sunset District, it's also a fine place for strolling.

EXPLORE

Baker Beach.

The centre of the Presidio is the **Main Post**, a complex of old buildings arrayed along parallel streets on the site of the original Spanish fort. Along with the main **Visitor Center** located in the Officers' Club (Building 50 Moraga Avenue, 1-415 561 4323), home to a well-stocked shop selling maps, books and gifts, you'll also find the fascinating **Walt Disney Family Museum** (*see p128*). Follow Sheridan Avenue west from the Main Post and you'll soon arrive at the **San Francisco National Cemetery**. Among the army officers (and their family members) laid here in hauntingly straightforward fashion are more than 450 'Buffalo Soldiers'. African-American servicemen known to many simply as the subject of the Bob Marley song of that name, they served not only alongside future president Theodore Roosevelt at the Battle of San Juan Hill, referenced by Marley, but also throughout the Civil War, the Indian Wars, the Spanish-American War and virtually every conflict up to the Korean War, after which the US armed services became officially integrated.

Continuing along Lincoln and taking the first right (McDowell Avenue), you'll soon stumble upon the **Pet Cemetery**. While its human counterpart sits high on a hill, its gravestones gleaming and its grass immaculately tidy, the cemetery in which servicemen buried their beloved animals has handmade markers, their endearing epitaphs – complete with poems and drawings – paying tribute to man's best friends.

Much of the rest of the Presidio is a jumble of former servicemen's quarters, now converted into private homes. Around 500 structures from the former military base remain, ranging from Civil War mansions to simple barracks. Some are utilitarian, but others, such as **Pilot's Row** on Lincoln Boulevard near the Golden Gate Bridge toll plaza, are truly delightful. In between these sometimes melancholic clusters run numerous hiking and cycling paths, all marked on the maps available from the visitors' centres. The hilly, unpaved **Coastal Trail** runs out past the Golden Gate Bridge to the beginning of the Pacific, with spectacular views of the Marin Headlands. The **Ecology Trail** begins directly behind the Officers' Club and follows a pastoral path on to **Inspiration Point**, which affords terrific views, and picturesque **El Polin Spring**.

A number of haunting old coastal batteries that once held guns capable of shooting 15 miles out to sea – thankfully never fired in anything other than practice – sit along the western edge of the park. **Batteries Godfrey** and **Crosby** are both easily accessible on foot. The last pictures taken by photographer Ansel Adams were of these concrete bunkers and they offer stunning views of the Golden Gate Bridge, making them the perfect place to enjoy a romantic bottle of wine at sunset. Below them is **Baker Beach**

(*see p126* **Shore Things**), a favourite getaway among locals where, in 1986, the first 'Burning Man' was the spark that began one of the biggest festivals in the country. To the south of the Presidio sits the relaxing idyll of **Mountain Lake Park** (access at Lake Street and Funston Avenue). Just next to it is the public **Presidio Golf Course**, formerly a private club favoured by presidents and generals.

Sights & Museums

🆓 Fort Point
Marine Drive, beneath Golden Gate Bridge (1-415 556 1693, www.nps.gov/fopo). Bus 28. **Open** 10am-5pm Fri-Sun. **Admission** free. **Map** p116 A1 ③⓪

The spectacular brick-built Fort Point was built between 1853 and 1861 to protect the city from a sea attack. The assault never came; the 126 cannons remained idle, and the fort was closed in 1900. Today the four-storey, open-roofed building houses various military exhibitions; children love to scamper among the battlements and passageways. Climb on to the roof for a fabulous view of the underbelly of the Golden Gate Bridge, which was built more than seven decades after the fort was completed. The fort's pier is famous as the spot where Kim Novak's character attempts suicide in Hitchcock's *Vertigo*.

★ 🆓 Golden Gate Bridge
1-415 921 5858, www.goldengatebridge.org. Multiple bus routes from downtown & Fisherman's Wharf. **Open** *East pedestrian walkway mid Mar-Oct* 5am-9pm daily. *Nov-mid Mar* 5am-6.30pm. **Map** p116 A1 ③①

Luminous symbol of San Francisco and California itself, the Golden Gate Bridge is one of the Seven Engineering Wonders of the World. Completed in 1937, it's truly immense: the towers are 746 feet high, the roadway runs for 1.75 miles, and enough cable was used in its construction to encircle the globe three times. However, raw statistics can't convey the sense of awe the bridge inspires, and no trip to the city is complete without walking across it.

The man mainly responsible for making it a reality was Joseph Strauss, a pugnacious Chicagoan engineer. Strauss spent over a decade lobbying to build a bridge, circumventing innumerable financial and legal hurdles in the process. But it was a little-known freelance architect named Irwin F Morrow who eventually designed it, his brilliantly simple pitch selected in preference to Strauss's hideous and complicated cantilever plans.

The bridge's name has nothing to do with its colour, and everything to do with the name of the strait it spans. The Golden Gate strait was named by Captain John Fremont – not after the Gold Rush, as many believe, but after Istanbul's Golden Horn, the geologically similar channel that links the Black Sea to the Mediterranean. The stroke-of-genius orange

EXPLORE

colour was also an accident of fate: San Franciscans were so delighted by the reddish tint of the bridge's primer paint that the builders decided to stick with it, rather than paint it in the traditional grey or silver.

Reputedly five times stronger than it needs to be, the bridge has survived hurricane-force winds, earthquakes and almost 80 years of abuse without the slightest sign of damage. Built to flex under pressure, it can sway more than 21 feet and sag ten feet while withstanding 100mph winds. Although large portions of the Marina were totally devastated by the 1989 earthquake, the bridge survived unscathed. But the virtual certainty of another earthquake of a similar (if not greater) magnitude prompted officials to undertake a seismic refitting project. Vehicle tolls were hiked to help pay for the reinforcements, which will require around 22 million pounds of structural steel and 24,000 cubic yards of concrete.

Society of California Pioneers
Presidio Main Post, Pioneer Hall, 101 Montgomery Street, at Sheridan Avenue, suite 150 (1-415 957 1849, www.californiapioneers.org). **Open** 10am-5pm Wed-Sat. **Admission** free. **Map** p116 C3 ㉜
Operated by descendants of the state's first settlers, this small museum is a treasure trove for the historically inclined, presenting exhibitions focused on California art, history and culture. The library collection includes some 10,000 books, 50,000 prints and all kinds of other ephemera, such as 19th-century paintings, sculpture and furniture. Free guided tours are offered with advance reservations.

★ Walt Disney Family Museum
Presidio Main Post, 104 Montgomery Street at Sheridan Avenue (1-415 345 6800, www. waltdisney.org). Bus 28, 43. **Open** 10am-6pm Mon, Wed-Sun. **Admission** $20 adults; $12-$15 reductions; free under 6s. **Map** p116 C3 ㉝
Opened in 2009 by the Walt Disney Family Foundation, the museum is geared as much to adults as to kids, offering a fascinating, in-depth look at Disney's life, career and art. Housed in beautifully repurposed brick army barracks, its galleries follow a chronological history, from Walt's early attempts at cartooning to his death in 1966. Along the way, there's an interactive gallery showing Disney's innovations in sound; absorbing audio stations that recount tales of brothers Roy and Walt's early successes and the swindlers who tried to cash in on them; an original multiplane camera that shows how Disney developed dimensional animation; and a look at the financing and making of his first full-length feature, *Snow White and the Seven Dwarfs*.

Restaurants & Cafés

★ The Commissary
Presidio Main Post, 101 Montgomery Street, at Sheridan Avenue (1-415 561 3600, www.the commissarysf.com). Bus 28, 43. **Open** 5.30-9pm

Mon-Thur; 5.30-9.30pm Fri, Sat. **Main courses** $24-$32. **Map** p116 C3 ㉞ **California**
Local phenom chef Traci Des Jardins and the Presidio Trust partnered to deliver this gracious restaurant set inside a former army mess hall, serving Spanish-influenced California cuisine. Reclaimed lighting fixtures and salvaged wood tabletops merge with a metal bar and leather chairs for a clean, contemporary feel. Highlights of the menu include Alaskan halibut with chorizo and fennel broth, and grilled octopus with potatoes, olive, and lemon. All ingredients are sustainably sourced, and local and organic where possible. Front porch seating makes this an excellent spot to survey the lively scene on the lawn of the Main Parade grounds.

Presidio Social Club
563 Ruger Street, Building 563, at Lombard Street (1-415 885 1888, www.presidiosocialclub.com). Bus 41, 43, 45. **Open** 11.30am-10pm Mon-Fri; 10am-10pm Sat; 10am-9pm Sun. **Main courses** $23-$26. **Map** p117 E3 ㉟ **American**
Housed in a 1903 wooden army barracks, the airy, window-lined interior features a long bar stretching along almost the entire length of the space, plus a communal table. Both are perfect spots for soaking up the atmosphere while the foghorn moans outside. The menu features unfussy classics of the comforting steaks and chops variety, simply prepared using local ingredients. Brunch is a lively affair, especially when accompanied by bellinis, mimosas, and rum-pineapple concoctions like the Painkiller.

Shops & Services

★ SenSpa
1161 Gorgas Avenue, off Presidio/Crissy Field exit (1-415 441 1777, www.senspa.com). Bus 28, 29, 43, 76/PresidiGo shuttle. **Open** 10am-9pm Mon-Fri; 9am-8pm Sat, Sun. **Map** p117 E3 ㊱ **Health & beauty**
A World War I hospital-storage barracks might seem an unlikely place for an Asian-inspired holistic retreat, but somehow it works, transformed by walls of falling water, plants and skylights. The voluminous treatment menu encompasses everything from standard spa fare like body scrubs and facials to Rolfing, oncology massage and 'rhythm entrainment' designed to stimulate creativity.

Sports Basement
610 Old Mason Street, at Crissy Field (1-415 437 0100, www.sportsbasement.com). Bus 23, 30, 43, 91. **Open** 9am-9pm Mon-Fri; 8am-8pm Sat, Sun. **Map** p116 D2 ㊲ **Sports**
Size is everything at Sports Basement: this large emporium includes end-of-line goods from top-tier brands (North Face, Teva, Pearl Izumi), offered at reductions of 30% to 60%.
Other location 1590 Bryant Street, Potrero Hill (1-415 575 3000).

EXPLORE

COOKING WITH GAS
San Francisco's food truck culture has kicked into high gear.

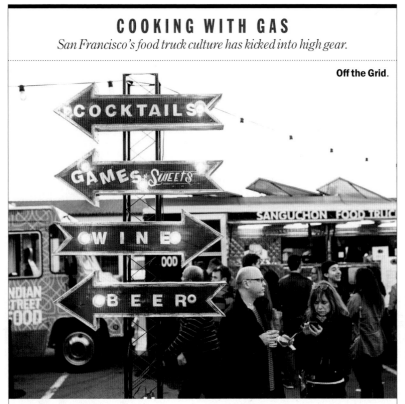

Off the Grid.

EXPLORE

While San Francisco isn't the birthplace of the gourmet food truck, it has definitely revved up mobile street food to new gastronomic heights. On any given day, the city's gastro-fleet dispenses everything from fried oyster and bacon sandwiches to Moroccan curry goat tacos and frozen confections to rival the best bricks-and-mortar ice-cream shops.

The truck collective, **Off the Grid** (www.offthegridsf.com), offers a dozen weekly markets, with stops at Civic Center, Haight Street and Fort Mason among others. A combination street festival/eating extravaganza, it features a mind-boggling melting pot of ethnic and fusion cuisines, plus music, crafts, beer gardens and activities. Families shouldn't miss **Picnic at the Presidio** on Sundays (Apr-Oct), a giant gathering on the lawn of the Presidio's Main Post (see p127) overlooking the Golden Gate that usually includes free lawn games,

music and a 'bubble bar' for grown-ups. **Twilight at the Presidio** (Ap-Oct) is a Thursday night 'campout' with lantern-lit dining cabanas, cocktail service, Adirondack chairs, fire pits and live music.

Across town, urban-hip **Streat Food Park** (www.somastreatfoodpark.com) is a permanent address for a revolving array of trucks, wedged between the elevated freeway and the Costco market in SoMa. On any given day, a dozen or more trucks ring the festive picnic tables and tent pavilion at this decidedly urban gathering. Entertainment ranges from arts and crafts bazaars and karaoke to comedy, trivia contests and the popular bottomless mimosa brunch.

To get an idea of who's serving up what and where, go to www.roaminghunger.com/sf, which tracks food trucks day and night, and offers real-time locations of everything from the Crème Brûlée Cart to the infamous Bacon Bacon truck.

Western Addition

Perhaps no other area of San Francisco has seen more transition than the Western Addition – its fortunes rising and falling since it became part of the city proper in 1855. Once a parcel in the 'Outside Lands' that extended beyond the city borders, it originally encompassed around 500 square blocks from Larkin Street to Divisadero Street. That area has been drastically reduced to a swathe that runs roughly between Masonic Avenue and Fell, Franklin and Pine Streets, with several micro-neighbourhoods divvying it up further. The district's personality reflects these shifting demographics: it has alternately been the heart of the West Coast jazz scene, the victim of 'urban renewal', the centre of the Japanese community and a gentrification hotspot. Sandwiched among its preserved blocks of 'Painted Lady' Victorian houses are tenement buildings, funky clubs, trendy bistros, noodle bars and artisan coffee roasters.

EXPLORE

Alamo Square.

Don't Miss

1 **Alamo Square** Home of the city's gorgeous 'Painted Ladies' (p132).

2 **The Mill** Trust us, the $4 toast is worth every penny (p132).

3 **The Fillmore** Catch a gig where the San Francisco Sound was born (p136).

4 **State Bird Provisions** Do what you must to snag a seat at this hotspot (p137).

5 **Kabuki Springs & Spa** A tranquil Japanese-style retreat (p139).

EXPLORE

The Western Addition was not only the city's first suburb, but also its first multicultural neighbourhood. Mapped out in the 1860s to accommodate the post-Gold Rush population boom, the area was home to a thriving Jewish community in the 1890s. After the 1906 earthquake, the Fillmore District, the area's heart, sprang to life as displaced residents, many of them Japanese, began arriving.

After the Japanese were sent to internment camps following Pearl Harbor, thousands of African-American Southerners, who had come west for work, moved into their houses. Because the area didn't observe the racial covenant laws that prevented African-Americans from owning land elsewhere in the city, the Western Addition soon developed into what became known as the 'Harlem of the West'.

Today, it still has a very distinct character, with a mix of African-Americans, European immigrants and UCSF students who live in everything from amazing Victorian buildings – some of the oldest in the city – to bland highrises. Gentrification has crept in, but the area's shopping remains mostly chain-free.

The most notable sign of mindshift in the area is the adoption of the acronym **NoPa** for the neighbourhood North of the Panhandle. Once a term used exclusively by real estate agents to entice a more affluent clientele, it's become an accepted moniker for the young, creatively inclined, social-minded and mostly monied new establishment that has moved here over the last decade. The bellwether of this sea change is **Nopa** (*see p134*), one of the hottest restaurants in town, with an earth-conscious cuisine and clientele that embodies the new neighbourhood aesthetic.

San Francisco is crammed full of handsome Victorian-era houses (commonly known as 'Victorians'). However, most tourists choose not to roam the city and discover them at random; instead, they head to the 'Postcard Row' of tidy pastel Victorians on the east side of **Alamo Square**, which are juxtaposed wonderfully against the sweeping view of downtown behind them. While these 'Painted Ladies' are certainly the most famous (they're featured in numerous films and TV shows), there are other fine Victorians nearby to visit, chiefly the ornate Italianate **William Westerfeld House**, at the corner of Fulton and Scott Streets, which dates back to 1889; and the **Chateau Tivoli** (1057 Steiner Street at Golden Gate Avenue), an opulent 1892 Victorian mansion that is now a bed and breakfast inn. The square itself is a tidy, flowery park popular with kite fliers (it gets breezy) and dog walkers that also features a tennis court and kids' playground.

On Oak Street just west of Divisadero Street, the **Abner Phelps House**, built circa 1850, is the city's oldest residence, tucked off the street and almost hidden behind manicured hedges and shrubs. Near the corner of Divisadero and Fulton, past the incense emporiums and African-American barbershops, sit notable businesses that include **The Mill**, serving up locally roasted Four Barrel Coffee and its infamous (and worth every dime) $4 toast, and deep-dish kings, **Little Star Pizza**.

Restaurants & Cafés

Bar Crudo

655 Divisadero Street, at Grove Street (1-415 409 0679, www.barcrudo.com). Bus 5, 21, 24. **Open** 5-10pm Tue-Thur, Sun; 5-11pm Fri, Sat. **Main courses** $14-$26. **Map** p133 C3
❶ Seafood

This popular raw bar serves up plates of oysters, clams, prawns, mussels, Dungeness crab and all manner of seasoned and marinated fish at very reasonable prices. Stop in during happy hour (5-6.30pm) and you can fill up on buttery, flaky rock cod tacos piled with salsa, guacamole, pickled onions and cotija cheese, or the rich seafood chowder for just $6. While you can find $1 oyster deals throughout the city, Bar Crudo caters to those with discerning tastes. It's also a destination for beer snobs, serving rotating saisons, strong ales, tripels, pilsners, kolshes and hefeweizens on tap.

★ $ The Mill

736 Divisadero Street, between Fulton & Grove Streets (1-415 345 1953, www.themillsf.com). Bus 24. **Open** 7am-9pm Mon; 7am-7pm Tue-Thur; 7am-8pm Fri-Sun. **Pastries** $3.50-$5. **Map** p133 C4 ❷ Café

Love it or mock it, the minimalist bakery inside Four Barrel Coffee came into prominence thanks to its now-notorious $4 toast. The label sells this café/bakery way short. The Mill is the love child of Josey Baker (his real name), who turns out legendary loaves of sumptuous sour wheat, country, rye and Wonder breads, along with chocolate claws, gouda tarts, morning buns, and pistachio-and-blackberry croissants. But frankly, it's the thick, chewy slabs of toast – slathered with seasonal toppings ranging from almond butter with Maldon sea salt to cinnamon sugar, pumpkin spread and cream cheese with honey – that people line up for in droves. On the coffee side, Four Barrel is a stickler for quality and flavour, sourcing their beans from small fair-trade farms around the world, and roasting them daily on a vintage German roaster.

Little Star

846 Divisadero Street, at McAllister Street (1-415 441 1118, www.littlestarpizza.com). Bus 5, 21, 24. **Open** 5-10pm Mon-Thur; 4-11pm Fri; noon-11pm Sat; noon-10pm Sun. **Main courses** $13.25-$25.75. **Map** p133 C4 ❸ Italian & pizza

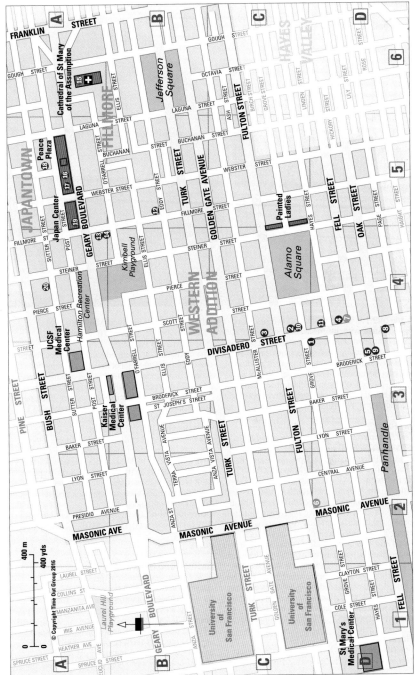

EXPLORE

Nopalito.

EXPLORE

Little Star has successfully won over its share of thin-crusters with its fresh take on Chicago-style deep-dish pizza, starting with a crunchy cornmeal crust that stands up to robust toppings such as tangy, chunky tomato sauce, salty feta, piquant green olives, red peppers, artichoke hearts and whole-milk mozzarella. The Mediterranean chicken pizza, made with house-baked chicken seasoned with pepperoncini juice and garlic, will make you a believer.

★ Nopa

560 Divisadero Street, at Hayes Street (1-415 864 8643, www.nopasf.com). Bus 5, 21, 24. **Open** 6pm-1am Mon-Fri; 11am-2.30pm, 6pm-1am Sat, Sun. **Main courses** $18-$29. **Map** p133 D4 ❹ California

One of the hottest restaurants in town, Nopa's attractions include the wood-fired oven and the late hours – unusual in a city where many kitchens pack up at 10pm. Italian- and Med-inspired ('urban rustic') dishes offer inventive twists with local, seasonal ingredients – Moroccan vegetable tagine and house-made pappardelle with lamb sugo, for example. Others are more classic – the likes of country pork chop with fresh beans and grilled peaches. Don't skip the luscious desserts, such as cornmeal honey crêpes with plums, raspberries and burnt honey ice-cream. Weekend brunch is hugely (and deservedly) popular.

Nopalito

306 Broderick Street, between Fell & Oak Streets, (1-415 535 3969, www.nopalitosf.com). Bus 16X, *44, 71.* **Open** 11.30am-10pm Mon-Thur, Sun; 11.30am-11pm Fri, Sat. **Main courses** $13-$22. **Map** p133 D3 ❺ Mexican

The antithesis of slapped-together street food, this Nopa (*see left*) offshoot makes everything from scratch using local, sustainable and organic ingredients. Dishes are carefully composed with subtle flavours to create deliciously complex interpretations of traditional Mexican dishes: *carnitas* is slow-cooked and braised in orange, bay leaf, milk, cinnamon and beer; Mole Coloradito con Pollo is made with toasted chiles, almonds, Ibarra chocolate, dried plums and a huge array of spices. Don't miss any version of tangy, tender *nopales* (cactus leaves), frequently on the menu in the form of tamales or in dishes such as Queso Flameado con Chorizo y Nopales (flamed Oaxacan and jack cheese with grilled cactus and chorizo).

Other location 1224 9th Avenue, between Lincoln Way & Irving Street (1-415 233 9966).

Bars

Barrel Head Brewhouse

1785 Fulton Street, between Masonic & Central Streets (1-415 416 6989, www.barrelheadsf.com). Bus 5, 43. **Open** 4pm-midnight Mon, Tue; 4pm-2am Wed-Sat; noon-midnight Sun. **Map** p133 D2 ❻

Catering to a mixed-age crowd of hipsters, sports fans, USF students and their parents, this boisterous bi-level brewpub leans towards Belgian and fruit-infused beers. Its menu strives to complement the drinks, using elements that incorporate sweet, salty and sour flavours. Pair your Fruitfly Framboise (raspberry wheat ale) or Simon Says Persimmon Saison with barbecued pulled pork sandwiched in Indian naan bread, alongside cucumbers, cilantro and tzatziki sauce, and served with a side of chickpea fries. Or try a refreshing Knify-Spoony Down Under Lager with some decadent poutine – thick-cut French fries slathered in beef gravy and cheese curds. On weekends, Barrel Head draws a neighbourhoody brunch crowd for baked apple pancakes and brisket hash.

Madrone Art Bar

500 Divisadero Street, at Fell Street (1-415 241 0202, www.madroneartbar.com). Bus 5, 21, 24. **Open** 4pm-2am Mon-Sat; 3pm-1.30am Sun. **Map** p133 D4 ❼
This funky lounge and art gallery brought joy to the neighbourhood when it revived a fine Victorian from almost total dilapidation – the building now flaunts a beautifully restored exterior. Inside, draught beers, a speciality cocktail list and a bar menu keeps patrons occupied while digging DJs, independent film screenings or live music.

Shops & Services

Cookin'

339 Divisadero Street, between Oak & Page Streets (1-415 861 1854). Bus 6, 21, 24, 71. **Open** noon-6.30pm Tue-Sat; 1-5pm Sun. **Map** p133 D4 ❽
Homewares
A staple on Divisadero since 1981, Cookin' is the holy grail of vintage cookware, catering to esteemed Bay Area chefs as well as budget-conscious home cooks. Owner Judy Kaminsky collects much of her store's stash in French flea markets. The assortment includes cast-iron pots and pans (including colourful enamelled pots and casseroles by Le Creuset), kitschy cake stands and baking accessories, barware, servers and dishes. Though Kaminsky, who lives upstairs and is often behind the register, may come off more cranky than charming, regulars consider her a local treasure.

Falletti Foods

308 Broderick Street, between Fell & Oak Streets (1-415 626 4400, http://fallettifoods.com). Bus 6, 21, 24. **Open** 7am-9pm daily. **Map** p133 D3 ❾
Food & drink
Falletti has been synonymous with San Francisco groceries since 1941, when Lou Falletti opened his first store (he went into business with his brother Jim after the war). The L-shaped NoPa market, which opened in 2006, sells nationally known products like Muir Glen organics alongside local favourites such as Straus Family Creamery's butter, milk and ice-cream. There's also an exceptional selection of cheese, meat, wine and produce. If you're looking for lunch, head to the deli – we're huge fans of the Italian

Perish Trust.

cold cuts sandwich on foccacia, which includes a healthy portion of wine-infused salami.

★ Perish Trust

728 Divisadero Street, between Fulton & Grove Streets (www.theperishtrust.com). Bus 5, 21, 24. **Open** 11am-6pm Mon, Wed-Sun. **Map** p133 C4 ❿ Gifts & souvenirs/homewares
You wouldn't be the first shop visitor to fantasise about wrapping yourself in a Pendleton throw, settling into the broken-in leather armchair and never having to leave. This eclectic gift and home-furnishings shop is the brainchild of prop stylist Rod Hipskind and photographer Kelly Ishikawa. As one might expect, every surface and nook is impeccably styled. The vibe is rustic and nautical-cool, from the anchor motif to the collection of vintage typewriters. The goods include housewares, ceramics, jewellery and industrial-era decor arranged throughout the moodily lit space to artful effect. The back area contains the SF outpost for Oakland-based kitchen and barware shop Umami Mart, where you can peruse Japanese imports and gold-plated cocktail shakers, shatter-resistant highball glasses, exotically flavoured bitters and beautiful ceramic cookware.

Rare Device

600 Divisadero Street, between Grove & Hayes Streets (1-415 863 3969, www.raredevice.net). Bus 21, 24. **Open** noon-8pm Mon-Fri; 11am-7pm Sat; 11am-6pm Sun. **Map** p133 D4 ⓫
Gifts & souvenirs

EXPLORE

This colourful shop is headed up by Giselle Gyalzen, who has a penchant for hand-crafted, thoughtfully designed and eminently giftable goods. That haul includes affordable art prints, ceramics and tableware, gourmet foodstuffs, locally designed jewellery, beauty products, design tomes and kids' toys. (Plus, several twirling racks filled with letterpress cards for topping off impromptu gifts.) The space also doubles as a gallery, with a focus on Bay Area-based illustrators and screen-printers. Take a spin through the store after brunch, then stroll through the Divisadero Farmers' Market, which unfurls every Sunday just across the street.

THE FILLMORE DISTRICT

The Fillmore neighbourhood was a mecca for jazz and blues musicians in the 1940s and '50s. Several albums, among them Miles Davis's 1961 *In Person* recordings at the Black Hawk club, are testament to its pedigree. However, the locale was declared a slum by the San Francisco Redevelopment Agency in the 1960s and torn apart under the guise of urban renewal.

Happily, new life is being slowly and steadily breathed into the area. **State Bird Provisions** and next-door sister restaurant. **The Progress** have made the stretch of Fillmore between Geary and Eddy Streets a destination dining spot, while **1300 On Fillmore** has brought soul food and jazz back to the hood.

Based in the city for more than three decades, the **African Orthodox Church of St John Coltrane** (1286 Fillmore Street, at Eddy Street, 1-415 673 7144, www.coltranechurch.org) continues to hold jazz-driven services-cum-jam sessions. Coltrane's seminal invocation of the divine, *A Love Supreme*, is the key work – every Sunday at noon.

Legendary auditorium the **Fillmore** (1805 Geary Boulevard, at Fillmore Street; *see p218*) is still going strong, booking top-flight rock and independent bands. So close you can almost hear the ghosts is the now-defunct Winterland (formerly at the northwest corner of Post and Steiner Streets), where the Band filmed *The Last Waltz* and Johnny Rotten asked the audience 'Ever get the feeling you've been cheated?' at the final Sex Pistols show in 1978.

Yards away, on the wall of the **Hamilton Recreation Center** at the corner of Post and Steiner, is a huge musical mural, created by local musician and painter Santie Huckaby. The mural features dozens of musicians with an SF connection: some lived here, some simply played here, and one, bluesman John Lee Hooker, even opened his own club here. Hooker died in 2001, but the **Boom Boom Room** (1601 Fillmore Street, at Geary Boulevard; *see p223*) lives on. Next to the Fillmore, at 1849 Geary Boulevard, is an eerier landmark. A post office has stood

here in recent years, but from 1971 to 1977 this site was the home of the notorious Jim Jones and his People's Temple. Despite running his own legendarily cultish church, Jones was considered a respectable citizen. However, when reports emerged of physical and sexual abuse within the church, he moved it from here to a settlement he named Jonestown located in French Guyana. The following year, Jones and more than 900 disciples, the majority former Fillmorites, committed mass suicide or were murdered in the now-infamous Jonestown Massacre.

Restaurants & Cafés

1300 On Fillmore

1300 Fillmore Street, at Eddy Street (1-415 771 7100, www.1300fillmore.com). Bus 5, 22, 31, 38. **Open** 5.30-10pm Tue-Thur; 5.30pm-11pm Fri, Sat; 10.30am-2.30pm, 5.30pm-10pm Sun. **Main courses** $18-$28. **Map** p133 B5 ➋ **American**
Part of the revival of the historic Fillmore Jazz District, this soul-food eaterie is a welcome addition to the area. The Southern-influenced fare is anchored in classics: fried chicken, barbecued shrimp with hushpuppies, roasted catfish and peach cobbler. The room has a supper-club atmosphere, with big leather chairs and classic jazz streaming through the joint; on Friday and Saturday nights there's live music. Don't miss the Heritage Wall in the lounge, with a collection of historic photos and TV screens scrolling through images of jazz greats who once played in the neighbourhood.

State Bird Provisions

The Progress

1525 Fillmore Street, between Geary Boulevard & O'Farrell Street (1-415 673 1294, www.the progress-sf.com). **Open** *5.30-10pm Mon-Thur, Sun; 5.30-11pm Fri, Sat.* **Prix fixe** *$65.* **Map** p133 A4 **⑬ American creative**

The most hotly anticipated restaurant opening of 2015, the Progress is the sequel and next-door neighbour to Stuart Brioza and Nicole Krasinski's insanely popular and acclaimed State Bird Provisions *(see below)*. Family-style shared plates showcase the entirely local and custom-made experience (even the artisan earthenware dishes were made specifically for the restaurant). Menus give diners a choice of six courses from about 20 different dishes for a fixed price of $65, with additional small bites that emerge from the kitchen. The regularly changing menu might include genre-bending offerings like spiced lamb tartare with 'mix-in' condiments, black rice-fried Hog Island oysters with butter-clam kimchi, and rabbit with eggplant vinaigrette and Oaxacan red-bean salsa. Happily, the Progress is considerably larger than its sister, so reservations should (in theory) be a little easier to come by.

★ State Bird Provisions

1529 Fillmore Street, between Geary Boulevard & O'Farrell Street (1-415 795 1272, www.statebirdsf. com). **Bus** *22, 38, 92.* **Open** *5.30-10pm Mon-Thur, Sun; 5.30-11pm Fri, Sat.* **Main courses** *$9-$22.* **Map** p133 A4 **⑭ American creative**

Michelin-starred State Bird Provisions (and its newer sister, the Progress) have amassed such a following that foodie hackers have devised programmes to attempt to beat its online reservation system, or hire surrogates to stand in line when the restaurant opens at 5.30pm hoping to snag one of the coveted walk-in spots or a seat at the chef's counter. The menu is divided into Provisions, Pancakes, and Commandables – the latter two served as à la carte items, such as the signature CA State Bird (crispy fried quail with pickled sautéed onions) and sourdough pancakes with sauerkraut, pecorino and ricotta. But the real fun comes with the Provisions – dim sum-style rolling carts bring dish after dish of inventive small bites from the kitchen, from duck liver mousse with almond cakes to smoked trout-avocado 'chip and dip'.

JAPANTOWN

Three commercial blocks and a compound-like shopping mall are all that remains of what was once one of the largest Japanese communities in the US. Devastated by the forced relocation of Japanese-Americans to internment camps during World War II, the area is now home to only a tiny percentage of residents. But the locale still provides support for the elderly, history lessons for the young, and a banquet of aesthetic and pop-culture delights for anyone interested.

At the heart of Japantown is the **Japan Center** (between Geary, Post, Fillmore and Buchanan Streets), a mostly underground maze of shops, restaurants and unique businesses that cater to Japanese residents. The **Kinokuniya Bookstore** (1581 Webster Street, at Post Street, 1-415 567 7625, www.kinokuniya.com/us) is a fascinating clearing-house of J-pop culture, manga comics and Japanese-language books, while across the street, **Paper Tree** (1743 Buchanan Street, at Sutter Street, 1-415 921 7100,

www.paper-tree.com) specialises in origami supplies. The **Sundance Kabuki Theater** (1881 Post Street, at Fillmore Street, 1-415 929 4650, www.sundancecinemas.com) is the flagship cinema of actor/activist Robert Redford's film company. Seven screens with stadium seating feature the latest independent films and the winners of Redford's renowned Sundance Film Festival. There are two bars inside; the one at the top offers wine, beer, and a light fare menu – and you can bring drinks into the theatre.

Outside, the **Japantown Peace Plaza** with its towering five-tier **Peace Pagoda** designed by Japanese architect Yoshiro Taniguchi, was presented to the city as a symbol of friendship from sister city, Osaka, in 1968. Across Post Street on Buchanan Street is the pedestrian-only **Buchanan Mall**, where you'll find Japanese stores such as **Soko Hardware** (1698 Post Street, 1-415 931 5510), a trove of gardening tools, handy kitchen items, knives, and knick-knacks ranging from tea sets to paper lanterns and rice cookers.

Peace Pagoda.

To gain a bit of cultural context, visit the **National Japanese American Historical Society** (1684 Post Street, between Buchanan & Laguna Streets, 1-415 921 5007, www.njahs. org) or the nearby **Japanese American Community Center** (1840 Sutter Street, at Webster Street, 1-415 567 5505, www.jcccnc. org), which hosts exhibitions on the Japanese-American way of life. Meanwhile, just east of the Japan Center, is the decidedly non-Japanese, impressively modern **Cathedral of St Mary of the Assumption**.

Sights & Museums

FREE Cathedral of St Mary of the Assumption
1111 Gough Street, at Geary Boulevard (1-415 567 2020, www.stmarycathedralsf.org). Bus 2, 3, 4, 38. **Open** 6.45am-4pm Mon-Fri, Sun; 6.45am-5.30pm Sat. **Admission** free. **Map** p133 A6 ⓖ
Dominating the skyline, the exterior of this 1971 cathedral is stark, a modern, sculptural structure (some say it resembles the blades of a washing machine) reaching 190ft into the sky. The four corner pylons were designed to support millions of pounds of pressure and extend 90ft down to the bedrock beneath the church. Inside, the staggering structure of the cupola is revealed in 1,500 triangular coffers, in over 128 sizes, meant to distribute the weight of the roof. The trumpets of the huge organ, on a raised pedestal that floats above the congregation, appear capable of blasting down the walls of Jericho. Large corner windows allow views of the city.

Restaurants & Cafés

Isobune
Japan Center, 1737 Post Street, between Buchanan & Webster Streets (1-415 563 1030, www.isobune sushi.com). Bus 2, 3, 38. **Open** 11.30am-9.30pm daily. **Sushi** $4.75-$28. **Map** p133 A5 ⓖ **Japanese**
Isobune may not garner top honours among critics, but it's undoubtedly the most entertaining sushi spot in the city. The original sushi boat restaurant opened in 1982, delivering high-quality, affordable delicacies to diners via dishes set on small wooden boats that circulate on a canal around the bar. The tradition continues in the Japan Center mall, where you'll find boisterous crowds plucking colourful rolls, sushi and sashimi from the vessels and toasting the chefs with shots of saké. Each plate pattern has a different price and the plates are tallied at the end of your meal. This is a great place to introduce kids and novices to the delights of raw fish.

$ Mifune
Japan Center, 1737 Post Street, between Buchanan & Webster Streets (1-415 922 0337, www.mifune. com). Bus 2, 3, 22, 38. **Open** 11am-9.30pm daily. **Main courses** $14. **Map** p133 A5 ⓖ **Japanese**

Mifune's motto is 'It's okay to slurp your noodles', which gives you an idea of the atmosphere and focus of this place. Here you'll find the lowly noodle prepared in at least 30 different ways. Orders come quickly, and the food is that appealing combination: inexpensive and delicious. Good for children and vegetarians.

★ $ Ramen Yamadaya
1728 Buchanan Street, between Post & Sutter Streets (1-415 359 9983, www.ramen-yamadaya. com). **Open** 11.30am-3pm, 5.30-10pm Mon-Fri; 11.30am-10pm Sat, Sun. **Main courses** $7.95-$10.95 **Map** p133 A5 ⓖ **Japanese**
Tonkatsu – broth made from pork bones cooked for 20 hours – and house-made ramen noodles topped with *chashu* (thin-sliced pork), bamboo shoots, marinated eggs, pork belly strips and other delicacies, are the hallmark of this immensely popular LA transplant. The menu is deceptively simple, but the complexity of flavours in the soups is anything but. Try the level 1-2-3 spicy or the Yamadaya. There's also an extensive sushi menu and bento box meals with karaage chicken and katsu curry.

Shops & Services

★ Kabuki Springs & Spa
Japan Center, 1750 Geary Boulevard, at Fillmore Street (1-415 922 6000, www. kabukisprings.com). Bus 2, 3, 22, 38. **Open** 10am-9pm daily. *Men only* Mon, Thur, Sat. *Women only* Wed, Fri, Sun. *Mixed* Tue. **Map** 133 A5 ⓖ **Health & beauty**
This tranquil, dimly lit bathhouse feels not only like an escape from city life, but also from the city itself. As you soak in a steaming communal pool or succumb to a sense-scrambling Eastern-influenced massage, you'll have to keep reminding yourself that you are indeed smack dab in the middle of San Francisco. Or maybe an invigorating plunge in the cool pool will snap you back to reality. Bath rates start at $25; $15 with a treatment.

Song Tea & Ceramics
2120 Sutter Street, between Pierce & Steiner Streets (1-415 885 2118, www.songtea.com). Bus 2, 3, 24, 31, 38. **Open** 11am-6pm Tue-Sat. **Map** p133 A4 ⓖ **Food & drink/gifts & souvenirs**
After serving as a partner and buyer at Red Blossom for years, Peter Luong opened this tearoom and shop in 2014. The space is a modernist design geek's dream, awash in white, concrete and wood. Tastings happen at a long wooden table, where Luong delves into each tea's history, origin and preparation. He takes tea pilgrimages across southern China and Taiwan to hand-pick new offerings each season. Opposite the teas, you'll find a gorgeous assortment of ceramics from his travels, including a small collection of one-of-a-kind wood-fired pieces by Taiwanese artisans.

EXPLORE

The Haight & Hayes Valley

Mention the words Haight-Ashbury, or even just the Haight, and members of a certain generation will either sigh with nostalgic longing or groan in exasperation, depending on their political leanings and/or their connection to 1967's legendary Summer of Love. However, once the crowds had tuned out, turned off and dropped back in again, the neighbourhood resumed duty as one of the most liveable in San Francisco.

Bordering the Haight and Civic Center, Hayes Valley emerged from the rubble of the 1989 Loma Prieta earthquake minus one eyesore freeway overpass. Since then, a tree-lined boulevard and park, a state-of-the-art jazz centre, chic boutiques, trendy furnishings stores and a trove of bars and restaurants have helped reshape the enclave as one of San Francisco's hippest districts.

Zuni Cafe.

Don't Miss

1 Amoeba Music The longstanding behemoth proves the record store ain't dead yet (p146).

2 Magnolia Gastropub & Brewery Toast the Haight's hippie legacy at this fine brewpub (p146).

3 Zuni Café Seminal spot for NorCal cuisine (p151).

4 Hayes Street Hit the blissfully chain-free strip for indie shops galore (p151).

5 Fatted Calf Pig out at this charcuterie (p153).

THE HAIGHT

The Haight's history is written in its Victorian buildings, many of them painstakingly restored and elaborately painted. Despite being three miles from the ocean, the neighbourhood was considered a beach town in the mid-19th century and many wealthy families from Nob Hill kept vacation homes here. In 1870, the first San Francisco Park Commission was appointed. As development began on Golden Gate Park, the neighbouring Haight began to expand, and it was to thrive still further in the years following the 1906 earthquake, from which it emerged relatively unscathed.

As the 1950s phenomenon of 'white flight' swept through urban areas, families left for the suburbs, and the Victorian houses of the Haight were increasingly left both vacant and affordable. Inevitably, the city's students and post-war bohemian culture kids moved in. An offshoot of the North Beach beat scene of the late 1950s, the Haight went on to become the epicentre of hippie culture, the most famous youth movement in history. The beats, however, were scornful of the monied, pleasure-seeking hippies, considering them a kind of 'beatnik-lite': the word 'hippie' is itself said to have derived from a derogatory beatnik term meaning 'little hipster'.

In Berkeley and Oakland, the Free Speech and Black Power movements were already bringing a new political consciousness to the Bay Area. Duly inspired, the hippies were the driving force behind the anti-Vietnam War protests in San Francisco in the 1960s, and a new counterculture emerged. In January 1967, 25,000 gathered for the Human Be-In at the Polo Grounds in Golden Gate Park, a proto-hippie gathering where psychologist and LSD proponent Timothy Leary famously coined the phrase 'Turn on, Tune in, Drop Out'.

After 1967's Summer of Love, speed and heroin replaced marijuana and LSD as the drugs of choice, and free love turned into grim disaffection. Unsavoury types such as Charles Manson (who lived at 636 Cole Street) emerged as gurus to the impressionable youth, counteracting the work of idealistic political groups such as the Diggers, and guerrilla theatre pioneers the San Francisco Mime Troupe, which still performs today (its anti-war message regained currency with the conflicts in Iraq and Afghanistan).

Just as the bold and the beautiful still flock to Hollywood from all over the world hoping to be 'discovered', so teenage runaways still gravitate to **Haight Street** looking for peace, love, understanding and spare change. Traces of the radical past linger at anarchist-run bookshop **Bound Together** (1369 Haight Street, at Masonic Avenue, 1-415 431 8355) and the **Haight-Ashbury Free Clinic** (now called HealthRight 360, *see p294*),

Magnolia Gastropub & Brewery.
See p146.

while the mellow coffee houses hark back decades. Famous for its vehement anti-corporate stance (attempts to build a chain drugstore in 1988 were met with an arsonist's firebomb), the Haight appears to be shifting ever-so-slightly towards the dreaded 'establishment', with the opening of a **Whole Foods** at the corner of Haight and Stanyan Streets, and the closure of a recycling centre that long served as an ersatz homeless hangout.

Haight-Ashbury

The stretch of Haight Street that sits between Masonic and Stanyan Streets, known both as Haight-Ashbury and Upper Haight, makes for a lively scene on weekends and warm-weather days. Stores hawk New Age and Eastern esoterica, hand-blown glass smoking paraphernalia, edgy and vintage clothing, funky shoes and, at the vast **Amoeba Music** (*see p146*), mountains of records and CDs. Shoppers also have to duck the buskers and bums, who add more local flavour than some tourists were expecting. Just west of Amoeba, across Stanyan Street, is **Golden Gate Park**. A couple of blocks north is the **Panhandle**, the park's grand entrance; at the height of the hippie era, local bands that went on to fill stadiums (the Grateful Dead, Janis Joplin *et al*) played free shows here.

More evidence of the neighbourhood's past can be found at **Jammin On Haight** (1400 Haight Street, 1-415 817 1027, www.jamminon haight.com), which sells groovy tie-dye gear and hippie ephemera, and the **Magnolia Gastropub & Brewery** (*see p146*). This former pharmacy served as a hippie haven called the Drogstore Café [sic] back in the 1960s, before becoming the base for Magnolia Thunderpussy and her erotically themed desserts. The new owners named their brewpub in her honour and covered the walls in psychedelic 1960s murals.

At the corner of Haight Street and Central Avenue is the aptly named, beautifully wooded **Buena Vista Park**, the oldest designated park in the city and the unofficial eastern terminus of Upper Haight. In 1867, when the land was still known as Hill Park, the city paid squatters $88,250 to gain rights to the park. It was a wise investment, not only for the city, but in terms of the example it set for the zealous culture of land preservation that still flourishes today across Northern California. The paths on the west side of the park are lined with marble gutters and a retaining wall built by WPA workers using Victorian headstones, some laid face up with their inscriptions visible. The walk to the park's 589-foot peak is worth the effort: the views over the city and (on clear days) out to the Golden Gate Bridge and Marin Headlands are commanding.

EXPLORE

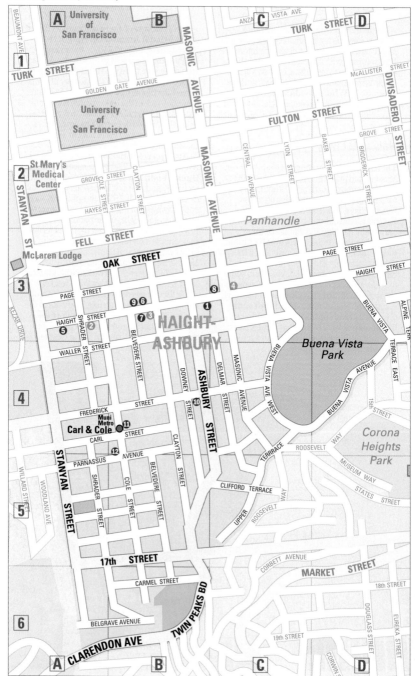

The Haight & Hayes Valley

EXPLORE

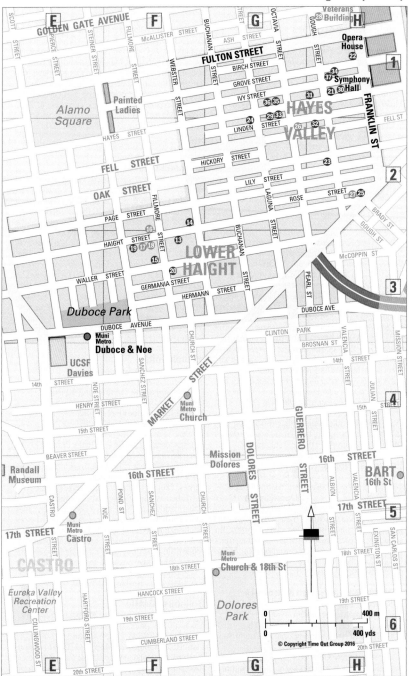

Restaurants & Cafés

$ Pork Store Café
1451 Haight Street, between Ashbury Street & Masonic Avenue (1-415 864 6981, www. porkstorecafe.com). Bus 6, 33, 37, 43, 71.
Open 7am-3.30pm Mon-Fri; 8am-4pm Sat, Sun.
Main courses $7-$9.50. **Map** p144 B3 ❶ **Café**
Sit at the counter for a view of the skilled spatula-slingers manning the griddle. This narrow diner serves giant, steaming portions of food for under $10. It's an egg lover's dream, offering all manner of omelettes, scrambles and Benedicts. The speciality is Eggs in a Tasty Nest, which layers two over-easy eggs atop a heap of hash browns, bacon, bell peppers, tomatoes, onion, garlic and cheddar.

Bars

★ Alembic
1725 Haight Street, between Cole & Shrader Streets (1-415 666 0822, www.alembicbar.com). Metro to Cole & Carl/bus 33, 37, 43, 66, 71. **Open** 4pm-2am Mon-Fri; noon-2am Sat, Sun. **Map** p144 A3 ❷
Neighbourhood bar flies, cocktail nerds, foodies and hippies converge at this classic Haight-Ashbury hangout, where funky yellow walls and chalkboard menus foster a relaxed atmosphere. As a pioneer of the San Francisco craft cocktail movement, Alembic serves strong and pitch-perfect drinks using fresh ingredients. Half of the menu is devoted to well-loved classics, like the Sazerac, old-fashioned and French 75; the other half house-devised concoctions that embrace seasonal ingredients, such as the Bait and Switch (a fruity and smoky mix of mescal, Chareau Aloe Liqueur, strawberries, lemon juice, peppercorn syrup and green strawberry bitters). The knowledgeable, amiable bartenders can help curious drinkers explore new flavours while swiftly supplying regulars with old standbys.

Hobson's Choice
1601 Haight Street, at Clayton Street (1-415 621 5859, www.hobsonschoice.com). Metro to Cole & Carl/bus 6, 7, 33, 37, 43, 71. **Open** 2pm-2am Mon-Fri; noon-2am Sat, Sun. **Map** p144 B3 ❸
At this 'Victorian punch bar', bartenders ladle out tall glasses of tasty rum punch. For connoisseurs of the spirit, the place features more than 100 rotating rums. Fresh, grilled kebabs from the neighbouring Asqew Grill soak up the booze as it settles in the bellies of the collegiate-cum-jam-band set that fills the bar.

★ Magnolia Gastropub & Brewery
1398 Haight Street, at Masonic Avenue (1-415 864 7468, www.magnoliapub.com). Bus 6, 33, 37, 43, 71. **Open** 11am-midnight Mon-Thur; 11am-1am Fri; 10am-1am Sat; 10am-midnight Sun. **Map** p144 C3 ❹
This beloved brewpub's decor plays up its history: built in 1903, it was a focal point of hippie culture in

the 1960s, before being taken over by local dessert maven Magnolia Thunderpussy – hence the name. A staple for beer lovers and neighbourhood residents for more than 16 years, Magnolia's solid pub menu of house-made sausages, fish and chips, and outstanding burgers complements the excellent house-brewed beer selection, which includes cask ales. Owner Dave McLean expanded his brewery operation in 2014 with the Magnolia Brewing Company & Smokestack BBQ in Dogpatch (*see p176). Photos pp142-143.*

Shops & Services

★ Amoeba Music
1855 Haight Street, between Shrader & Stanyan Streets (1-415 831 1200, www.amoeba.com). Metro to Carl & Cole/bus 6, 33, 37, 43, 66, 71. **Open** 11am-8pm daily. **Map** p144 A3 ❺ **Books & music**
Amoeba Music remains a mighty presence. It's partly a matter of scale – 25,000sq ft of former bowling alley, to be exact – but mainly a matter of breadth: there's every imaginable type of music, both new and second-hand, the vast majority priced very fairly, as well as a massive DVD selection. The Berkeley branch used to be the stronger of the two, but the SF store now pips it. There are free gigs, too, with some surprisingly big names. The store also launched its own imprint: one of its first releases was a 1969 concert by Gram Parsons and the Flying Burrito Brothers at SF's Avalon Ballroom.

★ Booksmith
1644 Haight Street, between Belvedere & Clayton Streets (1-415 863 8688, www.booksmith.com). Metro to Carl & Cole/bus 6, 33, 37, 43, 66, 71. **Open** 10am-10pm Mon-Sat; 10am-8pm Sun. **Map** p144 B3 ❻ **Books & music**
This cheery bookstore near Golden Gate Park offers a welcome respite from the head shops and tie-dye tourist traps along Haight Street. Owner Christin Evans also runs Berkeley Arts & Letters, Berkeley's author event programme, and Booksmith is known for hosting a full schedule of readings, signings and book parties. Thoughtful staff recommendations are scattered liberally throughout the shelves, each including a short reader's pitch. This is a bookstore that goes above and beyond in a number of categories, whether it's the expansive kids section, hard-to-find international magazine editions, or the beautiful range of coffee table tomes. But locals swear by the customer service. If for some reason the shop doesn't have what you're looking for – a rarity – staff will order it on the spot and call you in a day or two when it arrives.

Dollhouse Bettie
1641 Haight Street, between Belvedere & Clayton Streets (1-877 342 1715, www.dollhousebettie. com). Bus 33, 37, 43, 66, 71. **Open** 11am-7pm Mon-Sat; noon-6pm Sun. **Map** p144 B3 ❼ **Fashion**
An unparalleled boudoir for Bettie Page wannabes, this shop is filled with pin-up inspired lingerie from

EXPLORE

SUMMER OF HAIGHT

They were going to change the world, starting here.

For most people, the Haight-Ashbury didn't exist before the Summer of Love. But in reality, it was in the years just prior to that vaunted summer of '67 that the Haight truly shone – a magnet for many talents that combined to produce an unprecedented explosion in virtually all forms of art, political discourse and even healthcare. As word spread about the new world of the Haight, people started to pour in, and Haight Street and the area surrounding it turned into a kind of hippie refugee camp virtually overnight.

Legions of people who are now household names lived in close proximity. Walking down Haight Street, one might encounter the likes of the **Grateful Dead**, **Jefferson Airplane** or **Janis Joplin**. The father of underground comics, **Robert Crumb**, might be scribbling away somewhere, while visionary musician **Frank Zappa** was hunched over a score, with rock-poster artist **Stanley Mouse** drawing up the playbill. *Howl* poet **Allen Ginsberg** (who once lived at 1360 Fell Street) might be found wandering the park in a trance. One might bump into **Crosby, Stills and Nash**, **Steve Miller**, **Sly and the Family Stone**,

Carlos Santana or **Jimi Hendrix** (the latter lived at 1524A Haight Street).

Those strapped for cash could visit the Free Store run by the **Diggers**, a semi-anarchic group dedicated to turning the Haight into a barter society, or get medical help at the **Haight-Ashbury Free Clinic**. The **Hell's Angels' clubhouse** (719 Ashbury Street), meanwhile, was located across the street from the Grateful Dead's residence (710 Ashbury Street). Although the Angels no longer own the building, the gang still starts its annual Thanksgiving run from the **People's Café** on Haight Street.

In his seminal work, *Fear and Loathing in Las Vegas*, **Hunter S Thompson**, who lived at 318 Parnassus Street, delivered a eulogy to the San Francisco of the '60s: 'There was a fantastic universal sense that whatever we were doing was right, that we were winning,' he wrote. 'And that, I think, was the handle – that sense of inevitable victory over the forces of Old and Evil… Our energy would simply prevail… We had all the momentum; we were riding on the crest of a high and beautiful wave…'

EXPLORE

the 1930s to '60s. The voluptuous mannequins are draped in silk, satin and lace; you'll find no itchy polyester here. Though the bulk of the merchandise consists of peek-a-boo bras, panties and vintage slips, there's all manner of alluring extras, including tassels, garters, corsets, lace thigh-highs, girdles and feathered toys. The shop also carries pin-up inspired styles from contemporary brands like Mary Green, What Katie Did, and Felina & Jezebel.

Shoe Biz

1420 Haight Street, between Ashbury Street & Masonic Avenue (1-415 861 0313, www. shoebizsf.com). Bus 6, 33, 37, 43, 66, 71. **Open** 11am-7pm Mon-Sat; 11am-6pm Sun. **Map** p144 C3 ❽ **Accessories**
This local empire has four stores in the city, but the best stocked are the pair on Haight Street. The 'Super' store at 1420 Haight is packed with fashionable but practical shoes for city life. Women will find an array of flats – ballet, D'Orsay, smoking slippers and Oxfords – as well as hardy wood-soled sandals and clogs. Men can browse chukka boots, dress shoes, and casual leather lace-ups. With lower-priced labels like Seychelles, Dolce Vita and Report, this is a great place to find a deal. Down the street at 1553 Haight, the Shoe Biz Dinostore – so called for the large dinosaur sculpture guarding the door – specialises in sneaker

and streetwear brands, including Nike, New Balance, Supra, Puma and Adidas. When new releases hit, you'll frequently find a line forming before it opens. **Other locations** throughout the city.

Wasteland

1660 Haight Street, between Clayton & Cole Streets, (1-415 863 3150, www.shopwasteland. com). Metro to Carl & Cole/bus 6, 33, 37, 43, 66, 71. **Open** 11am-8pm Mon-Sat; noon-7pm Sun. **Map** p144 B3 ❾ **Fashion**
Wasteland has long been a Haight Street standby for second-hand attire. It's split into vintage (largely from the 1960s to '90s) and 'vintage inspired' clothing from the noughties on. The buyers here are more discerning than at resale stores Buffalo Exchange or Crossroads down the street, resulting in higher-end brands and slightly higher prices. The modern section is aggressively trendy: denim jumpsuits, neon '80s prints, grungy plaid and the like, but much of the vintage stock can be incorporated into a modern wardrobe without feeling overtly costumey. The gently worn shoes are mostly contemporary and in good condition. It's a cavernous store compared to some of its neighbours, and those on the hunt can easily devote an afternoon flipping through dozens of racks. The staff maintain a coolly disaffected air; you're here for the low-priced gems, not the friendly service.

Wasteland.

Cole Valley

It's only a few blocks from the bustle of Haight-Ashbury, but the cosy enclave of Cole Valley is a different world altogether: low-key, smart and upscale. The businesses here are all clustered around a two-block area of Cole and Carl Streets. **Zazie** is a great spot for brunch or lunch. Alternatively, you can pick up supplies from **Say Cheese** (856 Cole Street, at Carl Street, 1-415 665 5020), which sells vast selections of gourmet cheeses, meats and wines, and enjoy a picnic on **Tank Hill**. Head one block west from Cole Street to Shrader Street and continue south up the hill until you reach Belgrave Street; turn left on to Belgrave and take the rustic stairway at the end of the street to the top of the hill. It's a bit of a slog, but well worth the effort. Once home to a water tank (hence the name), the 650-foot peak offers some of the city's best views.

Restaurants & Cafés

$ Bacon Bacon Café
205A Frederick Street, at Ashbury Street (1-415 218 4347, www.baconbaconsf.com). Bus 6, 37, 43. **Open** 7am-3pm Mon-Fri; 8am-3pm Sat, Sun. **Main courses** $8-$10. **Map** p144 B4 ⑩ **Café**
The brick-and-mortar offshoot of Jim Angelus's ridiculously popular Bacon Bacon food truck came sizzling back after a grease fire in 2013. At this small, breakfast-and-lunch spot, bacon lovers can pig out on double-bacon cheeseburgers, egg breakfast sandwiches with bacon jam, bacon-fried chicken, and BLTs loaded with lettuce, tomato, goat cheese and five strips of the café's namesake meaty treat.

$ Ice Cream Bar
815 Cole Street, at Carl Street (1-415 742 4932, www.theicecreambarsf.com). Metro to Carl & Cole/bus 6, 37, 43. **Open** noon-10pm Mon-Thur, Sun; noon-11pm Fri, Sat. **Ice-cream** $6-$16. **Map** p144 B4 ⑪ **Ice-cream**
A contemporary take on an old-fashioned ice-cream shop, Ice Cream Bar recalls the golden age of the soda fountain – complete with soda jerks in chevron hats and bow ties, an authentic 1930s fountain carted in from Mackinaw City, Michigan, and Streamline Moderne decor. The fountain features updated and upscale interpretations of 1940s and '50s ice-cream treats – cones, floats, sundaes, malts, milkshakes, ice-cream sandwiches and Lactarts (flavoured sodas made with lactart, a milk acid). There's also a savoury menu with nostalgic items such as tuna melts. Everything is made in-house, including the cones, the cookies for the ice-cream sandwiches and the hot dog buns. The art deco bar at the back offers grown-up fountain drinks, including 'remedies' like the Royal Red Milkshake: Duchesse De Bourgogne Flemish Red Ale, Sandeman Royal Ambrosante, 20-year-old sherry, cherry ice-cream, and turbinado syrup.

★ Zazie
941 Cole Street, at Parnassus Avenue (1-415 564 5332, www.zaziesf.com). Metro to Carl & Cole/bus 6, 37, 43, 66, 71. **Open** 8am-2pm, 5-9.30pm Mon-Thur; 8am-2pm, 5-10pm Fri; 9am-3pm, 5-10pm Sat; 9am-3pm, 5-9.30pm Sun. **Main courses** $19-$32. **Map** p144 B4 ⑫ **French**
This delightful spot oozes bonhomie and serves up lavish breakfasts and brunch (don't miss the lemon-ricotta pancakes), a small variety of lunch dishes (pasta, sandwiches), and a more traditional French menu for dinner (trout meunière, roast duck leg). Some see Zazie as a café, others a bistro, but it manages to pull off both.

LOWER HAIGHT

While Upper Haight still clings dreamily to its political past, the young, the disenchanted and the progressive have migrated down the hill to Lower Haight, on and around Haight Street between Divisadero and Octavia Streets. The area's main intersection is at Haight and Fillmore Streets, from which fashion shops, tattoo parlours, funky bars and ethnic eateries radiate in all directions. Beer-lovers would do well to try **Toronado**. It doesn't serve food, but you can get gourmet sausages next door at the **Rosamunde Sausage Grill** (545 Haight Street, 1-415 437 6851) and take them to the bar.

Restaurants & Cafés

$ Kate's Kitchen
471 Haight Street, between Fillmore & Webster Streets (1-415 626 3984, www.kates-kitchensf. com). Bus 6, 22, 71. **Open** 9am-2.45pm Mon; 8am-2.45pm Tue; 8am-2.45 pm, 5-9pm Wed, Thur; 8.30am-3.40pm Fri-Sun. **Main courses** $6.75-$15.50. **No credit cards**. **Map** p145 F3 ⑬ **Café**
Lower Haight's unofficial brunch HQ, this hotspot is an excellent choice when you've got a mountain of Sunday papers to wade through at your leisure. Ease into the day with a giant bowl of granola, a huge omelette, New England flannel hash, or one of their Southern-inspired dishes such as red beans with ham hocks and grits, or the signature hush puppies (drop pancakes made of cornmeal).

$ Rickybobby
400 Haight Street, at Webster Street (www. rickybobbysf.com). Bus 6, 71, 22. **Open** 6-10pm Tue-Thur; 6-11pm Fri, Sat. **Main courses** $9-$13. **Map** p145 F2 ⑭ **American**
The name alone (nabbed from the Will Ferrell movie *Talladega Nights: The Ballad of Ricky Bobby*) should tell you that you're in for a ridiculously over-the-top experience, and Rickybobby doesn't disappoint. The signature beef and bacon burger puts a gluttonous spin on a double cheeseburger. The

EXPLORE

two meats are ground together and formed into two separate patties that are grilled and topped with two slices of American cheese. Sandwiched in a buttery bun, the sumptuous sandwich is finished off with pickled onions, house-made mayo, plus a side of pickles. If that's not enough, pair it with crunchy Sweet Potatertots, a fabulous twist on the childhood favourite.

Thep Phanom

400 Waller Street, at Fillmore Street (1-415 431 2526, www.thepphanom.com). Bus 6, 22, 71. **Open** 5.30-10.30pm daily. **Main courses** $10-$17. **Map** p145 F3 ⓰ **Thai**
Be sure to book a table at Thep Phanom in advance, and once you're there, order the *tom ka gai* (coconut chicken soup) to start. The 'angel wings' (fried chicken wings stuffed with glass noodles), grilled prawns stuffed with crabmeat, and prawn and pumpkin curry are universally popular choices. After more than 25 years, chef Pat Parikanont's neighbourhood fave is still going strong, often touted as one of the top Thai restaurants in the city.

Bars

Mad Dog in the Fog

530 Haight Street, between Fillmore & Steiner Streets (1-415 626 7279, www.themaddoginthefog. com). Metro to Duboce & Church/bus 6, 7, 22, 71. **Open** 3pm-midnight Mon; 11am-2am Tue; 3pm-2am Wed-Fri; 10am-2pm Sat; 10am-midnight Sun. **Map** p145 F2 ⓰
Lower Haight is dotted with unpretentious sports bars, but Mad Dog, a great place to watch European soccer and rugby, stands above the rest. The bar is known for drawing anglophile and expat crowds as early as 5am on a weekday for big games. It's a good spot for large groups, as there are several big booths, including one that has its own self-serve beer tap. The bar is stocked with an evolving selection of over 150 different beers from across the world, while the food is straightforward with dishes like buffalo wings, bangers and mash, and hearty nachos layered with jack cheese, black beans, jalapeños, sour cream and fresh salsa. And for those early morning matches? Ask for an English breakfast.

Noc Noc

557 Haight Street, between Fillmore & Steiner Streets (1-415 861 5811, www.nocnocs.com). Metro to Duboce & Church, bus 6, 7, 22, 71. **Open** 5pm-2am daily. **Map** p145 F3 ⓱
If Dr Seuss and Trent Reznor had gone into the bar business together, this is what they'd have come up with. The decor is described as post-apocalyptic industrial, and the whole place has a peculiarly organic Gaudi feel. Always plunged in near darkness and with a mellow chill-room vibe, Noc Noc attracts an appropriately odd mix of beer and saké drinkers.

★ Toronado

547 Haight Street, between Fillmore & Steiner Streets (1-415 863 2276, www.toronado.com). Bus 6, 7, 22, 66, 71. **Open** 11.30am-2am daily. **No credit cards. Map** p145 F3 ⓲
Can a dive boast one of the best beer selections in the city? If so, this is it. You'll find the largest selection of sour beers in town, as well as a wide assortment from local breweries, most for around $5. It's a loud, dark, no-BS spot: the walls are collaged in stickers, the bathroom is covered in graffiti, and the music – usually metal or punk – is blasting overhead. The ambience, or lack thereof, weeds out girlfriend catch-up dates. Toronado regulars are here to drink (and occasionally yell at each other across the bar). For sustenance, grab a sausage from Rosamunde's next door.

Shops & Services

Idle Hand Tattoo

575 Haight Street, at Steiner Street (1-415 552 4353, www.idlehandsf.com). Bus 6, 22, 71. **Open** noon-8pm daily. **Map** p145 F3 ⓳ **Tattoos**
Hands are anything but idle here: the eclectic roster of tradition-inclined inkers includes the exceptional portrait artist (and founder) Holly Ellis. The shop's eccentric interior reflects the sensibilities of the Lower Haight neighbourhood – the walls are decorated with boar and stag heads and original illustrations of classic American tattoo motifs sketched by the staff.

Revolver

136 Fillmore Street, between Germania & Waller Streets (1-415 795 1748, www.revolveronline.com). Bus 6, 22, 71. **Open** 11am-7pm daily. **Map** p145 F3 ⓴ **Fashion**
This clothing store offers a mash-up of styles for men and women: a little bit nautical, a little bit surf, slightly buttoned-up, but with a dash of Mission plaid. If you're looking for solid basics, you'll find button-downs, henleys, wool coats, and jeans from brands like General Assembly, Alternative Apparel, Fidelity, and Scotch & Soda. But owner Robert Patterson, who also runs Voyager SF in the Mission, prides himself on importing high-quality international brands you won't find anywhere else in the city. Those looking to stretch themselves sartorially can get into printed shirts and knits by Parisian label Etudes, bomber jackets by Aussie brand Zanerobe, and Yuketen mocs and suede lace-ups by the Japanese-born Yuki Matsuda. Don't skip the tiny back room, packed with sale racks and gifts like handmade ceramics, alpaca throws and cedar saké cups.

HAYES VALLEY

Hayes Valley, just west of the Civic Center, was literally overshadowed by the Central Freeway for years. But when the 1989 earthquake irreparably damaged the roadway, its demolition transformed the area from a drug-riddled slum to perhaps the hippest urban shopping area in town. Streets that once sat under a tangle of concrete overpasses now have sidewalk cafés, local designer boutiques, galleries and even a specialist saké shop. It perhaps proved prescient that director Erich von Stroheim filmed part of his 1924 classic, *Greed*, in the neighbourhood.

The locals know how good they've got it. The community association is active here, and gets results: it has fought to keep out the chains (current score: Hayes Valley 1, Starbucks 0), won the battle to close the major Fell Street highway off-ramp, and established a tree-lined boulevard and mini-park along Octavia Street that features rotating sculpture exhibits.

It's a great neighbourhood for strolling – not just for window-shopping, but for its gorgeous Victorians and tiny alleys of shotgun cottages. During the day, **Hayes Street** gets busy with well-dressed millennials shopping for modernist furniture at **Propeller** (555 Hayes Street, 1-415 701 7767), Italian shoes at **Bulo** (*see p153*), and brunching on champagne and oysters at **Absinthe**, a belle époque French restaurant with tables that spill on to the pavement. In the evenings, the nearby **SFJAZZ Center** (201 Franklin Street, *see p223*) and performing arts venues around Opera Plaza make this a hub for pre- and post-performance dining and drinking.

Restaurants & Cafés

Absinthe

398 Hayes Street, at Gough Street (1-415 551 1590, www.absinthe.com). Metro to Van Ness/bus 5, 21, 47, 49, 90 & Market Street routes. **Open** 11.30am-midnight Mon-Fri; 11am-midnight Sat; 11am-10pm Sun. *Bar* until 2am Thur-Sat. **Main courses** $16-$32. **Map** p145 H1 ❹ **French**
The spirit of bohemian France pervades this boisterous and glamorous brasserie. Among the notable classics are an excellent coq au vin and cassoulet. Start with the seafood platter. True to its name, the bar offers genuine absinthe, along with an extensive classic cocktail menu, and the wine list of French vintages is exhaustive (four pages of Meursault selections alone). If you'd like to take some home, the owners also run Arlequin Wine Merchant (*see p153*) down the street.

Jardinière

300 Grove Street, at Franklin Street (1-415 861 5555, www.jardiniere.com). BART & Metro to Civic Center/bus 5, 21, 47, 49, 90. **Open** 5-10pm daily. **Main courses** $25-$34. **Map** p145 H1 ❷ **French**
This beautiful, whimsically designed restaurant (it's meant to resemble an overturned champagne glass) is one of the best high-dollar special-occasion establishments in the city. Located a short walk from Davies Symphony Hall and the Opera House, it delivers a menu as opulent as the decor. Chef Traci Des Jardins

continues to seek out the best local ingredients for a menu that features caviar, oysters, black truffles, duck breast confit, diver scallops, and bacon-wrapped rabbit. If you want to go all out, splurge on the the prix fixe menu with wine pairings and the cheese course. The wine list includes an extensive selection of champagne and sparkling wines.

► *Traci Des Jardins also runs Public House at AT&T Park (see p79) and the Commissary in the Presidio (see p128).*

★ Rich Table

199 Gough Street, at Oak Street (1-415 355 9085, www.richtablesf.com). Bus 6, 16X, 21, 71. **Open** 5.30-10pm Mon-Thur, Sun; 5.30-10.30pm Fri, Sat. **Main courses** $17-$33. **Map** p145 H2 ❷⓭ **American creative**
One of the most exciting new restaurants to open in the last five years, Rich Table melds San Francisco's famed farm-to-table credentials with a marvellous mélange of unique flavours and ingredients. Starters such as house-made wild fennel levain bread, delicate sardine chips with horseradish dip, and dried porcini doughnuts will make you wonder why no one thought of these dishes before. Main courses change constantly according to what's on market, ranging from pasta with Dungeness crab and sea urchin to black cod with mustard greens, mango and chanterelles. Reservations, as you'd expect, are worth their weight in gold, and can be made as far as 30 days in advance.

Suppenküche

601 Hayes Street, at Laguna Street (1-415 252 9289, www.suppenkuche.com). Bus 5, 21. **Open** 5-10pm daily. **Main courses** $12-$21. **Map** p145 G2 ❷⓬ **German**
If you're hungry for something that's going to last you all day, then Suppenküche is a good bet. Its menu, which covers *spätzle*, sausages and dense, dark breads, is authentically German, and not for the faint of belly. An impressive array of flavoursome German beers is served in tall glasses and steins; seating is on benches.

★ Zuni Café

1658 Market Street, at Rose Street (1-415 552 2522, www.zunicafe.com). Metro to Van Ness/ streetcar F/bus 6, 9, 14, 47, 49, 71, 90. **Open** 11.30am-11pm Tue-Thur; 11.30am-midnight Fri, Sat; 11am-11pm Sun. **Main courses** $29-$48. **Map** p145 H2 ❷⓮ **California**
Since it opened in 1979, Zuni has developed a dedicated following as a destination restaurant that's on a par with Berkeley's Chez Panisse. One of a handful of restaurants that helped define San Francisco's fresh, seasonal and regional style back in the 1980s, it's still considered one of the best in the city. There's simply no equal for Zuni's signature Caesar salad and brick-oven roasted chicken for two. The French-and Italian-inspired cuisine also includes a fabulous burger, fresh pasta and, at lunch, heavenly pizzettas.

EXPLORE

Biergarten.

The art-filled space comprises four separate dining rooms and can be quite a scene before and after symphony and opera events.

Bars

★ Biergarten
424 Octavia Street, between Fell & Linden Streets (www.biergartensf.com). Bus 21. **Open** *Nov-Mar* 2-8pm Wed-Sat; 1-7pm Sun. *Apr-Oct* 3-9pm Wed-Sat; 1-7pm Sun. **Map** p145 G2 ㉖
Rarely in San Francisco do you get to enjoy beer in the style to which the Germans are happily accustomed. The semi-permanent spinoff of German restaurant Suppenküche down the street, this über-hip beer garden consists of picnic tables and a bar/kitchen carved out of metal shipping containers, sidled up against the side of the SFJAZZ Center. On warm afternoons and even cool ones (the bar provides wool blankets), the young, bearded and thirsty kick back with litres of Stiegel Pils and hefeweizen and celebrate…whatever. The munchies menu provides a tasty Teutonic base for all that beer: bratwurst, burgers, potato salad and giant chewy pretzels topped with mustard and horseradish or stuffed with cheese and charcuterie.

Hotel Biron
45 Rose Street, between Market & Gough Streets (1-415 703 0403, www.hotelbiron.com). Metro to Van Ness/streetcar F/bus 6, 7, 26, 71. **Open** 5pm-2am daily. **Map** p145 G2 ㉗

This stylish yet unpretentious wine bar and gallery is named after the Hôtel Biron in Paris, which houses the Rodin Museum. The walls showcase the work of local artists; the impressive wine list boasts 80 wines by the bottle and 35 or so by the glass, plus a selection of beers and a small but appealing menu of cheeses, caviar and olives. A great low-key place for drinkers who like to talk.

Smuggler's Cove
650 Gough Street, between Ash & McCallister Streets (1-415 869 1900, www.smugglerscovesf. com). Bus 6, 47, 49, 71, 90. **Open** 5pm-1.15am daily. **Map** p145 H1 ㉘

With an extensive menu of complex cocktails and an interior worthy of a movie set, it's not hard to understand why Smuggler's Cove is one of the most lauded tiki bars in the world. Patrons plunge straight into a pirate fantasy as they gaze at the three-storey interior bedecked with a ship's bow and a waterfall. But the fanciful decor belies a sophisticated cocktail programme. The hefty drinks list showcases traditional Caribbean and speciality creations expertly mixed, shaken and blended using a stunning array of fresh ingredients – as many as a dozen in a single drink – and spirits that include seriously boozy overproof rum. Alongside the classics are lesser-known delights like the Batida (coconut cream, fresh passion fruit purée and condensed milk blended with the Brazilian sugarcane spirit cachaça. The Cove also offers a serious selection of more than 200 rums.

Shops & Services

Alla Prima Fine Lingerie
539 Hayes Street, between Laguna & Octavia Streets (1-415 864 8180, www.allaprimalingerie. com). Bus 5, 6, 21, 71. **Open** 11am-7pm Mon-Sat; noon-5pm Sun. **Map** p145 G1 ❷ **Fashion**
Known for its thorough fittings and sky-high designer prices, Alla Prima stocks everything from Eres, Andres Sarda and La Perla lingerie to sublime swimsuits and thigh-high fishnets.
Other location 1420 Grant Avenue, between Green & Union Streets, North Beach (1-415 397 4077).

Arlequin Wine Merchant
384A Hayes Street, between Franklin & Gough Streets (1-415 863 1104, www.arlequinwine merchant.com). Bus 5, 6, 21, 71. **Open** 11am-7pm Mon; 11am-8pm Tue-Sat; noon-7pm Sun. **Map** p145 H1 ❸ **Food & drink**
The owners are thoroughly unpretentious, yet savvy enough in their choice to satisfy any armchair quaffer. Taste (and then, most likely, buy) elusive domestic bottles and coveted imports, ranging from under $10 to over $200.

★ Bulo
418 Hayes Street, between Gough & Octavia Streets (1-415 255 4939, www.buloshoes.com). Bus 5, 6, 21, 71. **Open** 11am-7pm Mon-Sat; noon-6pm Sun. **Map** p145 H1 ❸ **Accessories**
Bulo is the place to go for Cydwoq sandals and boots, handmade in California, as well as oxfords from Hudson Shoes and hard-to-find European (mostly Italian) designers. Considering the quality, prices are quite reasonable. On big sale days, expect a queue. The well-honed selection also includes a nice assortment of sunglasses and handbags.

★ Fatted Calf
320 Fell Street, between Gough & Octavia Streets (1-415 400 5614, www.fattedcalf.com). Bus 16X, 21. **Open** 10am-8pm daily. **Map** p145 H2 ❷ **Food & drink**
You know you'll be in hog heaven at any place that offers a weekly Butcher's Happy Hour. On Wednesday evenings (5.30-7pm), staff butcher a whole pig, and guests get to sample all the trimmings accompanied by other small bites and wine/beer. The artisan butcher and charcuterie also offers daily sandwiches that showcase its premium salumi, roasted and smoked meats and succulent pork products.

Flight 001
525 Hayes Street, between Laguna & Octavia Streets (1-415 487 1001, www.flight001.com). Bus 5, 6, 21, 71. **Open** 11am-7pm Mon-Sat; 11am-6pm Sun. **Map** p145 G1 ❸ **Travel**
If you like to travel in style, Flight 001 is the place to go. The sleek, streamlined store sells chic contemporary jet-set accoutrements, from Japanese metal suitcases to accessories like eye masks, neck pillows and all manner of adaptors, chargers and practical gadgets.

MAC (Modern Appealing Clothing)
387 Grove Street, between Franklin & Gough Streets (1-415 863 3011, www.modernappealingclothing. com). Bus 5, 21, 47, 49, 90. **Open** 11am-7pm Mon-Sat; noon-6pm Sun. **Map** p145 H1 ❸ **Fashion**
Belgian and Japanese designers, plus some local talent, get the exposure they deserve at this brother-and sister-owned boutique that resembles a chic pied-à-terre. Men, in particular, who are willing to open their wallets wide will discover great items by Dries Van Noten, Sofie D'Hoore and Comme des Garçons.
Other location 1003 Minnesota Street, Dogpatch (1-415 285 2805).

★ Reliquary
544 Hayes Street, between Laguna & Octavia Streets (1-415 431 4000, www.reliquarysf.com). Bus 5, 21. **Open** 11am-7pm Mon-Sat; noon-6pm Sun. **Map** p145 G1 ❸ **Accessories/fashion**
Leah Bershad's boutique is stocked with a mix of effortlessly cool clothing (Bay Area brand CP Shades and California-born Creatures of Comfort are mainstays) and accessories for men and women. But jewellery is the real highlight. Bershad travels around the world to find antique and vintage pieces; the eclectic stash encompasses glittering cocktail rings and cameo necklaces from the Victorian and Edwardian periods, offbeat charms, chunky skull rings and turquoise. Contemporary collections are here too, including Kate Jones's Ursa Major label and Polly Wales.

True Sake
560 Hayes Street, between Laguna & Octavia Streets, Hayes Valley (1-415 355 9555, www.true sake.com). Bus 5, 6, 21, 71. **Open** noon-7pm Mon-Fri; 11am-7pm Sat; noon-6pm Sun. **Map** p145 G1 ❸ **Food & drink**
A beautiful and elegant place, this is the first US shop devoted entirely to saké. Owner Beau Timken is every bit as helpful and knowledgeable about the rice-fermented beverage as you might hope, even suggesting food pairings for your purchase.

Welcome Stranger
460 Gough Street, at Ivy Street (1-415 864 2079, www.welcomestranger.com). Bus 5, 16X, 21. **Open** 11am-7pm daily. **Map** p145 H1 ❸ **Fashion**
If Unionmade is the gold standard for the stylish SF guy, Welcome Stranger is a little more rugged. It's a store for the outdoorsy guy who wants to look put-together, but not like he's trying too hard. The clothes are scattered among vintage trunks and camping equipment, adding to the urban woodsman feel. The emphasis is on fit and functionality, with finds like Jungmaven T-shirts, APC jeans, Zig-Zag shoes and Barbour waxed canvas jackets. The store clerks are unobtrusive, but knowledgeable about fabric, fit and styling.

EXPLORE

The Mission & the Castro

The heady cultural mix of the Mission, the Castro and Noe Valley makes for a uniquely San Franciscan melting pot. The Mission is the centre of Latin/hipster life, while the Castro is the historically gay hub in what many consider the gayest city on earth. Here, rainbow-swathed muscle-shirt boutiques rub shoulders with beautifully renovated Victorian homes, and pristine temples to gastronomy give way to bare-bones joints serving burritos the size of a baby's arm. These close-knit enclaves of all things queer, yuppie, hip and Latino provide a colourful snapshot of the city's remarkably diverse charm.

On the slopes of Potrero Hill, art galleries and design houses mingle with cosy cafés and boutique shops, while at the bottom of the hill to the east, creative do-it-yourselfers have taken up residence in the sunny nooks and crannies of formerly industrial Dogpatch.

EXPLORE

Don't Miss

1 **Mission Dolores** The simple church that gave the nabe its name (p157).

2 **Tartine Bakery** In a city obsessed with bakeries, this takes the cake (p164).

3 **Paxton Gate** Browse natural curiosities, taxidermy and gardening supplies (p168).

4 **Mission murals** Tour an open-air museum of eye-popping street art (p162).

5 **Sightglass Coffee** A hub for java purists (p164).

Mission murals

THE MISSION

First settled by the Spanish in the 1770s and later home to Irish, German, Italian and Asian immigrants, the Mission today is a not-always-harmonious confluence of Latin and tech culture. The once-steady influx of families and workers from Mexico and South and Central America lent the neighbourhood its distinctive character, especially on **Mission Street** between 14th and Cesar Chavez Streets. Here, cheque-cashing operations, bargain shops, taco stands and grocery stores (selling such exotica as sugar cane and prickly pears) conduct brisk business, while Banda (the Mexican music descended from the oompah bands of German immigrants) drifts out of open doors and windows. In a few places, the narrow, crowded sidewalks seem like a scene straight out of Guadalajara; it's especially atmospheric in autumn, when Mexican-run shops and art galleries fill with traditional ghoulish items in advance of Dia de los Muertos (Day of the Dead) in November. Note, however, that the neighbourhood can feel a little shady east of Mission Street in the inner Mission, particularly north of 19th Street and its environs, which still has its share of drug addicts and gangs.

Tourist buses tend to limit their explorations to the admittedly fascinating Mission Dolores, but there are other worthwhile stops. On Mission Street, the **Mission Cultural Center** (no.2868, at 25th Street, 1-415 821 1155, www.missionculturalcenter. org) contains a theatre and a gallery displaying works by under-the-radar artists. The nearby **Precita Eyes Mural Arts & Visitors Center** (*see p162* **Painting the Town**) offers weekend guided walks of the district's 200-plus murals.

At this juncture it's important to acknowledge the centrality of food to the Mission experience. It's one of the area's main attractions, and no discussion of Mission food would be complete without mentioning the mythical creation that is the Mission Burrito: a glory to behold, this steamed tortilla is an object of fanatical devotion. Packed with meat, cheese, beans, guacamole, spicy salsa, and often rice, it has become as ingrained in San Francisco culture as sourdough and artisanal coffee. Fast, cheap and portable, it takes under five minutes to prepare and costs about $8. Needless to say, competition is fierce. Some of the area's best are **La Taqueria** (2889 Mission Street, 1-415 285 7117), **Taqueria Cancun** (2288 Mission Street, 1-415 252 9560) and the place that lays claim to creating the original Mission burrito, **Taqueria La Cumbre** (515 Valencia Street, 1-415 863 8205). At **Pancho Villa** (3071 16th Street, at Valencia Street, 1-415 864 8840, www.sfpanchovilla.com), rocker Beck has been spotted sitting in for the *taqueria*'s regular serenading mariachi.

While Mission Street retains a Latino feel, most of the storefronts on **Valencia Street**, parallel to

Mission and just two blocks west, have been taken over by well-paid boho types, who dine on gourmet pizzettas, drink pour-overs in cult coffee shops, fill seats at the art-house **Roxie Theater** (3117 16th Street; *see p198*), and tip hand-muddled cocktails while listening to alternative avant-garde music at the **Chapel** (777 Valencia Street; *see p217*).

The strip is also lined with boutiques, with nary a chain store in sight. Bibliophiles can browse at **Dog-Eared Books** (no.900; *see p167*), among other bookstores, while **Aquarius Records** (no.1055; *see p167*) satisfies the area's vinyl junkies. Local designers also have a presence here, at shops such as **Dema** (no.1038; *see p167*), while at **Paxton Gate** (no.824; *see p168*), a cadre of creative landscapers and taxidermists sells gardening equipment and stuffed vampire mice. However, the most notable commercial landmark is the **Pirate Supply Store** at 826 Valencia (*see p168*). It's said that owner Dave Eggers, bestselling author and the brains behind publishing house McSweeny's, opened the shop to meet a commercial storefront zoning code: in reality, its main purpose is to support the centre for young writers located inside.

Although gentrification has largely displaced the neighbourhood's early adopters – the artists and musicians who were ensconced there for decades before skyrocketing rents forced them to find cheaper digs – its arty reputation is still evident in the numerous galleries and performance stages on Valencia Street or just off it. The **Women's Building** (3543 18th

Mission Dolores.

Street, between Valencia & Guerrero Streets, 1-415 431 1180, www.womensbuilding.org) is home to a dozen feminist non-profit groups. Meanwhile, three groups on Valencia Street – **Artists' Television Access** (no.992, 1-415 824 3890, www.atasite.org), the **Marsh** (no.1062; *see p232*) and **Intersection for the Arts** (no.446, 1-415 626 2787, www.theintersection.org) – offer a forum and mentoring for genre-smashing filmmakers, actors, playwrights, artists and musicians.

A walk along 16th will lead you to the building that gave the city its name: the 225-year-old Misión San Francisco de Asís, better known as **Mission Dolores**. Just south of here, bordered by Dolores, Church, 18th and 20th Streets, is the recently renovated **Dolores Park**, a bastion for sunbathers, tennis players, and kids who play on the creatively revamped playground. Summer and autumn evenings also offer free film screenings.

Sights & Museums

★ **Mission Dolores**

3321 16th Street, at Dolores Street (1-415 621 8203, www.missiondolores.org). BART to 16th Street/Metro J to Church/bus 22, 33. **Open** 9am-5pm daily. **Admission** $3-$5. **No credit cards. Map** p158 B2 ❶
Founded by a tiny band of Spanish missionaries and soldiers in 1776, and completed 15 years later, Mission Dolores is the oldest structure in the city and San Francisco's Registered Landmark No.1.

The building was originally called the Misión San Francisco de Asís (after St Francis of Assisi), and provided the town with its name. However, it takes its common name from Laguna de los Dolores, the long-gone lagoon on the shores of which it was allegedly built. Although the original mission became an expansive outpost, housing more than 4,000 monks and converts, today only the tiny old church remains. The adobe structure, constructed from 16,000 earthen bricks and four feet thick (a display at the back offers a peek inside the walls), survived the 1906 and 1989 earthquakes unscathed, while the new church next door crumbled. Small wonder that the cool, dim interior looks and feels authentic: almost everything about it is unreconstructed and original, from the redwood logs holding up the roof to the ornate altars brought from Mexico centuries ago. (The modern-day church next door is a 20th-century basilica with no real architectural significance; it does, however, handle all the mission's religious services.) A small museum on the mission premises offers volunteer-led tours. The picturesque, flower-filled cemetery contains the remains of California's first governor and the city's first mayor, as well as assorted Spanish settlers and the mass grave of 5,000 Costanoan Indians who died in their service. Film buffs may recall that in Hitchcock's *Vertigo*, an entranced Kim Novak led Jimmy Stewart to the gravestone of the mysterious Carlotta Valdes in this very cemetery. You won't find Carlotta's stone, though: it was a prop and was removed after filming.
▶ *For more about the founding of Mission Dolores, see p254.*

EXPLORE

Restaurants & Cafés

Aster

1001 Guerrero Street, at 22nd Street (1-415 875 9810, www.astersf.com). **Open** 5.30-10pm Mon-Thur, Sun; 5.30-10.30pm Fri, Sat. **Main courses** $23-$27. **Map** p158 C4 ❷ **California**

Chef-owner Brett Cooper earned his stripes under acclaimed chefs Stuart Brioza (State Bird Provisions), Daniel Patterson (Coi), and Josh Skenes (Saison), before branching out on his own to open Aster. Farm-to-table Northern California food to its core, Cooper marries heirloom grains, heritage meats, and hand-picked produce for unusual combinations: pork shoulder with sweet potato and rhubarb, milk-fed lamb with smoked eggplant, and potato-nettle dumplings with maitake and peas. Everything is made on the premises, down to the house-churned butter.

$ Atlas Café

3049 20th Street, at Alabama Street (1-415 648 1047, www.atlascafe.net). Bus 9, 12, 27, 33, 90. **Open** 6.30am-10pm Mon-Fri; 8am-10pm Sat; 8am-8pm Sun. **Main courses** $7-$10. **No credit cards.** **Map** p159 E3 ❸ **Café**

This comfortable, popular café is one of the outer Mission's best hangouts, with people lining up for fresh breakfast pastries in the morning, and settling into lattes for the afternoon and even California microbrews in the evening. A daily list of grilled sandwiches includes many vegetarian varieties (try the beet loaf), and is supplemented by soups, salads and pizza. The atmosphere is enhanced by live music (usually bluegrass and jazz) on Thursday and Friday evenings. On warm days, try to snag a sunny seat on the patio at the back (where dogs are allowed).

EXPLORE

Bar Tartine

*561 Valencia Street, between 16th & 17th Streets
(1-415 487 1600, www.bartartine.com). BART to
16th Street Mission/bus 22, 23.* **Open** 5.30-10pm
Mon-Thur, Sun; 5.30-10pm Fri, Sat. **Main courses**
$15-$29. **Map** p158 C2 ❹ **American creative**
At the restaurant arm of Liz Pruiett's and Chad
Robertson's revered Tartine bakery, co-chefs Nick
Balla and Cortney Burns give a Japanese and occasional Eastern European spin to dishes like sausage
with squash and burr gherkins, and pork belly with
shishito peppers. The menu capitalises on fresh,
local ingredients pickled, fermented and aged in-
house, served with amazing breads from the bakery.

Beretta

*1199 Valencia Street, at 23rd Street (1-415 695
1199, www.berettasf.com). BART to 24th Street
Mission/bus 12, 14, 48, 49, 67.* **Open** 5.30pm-1am
Mon-Fri; 11am-1am Sat, Sun. **Main courses** $17-
$22. **Map** p158 C4 ❺ **Italian & pizza**
Creative cocktails are on equal footing with the
food menu at this smart, stylish southern Italian
eatery, where a hip crowd squeezes in and min-
gles over concoctions such as the nuestra paloma
(tequila, elderflower, cointreau, grapefruit and
bitters) while sampling a wide array of antipasti;
the selection might include eggplant caponatina
with burrata; crescenza and broccoli rabe brus-
chetta; or Dungeness crab arancini. Anchoring the
main courses are perfectly fired thin-crust pizzas
topped with a variety of seasonal ingredients,
and there is also a selection of risottos and a
nightly meat or seafood special, such as cioppino
or manzo short ribs.
▶ *The same team runs Starbelly, see p171.*

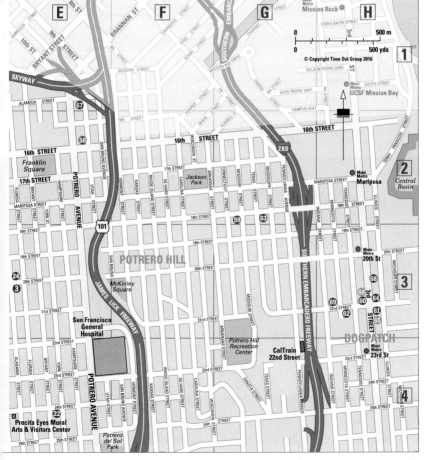

$ Bi-Rite Creamery & Bakeshop

3692 18th Street, between Dolores & Guerrero Streets (1-415 626 5600, www.biritecreamery.com/icecream). Metro to Church & 18th Street. **Open** 11am-10pm Mon-Thur, Sun; 11am-11pm Fri, Sat. **Ice-cream** $4.50-$8.50. **Map** p158 B3 ❻ Ice-cream

Bi-Rite's creamy salted-caramel ice-cream launched the craze for this heavenly pairing in San Francisco, and it's still the bar that all others strive to reach. Since then, it has introduced other taste sensations that have garnered cult followings, among them balsamic strawberry, brown sugar with ginger caramel swirl, honey lavender, basil and ricanelas (cinnamon with snickerdoodle cookies). Next door, the Bakeshop features house-made cupcakes, cookies and seasonal sweets. The Creamery is the offshoot of the gourmet Bi-Rite Market down the street, so if the line is too long, you can always opt for a pint or a quart from the store.

$ Craftsman and Wolves

746 Valencia Street, between 18th & 19th Streets (1-415 913 7713, www.craftsman-wolves.com). BART to 16th Street Mission/bus 14, 22, 33. **Open** 7am-7pm Mon-Thur; 7am-8pm Fri; 8am-8pm Sat; 8am-7pm Sun. **Baked goods** $4-$12. **Map** p158 C3 ❼ Bakery/café

This Mission District hotspot is among a new wave of café/bakeries that eschew comfy sofas and crumb-laden tables in favour of a minimalist style that puts the focus firmly on what's behind the counter and in the display cases. The self-described 'contemporary patisserie' offers a beautifully curated selection of sweet and savoury treats, from muscovado morning buns and exquisite little cube cakes made with chocolate and blood orange to the signature Rebel Within – a soft-cooked egg inside a muffin made with asiago, green onion and Boccalone sausage.

Delfina

3621 18th Street, between Dolores & Guerrero Streets (1-415 552 4055, www.delfinasf.com). BART to 16th Street Mission/Metro to Church & 18th Street/bus 14, 22, 33, 49. **Open** 5.30-10pm Mon-Thur; 5.30-11pm Fri, Sat; 5-10pm Sun. **Main courses** $10-$30. **Map** p158 C3 ❽ Italian

Chef/owner Craig Stoll favours simplicity over whimsy, and tradition over fashion. Yet his food is never ordinary: fresh pasta, fish and braised meats find the perfect balance of flair and flavour. The menu changes daily, reflecting Stoll's desire to stay on his toes. Recent standouts include garganelli pasta with liberty duck ragù and pancetta-wrapped rabbit saddle. Stoll's casual Pizzeria Delfina (1-415 437-6800) is next door, serving some of the best thin-crust pizzas in town. The Clam Pie with cherrystone clams and hot peppers is a perennial favourite.

Dosa on Valencia

995 Valencia Street, at 21st Street (1-415 642 3672, www.dosasf.com). Bus 2, 3, 22, 92. **Open** 5.30-10pm Mon-Wed; 5.30-11pm Thur; 5.30pm-midnight Fri; 11.30am-3.30pm, 5.30pm-midnight Sat; 11.30am-3.30pm, 5.30-10pm Sun. **Main courses** $10-$25. **Map** p158 C3 ❾ Indian

Thin rice and lentil crêpes and flatbreads (dosas and uttapams) stuffed and topped with everything from sweet potatoes and chickpea masala to spicy potatoes, fennel and spinach are the focus of this southern Indian eatery. In addition to dosas, the restaurant offers a wide array of chaat, small plates and curries.

Other location 1700 Fillmore Street, at Post Street, Fillmore District (1-415 441 3672).

★ Flour + Water

2401 Harrison Street, at 20th Street (1-415 826 7000, www.flourandwater.com). Bus 12, 14, 14L, 27. **Open** 5.30-11pm Mon-Wed, Sun; 5.30pm-midnight Thur-Sat. **Main courses** $16-$32. **Map** p158 D3 ⑩ **Italian & pizza**
As the name suggests, flour and water are the two main ingredients here, but what the kitchen does with them is nothing short of art. Pastas are slavishly nurtured to melt-in-your-mouth perfection; super-thin pizzas emerge exquisitely blistered from the 900-degree Italian wood-fired oven; salumi (from whole animals butchered on site) turns up in everything from pork trotters to prosciutto-wrapped petrale sole. The menu also includes two to three meat, poultry and fish options. Reservations are notoriously hard to come by, so book as far in advance as you can. Or get there at 5.30pm and try for one of the walk-in spots.

★ Foreign Cinema

2534 Mission Street, between 21st & 22nd Streets (1-415 648 7600, www.foreigncinema.com). BART

Flour + Water.

to 24th Street Mission/bus 12, 14, 48, 49, 67. **Open** 6-10pm Mon-Thur; 5.30-11pm Fri; 11am-11pm Sat; 11am-10pm Sun. *Bar & gallery* until 2am daily. **Main courses** $25-$39. **Map** p158 D3 ⑪ **Mediterranean**
Opened in 1999, Foreign Cinema is now something of a venerable elder on the Mission hipster scene. But thanks to chef/owners Gayle Pirie and John Clark it's not showing its age; we think the restaurant has improved over time. The interior features an open-air courtyard where classic foreign films are screened against the back wall (there are tableside speakers for those who want to listen). But the focus is still the exceptional food, a seasonal selection of locally interpreted Mediterranean dishes such as lamb mixed grill with couscous, chickpea and lentil tagine, house-cured anchovies, and more than 20 varieties of oysters. At the hugely popular brunch, the organic fruit 'pop tarts' are a must. Or stop by for happy hour at the cool adjacent bar, Laszlo.

$ Gracias Madre

2211 Mission Street, at 18th Street (1-415 683 1346, www.gracias-madre.com). BART to 16th Street Mission/bus 14, 33, 49. **Open** 11am-11pm daily. **Main courses** $8-$16. **Map** p158 C3 ⑫ **Mexican/vegetarian**
Mexican and vegan are not terms you would expect to sidle up to each other in a restaurant concept, but Gracias Madre has not only married the ideas, it's done so with spectacular success. Antojitos (street food-inspired starter snacks) such as grilled potato-masa gorditas topped with salsa verde and cashew cream, and sweet potato and caramelised onion quesadillas topped with cashew cheese and pumpkin-seed salsa, are full of piquant flavour and meaty textures, and don't suffer in the least from their lack of animal ingredients. Main plates such as nopales (prickly pear cactus) topped with pico de gallo and cashew cheese, accompanied by black beans, rice and handmade tortillas, and an heirloom masa tamale stuffed with seasonal veggies, will leave you satisfied and possibly rethinking your preconceived notions of vegan food. Desserts are also excellent, especially the peach cobbler.

Hog & Rocks

3431 19th Street, at San Carlos Street (1-415 550 8627, www.hogandrocks.com). BART to 16th Street Mission/Metro to Church & 18th Street/ bus 14, 22, 33, 49. **Open** 5-11pm Mon-Thur; 5pm-1am Fri; 11am-2.30pm, 5pm-1am Sat; 11am-2.30pm, 5-11pm Sun. **Main courses** $12-$27. **Map** p158 C3 ⑬ **Gastropub**
The unlikely pairing of ham and oysters (clearly not for the kosher) has been a hit in this comfortable-chic hobnobbing gastropub. Neighbourhood denizens belly up to the bar or tall communal tables for classic cocktails, plates of cured pork – Serrano, prosciutto and more – and bivalves from California and beyond. There is also

EXPLORE

PAINTING THE TOWN

The famous Mission murals mix Latino culture with political activism.

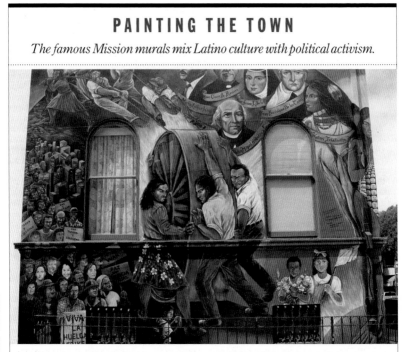

San Francisco's tradition of public art – both officially sanctioned and otherwise – has made the city a grand canvas, with works that adorn façades, plazas, alleyways and the exterior walls of burrito joints. The Mission District is as vibrantly illustrated as many of the tattooed residents who live and work among over 90 documented murals and hundreds of others.

A blend of Mexican, Cuban, Salvadoran, Guatemalan and American culture, 24th Street east of Mission Street is awash with public art – even the local McDonald's on the corner of Mission and 24th has a Technicolor coat. In the vicinity, world-class painters have created staggeringly complex pieces at a scale (sometimes covering entire three-storey buildings) that is meant to be both examined in detail and admired from afar. The vivid displays are largely thanks to the vision of one woman, Susan Cervantes, founder of **Precita Eyes Mural Arts & Visitors Center** (2981 24th Street, at Harrison Street, 1-415 285 2287, www.precitaeyes.org), which has mentored mural artists since 1997. The centre has a shop that carries maps, decorated T-shirts and postcards. Precita Eyes also runs walking tours every Saturday and Sunday at 11am and 1.30pm ($20); private tours are available by appointment.

If you can't take the tour, be sure to check out the murals along Balmy Alley, between 24th & 25th Streets, and Treat & Harrison Streets. These hark back to the mid 1980s, when the community was expressing outrage over human rights abuses in Central America. On 24th Street, at the corner of Florida Street, *500 Years of Resistance* by El Salvador muralist Isaias Mata honours the local migrant community. Although its message never faded, its colours did; the artist returned to restore it to its original glory in 2013.

Further north on Clarion Alley (between 17th & 18th Streets, and Mission & Valencia Streets), murals boil with social activism, commenting on everything from corporate takeovers to prison policies. Around the corner at 3543 18th Street, the Women's Building's *MaestraPeace* mural is a work of monumental scope by seven female artists including Susan Cervantes, Miranda Bergman and Juana Alicia. Covering some 12,000 square feet, it includes figures and images representing cultures, achievements and belief systems of women throughout history and around the world.

a lavish brunch, very good fish and chips and other dishes, but the mingling crowd gravitates towards the well-mixed manhattans and mai tais.

$ Humphry Slocombe

2790A Harrison Street, at 24th Street (1-415 550 6971, www.humphryslocombe.com). Bus 12, 27, 48, 67. **Open** noon-9pm Mon-Thur, Sun; noon-10pm Fri, Sat. **Ice-cream** $4-$9. **Map** p158 D4 ❹ **Ice-cream**

Humphry Slocombe caters to a decidedly grown-up crowd of ice-cream aficionados, with intriguing sweet-savoury flavour combos that occasionally sound dubious, but taste fabulous. Popular choices on the constantly changing menu include Secret Breakfast, made with a base of anglaise ice-cream, mixed with bourbon and corn flake cookies; pink grapefruit tarragon; Blue Bottle Vietnamese coffee; Russian Imperial Stout and Limoncello. The Mission District location is the main shop, but there's a small outlet at the Ferry Building Marketplace.

$ La Taqueria

2889 Mission Street, at 25th Street (1-415 285 7117). BART to 24th Street Mission/bus 12, 14, 48, 49, 67. **Open** 11am-9pm Mon-Sat; 11am-8pm Sun. **Main courses** $3.75-$9.20. **Map** p158 D4 ❺ **Mexican**

The Mission burrito, as iconic to San Francisco as fog and cable cars, is the star at La Taqueria, a stalwart of the district for more than 40 years. How great is it? Statistics guru Nate Silver recently analysed data from 67,391 restaurants to crown it the best burrito in America. While some quibble over the exclusion of rice, no one argues over the tastiness of these behemoth foil-wrapped bombs, filled with beans, cheese, salsa and meats ranging from carne and pollo asada to carnitas, chorizo and lengua. The tidy no-frills spot also features tacos, quesadillas and a full selection of aguas frescas. Whatever your preference, start off with a basket of chips and the super-fresh guacamole.

$ Lers Ros

3189 16th Street, at Guerrero Street (1-415 638 6909, www.lersros.com). BART to 16th Street Mission/bus 14, 22, 33, 49. **Open** 11.30am-10pm Mon-Thur, Sun; 11.30am-11pm Fri, Sat. **Main courses** $10-$15. **Map** p158 C2 ❻ **Thai**

Don't let the hard-to-pronounce name (something approximating Lairt Rot, but with soft Ts) or the six-page menu deter you from trying owner-chef Tom Silargorn's take on Thai cuisine. Traditional curries, stir-fries and pad thai noodle dishes get original spins here in dishes such as Pad Kra Prow Moo Krob (pan-fried noodles with crispy pork belly), garlic and pepper rabbit, shredded green papaya salad with salted eggs, and Lers Ros's signature duck *larb* – a salad of roast duck, red onions and lettuce wedges seasoned with chilli, herbs and tangy-salty lime dressing.

Other locations 730 Larkin Street, between Ellis & O'Farrell Streets, Tenderloin (1-415 931 6917); 307 Hayes Street, between Franklin & Gough Streets, Hayes Valley (1-415 874 9661).

Limón

524 Valencia Street, at 16th Street (1-415 252 0918, www.limonrotisserie.com). BART to 16th Street Mission/bus 14, 22, 33, 49. **Open** noon-10pm Mon-Thur, Sun; noon-10.30pm Fri, Sat. **Main courses** $11-$30. **Map** p158 C2 ❼ **Peruvian**

One of a handful of local eateries specialising in Peruvian food, this chic, packed, low-lit hotspot serves a culture-bending menu of traditional dishes creatively infused with influences ranging from China and Japan to Spain and Africa. Dishes such as crispy ceviche (petrale sole and yucca with a shot of leche de tigre) and lomo saltado (beef stir-fried with french fries, tomatoes and onions) are popular, but it's the rotisserie chicken that's made Limón a household name – marinated and slowly roasted over an open flame to a garlicky, lemony goodness.

$ Mission Pie

2901 Mission Street, at 25th Street (1-415 282 4743, www.missionpie.com). BART to 24th Street Mission/bus 14, 49. **Open** 7am-2pm Mon; 7am-10pm Tue-Fri; 8am-10pm Sat; 9am-10pm Sun. **Pies** $4 slice, $22 whole. **Map** p158 D4 ❽ **Café**

Wholesome, handmade pies – from strawberry-rhubarb to banana cream – and fresh-brewed fair-trade coffee are turned out by local youth, who gain valuable work skills and learn about sustainable farming practices. The feel-good atmosphere seems to be baked right into the sweet and savoury treats, tempting you to linger in this homey coffee shop.

$ Philz Coffee

3101 24th Street, at Folsom Street (1-415 875 9370, www.philzcoffee.com). BART to 24th Street Mission/bus 12. **Open** 6am-8.30pm Mon-Fri; 6.30am-8.30pm Sat, Sun. **Coffee** most $3. **Map** p158 D4 ❾ **Café**

If drip is your thing, your best cup of coffee is at Philz, where more than 20 different secret blends known only to founder Phil Jaber and his son, Jacob, are individually filter-drip brewed and poured to your exact specifications. The original café on Folsom and 24th Street that opened in 2003 has since been augmented with nine city locations, plus more sprinkled throughout the North, East and South Bays. The formula remains the same: walk up to the bar and the barista will help you choose a blend that they think you'll like, watch it being made, then add milk and sugar to taste. Local favourite blends include nutty Jacob's Wonderbar, rich Mocha Tesora, and the ultra-strong Code 33, crafted for the SFPD.

Other locations throughout the city.

EXPLORE

Range

842 Valencia Street, between 19th & 20th Streets (1-415 282 8283, www.rangesf.com). BART to 16th Street Mission/Metro to Church & 24th Street/ bus 14, 33, 49. **Open** 6-10pm Tue-Thur; 5.30-11pm Fri-Sun. **Main courses** $27-$38. **Map** p158 C3 ㉓ **American**

Range is consistently rated among San Francisco's best restaurants, and for good reason: the concise and constantly changing menu never fails to have something on it that you really want to eat – egg noodle pasta with roasted sweet tomatoes and goat's milk ricotta, or coffee-rubbed pork shoulder with creamy hominy and collard greens, for example. For dessert, the goat's cheesecake with spiced pecan spelt shortbread and lemon curd is everything you'd expect.

Ritual Roasters

1026 Valencia Street, between 21st & Hill Streets (1-415 641 1011, www.ritualroasters.com). BART to 24th Street Mission/bus 14, 49. **Open** 6am-8pm Mon-Thur; 6am-10pm Fri; 7am-10pm Sat; 7am-8pm Sun. **Map** p158 C3 ㉑ **Café**
See p174 **Grounds Control**.

$ St Francis Fountain

2801 24th Street, at York Street (1-415 826 4210, www.stfrancisfountainsf.com). Bus 9, 10, 27, 33, 48, 90. **Open** 8am-3pm Mon-Fri; 8am-4pm Sat, Sun. **Sandwiches** $7-$10.50. **Map** p159 E4 ㉒ **Café**

An almost classical link from old Mission to new, this ancient soda fountain has been given a new lease of life in recent years thanks to the attention lavished on it by new owners a few years back. The menu offers a few nods to the 21st century, but it's mainly a wonderfully retro experience, from the Formica tabletops to the magnificent mac and cheese and ice-cream sodas.

St Vincent

1270 Valencia Street, at 24th Street (1-415 285 1200, www.stvincentsf.com). Bus 12, 48, 67. **Open** 6-10pm Mon-Thur; 6-11pm Fri, Sat. **Main courses** $26-$29. **Map** p158 C4 ㉓ **American**

Sommelier extraordinaire David Lynch's first foray as a restaurateur, St Vincent offers big, bold flavours that tantalise the palate – and we're not just talking about wine selections. Dishes such as charred chicken wings with sansho pepper and rockfish with gigante beans, chorizo, clams and padrón peppers are carefully paired to complement the deep and detailed wine list. And all bottles are also available for sale to take with you.

★ $ Sightglass Coffee

3014 20th Street, between Alabama & Florida Streets (1-415 861 1313, www.sightglasscoffee. com). Bus 12, 27. **Open** 7am-7pm Mon-Sat; 8am-7pm Sun. **Map** p159 E3 ㉔ **Café**

Brothers Jerad and Justin Morrison are perfectionists who oversee every detail that goes into a cup of their single-origin tiny-production coffee. From sourcing green coffee at farms from Rwanda to Ethiopia and Peru, to painstakingly determining the correct roast for each batch of beans and perfecting the process on their 1969 five-kilo Probat roaster, no bean goes unturned. The love of coffee shines all the way through to the warm woody ambience of their cafés and the foam hearts on the top of your creamy cappuccino.
Other location 270 7th Street, between Folsom & Howard Streets, SoMa (1-415 861 1313).

$ Tacolicious

741 Valencia Street, between 18th & 19th Streets (1-415 626 1344, www.tacolicious.com). Bus 14, 33, 49. **Open** 11.30am-midnight daily. **Main courses** $4-$15. **Map** p158 C3 ㉕ **Mexican**

Tacolicious sits on a block that's at the heart of the Mission gentrification, bridging the gap between the old Hispanic district and the young tech hub. Here, traditional Mexican street food – tacos, enchiladas, sopes, tostadas – is interpreted with local, seasonal and supremely fresh ingredients. Sit at one of the tall tables, belly up to the bar, or bask under Paul Madonna's cityscape mural on the patio in the company of bearded hipsters discussing their latest DIY projects. Whether you order albacore tuna tostadas with crispy leeks and chipotle mayo, or one of a dozen taco offerings like guajillo-braised beef short ribs, all come with three kinds of salsa (the habanero with turmeric and rice vinegar may require one of the 100 speciality tequilas to cool you down).

★ $ Tartine Bakery

600 Guerrero Street at 18th Street (1-415 487 2600, www.tartinebakery.com). BART to 16th Street Mission/Metro to Church & 18th Street/ bus 14, 22, 33, 49. **Open** 8am-7pm Mon; 7.30am-7pm Tue, Wed; 7.30am-8pm Thur, Fri; 8am-8pm Sat; 9am-8pm Sun. **Sandwiches** $13-$15. **Map** p158 C3 ㉖ **Bakery/café**

If there's such a thing as baking royalty, Chad Robertson and Liz Pruiett are it. The husband/wife team has won awards and accolades from nearly every critic and baker in the country. The couple's quintessentially French and quintessentially local bakery, Tartine, turns out heavenly country bread – locals line up around the block when the loaves emerge from the ovens after 4.30pm. Other delectable creations include perfect croissants, fresh fruit bread puddings, frangipane tarts, lemon meringue cakes and morning buns to make you weep. The hot-pressed sandwiches include glorious, globe-trotting variations on grilled cheese and croque-monsieur.

$ Wise Sons Delicatessen

3150 24th Street, at Shotwell Street (1-415 787 3354, www.wisesonsdeli.com). Bus 12, 48, 67. **Open** 8am-9pm Mon-Sat; 9am-3pm Sun. **Main courses** $9.75-$14.50. **Map** p158 D4 ㉗ **American**

Tacolicious.

For all San Francisco's multicultural culinary chops, the city has never successfully done Jewish deli. All that changed in 2012 with the opening of Wise Sons. Evan Bloom and Leo Beckerman have not only nailed it, but done so in a uniquely Northern California way with reinterpreted classics such as house-smoked pastrami on rye with handmade pickles, just-salty-enough chopped liver, and rich, veggie-filled matzo ball soup (self-deprecatingly described as 'not as good as your bubbe's'). The amazing burger, made with a mix of ground chuck and pastrami, is schmeared with beet-horseradish spread and served on a challah bun.

Bars

20 Spot

3565 20th Street, at Lexington Street (1-415 624 3140, www.20spot.com). BART to 16th or 24th Street Mission/bus 14, 22, 33. **Open** 5pm-midnight Mon-Thur; 5pm-1am Fri, Sat. **Map** p158 C3 ㉓

In an old record store that's been converted into a Don Draper-worthy den (down to the hand-curated vintage vinyl soundtrack), tiny 20 Spot is perfectly positioned between wine bar and restaurant. Owner Bodhi Freedom offers a wine list that's heavy on Pinots and Rieslings, and a menu that manages to create intricate, innovative dishes – king trumpet mushrooms and sunchokes in cheese sauce, pork belly barbecue, potted crab – all without a stove (meat is cooked sous vide). If you only want a glass and a small bite, don't miss the Della Fattoria bread plate with housemade butter or the devilled eggs with trout roe. Food is served until 11pm – a rarity in this town.

★ ABV

3174 16th Street, between Albion & Guerrero Streets (1-415 400 4748, www.abvsf.com). BART to 16th Street Mission. **Open** 2pm-2am Mon-Fri; 11am-2am Sat, Sun. **Map** p158 C2 ㉙

Cocktail luminaries Ryan Fitzgerald and Todd Smith, who helped kick off the drinks programme at Bourbon and Branch in the noughties, bring a subtle and well-balanced approach to simple but elegant, three- or four-ingredient drinks at this narrow bar. The design of the sophisticated spot incorporates recycled materials, including charming gin-bottles-turned-candle-holders, corroded mirrors fashioned into shimmering chandeliers and a reclaimed-wood bar. Standout tipples include the smooth and smoky Whisky in Church (scotch, oloroso sherry, maple-smoked pear bitters) and the refreshing, slightly bubbly Tarragon Collins (gin, lemon, tarragon and soda). To go with the cocktails are rich bites, such as the mapo 'sloppy joes' made of tangy pork stuffed into fluffy white Chinese bread, cheese boards, kimchi fritters and trays of pickled seasonal vegetables.

Doc's Clock

2575 Mission Street, between 21st & 22nd Streets (1-415 824 3627, www.docsclock.com).

EXPLORE

BART to 24th Street Mission/bus 12, 14, 26, 48, 49, 67. **Open** 5pm-2am Mon-Thur; 4pm-2am Fri, Sat; 3pm-2am Sun. **No credit cards**. **Map** p158 D3 ③⓪

Like many Mission dives, this place has had a makeover – the mahogany bar has been buffed up, the booze selection expanded, and the CD-changer now spits out anything from Air to Sufjan Stevens. Down the road is the similarly revamped Mission Bar (2695 Mission Street, 1-415 647 2300), which lacks both the shuffleboard table and the magnificent neon sign of Doc's, but has a great jukebox and adds some of the area's strongest drinks.

El Techo de Lolinada

2518 Mission Street, between 21st & 22nd Streets (1-415 550 6970, www.eltechosf.com). BART to 24th Street Mission/bus 12, 14, 48, 49, 67. **Open** 4-11pm Mon-Thur; 4pm-1am Fri; 11am-1am Sat; 11am-11pm Sun. **Map** p158 C3 ③①

Stunning views of San Francisco that sweep from Mission Street all the way to the Bay, complex tequila cocktails and well-seasoned plates of Latin American food make this spacious rooftop bar above Lolinda steakhouse the perfect weekend afternoon or late-night stop. Bartenders serve bright, refreshing drinks with roots in South America – caipirinhas, piña coladas and margaritas using fresh coconut and carefully selected cachaca, and other rum-, tequila-, and pisco-inspired originals. One of the best kitchens in the city turns out upscale food inspired by street-cart fare – small plates of fresh guacamole, corn on the cob, ceviche, skewers and chicharrones de carne (roasted and fried chunks of pork shoulder served with housemade tortillas, lime, salsa and fish).

Monk's Kettle

3141 16th Street, at Albion Street (1-415 865 9523, www.monkskettle.com). BART to 16th Street Mission/bus 22. **Open** noon-2am daily. **Map** p158 C2 ③②

This wood-accented gastropub curates an impressive list of roughly 200 rotating beers (more than 20 draught, 180 bottled and 15 vintage pours from the cellar) that spans European and American styles and includes a large selection of local brews. Beer nerds will revel in rare suds, some costing as much as $79 for a 750ml bottle, such as the barrel-aged AleSmith Old Numbskull from San Diego. The small space is in inverse proportion to the expansive beer selection, so come early or be prepared to wait. The staff provides well-informed, if sometimes surly, drink suggestions to those who manage to secure a seat at the bar. Small groups can also snag booths along the wall.

Southern Pacific Brewing Company

620 Treat Avenue, at 19th Street (1-415 341 0152, www.southernpacificbrewing.com). Bus 12, 27. **Open** 11am-midnight Mon-Wed, Sun; 11am-2am Thur-Sat. **No credit cards**. **Map** p158 D3 ③③

Nestled in a quiet corner, Southern Pacific Brewing Company offers a sun-drenched patio prime for cold pints of draught beer and tasty burgers – not to mention great people- and dog-watching opportunities. Brewmaster Andy French brings clean flavours to a wide variety of beers. The on-site bar features 21 taps and a range of styles, including porters, IPAs, Belgians, ambers and lagers. Pair the brews with robust bar food like burgers, mac and cheese, fish and chips, pizza and wings. If the weather's chilly, retreat to the bar's cavernous, warehouse-style interior.

Monk's Kettle.

Uptown

200 Capp Street, between 17th & 18th Streets (1-415 861 8231). BART to 16th Street Mission/bus 14, 33, 49. **Open** *4pm-2am Mon-Thur, Sat, Sun; 2pm-2am Fri.* **No credit cards. Map** p158 C2 ③

There aren't many surprises at Uptown, which is exactly why we like it. Though it's in the trendy Mission, surrounded by more glamorous drinkeries, the no-frills joint keeps it real. Join the regulars lazing on grimy but strangely inviting couches, catch the game on one of two TVs above the bar, have a game of pool or Simpsons pinball, and peruse the eclectic tunes on the jukebox. Bartenders serve a solid selection of cheap beers – including PBR, naturally – and are ready to provide a friendly ear and the voice of reason. Just make sure to bring some cash, and you're set for the night.

Zeitgeist

199 Valencia Street, at Duboce Avenue (1-415 255 7505, www.zeitgeistsf.com). Bus 14, 49. **Open** *9am-8pm daily.* **Map** p158 C1 ③

San Francisco is a chill city, and it doesn't get chiller than this outdoor spot. Sipping a beer at one of Zeitgeist's sunny picnic tables with very relaxed smokers is a definitive SF experience. The beer garden stretches across a wide, open area defined by wooden fences, but large trees provide shady spots for those who prefer to stay out of direct sun. Inside, the bar taps dispense more than 40 beers – many of them from microbreweries – available by the pint or the pitcher, and a full kitchen serves excellent renditions of simple favourites like hamburgers, bratwurst and grilled cheese.

Shops & Services

Aquarius Records

1055 Valencia Street, between 21st & 22nd Streets (1-415 647 2272, www.aquariusrecords.org). BART to 24th Street Mission/bus 14, 49. **Open** *noon-8pm Mon-Fri; 11am-9pm Sat; 11am-7pm Sun.* **Map** p158 C4 ㊱ **Books & music**

This splendid little neighbourhood record store could be classed as a boutique, were the staff not so wonderfully lacking in pretension (tiny handwritten notes attached to numerous CD covers reveal their enthusiasm). Expect carefully curated selections and rarities in everything from art rock to sludge metal.

★ Dandelion Chocolate

740 Valencia Street, between 18th & 19th Streets (1-415 349 0942, www.dandelionchocolate.com). BART to 16th Street Mission/bus 14, 33, 49. **Open** *10am-9pm Mon-Thur, Sun; 10am-10pm Fri, Sat.* **Map** p158 C3 ㊲ **Food & drink**

At this 'bean to bar' chocolate factory and café, everything is crafted by hand in small batches. Watch the staff roast, winnow, grind, temper, mould and wrap their creations before you sample

---

IN THE KNOW THE MISSION BY NUMBERS

Unlike the convention in the downtown and SoMa areas, the street numbering along Mission and Valencia Streets in the Mission doesn't correspond to the numbered streets that cross them. For example, 2000 Mission Street is not at the junction of 20th Street, as you might expect, but of 16th Street; similarly, 2800 Mission is actually at 24th Street. It's a similar story two blocks away: 500 Valencia Street sits at the junction with 16th Street, while 1300 Valencia is at 24th Street. Still, while the numbering doesn't match the streets, it does at least increase at the standard rate of 100 per block, which makes it easy to figure out how far you have to walk.

---

the results. Tours and talks are offered Wednesday through Saturday. Along with single-origin chocolate bars, the café offers a menu of thick-enough-to-stand-a-spoon-in drinking chocolates and mochas, plus desserts such as a decadent, dark-chocolate red velvet beet cake, nib-infused panna cotta and a PB&J cup that crushes Reese's.

Dema

1038 Valencia Street, at Hill Street (1-415 206 0500, www.godemago.com). BART to 24th Street Mission/bus 14, 33, 49. **Open** *11am-7pm Mon-Fri; noon-7pm Sat; noon-6pm Sun.* **Map** p158 C4 ㊳ **Fashion**

Local designer Dema Grim specialises in blouses, skirts, dresses and sheaths in gloriously fun prints. Her modern interpretations of vintage classics are timeless, standing up to fashion's fickle whims.

★ Dog Eared Books

900 Valencia Street, at 20th Street (1-415 282 1901, www.dogearedbooks.com). Bus 14, 33, 49. **Open** *10am-10pm Mon-Sat; 10am-9pm Sun.* **Map** p158 C3 ㊴ **Books & music**

With a storefront splashed in colourful murals, windows lined with pulp paperbacks, and vibrant papel picado banners draped overhead, this 20-year-old bookstore in the heart of the Mission is very much a reflection of its surrounding community. Signs designating the genres are hand-lettered, and the shelves are dotted with stickers left behind by self-promoting browsers. The store sells both used and new books, and the long tables in the centre of the store offer deals on both. Though the emphasis here is on local authors, small presses and the Beats, a little bit of everything is interspersed throughout. Look up: the paintings displayed above the bookshelves are for sale as well – all the work of local artists, of course.

EXPLORE

★ Gravel & Gold

3266 21st Street, between Lexington & Valencia Streets (1-415 552 0112, www.gravelandgold.com). BART to 24th Street Mission/Bus 14, 49. **Open** noon-7pm Mon-Sat; noon-5pm Sun. **Map** p158 C3 ㊵ **Fashion**

This weirdly, wonderfully San Franciscan store isn't afraid to be irreverent: the best-selling Boob Bag is covered with a black-and-white print of breasts (the pattern is also splashed across tees, tanks and pillowcases). The in-house designed G&G collection often draws upon the talents of local illustrators, painters and designers, but never skews twee or kitsch. If you're not a fan of over-the-top prints, fear not – the store also stocks understated striped tanks, dresses and tees galore. Many of the shop clerks are also designers and artists themselves. Look out for leather sandals by sometime-shopgirl Rachel Corry, Jenny Pennywood bags and clutches by local fine artist Jen Garrido, and Ursa Major jewellery by New York transplant Kate Jones.

Little Paper Planes

855 Valencia Street, between 19th & 20th Streets (1-415 643 4616, www.littlepaperplanes.com). Bus 14, 33, 49. **Open** noon-7pm Mon-Sat; noon-6pm Sun. **Map** p158 C3 ㊶ **Gifts & souvenirs**

After founding Little Paper Planes as a web-only store for art, home decor and accessories in 2004, Kelly Jones graduated to a brick-and-mortar space on a retail-packed strip of the Mission in 2013. The interior is modern and gallery-like, and neon and metallic wares pop against pristine white walls. Jewellery, table-top items and small home accessories cover the large central table, while neat shelves are filled with design books, art prints, zines, and stationery. Jones herself designs Uniforma, a line of bags and small leather good in simple, easy-to-wear silhouettes and bright hues. The Little Paper Planes residency programme takes over the blank white box in the rear of the shop, whether for performances, interactive art events or a more traditional exhibition.

Mira Mira

3292 22nd Street, at Valencia Street (1-415 648 6513, www.miramirasf.com). Bus 12, 14, 48, 49.

Open noon-7pm Tue-Sat; noon-6pm Sun. **Map** p158 C4 ㊷ **Fashion**

Situated just off Valencia's main shopping drag, this narrow store doubles as a local hangout and stopover for fashion emergencies. Owner Mira Pickett buys with an eye for the season's trends in a way that feels current, but not fleeting. You'll find flattering rompers, cut-outs even a non-model can pull off, cheeky prints and boho-cool jewellery. Though Pickett is an unabashed proponent of prints and colour, you'll never be a fashion victim here: she's her shoppers' best stylist, often posting shots of her favourite looks on Instagram and the store blog, and she relishes matching women with the ideal, occasion-appropriate dress.

Painted Bird

1360 Valencia Street, between 24th & 25th Streets (1-415 401 7027, www.paintedbird.org). BART to 24th Street Mission/bus 12, 14, 48, 49, 67. **Open** noon-8pm daily. **Map** p158 C4 ㊸ **Fashion**

Cooler than cool and extremely well priced, this brilliantly edited vintage outpost has become a must-shop for hipsters in search of granny sundresses, glam disco bags, flash but cute jewellery and styling shoes and boots from the 1980s, '70s and earlier eras.

★ Paxton Gate

824 Valencia Street, between 19th Street & Cunningham Place (1-415 824 1872, www. paxtongate.com). Bus 14, 33, 49. **Open** 11am-7pm Mon-Wed, Sun; 11am-8pm Thur-Sat. **Map** p158 C3 ㊹ **Gifts & souvenirs**

A taxidermy 'unicorn' is stationed at the door of this eclectic den of plants, animalia and various oddities, drawing gawking window shoppers in off the street. The store has an off-kilter, mystical feel inspired by plants and the natural sciences. Anatomical posters and scientific illustrations adorn the walls and glass cases contain jewel-toned entomology specimens, small pieces of taxidermy (including tiny stuffed mice dressed as religious figures), fossils, earrings fashioned from butterfly wings, animal bones and pocketknives. All are interspersed with an assortment of garden supplies, from hummingbird feeders to hanging planters. Work your way back past the greenhouse to the peaceful landscaped courtyard. All the plants at Paxton Gate are for sale, including flowers, ferns and air plants.

Pirate Supply Store

826 Valencia Street, between 19th Street & Cunningham Place (1-415 642 5905 ext 201, www.826valencia.org/store). Bus 14, 33, 49. **Open** noon-6pm daily. **Map** p158 C3 ㊺ **Gifts & souvenirs**

Need to track down a bottle of Scurvy Begone or a tin of Mermaid Bait? Thank goodness, then, for the Pirate Supply Store, the retail front of nonprofit

---

IN THE KNOW HUNGER GAMES

Getting a reservation at one of the Mission's 'it' restaurants can be a competitive sport. When all else fails: 1) Arrive at 5.30pm or after 9pm. 2) Sit at the bar, where there's often no-reserve seating. 3) Chance it – many hotspots hold a decent percentage of tables for walk-ins. 4) Go for lunch – a number of top restaurants are open midday, and you probably won't need reservations.

youth writing centre 826 Valencia (which is also the brainchild of local lit-god Dave Eggers). There are treasures hidden behind every door and inside every drawer in the ship-shape, wood-panelled interior, which is designed for exploring. The tongue-in-cheek pirate gear and paraphernalia includes skull and crossbones dice, peg leg sizing charts, eye patches, hooks and gold coins. The kids' classroom is in the back, where the organisation hosts writing workshops, after-school programmes and field trips.

Taylor Stitch

383 Valencia Street, at 15th Street (1-415 621 2231, www.taylorstitch.com). Bus 14, 22, 49. **Open** 11am-7pm daily. **Map** p158 C2 ⑩ **Fashion**
Co-owners Michael Maher, Michael Armenta and Barrett Purdum set up shop in 2008 focusing on one menswear staple – the button-down shirt. Nowadays, you'll find their brand everywhere from indie stores in Oakland to New York (they did a shirting collab with Banana Republic a few years back), and the trio has made forays into small-batch collections of blazers, trousers, tees and jeans as well. But the small Mission store still churns out the best new iterations of the basic button-down. You'll find them in 'sun-bleached' Italian denim, chambray cotton, rugged woven canvas and lightweight gingham. The brand's loyal client base may be its one downside: sizes tend to sell out quickly with each new release.

THE CASTRO

The Castro is an international gay centre. Along this rainbow flag-festooned stretch of trendy shops and see-and-be-seen cafés and bars, most of them gay-owned, a predominantly male populace enjoys a hard-won social and political influence.

A working-class Irish-Catholic stronghold for nearly a century, the Castro changed rapidly in the 1970s, when gay residents began buying businesses and battered Victorian and Edwardian properties at rock-bottom prices, renovating them into what's now some of the city's prettiest and priciest real estate. No place exemplifies the change more than the landmark **Twin Peaks Tavern** (*see p209*): its 1973 metamorphosis from traditional pub to gathering place for a conspicuously gay clientele began just as the Castro was, so to speak, coming out. The bar's location on what was fast becoming the gayest corner of the gayest street in the country drew an ever-larger crowd, and socialising unashamedly behind its daring, pavement-fronting windows became more of a political act than a mere evening's entertainment.

While the Castro today is still predominantly gay, the LGBT community has spread across

Pirate Supply Store.

IN THE KNOW PLAYTIME

A haven for game geeks and beer lovers in the Castro, **Brewcade** (4121 18th Street, at Castro Street, www.brewcadesf.com), is a combination bar and retro video arcade, offering 25 craft beers on tap and more than 20 classic coin-operated machines.

the city, and the urgency of those early days has receded. Most weekdays, the streets seem no different than any other neighbourhood, filled with commuting office workers, couples grabbing coffee or dinner in one of the local restaurants and buying groceries at the corner store. On weekends, however (and, of course, during Pride Week), the area around Castro and 18th Streets is overrun with visitors and locals who come to mix it up at **Harvey's** (see p206) or **Moby Dick's** (see p208), and revel in the exuberantly queer party atmosphere.

Gay landmarks abound here. In addition to the huge rainbow flag that flies over **Harvey Milk Plaza** (the Muni stop at the corner of Market and Castro Streets), the **GLBT History Museum** celebrates 100 years of the city's queer past.

The other must-see local landmark is the dazzling art deco **Castro Theatre** (see p198).

Constructed in 1922, it's one of the few American movie palaces that has remained in constant operation. It was designed by noted Bay Area architect Timothy L Pflueger, and became the 100th structure to be designated a US National Historic Landmark, 55 years after its completion. The theatre (motto: 'an acre of seats in a palace of dreams') has retained its original vibe, with an organist hunched over the mighty Wurlitzer pipe organ banging out show tunes before each night's screening. Programming includes large-scale film festivals, premières, themed film series and new prints of classic movies.

For a great view of the Castro from above, get lunch to go and wander up to **Corona Heights** – walk all the way up 16th Street to Flint Street, then take a right; the bare red rock of Corona will loom overhead. Along with beautiful vistas, you'll see plenty of Castro pooches out with their humans.

For gay bars and nightlife in the Castro, see p207 and p210.

Sights & Museums

GLBT History Museum

4127 18th Street, between Castro & Collingwood Streets (1-415 621 1107, www.glbthistory.org/museum). Metro to Castro/bus 24, 35. **Open** 11am-7pm Mon-Sat; noon-5pm Sun. **Admission** $5; $3 reductions. **Map** p158 A3 ⑰

Starbelly.

The GLBT History Museum opened in 2010, making history as the first full-scale, stand-alone museum of its kind in the United States. Coined the 'queer Smithsonian', the museum presents exhibits documenting 100 years of gay life in the city. The main gallery houses displays covering everything from Harvey Milk's assassination to AIDS activism, and gaybourhoods of yesteryear. The front gallery features rotating shows focusing on photography.

Restaurants & Cafés

Café Flore

2298 Market Street, at Noe Street (1-415 621 8579, www.cafeflore.com). Metro to Castro/streetcar F/bus 24, 33, 35, 37. **Open** 10am-midnight Mon-Fri; 8am-midnight Sat, Sun. **Main courses** $9.50-$20. **Map** p158 A2 ⓭ **Café**
The unofficial neighbourhood clubhouse, Café Flore draws a mixed crowed to its gorgeous patio day and night to check each other out, sip cappuccino or chow down on everything from brunchtime eggs benedict to comfort food like chicken pot pie and house-made ravioli at dinner. Stick around and you'll eventually meet all the local luminaries.

Chow

215 Church Street, at Market Street (1-415 552 2469, www.chowfoodbar.com). Metro J to Church & Market Streets/streetcar F/bus

22, 37. **Open** 8am-11pm Mon-Thur, Sun; 8am-midnight Fri, Sat. **Main courses** $7-$21. **Map** p158 B2 ⓭ **American**
Chow's hugely popular, well-priced, straight-ahead American fare ranges widely from roast chicken and burgers to Asian noodles, and the kitchen succeeds at most things it tries. Staff are pally, and the portions huge.
Other locations Park Chow, 1240 9th Avenue, between Irving Street & Lincoln Way, Sunset (1-415 665 9912).

Frances

3870 17th Street, at Pond Street (1-415 621 3870, www.frances-sf.com). Metro to Castro/bus 22, 37. **Open** 5-10.30pm daily. **Main courses** $22-$31. **Map** p158 A2 ⓮ **American creative**
Chef Melissa Perello opened this casual, cosy spot in the Castro in 2009 and the accolades – from *New York Times* write-ups to James Beard Award nominations – have been pouring in ever since. Her daily changing menu ebbs and flows with the seasons and never feels contrived or uptight. Among the recurring winning dishes: applewood smoked bacon beignets and bavette steak with roasted eggplant. Another draw: pay-for-what-you-drink house-blended wines served in pitchers ($1.50 per ounce).

Ike's Place

3489 16th Street, at Sanchez Street (1-415 553 6888, www.ilikeikesplace.com). Metro J to Church & 16th Streets/streetcar F/bus 22, 37. **Open** 10am-7pm daily. **Sandwiches** $8-$26. **Map** p158 A2 ⓮ **Sandwiches**
What started almost a decade ago out of a doorway has expanded to a dozen outlets around Northern California, as well as LA and Arizona, with a following that might make Taylor Swift jealous. More than 200 different sandwiches are offered on the menu (tip: look online before you go – the wall menu doesn't have room for nearly all the options), sporting names like Name of the Girl I'm Dating (hand-shredded chicken, honey mustard, avocado, pepper jack), Matt Cain (shredded turkey, roast beef, salami, Godfather Sauce, and provolone), and Favorite Sesame Street Character (cucumbers, lettuce, tomato, avocado, pesto, cream cheese). All sandwiches come with Ike's garlicky Dirty Sauce, which is spread over house-baked rolls. The line is invariably long, but the wait is worth it.

Starbelly

3583 16th Street, at Market Street (1-415 252 7500, www.starbellysf.com). Metro to Castro/streetcar F/bus 22, 35, 37. **Open** 11.30am-11pm Mon-Thur; 11.30am-midnight Fri; 10.30am-midnight Sat; 11am-11pm Sun. **Main courses** $14-$25. **Map** p158 A2 ⓮ **American**
In a neighbourhood not traditionally known for its cuisine, Starbelly is among a handful of restaurants setting out to change that. Chef Adam Timney

EXPLORE

turns out top-notch comfort food with California spin: chicken liver pâté, to-die-for house-made salumi platter, rotisserie chicken with butternut squash bread pudding. The relaxed setting – with communal tables and a large outdoor patio – adds to the enjoyment.

Shops & Services

Citizen Clothing

489 Castro Street, between 17th & 18th Streets (1-415 575 3560, www.citizensf.com). Metro to Castro/bus 24, 33, 35, 37. **Open** 10am-7pm Mon-Thur, Sun; 11am-8pm Fri; 10am-8pm Sat. **Map** p158 A3 ⓢ **Fashion**

Citizen is all about upscale utilitarian chic, meaning Scotch & Soda, Ben Sherman and Fred Perry appear alongside Penguin, Ted Baker, Jack Spade and Lacoste. Guys seeking something a bit more sporty head up the street to sibling establishment Body (450 Castro Street, 1-415 575 3562).

Rock Hard

518 Castro Street, between 18th & 19th Streets (1-415 437 2430). Bus 24, 33, 35. **Open** 9.30am-11pm Mon-Wed, Sun; 9.30am-midnight Thur; 9.30am-1am Fri. **Map** p158 A3 ⓢ **Sex shop**

There are many sex shops in the Castro. But Rock Hard stands apart from some of its cave-like contemporaries with an extensive selection, welcoming atmosphere and helpful staff. The majority of the clientele here is gay and male, and the merchandise is largely geared towards its neighbourhood base (if the Pride flag displayed in the front window wasn't enough of a tip-off). You'll find an assortment of sex toys, bondage accessories, strap-ons and lube (by the gallon!), neatly displayed against neutral grey walls.

★ Unionmade

493 Sanchez Street, at 18th Street (1-415 861 3373, www.unionmadegoods.com). Metro to Church & 18th Street/bus 33. **Open** 11am-7pm Mon-Sat; noon-6pm Sun. **Map** p158 B3 ⓢ **Fashion**

This Castro mainstay is credited with creating the daily uniform of the San Francisco man – not entirely in jest. The racks are filled with everything a casually stylish guy needs, including twill and waxed cotton jackets, nautical striped tees, hardy leather boots, jeans, plaid and chambray button-downs. Everything is selected with an eye for craftsmanship and quality, from the Golden Bear blazers and Hillside ties to weekend-wear like Chimala terry cloth tees and Todd Snyder sweatshirts. The store is divided into two rooms, one side bearing denim, button-downs, shoes, and giftables, the other devoted to outerwear and accessories. A midpoint of sorts between the Castro and the Mission, it draws regulars from both neighbourhoods, many who pop in to browse the book and magazine selection.

NOE VALLEY & BERNAL HEIGHTS

Quaint **Noe Valley**, roughly bordered by 20th, Dolores, 30th and Douglass Streets, is a self-contained village cut off from the rest of the city by steep hills on every side. In the 1970s it housed a fairly bohemian mix of straight, gay, working-class and white-collar residents, before growing more family-oriented in the 1980s and '90s – a sunny hamlet to which well-paid young couples could retreat to raise kids (or the dog equivalents) away from the chaos of the rest of the city. **Twin Peaks** overlooks the area from the west and its flanks offer attractive views of the East Bay.

Noe's main shopping strip, 24th Street, is substantially different from the funky stretch east of Mission Street. This part of 24th is lined with cafés, romantic restaurants and boutiques where owners and regulars are on first-name terms. The **24th Street Cheese Company** (No.3893, 1-415 821 6658, www.24thstreetcheese.com) has a terrific selection, both local and international, along with a variety of snacks and charcuterie. Noe Valley Ministry (1021 Sanchez Street, at 23rd Street, 1-415 282 2317, www.noevalleyministry.org) is a Presbyterian church that presents regular chamber music concerts in a small hall with great acoustics. A little bit further afield, **Mitchell's Ice Cream** (688 San José Avenue, at 29th Street, 1-415 648 2300, www.mitchellsicecream.com), has been serving up what many consider the city's best ice-cream since 1953.

Bernal Heights, meanwhile, boasts an eclectic mix of young families and hipsters priced out of the Mission, who frequent the restaurants, shops and cafés on and around Cortland Avenue. Attitude-free lesbian bar **Wild Side West** (*see p210*), is something of a local legend, first opened in 1962 across the Bay in Oakland and settling into Bernal Heights in the mid-1970s. Despite its LGBT cred, the bar welcomes patrons of all genders and proclivities. For those with energy to burn, a hike up the hill to **Bernal Park** affords spectacular 360-degree views of the city and Bay.

Restaurants & Cafés

Firefly

4288 24th Street, at Douglass Street, Noe Valley (1-415 821 7652, www.fireflyrestaurant.com). Metro to Church & 24th/bus 24, 35, 48. **Open** 5.30-9pm Mon-Thur, Sun; 5.30-10pm Fri, Sat. **Main courses** $21-$29. **Map** p158 A4 ⓢ **American**

White-topped tables aglow with soft lights and a room buzzing with good conversation are hallmarks of this neighbourhood restaurant. The eclectic menu might feature fried chicken (among the best in town), honey-braised lamb shoulder or rib-sticking

EXPLORE

chicken and dumplings. There are always a number of inventive seasonal vegetarian and gluten-free selections, and special menus for the Jewish holidays. Warm, romantic and utterly charming.

La Ciccia

291 30th Street, at Church Street, Noe Valley (1-415 550 8114, www.laciccia.com). Metro J to Church & Day Streets/bus 34, 26. **Open** 5.30pm-10pm Tue-Sat. **Main courses** $19-$27. Italian
This unpretentious family-owned Sardinian restaurant in outer Noe Valley has become a destination spot for seafood lovers from all over the city, drawn to husband-and-wife owners Massimiliano Conti and Lorella Degan's interpretations of their island's culinary heritage. Among the standouts: spicy baby octopus stew, fregola with sea urchin and smoked pancetta, and Sardinian ricotta and saffron cake. The couple's newest venture, pizzeria and prosciutteria La Nebbia (1781 Church Street, 1-415 874-9924, www.lanebbia.com), lies kitty corner to La Ciccia.

Little Nepal

925 Cortland Avenue, at Folsom Street, Bernal Heights (1-415 643 3881, www.littlenepalsf.com). Bus 24, 67. **Open** 5-10pm Tue-Sun. **Main courses** $15-$18. Nepalese
Tucked away at the end of Cortland Avenue, Little Nepal offers cuisine that falls gastronomically, as well as geographically, between India and Tibet. Kathmandu-trained chef/owner Prem Tamang honed his skills cooking for Himalayan climbers. His menu features tandoori, vegetable curries, and chicken and lamb dishes that are packed with flavour and fire.

$ Lovejoy's Tea Room

1351 Church Street, at Clipper Street, Noe Valley (1-415 648 5895, www.lovejoystearoom.com). Metro to Church & 24th Street/bus 48. **Open** 11am-6pm Wed-Sun. **Main courses** $9-$13. Café
Select from Lovejoy's six different teas, including the Queen's Tea ($28, complete with sandwiches, a scone with Devon cream and preserves, plus other goodies) and the Wee Tea ($17) for children. They're all served in a room furnished with a jumble of antiques and knick-knacks.

Shops & Services

Ambiance

3979 24th Street, between Noe & Sanchez Street, Noe Valley (1-415 647 5800, www.ambiancesf. com). Metro J to Church & 24th Street/bus 24, 35, 48. **Open** 11am-7pm Mon-Fri, Sun; 10am-7pm Sat. **Map** p158 B4 ⑤ Fashion
If you've got an occasion, this popular local women's clothing chainlet has the perfect outfit for it. The collection of retro-style dresses, saucy skirts and essential denim from mid-priced to upscale brands like BB Dakota, Free People, Joe's Jeans and Nicole Miller is arranged by colour for your convenience.

The sales staff are beyond friendly. The Noe Valley branch also features shoes and jewellery; the sales racks are in the back.
Other locations throughout the city.

POTRERO HILL & DOGPATCH

On the outskirts of the Mission, the quiet neighbourhood of **Potrero Hill** (loosely bordered by 16th Street, I-280, Cesar Chavez Avenue and Potrero Avenue) is often sunny, even when the rest of San Francisco is shrouded in fog. Home to a mix of families and hipsters, it's a little off the beaten track, but boasts a compact, lively commercial district. Art galleries, along with fashion, furniture and design houses, are increasingly occupying the former industrial buildings in the flatlands at the base of the hill. Along the main artery of 18th Street, a small cadre of good neighbourhood eateries and cafés includes **Plow** (*see p176*) and **Farley's** (No.1315 1-415 648 1545, www.farleyscoffee.com), a coffeehouse institution. Meanwhile, local bar **Blooms Saloon** (no.1318, 1-415 552 6707) is a scruffy but solid place to knock back a drink while taking in the panoramic views from the back deck. Heading down the hill, the aptly named **Bottom of the Hill** (1233 17th Street, at Missouri Street; *see p220*) is the place to go for punk, rockabilly, pop, and alt-rock bands, and is one of the host venues for the annual Noise Pop festival in February. The beautiful **Anchor Brewery** (1705 Mariposa Street, between Carolina & De Haro Streets, 1-415 863 8350, www.anchorbrewing.com) has an illustrious history as a pioneer of the American craft brewing movement. It created its first brew in 1896, and bottled its first 200 cases of Anchor Steam beer in 1971. Today, it produces various beers and spirits, including the much-admired Junipero Gin and Old Potrero Whiskey. Informative tours (ending in the tasting room, of course) take place twice a day, by reservation only (call four to six weeks in advance). Anchor has also started construction on an expansive new brewery at Pier 48, near AT&T Park in Mission Bay. The facility will offer daily tours and a restaurant.

Located on the east side of Potrero Hill along 22nd and Third Streets, **Dogpatch** is a formerly industrial neighbourhood of dry docks and steel mills that escaped the rampages of the 1906 earthquake with most of its gorgeous Victorians intact. Dozens of the city's oldest architectural gems built between 1870 and 1910 (mostly working-class housing for shipyard workers and employees of companies such as Union Iron Works) can still be found here; the Irving M Scott School (1060 Tennessee Street, now housing several nonprofit groups), built in 1895, is San Francisco's oldest public school building.

As the shipbuilding industry declined post-World War II, the area fell into disrepair, leaving

EXPLORE

GROUNDS CONTROL
Dip into San Francisco's distinguished coffee scene.

Seattle may lay claim to the first Starbucks, but more than a century before the first vente latte, San Francisco was already steeped in coffee culture. Pioneer Steam Coffee and Spice Mills was founded in San Francisco in 1850, but it became better known after James A Folger acquired it and renamed it in 1872. Folger's Coffee went on to become the largest coffee company in the world and the building at 101 Howard Street (now on the National Register of Historic Places) still has its name emblazoned on the side. The building at 2 Harrison Street was headquarters to another coffee pioneer, Hills Brothers. Founded in 1878 by brothers Austin and RW Hills, the company began as a market stall and exploded in 1900 after RW invented vacuum packing – a method still widely used today.

The beans were firmly planted, but it wasn't until 1966, when Alfred Peet opened Peet's Coffee, Tea & Spices at 2124 Vine Street in Berkeley, that the modern-day coffee revolution began. What distinguished Peet's coffee was the insistence on high-quality beans, freshly roasted in small batches and, crucially, much darker than was the norm at the time. The founders of Starbucks, Gordon Bowker, Zev Siegl and Jerry Baldwin, who met while students at the University of San Francisco, got their start researching roasters when Siegl got a job at Peet's. Later, they sourced their beans from Peet's

when they created Starbucks in 1971. Peet's focused on tea and coffee sales; Starbucks on coffee bars – and the rest is history.

While old-school cafés such as **Caffè Roma** (*see p101*) in North Beach still draw devoted followers for strong Italian and espresso roasts, San Francisco coffee culture has undergone a renaissance, with small-batch, single-origin 'third wave' artisanal roasters (the first wave was Folger's, the second wave Peet's) popping up all over town. The best known, downtown's **Blue Bottle Coffee** (*see p73*), is still 'grounds' zero for many, a pioneer of the five-light siphon bar and other de rigueur coffee-brewing methods. Mission roasters with fanatical followings include **Sightglass Coffee** (*see p164*), single-cup drip king **Philz** (*see p163*), and **Ritual Roasters** (*see p164*), whose meticulous approach to production and brewing borders on the religious.

As you'd expect in this geek-tech capital, the hunt for the latest, greatest, darkest, freshest, most perfectly brewed cup doesn't just rely on word of mouth – there's also an app for that. **Acceptable Espresso** provides an up-to-the-moment list of cafés serving 'espresso worth ordering'. (Their motto: We drank a bunch of crappy espresso, so you don't have to.) **Coffeeratings.com** assesses the best coffee spots in San Francisco on a ten-point scale, with ratings based on aroma, body and flavour, as well as ambience and presentation.

Sightglass Coffee.

crumbling structures and an inhospitable neighbourhood behind. In the noughties, an influx of artists and entrepreneurs, attracted by low rents, spacious live-work lofts, and a new Metro streetcar line, began to transform the district with a rapidly growing cache of hip restaurants and bars, local cottage industries, design studios, chocolatiers, wine bars and a top-flight brewery.

Across Third Street on the Bay side of Dogpatch, the historic shipyard at **Pier 70** (1-415 836-5980, www.pier70sf.com) is undergoing a renaissance. The 69-acre site has become a redevelopment hotspot, with plans for more artist studios, up to 600 middle- and working-class homes and a massive waterfront park.

Sights & Museums

Hosfelt Gallery
260 Utah Street, at 16th Street, Potrero Hill (1-415 495 5454, www.hosfeltgallery.com). Bus 9, 27. **Open** 10am-5.30pm Tue, Wed, Fri, Sat; 11am-7pm Thur. **Map** p159 E2 ㉝
An established gallery that relocated from neighbouring SoMa to this sprawling, light-filled converted door factory, Hosfelt has acted as an anchor for art in the area; four other large galleries, and several smaller ones, have joined the immediate neighbourhood since 2012. With a focus on contemporary art – not just painting and sculpture but also installations and new media such as Jim Campbell's LED light creations – Hosfelt is the perfect gateway to start exploring this emerging art enclave.

Restaurants & Cafés

Chez Maman
1401 18th Street, at Missouri Street, Potrero Hill (1-415 655 9542, www.chezmamansf.com). Bus 10, 22. **Open** 11.30am-10.45pm Mon-Fri; 10.30am-10.45pm Sat, Sun. **Main courses** $14-$21. **Map** p159 G2 ㉝ **French**
This homey, country French bistro from acclaimed restaurateur Jocelyn Bulow is among the best places in town for crêpes, classic steak frites, and mussels in sauce, but the burgers are the pièce de résistance. The juicy, thick beef patty is flecked with sautéed shallots, parsley and herbs and set on a grilled ciabatta roll, then topped with tomato and onions and spread with house-made aioli. Add to this your choice of goat's cheese, cheddar, Swiss or – *oh là là* – a chunk of aromatic Roquefort or a slab of melty brie. Then take it one decadent step further with sliced avocado, bacon or a fried egg.

$ Just for You Café
732 22nd Street, between 3rd & Tennessee Streets, Dogpatch (1-415 647 3033, www.justforyoucafe.com). Metro T to 23rd Street/bus 22, 48. **Open** 7.30am-3pm Mon-Fri; 8am-5pm Sat, Sun. **Main courses** $9-$15. **Map** p159 H3 ㉚ **Café**

This friendly neighbourhood joint serves breakfast with a side of sass. Of the Hangtown Fry, a plate heaped with cornmeal-battered oysters, bacon, eggs and grits, the menu chides, 'If this doesn't cure your hangover, you'd better just go back to bed.' Everything is served with a generous side of house-made jalapeño salsa, which regulars slather liberally across toast, cornbread and biscuits. The menu is an embarrassment of riches: three kinds of Benedicts (try the Crabby Bennie), four types of pancakes (buttermilk, cornmeal, oatmeal and buckwheat) and an international line-up of scrambles. They're not kidding about that hangover, either. The mimosas are served in pint glasses rather than standard flutes.

$ Mr and Mrs Miscellaneous
699 22nd Street, at 3rd Street, Dogpatch (1-415 970 0750). Metro T to 23rd Street/bus 48, 91. **Open** 11.30am-6pm Wed-Sat; 11.30am-5pm Sun. **Ice-cream** $2.75-$6.50. **Map** p159 H3 ㉛ **Ice-cream**
Started by two former pastry chefs, this artisanal ice-cream parlour offers kids' favourites like chocolate chip, peanut brittle and strawnana (strawberry banana) alongside sophisticated flavours such as candied violet, white sesame, and the wildly popular Ballpark – a blend of Anchor Steam beer ice-cream, roasted peanuts and chocolate-covered pretzels. In addition to daily changing scoops, frozen custard, White Rabbit (condensed milk and white chocolate) and sundaes with house-made hot fudge, butterscotch or pineapple sauce are decadent options.

★ Piccino
1001 Minnesota Street, at 22nd Street, Dogpatch (1-415 824 4224, www.piccino.com). Bus 48. **Open** 11am-10pm Tue-Sun. **Main courses** $12-$26. **Map** p159 H3 ㉜ **Italian & pizza**
Owners Margherita Stewart Sagan and Sheryl Rogat started Piccino in a tiny space in Dogpatch, with a pizza dough recipe passed down through generations from Sagan's mother. Since then, they've moved into a giant yellow barn next door and sparked a Dogpatch renaissance of butchers, bakers, and messenger-bag makers. Thin-crust pizzas are still the primary focus, topped with everything from house-made sausage and roasted mushrooms to pancetta and pea tendrils. But the menu has been augmented with main-course options such as pork and beef polpette, and milk-braised pork with chickpeas, hungarian peppers, and salsa verde. *Photos pp176-177.*

$ Plow
1299 18th Street, at Texas Street, Potrero Hill (1-415 821 7569, www.eatatplow.com). Bus 10, 12. **Open** 7am-2pm Tue-Fri; 8am-2pm Sat, Sun. **Main courses** $7.50-$15. **Map** p159 G2 ㉝ **American**
Simply outfitted with gleaming reclaimed wood tables and floor-to-ceiling windows, this breakfast-and-lunch spot is a beautiful space to spend a morning. You'll find standout dishes on the sweet

and savoury ends of the spectrum, from the legendary lemon ricotta pancakes to the house-made biscuits topped in honey butter, scallions and ham or sausage. (Nab a biscuit while you can – the place has been known to run out on busy mornings.) Even lighter fare is memorable here, like the chia seed pudding served with almond milk, bananas, coconut, almonds, honey and bee pollen.

Serpentine

2495 3rd Street, at 22nd Street (1-415 252 2000, www.serpentinesf.com). Metro T to 23rd Street/bus 22, 48. **Open** *11.30am-2.30pm, 6-10pm Mon-Thur; 11.30am-2.30pm, 6-11pm Fri; 10am-2.30pm, 6-11pm Sat; 10am-2.30pm Sun.* **Main courses** *$14-$27.* **Map** p159 H3 ❷ **American**
Housed in a former tin can factory, Serpentine champions the farm-to-table movement with offerings such as a house-made charcuterie platter and gnocchi with baby fava leaves, hedgehog mushrooms and English peas. Ingredients are seasonal and locally and sustainably sourced. Don't miss the Prather Ranch burger – one of the best burgers in the city.

Bars

★ Magnolia Brewing Company/ Smokestack

2505 3rd Street, between 22nd & 23rd Streets, Dogpatch (1-415 864 7468, www.magnoliabrewing. com). Metro T to 23rd Street/bus 22, 48. **Open** *11.30am-midnight Mon-Thur, Sun; 11.30am-2am Fri, Sat.* **Map** p159 H3 ❻
Magnolia in Dogpatch (big sister to the Haight-Ashbury's beloved Magnolia Gastropub & Brewery) was probably the most eagerly anticipated micro-brewery to open in the city in a decade, with cask-beer devotees waiting patiently through four years of construction delays and permitting red tape. By all accounts, it was worth it. Owner Dave McLean (whose resemblance to late Grateful Dead guitarist Jerry Garcia is only partially coincidental) has transformed a former can factory into a hip neo-industrial craft barbecue and beer lover's haven. Exposed pipes, reclaimed wood communal tables, and a bar hung with ladders that slide across a sheet metal wall of liquor provide the backdrop for some 15-17 draught and cask beers, as well as dozens of premium small-batch whiskies. Across the room, the Smokestack barbecue restaurant offers up brisket, hot pastrami, Wagyu beef back ribs, sausages, smoked duck and other meats by the pound, served on butcher trays.

Yield Wine Bar

2490 3rd Street, at 22nd Street, Dogpatch (1-415 401 8984, www.yieldandpause.com). Metro T to 23rd Street/bus 22, 48. **Open** *3-11pm Mon-Sat.* **Map** p159 H3 ❻
When this unassuming wine bar opened in Dogpatch in 2006, featuring a list of almost entirely sustainable, organic and biodynamic wines, there were sceptics aplenty. But Yield is still going strong, an anchor in a neighbourhood that's grown into a mecca for locavore restaurants, artisan food purveyors and craftspeople. Its popularity inspired

Piccino. See p175.

the owners to open a bigger, splashier spinoff in the up-and-coming mid-Market/Hayes Valley area. Yield draws a more low-key crowd than its sister, Pause, many of whom come to sample unusual varietals such as Italian Malvasia and Croatian Plavac Mali, while sampling inventive vegetarian and pescatarian fare (grilled flatbreads, chèvre-stuffed dates, cod sliders). If you needed another excuse to stop in, consider happy hour: half-bottle carafes for $12, every day from 4.30pm to 7pm.
Other location Pause, 1666 Market Street, between Haight & Rose Streets (1-415 241 9463).

Shops & Services

DZINE
128 Utah Street, at Alameda Street, Potrero Hill (1-415 674 9430, www.dzinestore.com). Bus 9, 27. **Open** 10am-6pm Mon-Fri; 11am-5pm Sat. **Map** p159 E1 ⓸ **Homewares**
Browsing this contemporary showroom is like meandering through an issue of *Architectural Digest*. It's a store for those who embrace boundary-pushing design – much of the furniture here doubles as art. The space showcases a range of contemporary European designers, with a particular emphasis on Italian brands. You'll find seating and lighting from Salone del Mobile favourites such as Moroso, Boffi, Flos and Kartell, as well as relative newcomers like Established & Sons. In 2015, the showroom introduced photography, paintings and sculpture into its repertoire, all curated by Alexa Ray of Five Senses Art Consultancy.

Poco Dolce
2419 3rd Street, between 20th & 22nd Streets, Dogpatch (1-415 255 1443, www.pocodolce.com). Metro T to 20th Street/bus 22, 48. **Open** 11am-5pm Mon-Fri; 11am-4pm Sat. **Map** p159 E2 ⓺⓼
Food & drink
Surrounded by locavore restaurants, artisan butchers and bakers, craft beer and wine makers, this confectionery and small storefront occupies a prime spot in the blossoming SFMade haven. Dark chocolate is topped with grey sea salt combinations, including signature tiles infused with such flavours as smoked almond and ghost chilli, sesame toffee, and burnt caramel. Truffles, bonbons, bars, brittles and boxed chocolates round out the selection. It's all good, but the popcorn toffee squares and sesame toffee bittersweet tiles are truly amazing.

Rickshaw Bagworks
904 22nd Street, between Indiana & Minnesota Streets, Dogpatch (1-415 904 8368, www.rickshawbags.com). Metro T to 20th or 23rd Street. **Open** 10am-6pm Mon-Fri; noon-4pm Sat, Sun. **Map** p159 H3 ⓺⓽ **Accessories**
Rickshaw began making custom messenger bags out of an old warehouse in 2007 and today, the label's bags are all over town – coveted by button-down office workers and casual bike commuters alike. Rickshaw's hand-sewn repertoire, crafted by about 30 employees on-site, includes sturdy, customisable bags for laptops and tablets, backpacks, briefcases, tote bags, computer sleeves and folios.

Sunset & Richmond

To many visitors, and some San Franciscans, the Richmond and Sunset districts are largely unexplored areas that sandwich the verdant expanse of Golden Gate Park, one of San Francisco's greatest attractions, three miles in length, half a mile wide and one of the largest manmade parks in the world. But that's fine with the residents, who tend to be a bit more unassuming, a bit less concerned with appearances and a bit more welcoming than those in other city neighbourhoods. This happy melange of active immigrant communities, students, families, working-class folk and, by the ocean, surfers, also enjoys the cutting-edge natural history museum, the California Academy of Sciences, and the city's very best coastal trails. Less touristy, less flashy and more foggy: for some, this is the real San Francisco.

Outerlands.

Don't Miss

1 Golden Gate Park See everything from bison to windmills in the massive man-made oasis (p181).

2 Outerlands Follow local gastronauts to this cosy culinary outpost (p181).

3 Green Apple Books A sprawling, appealingly quirky bibliophile hub (p187).

4 InnerFog Well-priced vino sans attitude (p181).

5 California Academy of Sciences A green paean to the natural world (p182).

IN THE KNOW
DEFINITELY SPEAKING

Though it may sound odd to out-of-town ears, locals always use the definite article when referring to neighbourhoods, even when the word 'district' is dropped – the Sunset, the Richmond, the Mission and so on.

SUNSET DISTRICT

This large southern neighbourhood, west of the Haight and south of Golden Gate Park, usually belies its own name. The sunsets in the Sunset are more often than not swathed in fog from June to September (though of late, global warming seems to be reducing the grey season considerably). If you are able to catch a fair day, however, they can be spectacular.

The stretch of **Irving Street** between 5th and 10th Avenues, in an area informally known as the **Inner Sunset**, is the area's shopping corridor. Just off Irving on 9th Avenue sit two fine eateries: sushi stop **Ebisu** and comfort food bistro **Park Chow** (no.1240, 1-415 665 9912, www.chowrestaurant. com). To the southeast is **Grandview Park**. Locally known as Turtle Hill, the small park sits at the top of a steep stretch of Moraga Street between 15th and 16th Avenues, and is home to locally endangered species that include the Franciscan wallflower and hairstreak butterfly. The best reason to visit, however, is the marvel of a mosaic-tiled stairway that leads to the top. Handcrafted by more than 300 neighbourhood residents in the early noughties, the 163 sparkling ceramic tiles depict birds, sea creatures, flora and fauna in a swirl of colour that begins at the ocean floor and climbs to the sun.

However, the Sunset's main attractions are way out west, where the turf meets the surf. Perhaps chief among them is sandy **Ocean Beach** (see p126 **Shore Things**), which runs for three and a half miles south from the **Cliff House** (see p185). It's a good spot for a contemplative wander, to spend time watching the surfers battling strong rip tides and chilly water. Take a warming break either over coffee at the **Java Beach Café** or with a garlic whole-roasted crab at Vietnamese restaurant **Thanh Long** (4101 Judah Street, at 46th Avenue, 1-415 665 1146, www.thanhlong.com).

The southernmost point of Ocean Beach is marked by **Fort Funston**, a large natural area in the far south-west of the city. Criss-crossed with hiking trails, promontories and jagged beaches, the reservation is popular with dog-walkers and hang-gliders, who launch themselves above the waves.

Just over a mile north of Fort Funston is **San Francisco Zoo** (see p193), one of very few zoos

to house koalas. Beyond the zoo is **Harding Municipal Park & Golf Course** (99 Harding Road, at Skyline Boulevard, 1-415 664 4690, www.tpc.com/tpc-harding-park). Cradled by picturesque Lake Merced and encircled by biking and jogging trails, the public course opened in 1925 and was completely renovated in 2002.

North of the lake is Stern Grove, just over 60 acres of eucalyptus and redwood that hosts the annual free **Stern Grove Festival**. Slightly further inland is **Mount Davidson**, which at 927 feet is the highest point in San Francisco. If you can ignore the enormous cross at its apex, the views are terrific. If you can't, you are not alone: the cross has been a source of controversy since it was first erected in 1923.

Restaurants & Cafés

$ Devil's Teeth Baking Company
3876 Noriega Street, at 45th Avenue (1-415 683 5533, www.devilsteethbakingcompany.com). Bus 16X, 18, 71, 71L. **Open** 7am-4pm Mon, Wed-Sun. **Sandwiches** $5.50-$6.75. Bakery/café
The ultimate morning-after breakfast can be found at Devil's Teeth Baking Company, an unfussy Outer Sunset shop where surfers, kids and dogs chow down side by side at the zigzag-shaped parklet out front. Although the spot serves an assortment of baked goods and sandwiches, the highlight is the 'special' breakfast sandwich: two eggs, pepper jack cheese, applewood-smoked bacon, avocado and lemon-garlic aioli served on a house-baked butter-milk biscuit.

Ebisu
1283 9th Avenue, between Irving Street & Lincoln Way (1-415 566 1770, www.ebisusushi.com). Metro N to 9th Avenue & Irving Street/bus 6, 43, 44, 66, 71. **Open** 11.30am-2pm, 5-10pm Tue-Thur; 11.30am-2pm, 5-11pm Fri; noon-2.30pm, 5-11pm Sat; noon-2.30pm, 5-10pm Sun. **Main courses** $12-$20. **Sushi** $5-$15. **Map** p316 C10. Japanese
This Inner Sunset stalwart has been going strong for more than 30 years and remains a locals' favour-ite for creative sushi and a festive atmosphere. The inevitable wait for a table passes quickly with a drink from the bar. Then settle in for signature elab-orate speciality rolls such as the Caterpillar (eel, cucumber, avocado), Behind the Green Door (skip-jack, shrimp tempura, Maui onions, tobiko), and whatever the chef is concocting as a nightly special. Those who don't want sushi won't be disappointed; there's a good selection of cooked items from teriyaki and tempura to sukiyaki.

$ Java Beach Café
1396 La Playa Boulevard, at Judah Street (1-415 665 5282, www.javabeachcafe.com). Metro to Ocean Beach/bus 18. **Open** 5.30am-11pm Mon-Fri; 6am-11pm Sat, Sun. **Sandwiches** $6.50-$9. Café

Java Beach is funky and civilised, with the wetsuits and grand Pacific views making it feel a bit like Hermosa Beach in Los Angeles – minus the permatans. Surfers, cyclists and ordinary passers-by pop in for a toasted sandwich, some soup or maybe a pastry.

$ Marnee Thai

1243 9th Avenue, between Lincoln Way & Irving Street (1-415 731 9999, www.marneethaisf.com). Metro N to 9th Avenue & Irving Street/bus 16X, 71. **Open** 11.30am-10pm daily. **Main courses** $11-$15. **Map** p316 C10. **Thai**
With a menu of more than 50 items (plus daily specials), Marnee Thai offers a deep dive into regional cuisine. Chef Chai Siriyarn's menu focuses mainly on Siamese fare from Central Thailand, but he also covers specialities from the north and south, including turmeric- and ginger-seasoned noodle curries and Indonesian-style chicken satay. Popular dishes include *hor mok* (steamed snapper in curry mousse with cabbage in a banana leaf bowl), and morning glory sautéed in soy bean and garlic sauce.

★ Outerlands

4001 Judah Street, at 45th Avenue (1-415 661 6140, www.outerlandssf.com). Metro N to Judah Street & 46th Avenue/bus 18. **Open** 9am-3pm, 5-10pm daily. No reservations. **Main courses** $13-$29. **American**
Deep in the sleepy Outer Sunset district, Outerlands has sparked a cultural renaissance in what has long been a culinary backwater. Amid salvaged fencewood walls, crocheted afghans, beer in mason jars, and the Pavlovian scent of simmering soups and baking bread, diners tuck into dishes like fennel a la plancha in mussel vinaigrette, pressed roast chicken and cast-iron-grilled cheese sandwiches made with heavenly house-baked bread. At brunch, don't miss Dutch pancakes baked in a cast-iron skillet, or 'eggs in jail' – hollowed-out house-made levain toast with eggs fried in the hole – and the array of delectable pastries.

Bars

★ InnerFog

545 Irving Street, at 7th Avenue (1-415 682 4116, www.innerfog.com). Metro N to 9th Avenue & Irving Street/bus 43, 44, 71. **Open** 4-10pm Mon; 4-11pm Tue; 4pm-midnight Wed, Thur; 4pm-1am Fri; 4pm-midnight Sat; 3-10pm Sun. **Map** p316 C10.
This Inner Sunset gem pours great wines by the glass without succumbing to the usual swirling, sniffing wine bar pretension. It's ideal for catch-up drinks or casual dates, but you won't feel uncomfortable just unwinding with a book or your laptop. Rather than some nondescript 'house' blend, the Fog offers a $6-per-glass happy hour selection (4-6pm Mon-Sat; 3-6pm Sun) of around a dozen wines from California, France, Argentina and beyond, all helpfully listed from the softest to the most robust. (The bartenders are eager to make recommendations,

if you can't decide.) Likewise, beers like Full Sail Brewing's Session lager and the Deschutes Inversion IPA from Oregon are just $3.50 apiece.

Shops & Services

3 Fish Studios

4541 Irving Street, between 46th & 47th Avenues (1-415 242 3474, www.3fishstudios.com). Metro N to Judah Street & 46th Avenue. **Open** 10am-6pm daily. **Gallery**
Husband-and-wife artists Eric Rewitzer and Annie Galvin moved their studio and gallery into the burgeoning Sunset District creative community in 2012. The gallery showcases San Francisco art, including Galvin's iconic 'I Love You California' bear and '49 Mile Scenic Drive' prints – the former was inspired by a 1913 sheet music cover, the latter is based on a 1950s road sign – and Rewitzer's Japanese movie monster linocuts, paintings and digital reproductions. The couple also represent local artists such as Alexander von Wolff, whose vintage San Francisco matchbook reproductions cover the walls of businesses around the city.

$ Arizmendi Bakery

1331 9th Avenue, between Judah & Irving Streets (1-415 566 3117, www.arizmendibakery.com). Metro N to 9th Avenue & Irving Street/bus 6. **Open** 7am-7pm Tue-Fri; 7.30am-6pm Sat, Sun. **Map** p316 C10. **Food & drink**
This worker-owned cooperative named for Basque priest and cooperative movement founder José María Arizmendiarrieta is the place to go for decadent carbo-loading: fresh berry scones, pecan rolls, cookie brittle, brioche knots and sourdough-crust pizzas (sold whole and by the slice) with toppings like arugula, caramelised onions, gorgonzola cheese and rosemary oil. A huge assortment of fresh-baked breads, from corn-oat molasses to provolone olive, is also available, with daily-changing specials.

GOLDEN GATE PARK

Roughly three miles long and half a mile wide, **Golden Gate Park** is one of the largest manmade parks in the world and a testament to perseverance – or, put another way, a gargantuan project that introduced non-native species and used vast resources in ways that would never have been approved in modern-day San Francisco. The ambitious task of creating this pastoral loveliness – 1,017 acres of landscaped gardens, forests and meadows – from barren sand dunes began in 1870 in an attempt to solidify San Francisco's position as a modern urban centre, to meet the growing public demand for a city park, and, on the part of the wealthy land speculators in the area, to stimulate property values.

William Ralston, founder of the Bank of California and builder of the Palace Hotel, first approached Frederick Law Olmsted, the visionary behind Manhattan's Central Park, to design the project. Believing that the arid landscape of the Outside Lands, as the virtually uninhabited area was then known, was a barren wasteland that could never support a park, Olmsted's original design instead proposed a green stretch that would take advantage of the large natural valley that ran through the city. However, once Olmsted left town, his plan was shelved; the valley is now Van Ness Avenue.

The project was next awarded to a young civil engineer named William Hammond Hall. The park's wealthy patrons, whose motives were more fiscal- than civic-minded, saw Hall as a sympathetic individual who would accede to their plans for the land development, and they were right. Olmsted even wrote to Hall, telling him that he 'did not believe it practicable to meet the natural but senseless demand of unreflecting people bred in the Atlantic states and the North of Europe for what is technically termed a park under the climatic conditions of San Francisco'.

Work continued, however, and while it cost the surrounding environment dearly, the result was clearly a marvel. Still, it wasn't until eccentric Scottish-born John McLaren took over stewardship in 1890 that the park finally came together. McLaren spent more than 50 years as park superintendent, expanding on Hall's innovations and planting by stages, to enable lakes, meadows and forests to evolve in ways that would allow the substrate to sustain them. In the process, he was responsible for planting more than a million trees.

The park made its public debut in 1894, when more than 1.3 million people visited for the Midwinter International Exposition. The fair filled more than 100 temporary buildings. Two still remain: the **Japanese Tea Garden** and the **Music Concourse**. As the park's fame spread, horticulturalists from all over the world sent in seeds and cuttings. Today, a rose garden, a Shakespeare garden, a rhododendron dell and a tulip garden are among the living delights.

Sampling all that the park has to offer, from the diverse natural attractions to the dramatic contemporary **de Young Museum**, would take days. The prospect is even more daunting when one adds in the natural history museum, the **California Academy of Sciences**, which was transformed in 2008 into the world's greenest museum.

However, one great way to see it over the course of a single afternoon is to stroll all the way from the entrance of the park along the pedestrian footpaths beside John F Kennedy Drive, the park's main east–west artery, to the ocean (*see p188* **Walk**). It takes a few hours if you stop along the way, but your reward will be the crashing waves of the Pacific. If you prefer to travel on wheels, bikes can be hired from the area behind the Music Concourse. Indeed, if you join the throngs of locals biking, walking, jogging and in-line skating along

JFK Drive on a Sunday afternoons (and Saturdays April through September) when the road is closed to traffic, you'll soon understand why the park is known as San Francisco's collective backyard.

If you're planning on entering Golden Gate Park from Haight-Ashbury, you can do so at the west end of Haight Street by crossing Stanyan Street. Otherwise, come in via the Panhandle, a couple of blocks north. This was once the grand entrance to the park, with paths wide enough to accommodate carriages. It brings you out next to the park headquarters in **McLaren Lodge**, where you can pick up information. For a self-guided tour of the park, *see p188* **Walk**.

Sights & Museums

★ Beach Chalet & Park Chalet
1000 Great Highway (visitor centre 1-415 751 2766, restaurant 1-415 386 8439, www.beach chalet.com, www.parkchalet.com). Bus 5, 18. **Open** *Visitor centre & Beach Chalet* 9am-10.30pm daily. *Park Chalet* noon-10.30pm daily.
A perfect spot for sunset cocktails, the Beach Chalet, a historic Willis Polk-designed building on the coast, is home to a fine restaurant and brewpub. The ground-floor walls are awash in WPA (Works Progress Administration) frescoes by Lucien Labaudt depicting notable San Franciscans, among them sculptor Benny Bufano and John McLaren; the staircase features elaborate woodcarvings of sea monsters, mermaids and octopuses by Michael Von Meyer. The visitor centre also displays memorabilia from the 1894 Mid-Winter Exposition. Upstairs, the views of the ocean are stupendous. The newer downstairs Park Chalet, billed as a 'coastal beer garden', faces Golden Gate Park, with a mellow vibe ideal for whiling away a sunny afternoon with a beer on the lawn in one of the Adirondack chairs. In the summer, the restaurant offers live music and an outdoor barbecue.

★ California Academy of Sciences
55 Music Concourse Drive (1-415 379 8000, www.calacademy.org). Bus 5, 44. **Open** 9.30am-5pm Mon-Sat; 11am-5pm Sun. **Admission** $35; $25-$30 reductions; free under-4s. Free 3rd Wed of mth. **Map** p316 B9.
The architecturally stunning natural history museum – twice awarded a LEED Platinum award – debuted in 2008 after a $500 million remodel. Renzo Piano's design, clearly inspired by the natural world, doesn't disappoint. The organically shaped living roof – a vast expanse of green, undulating domes – accommodates 1.7 million native flowers and plants that reduce energy needs for heating and cooling, convert carbon dioxide into oxygen, capture rainwater, and provide a habitat for dozens of species of birds and insects.

Inside, exhibits cover a huge spectrum of life on our planet – and worlds beyond. They include the country's largest planetarium; its 90ft-tall domed screen allows visitors to watch real-time NASA feeds.

A BASTION FOR BOOKSTORES
Word up.

Green Apple Books.

EXPLORE

While independent booksellers are a dying breed around the country, San Francisco's niche bookshops are still finding ways to thrive, with speciality bookstores for almost every literary leaning and fetish imaginable. Nerve centres of the active literary scene, some of the best bookstores in San Francisco – including the **Booksmith** (*see p146*) in the Haight and legendary beat landmark **City Lights** in North Beach (*see p100*) host regular readings, as well as events like **Litquake** (www.litquake.org) and **Writers with Drinks** (www.writerswithdrinks.com) that pair with booze for a party atmosphere. The wildly popular **Porchlight Storytelling Series** (www.porchlightsf.com) teams up with Friends of the San Francisco Public Library to present lively evenings of literary entertainment.

To scratch your literary itch, make your first stop **Green Apple Books** (*see p187*). This beloved Richmond District institution, founded in 1967, is a mecca for everything from local authors to graphic novels. The annex offers a huge collection of DVDs.

Architecture and design fiends should head to **William Stout Architectural Books** (804 Montgomery Street, at Gold Street, Financial District, 1-415 391 6757, www.stoutbooks.com). For lefty literature, **Bound Together Anarchist Collective Bookstore** (1369 Haight Street, between Central & Masonic Avenues, Haight-Ashbury, 1-415 431-8355, https://boundtogetherbooks.wordpress.com) offers stacks of radical lit and hosts an annual Anarchist Book Fair in the spring, as well as supporting the Prisoners' Literature Project. Foodies should head to tiny **Omnivore Books** (3885 Cesar Chavez Street, at Church Street, Noe Valley, 1-415 282 4712, www.omnivorebooks.com), which exclusively shelves tomes on food and drink. Sci-Fi, fantasy, and Stephen King fans will find plenty to occupy them at **Borderlands Books** (866 Valencia Street, between 19th & 20th Streets, Mission, 1-415 824 8203, www.borderlands-books.com), where the staff are all-knowing. **Bird & Beckett Books & Records** (653 Chenery Street, between Carrie & Diamond Streets, Glen Park, 1-415 586 3733, www.birdbeckett.com) stocks a wealth of books on jazz and poetry, and features live jazz Fridays and Saturdays.

Elsewhere, the 212,000-gallon tank of the Steinhart Aquarium is home to 4,000 fish and 1,500 colonies of living coral. The four-storey indoor rainforest takes visitors on a spiral walkway from ground level to above the tree canopy, where birds and butterflies fly free, then drops them via an elevator to the Amazon flooded basin, home to anacondas, piranhas and giant catfish, and to the aquarium. Other exhibits recreate an American subtropical swamp, with a rare albino alligator, and a zoological landscape of Africa with traditional dioramas and a live penguin display. The museum has an excellent café.

★ De Young Museum

50 Hagiwara Tea Garden Drive (1-415 750 3600, www.deyoung.famsf.org). Bus 5, 44. **Open** 9.30am-5.15pm Tue-Sun (*Apr-Nov* until 8.45pm Fri). **Admission** $10; $6-$7 reductions; free under-12s. **Map** p316 B9.

The most prominent feature of this controversial future-primitive building, designed by Herzog & de Meuron, is the massive tower that emerges from the surrounding canopy of trees, making all those who approach from the 10th Avenue entrance to Golden Gate Park feel like they've just stumbled across an ancient lost city or an abandoned mothership. Most people would agree that the design – a combination of agular metal and organic forms found in ancient structures – is at once overwhelming and electrifying. The exterior walls are made from patterned copper, designed to take on the colour of the surrounding greenery as it oxidizes. Along with its vast collections of American art from the 17th to 20th centuries, the museum showcases an extensive collection from New Guinea and Oceania, as well as contemporary crafts and textiles. With commanding views over the park, the soaring observation tower is worth the trip alone, and there's an excellent store and café with outdoor seating areas in a delightful sculpture garden – all of which can be entered without paying admission.

RICHMOND

Bordering the northern edge of Golden Gate Park, from beyond Arguello Boulevard to the Pacific Ocean, and from Fulton to California Streets, the largely residential neighbourhood of the Richmond District is a true cultural mix, with large concentrations of Russian, Chinese and Irish immigrants. Once a sandy waterfront wasteland, the region was developed after the construction of the Geary Boulevard tramway in 1906. Eastern European Jews formed a strong community after World War I, and a number of synagogues still thrive here.

The **University of San Francisco** and the peculiar **Columbarium** hover at the easterly edge of the area, but **Clement Street** is the district's primary commercial centre. Stretching from 2nd Avenue all the way to 34th Avenue, the area between Arguello and Park Presidio

California Academy of Sciences. See p182.

Boulevards arguably offers more authentic Chinese restaurants than those found in Chinatown. Literary types have long been enamoured of **Green Apple Books** (*see p187*). Just a block north is the **Antique Traders** (4300 California Street, at 5th Avenue, 1-415 668 4444, www.theantiquetraders.com), whose breathtaking collection of stained-glass windows, salvaged from the city's many Victorians, has countless out-of-town shoppers calculating shipping costs.

Numerous cafés, bakeries and dim sum parlours line Clement Street: the takeout dumplings from **Good Luck Dim Sum** (no. 736, at 8th Avenue, 1-415 386 3388) are authentic and cheap (you can get stuffed for under $6).

One block south of Clement is **Geary Boulevard**, Richmond's main thoroughfare. In the deep end of Outer Richmond, you will stumble across **Tommy's Mexican Restaurant** (*see p187*), with its mind-blowing selection of pure agave tequilas. The much-appreciated 'free wine while you wait' policy is an added bonus at **Pacific Café** (no.7000, at 34th Avenue, 1-415 387 7091), which serves fresh seafood.

Out at 34th Avenue, turn north back over Clement into Lincoln Park and you'll find the **Legion of Honor**, which was built by George Applegarth to pay homage to the Palais de la Légion d'Honneur in Paris. Just north of the car park is the **Holocaust Memorial**, created by George Segal. The surrounding park contains the 18-hole **Lincoln Park Golf Course** (300 34th Avenue, at Clement Street, 1-415 221 9911, www. lincolnparkgolfcourse.com), offering majestic views of the Golden Gate from several greens, and a number of well-maintained hiking trails, shaded by twisted cypresses that meander along the spectacular cliffs of Land's End.

At the westerly end of the Richmond, **Sutro Heights Park** is a tiny idyll, virtually empty except for a few Russians walking their dogs or playing chess. A statue of the goddess Diana is often decorated with flowers by local pagans. In the nearby garden, enjoy a secluded picnic and marvel at the view of the Pacific. Or head across the street below Sutro Heights Park to **Louis' Restaurant** (902 Point Lobos Avenue, 1-415 387 6330), a 79-year-old diner serving big breakfasts. The views of the ocean rival those from the somewhat touristy and pricey **Cliff House** down the road; both perch on the very edge of the city.

The Cliff House was the brainchild of silver baron and former mayor Adolph Sutro. The remains of Sutro's own mansion are at the western edge of Sutro Heights Park; below the Cliff House to the north are the ruins of Sutro Baths, built by the man himself in 1896 and once the world's biggest swimming baths. Fed by the Pacific, seven pools holding more than 1.5 million gallons of water could be filled by the tides in one hour. The neglected baths were destroyed by fire

in 1966, but the ruins are strangely photogenic. A windswept three-mile coastal path winds north towards the Golden Gate Bridge.

Sights & Museums

Cliff House

1090 Point Lobos Avenue, at the Great Highway (1-415 386 3330, www.cliffhouse.com). Bus 18, 38. **Open** *Bar/restaurant* 11.30am-3.30pm, 5-9.30pm daily. *Bistro* 9am-9.30pm Mon-Sat; 8.30am-9.30pm Sun. *Walkways* 24hrs daily.

After a fire in 1894, a magnificent, eight-storey Victorian turreted palace replaced the original 1860s house on this site. However, only a year after surviving the 1906 earthquake, the second building also burned. Its subsequent 'restorations' involved more demolition and rebuilding; the current neoclassical structure, completed in 2004, includes an upscale restaurant and bar with floor-to-ceiling glass walls that make the most of its breathtaking Pacific views. Public walkways allow the less well-heeled to amble around the building. The whimsical camera obscura, a 19th-century optical marvel, was saved after a public outcry halted its demolition and is still accessible on the walkway; it projects an image of the outside world, including a large stretch of Ocean Beach, on to a giant parabolic screen using mirrors and lenses.

FREE Columbarium

1 Loraine Court, off Anza Street (1-415 752 7891). Bus 31, 33, 38. **Open** 9am-5pm Mon-Fri; 10am-3pm Sat, Sun. **Admission** free. **Map** p316 D7.

This domed neoclassical rotunda is honeycombed with hundreds of niches, filled with lavishly decorated cremation urns. Among them are the remains of many of the city's first families. With the exception of the Presidio's military cemetery, it's the only active burial site in the city: a 1901 law made burial illegal within San Francisco, and all graves were moved south to the town of Colma. Indeed, most Richmond residents are unaware that their homes were built on a massive 167-acre cemetery now known as the Richmond District, which centred on the Columbarium.

Legion of Honor

Lincoln Park, at 100 34th Avenue (1-415 750 3600, www.thinker.org). Bus 1, 2, 18, 38. **Open** 9.30am-5.15pm Tue-Sun. **Admission** $10; $6-$7 reductions; free under-12s. Free 1st Tue of mth.

Built as a memorial to the Californians who died in World War I, and set in a wooded spot overlooking the Pacific Ocean, the Legion of Honor is San Francisco's most beautiful museum, its neo-classical façade and Beaux Arts interior virtually unchanged since it was completed in 1924. A cast of Rodin's *The Thinker* dominates the entrance; the French sculptor was the personal passion of Alma Spreckels, the museum's founder, and the collection of his work here is second only to that of the Musée Rodin in Paris. A glass

EXPLORE

Burma Superstar.

EXPLORE

pyramid acts as a skylight for galleries containing more than 87,000 works of art, spanning 4,000 years but with the emphasis on European painting (including works by El Greco, Rembrandt and Monet) and decorative art. An expanded garden level houses temporary exhibitions, the Achenbach Foundation for Graphic Arts and the Bowles Collection of porcelain.

Restaurants & Cafés

★ Aziza

5800 Geary Blvd, at 22nd Avenue, (1-415 752 2222, www.aziza-sf.com). Bus 29, 38. **Open** 5.30-10pm Mon, Wed-Sun. **Main courses** $19-$29. **Moroccan**

A perfect marriage of Moroccan flavours with Northern California ingredients, suffering from none of the clichés of either. With a Michelin star and an *Iron Chef* championship under his belt, chef-owner Mourad Lahlou has risen to the ranks of the city's elite, but Aziza remains grounded, turning out dishes – such as branzino with eggplant, mustard greens and peppers, and short ribs with carrot jam, mustard soubric and dates – that continue to surprise and delight. A destination in its own right, the bar serves cocktails with fruit and veg in imaginative combinations: try reposado tequila with arugula and turmeric root.

★ Burma Superstar

309 Clement Street, at 4th Avenue (1-415 387 2147, www.burmasuperstar.com). Bus 1, 2, 44. **Open** 11.30am-3.30pm, 5-9.30pm Mon-Thur, Sun; 11.30am-3.30pm, 5-10pm Fri, Sat. **Main courses** $9-$18. **Map** p312 C6. **Burmese**

This small, wildly popular eaterie falls gastronomically between Thailand and India, sharing ingredients and spices with both, but interpreting them in uniquely Burmese ways. Lines start forming a half-hour before opening for house specialities such as tea leaf salad, a deliciously crunchy combo of dried tea leaves, fried yellow beans and garlic, sesame seeds, tomatoes and dried shrimp; and pumpkin pork stew slow-cooked with kabocha squash and ginger. No reservations are taken – the best bet for immediate seating is to get there at 5pm for dinner.

$ Cinderella Bakery

436 Balboa Street, between 5th & 6th Avenues (1-415 751 9690, www.cinderellabakery.com). Bus 31, 44. **Open** 7am-7pm daily. **Main courses** $5-$12. **Map** p316 C7. **Café**

This quirky little Russian bakery and café is known for hard-to-find Old World specialities. Authentic *piroshki* and *pierogi* stuffed with everything from meat, egg and onions to cabbage and potatoes, *pelmeni* (boiled meat dumplings), blini, borscht, *hamentaschen* (jam-filled cookie pockets), and honey and napoleon cakes are just the tip of the Siberian iceberg. No matter what you end up trying, make sure to add a loaf of the fantastically moist and sour Russian rye bread.

$ Khan Toke Thai House

5937 Geary Blvd, between 23rd & 24th Avenues (1-415 668 6654, www.khantokethai.com). Bus 29, 38. **Open** 5-10pm daily. **Main courses** $9-$15. **Thai**

Slip off your shoes, sit on a low bench (with a padded back support) and enjoy fiery, colourful curries, excellent pad thai and noodle dishes, and specialities such as Saam Kasart – spicy beef, chicken and pork sautéed with young bamboo shoots in a secret berry sauce. At $25, the Thai Royal Dinner, which includes appetiser, soup, salad, two main dishes and dessert per person, is a bona fide bargain.

Ton Kiang
5821 Geary Blvd, between 22nd & 23rd Avenues, (1-415 387 8273, www.tonkiang.net). Bus 29, 38, 38AX, 38BX. **Open** 10am-9pm Mon-Thur; 10am-9.30pm Fri; 9.30am-9.30pm Sat; 9am-9pm Sun. **Main courses**: $9-$26. **Chinese**
Ton Kiang is a longtime local fixture for dim sum, invariably packed and noisy, especially during peak hours (10am-3pm). Dining rooms on two floors fill up with extended families, neighbourhood regulars and adventurous tourists, all clamouring to get the attention of the staff rolling around carts of Chinese dumplings, glistening roast duck, sticky rice wrapped in lotus leaves, clay pot stews and sweet egg custard tarts. For novices, the best strategy is to ignore the menu and just point at what looks and smells tasty. Don't miss the Shanghai dumplings, filled with meat and a shot of hot soup, or the Chinese doughnuts – deep-fried chewy puffs rolled in sugar.

Bars

Tommy's Mexican Restaurant
5929 Geary Boulevard, between 23rd & 24th Avenues (1-415 387 4747, www.tommysmexican. com). Bus 1, 2, 29, 31, 38. **Open** noon-11pm Mon, Wed-Sun.
Although there is a restaurant attached to the bar, it's all about the tequila, on which Julio Bermejo, son of late founder Tommy, is a legitimate and recognised global authority. Ask him for advice on which of the 240-plus varieties to sample; then sip, don't shoot. The house margarita, made with fresh Peruvian limes, agave nectar and top-shelf tequila, is a doozy; order it 'rocks, no salt'.

Trad'r Sam
6150 Geary Boulevard, between 25th & 26th Avenues (1-415 221 0773). Bus 1, 2, 29, 31, 38. **Open** 10am-2am daily. **No credit cards.**
A local hangout since 1939, this tiki bar serves the kind of cocktails that can only be described as dangerous. Planter's punch, mai tais, singapore slings, the ever-popular Volcano & Goldfish Bowl…there's a guaranteed hangover under every tiny umbrella.

Shops & Services

Aroma Tea Shop
302 6th Avenue, at Clement Street (1-415 668 3788, www.aromateashop.com). Bus 1BX, 2, 44, 92. **Open** 11am-7pm daily. **Map** p312 C6. **Food & drink**
This Inner Richmond shop is packed with more than 150 varieties of tea, including jasmine, white, green oolong, black and pu-erh varietals. Owner Haymen

Da Luz is both a connoisseur and a consummate showman, performing free tastings that touch on history, health benefits, harvesting practices and rituals. Any tea can be sampled, and Haymen offers notes as one would with a fine wine. Each canister is affixed with a picture and a silly or witty description of the rare leaves within.

★ Green Apple Books
506 Clement Street, at Sixth Avenue (1-415 387 2272, www.greenapplebooks.com). Bus 1BX, 2, 44, 92. **Open** 10am-10.30pm daily. **Map** p312 C6. **Books & music**
Green Apple Books was founded in 1967 as a 750-square-foot used-book nook. Since then, it has steadily upsized, taking over several storefronts on a block of the misty Inner Richmond. One bi-level storefront houses all new books, including an excellent section of staff picks and quirky categorising designations ('Lowbrow,' reads one). Head upstairs to browse an assortment of board games, journals, stationery and novelty gifts. Two doors down, the Green Apple annex contains finds ranging from antique classics and rare first editions to 1960s comic books and graphic novels, as well as an extensive CD and DVD collection.

Park Life
220 Clement Street, between 3rd & 4th Avenues (1-415 386 7275, www.parklifestore.com). Bus 2, 33, 38, 38BX, 44. **Open** noon-8pm Mon-Thur; 11am-8pm Fri, Sat; 11am-7pm Sun. **Gifts & souvenirs**
This 1,400-square-foot store is a champion of emerging artists and clever design. The colourful wares are spread across large tables stocked with books, and dozens of posters and prints cover the walls. The store's curated stash includes playful office accessories and housewares from Japan, Germany and Scandinavia, jewellery, T-shirts and stationery. Park Life maintains a time-stealing display of art, photography, and design books, including a handful of rare, out-of-print books and exhibition catalogues. Co-owner Jamie Alexander curates ten exhibitions per year in the Park Life gallery in the Mission (3049 22nd Street, at Shotwell Street, 1-415 757 0107).

EXPLORE

EXPLORE

WALK PANHANDLE TO THE PACIFIC
Cultural meets pastoral in Golden Gate Park.

Start your tour of **Golden Gate Park** at the **McLaren Lodge** (John F Kennedy Drive, 1-415 831 2700). Once the residence of John McLaren, the lodge is now the site of the park offices and visitors' centre (open 8am-5pm Mon-Fri). Strike out south from the lodge down the tree-lined path running parallel to Stanyan Street, bearing right until you come to **Alvord Lake**. Keep right by the lake and pass under Alvord Lake Bridge, which dates to 1889. It was the first reinforced concrete bridge in the US and one of few bridges to survive the 1906 earthquake.

Head through to **Mothers' Meadow** until you reach a fork. The left branch brings you to the inventively restored **Children's Playground**, the oldest municipal playground in the nation and home to the 62 hand-painted animals of the wonderful 1912 **Herschel-Spillman Carousel**. North, past the Sharon Art Building, is **Sharon Meadow**. You'll hear **Hippie Hill**, in the middle of the meadow, before you see it. The hill became the heart of the Summer of Love, and the never-ending pick-up drum jams are still going strong.

Follow the path north to the tennis courts and continue round their right-hand side. Cross John F Kennedy Drive after you emerge

from the trees to take in the gleaming, white-domed **Conservatory of Flowers** up to your left. The oldest glass-and-wood Victorian greenhouse in the western hemisphere, it's home to more than 10,000 plants.

Take the stairs up to JFK Drive and head along Middle East Drive. On your left is the 7.5-acre **National AIDS Memorial Grove**. It bears the names of some of the city's nearly 20,000 dead engraved in stone amid redwoods, oaks and maples. Free guided tours are offered third Saturday each month (March to October) 9am and noon, or call 1-415 765 0497 to schedule a tour. Opposite, a path leads north to the lovely **Lily Pond**. Follow it round the west side to the crossroads. On the right, a grove of ferns dates from 1898. Head straight on, taking the footpath to your left that parallels JFK Drive, to another botanical delight: the **John McLaren Rhododendron Dell**. Lovingly restored, it holds a statue of McLaren himself.

Here you have a choice: carry on west towards the **de Young Museum** (*see p184*) before heading south, or amble south along leafy walkways to the **California Academy of Sciences** complex (*see p182*). From either venue, walk across the **Music Concourse** (where free Sunday afternoon concerts are

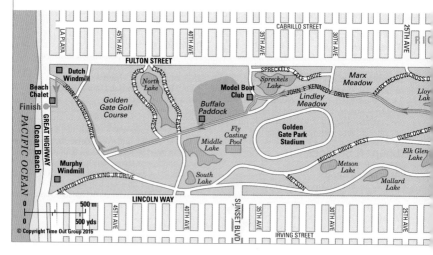

staged from April to September) to reach the **Japanese Tea Garden** (1-415 752 1171; $8). Built in 1893 for the Midwinter Exposition, the landmark garden was designed by Makoto Hagiwara, who is also credited with the invention of the fortune cookie, a treat first served by kimono-clad hostesses at the fair. Ironically, Hagiwara and his family were later evicted and sent to an internment camp during World War II. The garden still delights visitors with its steep bridges, bonsai, huge bronze Buddha and outdoor tearoom with kimono-clad servers. Another nice stopping-off point is the **Strybing Arboretum & Botanical Gardens** (1-415 661 1316), which house some 7,000 species from diverse climates. There's a fragrant garden designed for the visually impaired and a particularly appealing moon-viewing garden.

Return to MLK Drive, head west up the hill and take the stairs to **Stow Lake**. Wandering along the broad path on the south side of the lake, you'll come to the **Rustic Bridge**: cross here to explore **Strawberry Hill** island and its Chinese pavilion. A gift from the people of Taipei, it was shipped in 6,000 pieces and reassembled here in 1981. Head round the lake to the **Boathouse** (1-415 386 2531), where pedal- and rowboats are available for rent, and where you can stop for a snack at the refurbished café.

From the Boathouse, walk north up the path and you'll come out opposite **Rainbow Falls** and the **Prayer Book Cross**, which commemorates Sir Francis Drake's chaplain offering up prayers during a brief stay in the

Bay Area in 1579. Follow the little waterway west under Cross Over Drive Bridge and across Transverse Drive to **Lloyd Lake** and the **Portals of the Past**, the only memorial in the city devoted to the 1906 earthquake and fire. The ornate marble archway that now stands here was once the front entrance to the Towne Mansion at 1101 California Street; it was the last structure left standing in Nob Hill following the great fire. From there, JFK Drive takes you through meadows offering plenty of picnicking opportunities. After about half a mile, you'll come to **Spreckels Lake**, with its ducks and model sailing yachts.

When you're ready, get back on to JFK (passing the **San Francisco Model Yacht Club** on your right) and press ever west. Almost immediately, on your right, you'll pass the large **Buffalo Paddock**, where a small herd of bison roams on a 'prairie'. Pass Chain of Lakes Drive West on your right and keep going for about five minutes. Just beyond the golf course, you'll find a pleasant tree-lined pedestrian path that takes you round to the **Queen Wilhelmina Tulip Gardens**.

A gift from the eponymous Dutch monarch in 1902, the garden is shaded by the commanding **Dutch Windmill**, which boasts the world's largest windmill wings. It functioned as a huge pump, feeding water to the verdant urban wonderland that is now Golden Gate Park but was once barren sand dunes. Finally, head through the tunnel or across one of the wooded paths and you'll shortly arrive at journey's end: the historic **Beach Chalet** (see p182) overlooking the shore of the Pacific Ocean.

EXPLORE

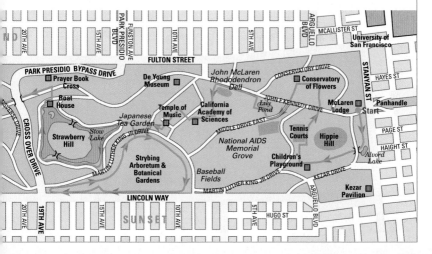

Arts & Entertainment

Children

Having a tête-à-tête with belching sea lions, watching whales spout off the coast, running wild in Golden Gate Park, driving down crazy, twisting Lombard Street – the City by the Bay is like a 49-square-mile amusement park. Luckily, not only are there enough attractions to keep children of all ages amused for weeks, but many of them will appeal to parents too. When it's time to recharge, there's a multitude of eateries offering fresh kid-friendly fare that goes way beyond standard chicken nuggets and hot dogs, including healthy picnics foraged from gourmet food trucks that you can enjoy while soaking up views of the Bay and the Golden Gate Bridge.

SIGHTSEEING & ENTERTAINMENT

In addition to the places listed below, San Francisco's gorgeous **Main Library** (*see p64*) has a Children's Center, which includes a storytelling room and a creative area for crafts and performances. A separate section for teens, styled as a creative studio, opened in 2015. If you're stuck for something to do, it's always worth contacting one of the 27 branches to see what events are being put on that week; full contact details can be found at www.sfpl.org.

There are many child-friendly attractions near **Fisherman's Wharf** (*see pp104-109*), including a pack of rather boisterous sea lions in permanent residence on the docks at Pier 39, where you'll also find a carousel, a games arcade and numerous street performers. The Wharf is also the departure point for trips to **Angel Island** and **Alcatraz Island**. Organised outings from here include the excellent **Fire Engine Tour** (1-415 333 7077, www.sanfranciscofireenginetours.com), which takes you to some of the city's major sights and across the Golden Gate Bridge on a vintage San Francisco fire truck, while clad in firefighters' gear.

It's also worth venturing further afield for family-centric activities. Across the Bay, Sausalito has a couple of standout destinations: the **Bay Area Discovery Museum** and **Marine Mammal Center**. The **Chabot Space & Science Center** (10,000 Skyline Boulevard, 1-510 336 7300, www.chabotspace.org) in Oakland is possibly the next best thing to space travel, and Berkeley's hands-on **Lawrence Hall of Science** (*see p238*) is also terrific.

Animals & Nature

If you're heading south, don't miss the world-renowned **Monterey Bay Aquarium** (886 Cannery Row, Monterey, 1-831 648 4800, www.montereybayaquarium.org).

Aquarium of the Bay

Pier 39, Embarcadero at Beach Street, Fisherman's Wharf (1-415 623 5300, www.aquariumofthebay.org). Streetcar F/bus 39, 47/cable car Powell-Mason. **Open** *June-early Sept* 9am-8pm daily. *Nov-Feb* 10am-6pm daily. *Mar-May* 10am-7pm daily. **Admission** $20; $12 reductions; free under-4s; $64 family. **Map** p312 L1.

The Aquarium puts kids in the middle of the aquatic action. Moving walkways rolling through 300 feet of clear, acrylic underwater tunnels give visitors a diver's-eye view of the Bay and its occupants. Upstairs, there are several touch tidal pools with urchins and bat rays. If you've got time, combine your visit with an island hop or Bay cruise. Blue & Gold Fleet (1-415 705 8200, www.blue and goldfleet.com) offers hour-long Bay cruises, as well as trips to Angel Island, departing from Pier 39. Alcatraz Island Cruises (1-415 981 7625, www. alcatrazcruises.com) offers two-and-a-half-hour and half-day tours of Alcatraz and Angel Islands, departing from nearby Pier 33; for details, *see p107*.

FREE Marine Mammal Center

2000 Bunker Road, Fort Chronkhite, Sausalito (1-415 289 7325, www.tmmc.org). Visitor centre 1049 Fort Cronkhite. Blue & Gold Fleet ferry from Pier 41, or Golden Gate ferry from Ferry Building. **Open** 10am-5pm daily. **Admission** free.

Visit the sea lions and sea otters being rehabilitated at this nonprofit centre. The organisation rescues sick or stranded animals, nurtures them back to health and returns them to the Pacific. Spring is pupping season, and also the period when you can see most animals. There are self-guided audio tours, and docent-led tours are available with reservations.

San Francisco Zoo

Sloat Boulevard, at 47th Avenue, Outer Sunset (1-415 753 7080, www.sfzoo.org). Metro to SF Zoo/ bus 18, 23. **Open** *Late May-early Sept Main zoo* 10am-5pm daily. *Children's zoo* 10am-4pm daily. *Early Sept-late May* 11am-4pm daily. **Admission** $20; $14-$17 reductions; free under-4s.

The three-acre African Savanna, Grizzly Gulch, and the expansive Lemur Forest are highlights of the zoo, where more than 1,000 species of animals make their home. Combine your visit with a walk along Ocean Beach and maybe lunch at the Beach Chalet or Park Chalet (*see p182*). Look out for whales in January and February.

Attractions & Museums

San Francisco institutions of equal interest to kids and grown-ups include the **Cable Car Museum** (*see p86*), the ships at **Maritime**

National Historical Park at Fisherman's Wharf (*see p107*), and the **Exploratorium**, which explodes the 'don't touch the exhibits' tradition with such cool displays as a *Hugo*-esque 22-foot-high Tinkerer's Clock manned by cut-out figures that kids can control.

Alcatraz

For listings, see p107.

The former island prison in the middle of the Bay, once home to notorious criminals such as Al Capone, George 'Machine Gun' Kelly, and Robert 'Birdman' of Alcatraz' Stroud, holds a fascinatingly creepy allure for kids and parents alike. The fun begins with a scenic ferry ride from Fisherman's Wharf. Once you've landed, pick up an audio cellhouse tour (included in ticket price) and hear first-hand from former inmates and guards about life in the maximum-security prison, including the numerous escape attempts, food riots, and the occupation by Native Americans in the 1970s. Book well in advance for the very popular night tour.

Bay Area Discovery Museum

East Fort Baker, 557 McReynolds Road, Sausalito (1-415 339 3900, www.baykidsmuseum.org). Blue & Gold Fleet ferry from Pier 41, or Golden Gate ferry from Ferry Building. **Open** 9am-5pm Tue-Fri (open Mon mid June-Aug) **Admission** $14; $13 reductions; free 1st Wed of mth.

This hands-on museum is located just below the north ramp of the Golden Gate Bridge and consequently offers spectacular skyline views. Activities for include the Lookout Cove, an expansive outdoor area with a sea cave, climbable shipwreck and miniature Golden Gate Bridge. Discovery Bay features rotating exhibits on everything from Curious George to space travel.

San Francisco Zoo.

ARTS & ENTERTAINMENT

Tot Spot gives toddlers their own indoor/outdoor nirvana, with a plastic trout-packed waterway, climbing structures and animal costumes.

California Academy of Sciences
For listings, see p182.
The combination aquarium, planetarium and natural history museum is a magnet for children and parents alike. Inside the four-storey rainforest dome, kids can interact with flitting butterflies and birds, then descend to an Amazonian 'flooded forest' to view magnified sea creatures from inside an acrylic tunnel. Interactive digital games, a 'living roof' with thousands of native plants, a shark and ray lagoon, all-digital planetarium, live penguin habitat, and a swamp featuring Claude, the albino alligator, round out the myriad exhibits. The Academy's kid-friendly dining options are also first-rate, featuring organic, sustainable food at the café as well as on the lovely garden terrace.

Children's Creativity Museum
Yerba Buena Gardens, 221 4th Street, at Howard Street, SoMa (1-415 820 3320, www.zeum.org). BART & Metro to Powell/bus 12, 14, 30, 45, 91 & Market Street routes. **Open** 10am-4pm Wed-Sun. **Admission** $12. **Map** p313 N6.
At this interactive art and technology museum, activities include a stop-motion animation studio, an innovation lab where kids are challenged to invent something, and a studio where they can record a music video using green screens. In the same complex, you'll also find a bowling alley, a great children's playground, an ice rink, a garden and a vintage carousel.

★ FREE Musée Mécanique
For listings, see p107.
At this museum-arcade hybrid, kids can discover a lost world of non-digital, coin-operated games and amusements: gypsy fortune tellers, giant mechanical-circus dioramas, carnival strength-testers, boxing and baseball games, player pianos, early pinball machines, and a looming Laffing Sal (a cackling mechanical relic salvaged from San Francisco's defunct Playland at the Beach amusement park). Afterwards, step out back to visit the USS *Pampanito*, a restored World War II submarine that's open for tours.

IN THE KNOW PRESIDIO PICNIC

When sitting in a restaurant is too confining for fidgety kids, head to **Picnic at the Presidio** (see p129), a weekly Off the Grid food truck gathering on the Presidio's Main Post, where you can spread out on the lawn, play with free games, listen to music, and indulge in a host of gourmet goodies while soaking up views of the Golden Gate.

Pier 39
Beach Street & the Embarcadero, Fisherman's Wharf (1-415 705 5500, www.pier39.com). Metro to Pier 39/bus 39, 47/cable car Powell-Mason. **Open** *Jan-mid Feb* 10am-7pm Mon-Thur, Sun; 10am-9pm Fri, Sat. *Mid Feb-mid Apr, Nov-Jan* 10am-8pm Mon-Thur, Sun; 10am-9pm Fri, Sat. *Mid Apr-Nov* 10am-9pm Mon-Thur, Sun; 10am-10pm Fri, Sat. **Map** p312 L1.
Pier 39 is a bustling tourist trap with mediocre chain restaurants. But it's popular with younger visitors for its fairly decent street performers, games arcade, bungee jump, carousel and kayak rentals. If you can handle the schlock, you might enjoy the beautiful views and playful (or bickering) sea lions on the K Dock.

SS Jeremiah O'Brien National Liberty Ship Museum
Pier 45, The Embarcadero, at Taylor Street, Fisherman's Wharf (1-415 544 0100, www.ssjeremiahobrien.org). Metro to Fisherman's Wharf/bus 39, 47/cable car Powell-Mason. **Open** *Sept-May* 10am-4pm daily. *June-Aug* 10am-6pm daily. **Admission** $12; $6-$8 reductions; free under-5s; $25 family. **Map** p312 K1.
There's plenty for history buffs big and small to explore aboard the *Jeremiah O'Brien*, a veteran of D-Day and the only US ship to sail to the 50th anniversary of the Allied invasion at Normandy. From the faithfully restored engine room to the officers' bunkrooms, it's a fascinating bit of World War II arcana. At nearby Maritime National Historic Park at Hyde Street Pier, you'll also find a flotilla of turn-of-the-19th-century ships, including the three-mast, square-rigged *Balclutha*.
▶ *For more about Hyde Street Pier and the Balclutha, see p107.*

★ Urban Putt
1096 S Van Ness Avenue, at 22nd Street, Mission (1-415 341 1080, www.urbanputt.com). BART to 24th Street Mission. **Open** 4pm-midnight Mon-Thur (last tee-off 11pm); 4pm-1am Fri (last tee-off midnight); 11am-1am Sat (last tee-off midnight); 11am-midnight Sun (last tee-off 11pm). Under-21s not admitted after 8pm. **Map** p316 K12.
A steampunk mini-golf course set inside a Victorian mortuary? Only in San Francisco. Putt your ball around the Transamerica Pyramid, inside a Jules Verne-esque submarine beneath the Bay, alongside cable cars, and even through the 1906 earthquake. Entertaining for families and non-parents alike, the place has a full bar and restaurant upstairs serving great California comfort cuisine and portable bar bites, including decadent duck poutine, chicken-and-waffle skewers, and cornmeal-crust deep-dish pizza. Downstairs, there's another bar that also dispenses soft-serve ice-cream.

STORY TIME WITH A TWIST

Once upon a time in San Francisco...

With its lively lit scene, San Francisco is known for storytellers. And the roster of readings extends to the younger set too. If your tyke simply can't take another bridge or museum, settle in for a session at one of these great venues.

Perhaps the most obvious places for book-related events, all branches of **San Francisco Public Library** (1-415 557 4400, www.sfpl. org) host story times. Check online or call for the most current schedule. Most Sundays, staff at the **Asian Art Museum** (*see p64*) recount stories tailored to the contents of its galleries – Indian myths to Chinese folktales (consult the museum's website for times).

The **de Young Museum** in Golden Gate Park (*see p184*) offers a range of fun and educational activities for children, including stories and free classes most Saturdays taught by 'artist-teachers'. Also in the park, the **San Francisco Botanical Garden Library** (9th Avenue, at Lincoln Way, Golden Gate Park, www.sfbotanicalgarden.org) hosts themed story times the first and third Sunday of each month (10.30am-11am), followed by a docent-led children's tour of the gardens.

The offspring of eclectic Mission emporium Paxton Gate (*see p168*), nearby **Curiosities for Kids** (766 Valencia Street, between 18th & 19th Streets, 1-415 252 9990, www.paxton gate.com) hosts a story time every Thursday from 11am until noon. Once you've perused the trove of mostly handmade or non-plastic toys, head to the main store, which offers such kid-appealing items as giant framed scarab beetles and taxidermied mice.

Walt Disney Family Museum

For listings, see p128.

Opened by a foundation headed by Walt Disney's daughter, Diane, the museum is not fully geared to kids, but still offers enough entertaining fare – including classic cartoons and listening stations – to ensure they won't get bored. Housed in repurposed army barracks, its galleries take a chronological look at Walt's life and work, from his early cartoons to his revolutionary innovations in dimensional animation and sound. Don't miss the gallery where children get to add sound effects to Disney's classic *Steamboat Willie*.

Performing Arts

Details for most special events, festivals and performances for kids can be found in the Sunday pink section of the *San Francisco Chronicle* (www.sfgate.com) or on the website **Red Tricycle** (http://redtri.com/san-francisco-kids).

Buddy Club

Randall Museum, 199 Museum Way, at Roosevelt Way, Corona Heights (1-510 236 7469, www.the buddyclub.com). Bus 37. **Shows** *July-Apr* 11am Sun. **Tickets** $8. **Map** p315 G10.

Since 1987, impresario Scott Gelfand has been presenting sold-out shows to adoring pint-size fans (ages two to 12) featuring a troupe of magicians, jugglers, singers, clowns, ventriloquists, acrobats and puppeteers. A perennially popular place for birthday parties. Note that in 2016 shows resume in autumn when the museum reopens following renovation.

Family Matinees at SFJAZZ

For listings, see p223. **Tickets** $5-$15. **Map** p316 K8.

Kids can get into the groove at these family-friendly Saturday-morning concerts at SFJAZZ Center, roughly once a month. One-hour performances are followed by interactive family workshops where

ARTS & ENTERTAINMENT

young musicians can join in on Orff percussion instruments (workshops are free with matinee tickets). Shows range from reinterpretations of Michael Jackson and Stevie Wonder and jazz poetry to African-American children's folk music and the SFJAZZ High School All-Stars Orchestra.

Young Performers Theatre

Fort Mason Center, 2 Marina Boulevard, at Buchanan Street, Building C, Room 300, Marina (1-415 346 5550, www.ypt.org). Bus 38, 45, 47, 49. **Shows** vary. **Tickets** $12.
Adaptations of classics (*Snow White, Beauty and the Beast*), as well as original works by local playwrights, are performed by kids, for kids, here. The institution, which aims to engender an early appreciation of theatre, offers year-round classes for children ages three to 15.

PARKS & PLAY SPACES

FREE Crissy Field

See p125.
This 130-acre restored waterfront wetlands area features a lovely walking and biking promenade, a sheltered beach and lagoon, picnic areas, and several kid-friendly attractions that include the House of Air trampoline park (www.houseofair. com) and Planet Granite climbing gym (www. planetgranite.com). Follow the bayfront path past the Greater Farallones National Marine Sanctuary Visitor Center, where you can feed an anemone or hold a shark tooth. Walk out onto Torpedo Wharf for a postcard-worthy photo of the Golden Gate Bridge, and make a pit stop at the Warming Hut for organic soups, sandwiches, and only-in-San-Francisco books, games and souvenirs. You can also pick up a *Mystery Trail* booklet with clues that kids can use to find bronze rubbing plaques along the waterfront path.

★ FREE Golden Gate Park

See p181.
A huge array of kid-friendly attractions make Golden Gate Park one of San Francisco's best family destinations, especially on weekends when the main drive is closed to cars (Sundays year-round, Saturdays April through September). Children will want to head straight for Stow Lake, where they can hike out to Strawberry Hill or rent bicycles, pedal- and rowing boats. Visit Spreckels Lake to marvel at the model boats (at Fulton Drive & 36th Avenue), then wander down to the buffalo paddock to see the small herd of bison that have been residents in the park since 1890. The younger set will enjoy the Koret Children's Quarter (http://sfrecpark.org). Built in 1887 as America's first municipal playground, it was remodelled in 2007 to incorporate state-of-the-art features such as a huge spiderweb net and a wave climbing wall. The old-school cement slides and neighbouring historic Herschell-Spillman Carousel are legacies from the original playground.
▶ *For a walk on the wilder side, head over to Ocean Beach (see p180).*

FREE Helen Diller Playground at Dolores Park

Dolores Street, between 18th and 19th Streets, Mission (sfrecpark.org/mission-dolores-helen-diller-playground). Metro J to 20th Street. **Map** p316 J11.
The playground in Dolores Park was completely revamped in 2012 with a huge array of whimsical structures, including a 40-foot super slide, a giant climbing net, swings, a suspension bridge and shipwrecked boats.

Rooftop at Yerba Buena Gardens

750 Howard Street, at 4th Street, SoMa (www. yerbabuenagardens.com). BART & Metro to Powell. **Open** 6am-10pm daily. **Map** p313 N6.
The inventive playground at Yerba Buena Gardens sits directly next to an ice rink, a bowling alley and the multimedia Children's Creativity Museum (*see p194*). Among the attractions are giant tube slides, a mini hedge maze, climbing structures, and a captivating interactive sculpture by Chico MacMurtrie in which you activate a bronze figure atop a giant globe by sitting down on a bench. Nearby is the beautifully restored Children's Creativity Carousel, hand-carved by Charles Looff in 1906 ($4 for two rides).

RESTAURANTS

In addition to good, local burger-and-fries chains like **Mel's Drive In** (four SF locations, www. melsdrive-in.com) and **Barney's** (locations in Noe Valley and Cow Hollow, www.barneyshamburgers. com), San Francisco abounds with grown-up restaurants that offer excellent kid options and special menus that are a big cut above the average hot dog and tater tots fare. In the Mission District, **Foreign Cinema** (*see p161*) draws sophisticated crowds for its California-Mediterranean cuisine, lively bar, and outdoor film screenings, but parents love it just as much for its three-course kids menus (at brunch and dinner), featuring everything from French toast and scrambled egg to fresh pasta and steak and potatoes. Steamy rolling carts dispensing dim sum – dumplings and buns stuffed with shrimp, sweet pork, egg custard, and other fillings – are a sure-fire hit at **Yank Sing** (*see p60*), where youngsters can order just by pointing at what looks (or smells) good. At **Tony's Pizza Napoletana** (*see p102*), kids can choose from ten types of pizza, including the pie that won owner Tony Gemingnani the title of World Champion Pizza Maker in Naples, then watch them emerge blistering from a 1,000-degree coal-fired oven. The popular North Beach restaurant also features a special kids' menu with pint-size pizzas, housemade breadsticks, and mac and cheese.

Film

With its distinctive neighbourhoods, its impossibly steep streets and spectacular bayside backdrop, San Francisco has long attracted film directors. But the city's long-standing love affair with the movies goes far beyond its reputation as one of the world's finest film locations. The city's fertile creative environment, combined with the Bay Area's status as America's premier tech hub, has fostered everything from the digital-effects revolution at George Lucas's Industrial Light & Magic and Pixar Studios to film festivals that fill every frame in the global cinematic reel.

CINEMAS

Like any US city, San Francisco has its share of massive, cookie-cutter multiplexes. SoMa's **AMC Metreon 16** and the nine-screen **Century San Francisco Centre** downtown (Westfield San Francisco Centre, 845 Market Street, between 4th & 5th Streets, 1-415 538 8422, www.cinemark.com) are typical examples, with all the ambience and individuality of an airport lobby. Still, they offer state-of-the-art IMAX and XD (Extreme Digital) screens, extremely comfortable seats and sound systems that are beyond reproach.

Centrally located movie houses offering a mix of new releases, indie, foreign and culturally focused fare include the **Presidio** (2340 Chestnut Street, between Scott & Divisadero Streets, Marina, 1-415 776 2388, www.lntsf.com), the vintage single-screen **Vogue Theatre** (3290 Sacramento Street, at Presidio Avenue, Presidio Heights, 1-415 346 2228, www.voguesf.com), and the city's three Landmark Theatres (www.landmarktheatres.com): **Opera Plaza Cinema** (601 Van Ness Avenue, at Golden Gate Avenue, Civic Center, 1-415 771 0183), **Embarcadero Center Cinema** (Building 1, Embarcadero Center, Battery Street, between Sacramento & Clay Streets, Financial District, 1-415 352 0835) and the **Clay Theatre** (2261 Fillmore Street, at Clay Street, Pacific Heights, 1-415 561 9921).

For the latest local listings and reviews, go to www.timeout.com/san-francisco.

Mainstream & first-run

AMC Metreon 16

135 4th Street, at Mission Street, SoMa (1-415 369 6207, www.amctheatres.com). BART & Metro to Powell/streetcar F/bus Market Street routes. **Tickets** $13.50-$20.50; $10.50-$19 reductions. **Map** p313 M6.

If you absolutely, positively have to see a just-released blockbuster in 3D IMAX with the latest sound system technology, this is the theatre to visit. Always at the cutting edge of movie-screening technology, the Metreon is either a feast for, or an assault on, the senses – probably depending on your age.

Sundance Kabuki

1881 Post Street, at Fillmore Street, Japantown (1-415 346 3243, www.sundancecinemas.com). Bus 2, 3, 22, 38. **Tickets** $10.50-$12.50. **Map** p312 H6.

Run by Robert Redford's Sundance Cinemas, this eight-screen complex contains cafés and a full bar – if you buy tickets for one of the frequent 21-and-over screenings, you can bring your drinks into the auditorium. The Kabuki serves as the main venue for the San Francisco International Film Festival.

Arthouse & revival

Built mostly between 1910 and 1930, San Francisco's single-screen neighbourhood cinemas flourished through World War II, but many have been lost in recent years to development and multi-screen complexes. There are signs of hope,

Castro Theatre.

however: set to open at the time of writing, the **Alamo Drafthouse New Mission Cinema** (2550 Mission Street, between 21st & 22nd Streets, www.drafthouse.com) is putting a contemporary spin on one of the city's classic movie palaces. The venue will feature five screens for new release, indie and repertory films and you can dine on comfort food and quaff local draught beer while you watch.

★ Castro Theatre

429 Castro Street, at Market Street, Castro (1-415 621 6120, www.castrotheatre.com). Metro to Castro/streetcar F/bus 24, 33, 35, 37. **Tickets** $11; $8.50 reductions. **No credit cards.** **Map** p315 H10.

One of San Francisco's finest and best-loved repertory cinemas, this glorious movie palace was built in 1922 by famed art deco architect Timothy Pflueger. It became a registered landmark 55 years later. These days it's a dream space of classical murals and rare old film posters, ceilings that shimmer with gold, and films introduced to the strains of a Mighty Wurlitzer organ.

▶ *For special-event gay and camp screenings at the Castro, see p211.*

Roxie Theater & Little Roxie

3117 16th Street, between Valencia & Guerrero Streets, Mission (1-415 863 1087, www.roxie.com). BART 16th Street/bus 14, 22, 26, 33, 49, 53. **Tickets** $10; $7.50 reductions. **No credit cards.** **Map** p316 J10.

The oldest continuously operated movie theatre in the United States and the second oldest in the world, the non-profit Roxie is community-run with an amazing range: world premières of cutting-edge documentaries, classic films noir and '60s horror flicks are only a taste of the adventurous programming. Next door, Little Roxie has a great projection set-up, a terrific sound system, and a programme of stuff too weird even for its wacky parent. The gritty atmosphere just adds to the funkiness.

OTHER INSTITUTIONS

Artists' Television Access

992 Valencia Street, at 21st Street, Mission (1-415 824 3890, www.atasite.org). BART 24th Street Mission/Metro to Church & 18th Streets/ bus 14, 26, 48, 49, 67. **Tickets** $5-$20. **No credit cards.** **Map** p316 K11.

An artist-run non-profit that specialises in experimental and unusual programming is home to both a screening venue and gallery. ATA hosts a broad variety of events, including open screenings, usually Thursday to Sunday.

Ninth Street Independent Film Center

145 Ninth Street, between Mission & Howard Streets, SoMa (1-415 625 6100, www.ninthstreet. org). Bus 14, 19. **Tickets** vary. **No credit cards.** **Map** p318 L8.

Look out for screenings from San Francisco Cinematheque (*see below*), the city-wide filmmakers group the Film Arts Foundation, LGBT film group Frameline, the Center for Asian American Media and more at this state-of-the-art facility.

Pacific Film Archive

2155 Center Street, at Oxford Street, Berkeley (1-510 642 1124, www.bampfa.berkeley.edu). BART Downtown Berkeley, then AC Transit bus 7, 51.

At presstime, the renowned Berkeley Art Museum/ Pacific Film Archive was set to reopen in January 2016 in a spectacular new building designed by Diller Scofidio + Renfro. The PFA features an amazing collection of more than 14,000 films and videos, including rare silent Soviet, US avant-garde and Japanese cinema (the largest collection of Japanese films outside of Japan). Committed not only to showing films, but also preservation, the PFA offers more than 480 programmes each year, many with appearances by filmmakers or accompanied by live music.

★ San Francisco Cinematheque

Various venues (1-415 522 1990, www. sfcinematheque.org). **Tickets** $5-$20.

For the stuff you simply can't see anywhere else, be it documentary, feature film, animation or experimental fare, this is the name to look for. The Cinematheque offers some 50 events a year from October to December and February to June. The annual spring festival Crossroads celebrates recent and rediscovered artist-made film, video and performance cinema at venues around the city, including the Victoria Theatre (2961 16th Street, between Capp & Mission Streets, Mission, 1-415 863 7576), Yerba Buena Center (*see below*), the Roxie Theater (*see p198*) and the Ninth Street Independent Film Center (*see p198*).

YBCA Screening Room

Yerba Buena Center for the Arts, 701 Mission Street, Galleries and Forum Building, 2nd floor, SoMa (1-415 978 2700, www.ybca.org/venues/screening-room). BART & Metro to Montgomery/bus 9, 9X, 10, 14, 30, 45, 71. **Tickets** $10; $8 reductions. **Map** p313 N6.

The screening room at Yerba Buena Center for the Arts showcases contemporary films made by local, national and international filmmakers. Series often focus on a single, provocative filmmaker or a genre, but documentaries and cult rarities also get a look in.

Recent offerings have included 'Shakey Pictures: The Films of Neil Young' and 'Hardcore Cronenberg'.

FOREIGN-LANGUAGE SPECIALISTS

Venues offering screenings of European films in their original languages include the **Alliance Française** (1345 Bush Street, between Polk & Larkin Streets, 1-415 775 7755, www.afsf.com) in Polk Gulch; the **Goethe-Institut** (530 Bush Street, between Grant Avenue & Stockton Street, 1-415 263 8760, www.goethe.de/ins/us/saf, *photo p200*), which sponsors the annual Berlin & Beyond Festival (*see p200*); and the **Instituto Italiano di Cultura** (601 Van Ness, Opera Plaza Suite F, 1-415 788 7142, www.iicsanfrancisco.esteri.it).

FILM FESTIVALS

The Bay Area's love affair with film is amply demonstrated by the volume and variety of its film festivals, many of which are both the longest running and largest of their kind in the nation – or the world. Ethnic and cultural groups in

Roxie Theater.

ARTS & ENTERTAINMENT

Goethe-Institut. See p199.

particular are well represented, with annual showcases for Asian, Native American, Black, Jewish, Arab and Latino filmmakers, among many others. Works by locals mingle with international productions, and the quality varies from high-minded to low-budget. Below are some of the major festivals, but several smaller festivals, such as the **Anti-Corporate Film Festival** (www.countercorp.org/film-festival), offer equally tantalising fare. You can find a complete list on the website of the **San Francisco Film Commission** (www.filmsf.org).

Berlin & Beyond
Castro Theatre (see p198) (1-415 263 8760, www.goethe.de/en). **Date** mid Jan.
Presented by the Goethe-Institut San Francisco, B&B focuses on the films of Germany, Austria and Switzerland. Celebrating its 20th anniversary in 2016, Berlin & Beyond Film Festival has been the leading festival of contemporary German cinema in the Americas. *Photo p202.*

CAAMFest
Various venues (1-415 863 0814, www.caamfest.com). **Date** mid Mar.
The largest and longest-running Asian-American filmmaking showcase in the US, CAAMFest presents more than 120 works at venues throughout the Bay Area. A production of the Center for Asian American Media (CAAM), the festival has become the premier event for Asian films in the United States and a significant launching pad for Asian-American filmmakers.

Frameline
Various venues (1-415 703 8650, www.frameline.org). **Date** late June.
An integral part of the month-long Gay Pride festivities, Frameline is both a potent political statement and an unbridled celebration, offering features, shorts, docs and experimental works.

IndieFest
Various venues (1-415 820 3907, www.sfindie.com). **Date** early-mid Feb.
The first IndieFest showed 85 films over 14 days and prompted organiser Jeff Ross to create three more festivals: Another Hole in the Head, highlighting the horror genre, and DocFest, both in the autumn, and the Winter Music Festival. IndieFest now runs concurrently with the Winter Music Festival, and with more music-themed films added to the schedule, there's always a lively crowd for screenings.

Jewish Film Festival
Various venues (1-415 621 0556, www.sfjff.org). **Date** late July-early Aug.
The world's largest Jewish film festival, the SFJFF presents two weeks of contemporary (and some archival) films.

ESSENTIAL SAN FRANCISCO FILMS

Six standouts starring the City by the Bay.

Vertigo.

VERTIGO
ALFRED HITCHCOCK (1958)

Hitchcock's swirling masterpiece has the hilly geography of the city built into its very plot. In long, wordless sequences, we watch James Stewart's retired detective chase down his obsession – the alluring Madeleine (Kim Novak) – on to Fort Point beneath the Golden Gate Bridge for her famous jump into the Bay, and fatefully, all the way to Muir Woods and Mission San Juan Bautista.

BULLITT
PETER YATES (1968)

Few movies show off the city as gloriously as Steve McQueen's action classic. During the film's famous 11-minute car chase, Hyde, Filbert and Laguna Streets get a coating of burned rubber. It's also worth noting that McQueen's character was based on SF's real-life supercop Dave Toschi, who saw his career become art while still on the job (hunting the Zodiac Killer).

DIRTY HARRY
DON SIEGEL (1971)

What can we say? San Francisco is the place to find cinema's great vigilante lawmen. Clint Eastwood's iconic character wields an enormous handgun and threatens a cowering perp ('You've got to ask yourself one question: "Do I feel lucky?" Well, *do ya*, punk?'). Elsewhere, Harry is led on a night pursuit around Washington Square and North Beach, all in defence of a city that questions his every move.

THE CONVERSATION
FRANCIS FORD COPPOLA (1974)

This paranoid thriller – finished the same year as *The Godfather: Part II* – is the director's dark valentine to the City by the Bay. Starring Gene Hackman as a nervous loner and surveillance expert, the movie centres on a long, aerial shot of two illicit lovers in Union Square, a rendezvous that slowly reveals itself to be more than it seems.

INVASION OF THE BODY SNATCHERS
PHILIP KAUFMAN (1978)

Discerning viewers know this nightmarish remake to be superior to the 1956 original, not least for turning San Francisco into a player itself. A freaky, funky town where the counterculture hangs on to its strangeness, the movie's metropolis might be getting overrun by yuppies – or perhaps they're from another planet entirely. Over everyone looms the Transamerica Pyramid, an antenna of doom.

TIME AFTER TIME
NICHOLAS MEYER (1979)

Sadly, largely forgotten now, Meyer's inventive thriller – about a time-travelling HG Wells who hunts down serial killer Jack the Ripper into the future – gorgeously shows off the city in a way that's instantly nostalgic for residents. Golden Gate Park, the Embarcadero, Chinatown and Ghirardelli Square are just a handful of the dozens of locations used to frame a classic battle of wits.

Berlin & Beyond. See p200.

Mill Valley Film Festival

Various venues in Marin County (1-415 383 5256, www.mvff.com). **Date** early-mid Oct.
Founded in 1977, the Mill Valley Film Festival is one of California's most influential annual film events. Make an excursion across the Bay to picturesque Marin County for 11 days of films, panels, tributes to actors and filmmakers, workshops and more – including the chance to gawk at celebrities.

Noir City

Castro Theatre, see p198 (www.noircity.com). **Date** Jan.
With 24 films shown over ten days in January, the Noir City festival now packs the lavish, historic Castro Theatre with film noir devotees from all around the world. Presented by the Film Noir Foundation (www.filmnoirfoundation.org), which counts author James Ellroy among its advisory council, Noir City is the highlight of the foundation's public exhibitions.

Ocean Film Festival

Cowell Theater, Fort Mason Center, Marina Boulevard at Laguna Street (1-415 561 6251, www.oceanfilmfest.org). **Date** mid Mar.
The Ocean Film Festival was launched in 2004. It's aim was 'to increase public understanding of the environmental, social and cultural importance of marine ecosystems and foster a spirit of ocean stewardship', and it's one of only two such festivals in the world. More than 40 films are screened over a period of more than three days in March, ranging from conservation documentaries to wildlife and adventure films.

IN THE KNOW REEL LIFE

Have dinner and a movie – simultaneously – at Mission District eaterie **Foreign Cinema** (*see p161*), which screens foreign and classic films in an outdoor courtyard. Or catch a flick while working up a sweat on the treadmill at the **Alhambra Crunch** (2330 Polk Street, between Green & Union Streets, Russian Hill, 1-415 292 5444, www.crunch. com). Housed in what was once an art deco movie palace, the gym shows films in the main exercise area. Movie-themed laundromat **Star Wash** (392 Dolores Street, at 17th Street, Castro, 1-415 431 2443) lets diehard cinephiles gaze at stills of screen idols during the rinse cycle.

San Francisco International Film Festival

Various venues (1-415 561 5000, www.sffs.org). **Date** mid Apr-early May.
Launched in 1957, this is North America's longest-running film festival, and one of the best, screening more than 180 films. The event sees around 200 filmmakers and other industry luminaries in attendance.

San Francisco Silent Film Festival

Castro Theatre, see p198 (1-415 777 4908, www.silentfilm.org). **Date** early-mid July.
Screenings at this three-day event are accompanied by a pianist, a Wurlitzer organist, or anything from Indian duos to avant-garde chamber groups.

ARTS & ENTERTAINMENT

Gay & Lesbian

San Francisco's status as the capital of gay America is constantly up for debate. There are other cities with larger LGBT populations (though SF still leads on a per capita scale) and municipalities that claim their hotspots make them number one. But there's no denying that the city is still at the forefront of gay activism. The landmark 2015 Supreme Court's ruling holding that gay marriage is a constitutional right came out of a decade-long struggle that started when then-mayor Gavin Newsom defiantly issued marriage licences to same-sex couples in 2004 in spite of state law. Before that, there were the pre-Pride days of gay liberation and the election of Harvey Milk, California's first openly gay politician. This sense of freedom translates to nightlife. SoMa's leather bars and the riot of LGBT art, music and attitude in the Mission are just two of the ever-changing scenes.

NEIGHBOURHOODS

Polk Street, the Tenderloin, North Beach, Haight-Ashbury and SoMa were the neighbourhoods of choice for gays and lesbians back in the 1970s, but the **Castro** – with its street fair, flourishing restaurants and bars, and talismanic **Castro Theatre** (*see p198*) – soon became the preferred destination. Today, the area remains vibrant, with trendy, expensive houses and streets brimming with Pride flags and gay-centric bars, eateries and shops. But the Castro is having an identity crisis, as more and more young, straight families move in and dilute its world-famous gay identity. Still, the history and imagery of the gay rights movement is so firmly woven into the fabric of the neighbourhood by now that it's doubtful it will ever completely go away.

Middle-class lesbians with kids and dogs have settled in cheery residential neighbourhoods such as **Bernal Heights** and the **Outer Mission**. Affluent queer folk thrive in villagey and ultra-gentrified **Noe Valley**, filled with chic shops and cosy cafés, and **Hayes Valley**, home to trendy restaurants and wine bars. Gay men still gravitate towards **SoMa**, which contains almost all of the gay clubs and many good gay bars, sex clubs and

dance joints frequented by the brawny, bear-like and well toned. **Duboce Triangle** (between Market, Waller and Castro Streets) and **Potrero Hill** both also draw queer crowds.

THE QUEER CALENDAR

San Francisco Pride (www.sfpride.org), the most prominent gay carnival in the world, is the highlight of the year. While activities span virtually the entire month of June, the main Pride Celebration takes place over the final weekend, including the spirit-buoying **Trans March** on Friday (www.transmarch.org), the boisterous Saturday night women-only **Dyke March** (www.thedykemarch.org), both with onlookers of any gender cheering from the sidelines, and Sunday's **Pride Parade** (*see p32*). The crowds stream up Market Street to Civic Center Plaza to watch the leather-and-lace Dykes on Bikes leading the parade with their full-throttled Harley power and roar. Almost as crucial as the parade is **Frameline**, the San Francisco International LGBTQ Film Festival (*see p200*), a two-week buffet of shorts, documentaries and features.

The annual leather-besotted **Folsom Street Fair** (www.folsomstreetfair.com; *see p32*), held

Women's Building.

ARTS & ENTERTAINMENT

in September, is a mixed affair, but with a preponderantly gay theme. Folsom's 'dirty little brother', **Up Your Alley Fair** (www.folsomstreetevents.org/upyouralley), a cruisey and risqué S&M festival in late July, also takes place in SoMa. The Castro's other major street celebration, Halloween, has been all but shut down in recent years due to dangerous overcrowding and an unsavoury atmosphere.

On a more sombre note, the city marks and fights the devastation of AIDS with several events: the **AIDS Candlelight Vigil**, along Market Street to the Main Library in May, the **AIDS Walk San Francisco** (www.aidswalk.net/sanfran) in July, and **World AIDS Day** on 1 December, which sees events across the city.

INFORMATION, MEDIA & CULTURE

Queer San Francisco past and present can be explored at the Reading Room in the **SF LGBT Center**, and at the James C Hormel Gay & Lesbian Center at the **Main Library** (*see p64*). **Cruisin' the Castro** (1-415 255 1821, www.cruisinthecastro.com) is a mazy walking tour, hosted by 'Leader of the Pack' Kathy Amendola, that covers the history of SF's famous gay neighbourhood. The Castro is also home to the new **GLBT History Museum**.

The free weekly *San Francisco Bay Times* (www.sfbaytimes.com) and *Bay Area Reporter* (www.ebar.com) both cover LGBT news. The **Women's Building** in the Mission District (*see p156*) is a hub of resources and services. Man-about-town Larry-bob Roberts keeps a voluminous and constantly updated calendar of event listings at www.sfqueer.com.

GLBT History Museum

For listings, see p170.
This first-of-its-kind repository of gay history took its inevitable place in the Castro in 2011. Though small, it contains an impressive collection of media and artefacts, chronicling LGBT history in San Francisco and around the world. Recent exhibits include a look at the life and times of legendary drag opera star and community leader Jose Sarria, the lives of same-sex lovers in World War II internment camps, and the history of San Francisco's historic 'gaybourhoods' outside of the Castro, from North Beach to Valencia Street.

San Francisco LGBT Community Center

1800 Market Street, at Octavia Boulevard, Hayes Valley (1-415 865 5555, www.sfcenter.org). Metro to Van Ness/streetcar F/bus 6, 7. **Open** noon-10pm Mon-Thur; noon-6pm Fri; 9am-6pm Sat. **Map** p316 J8.
Opened in 2002, the LGBT Community Center is the only non-profit in San Francisco serving the entire acronym, helping the L, the B, the G and the T find work, housing, counselling and health services and

even arts and culture free of discrimination and needless hurdles. For visitors, it can be a handy resource to find queer events, performances and parties – or just a friendly face – while you're in town.

WHERE TO STAY

For accommodation across the city, *see pp272-289*. Noteworthy gay-owned, gay-friendly or simply delightful places are listed below.

Beck's Motor Lodge
2222 Market Street, at 15th Street, Castro (1-415 621 8212, www.becksmotorlodge.com). Metro to Castro/streetcar F/bus 22, 24, 37. **Map** p316 H10.
Relatively cheap rates, a sun deck, private baths and, above all, a prime Castro location, help Beck's retain its popularity. Inside, the tacky carpets and garish soft furnishings offer a glimpse of quintessential motel Americana. Beware – or not – its reputation for being a very cruisey place to stay.

★ Hayes Valley Inn
417 Gough Street, at Hayes Street, Hayes Valley, (1-415 431 9131, www.hayesvalleyinn.com). Bus 5, 21, 47, 49, 90. **Map** p316 J8.
This 28-room lodging is in the centre of lively and lovely Hayes Valley, adjacent to the One Sushi restaurant. There's an on-site bar, and pets are welcome too. A kitchen and parlour are available to guests, but bathrooms are shared (although rooms have their own sinks).

Inn on Castro
321 Castro Street, at Market Street, Castro (1-415 861 0321, www.innoncastro.com). Metro to Castro/streetcar F/bus 24, 33, 35, 37. **Map** p316 H10.
In a beautifully restored Edwardian property, the inn offers eight rooms and four apartments decorated with contemporary furnishings, original modern art and elaborate flower arrangements. The sumptuous breakfast includes delicious house-made muffins and fresh fruit.

Metro
319 Divisadero Street, at Page Street, Western Addition (1-415 861 5364, www.metrohotelsf.com). Bus 6, 21, 24, 71. **Map** p315 G8.
The Metro is a gay-friendly establishment with a large patio and 24 well-appointed rooms with private baths in up-and-coming NoPa (North of Panhandle). Hip boutique shopping and unique eateries are practically on the doorstep.

Willows Inn
710 14th Street, between Belcher & Church Streets, Castro (1-415 431 4770, www.willows sf.com). Metro to Castro/streetcar F/bus 22, 37. **Map** p316 H9.
The 12 comfy guest rooms in this Edwardian B&B have bent-wood willow and antique furnishings. Bathrooms are shared, but all rooms are equipped with vanity sinks. Soft kimono bathrobes are provided, and complimentary breakfast and cocktails are served daily.

RESTAURANTS & CAFÉS

San Francisco was one of the first cities in America where same-sex couples could hold hands over a romantic dinner and not have to worry. That's now normal almost anywhere (phew!), but there's still a special sense of belonging in some places. The following is a selection of our favourite spots.

The Castro

★ Café Flore
For listings, see p171.
Flore has been the see-and-be-seen spot practically since it opened in 1973, its gorgeous patio crowded day and night with cruisers, coffee sippers and foodies (brunch is a must). Deep house and lounge tunes pump from the DJ booth.

Catch
2362 Market Street, at Castro Street (1-415 431 5000, www.catchsf.com). Metro to Castro/streetcar F/bus 24, 33, 35, 37. **Open** 11.30am-2.30pm, 5.30-9pm Mon, Tue; 11.30am-2.30pm, 5.30-10pm Wed, Thur; 11.30am-2.30pm, 5.30-11pm Fri; 11am-3.30pm, 5.30-11pm Sat; 11am-3.30pm, 5.30-9.30pm Sun. **Main courses** $18-$36. **Map** p316 H10.

ARTS & ENTERTAINMENT

This seafood restaurant has an enclosed heated outdoor deck and live piano music. Dishes are well turned out, but not exceptional. No one seems to mind, though: the bar fills up with local yuppies on a date (or looking for one) and a broad selection of gym rats. You'll need to book at weekends.

Firewood Café

4248 18th Street, between Collingwood & Diamond Streets (1-415 252 0999, www.firewoodcafe.com). Metro to Castro/streetcar F/bus 24, 33, 35, 37. **Open** 11am-10pm Mon-Thur, Sun; 11am-11pm Fri, Sat. **Main courses** $11-$18. **Map** p315 G11.
There's sometimes a queue outside the door for dinner here, but the loyal customers are willing to wait. Menu standouts include melt-in-the-mouth roast chicken, pasta dishes and thin-crust pizzas.

Harvey's

500 Castro Street (1-415 431 4278, www.harveyssf.com). Metro to Castro/streetcar F/bus 24, 33, 35, 37. **Open** 11am-11pm Mon-Fri; 9am-2am Sat, Sun. **Main courses** $10-$17. **Map** p316 H11.
Renamed in honour of activist Harvey Milk in 1996, this bar-restaurant was the site of an infamous brawl with cops during the 1979 White Night riot, which followed the lenient sentencing of his assassin. These days, it's a congenial place to grab bar food and soak up the neighbourhood's history.
▶ *For more on the Harvey Milk story and the White Night riot, see p263.*

La Mediterranée

288 Noe Street, between Market & 16th Streets (1-415 431 7210, www.cafelamed.com). Metro to Castro/streetcar F/bus 24, 33, 35, 37. **Open** 11am-10pm Mon-Thur, Sun; 11am-10.30pm Fri, Sat. **Main courses** $10-$15. **Map** p316 H10.
Everything here is keenly priced, with terrific hummus and baba ganoush, plus an excellent filo pastry combination plate. The menu makes brilliant use of fresh ingredients and the place feels like a genuine Mediterranean escape.
Other location 2210 Fillmore Street, Pacific Heights (1-415 921 2956).

Orphan Andy's

3991 17th Street, at Castro Street (1-415 864 9795). Metro to Castro/streetcar F/bus 24, 33, 35, 37. **Open** 24hrs daily. **Main courses** $10-$15. **Map** p316 H10.
Any neighbourhood famed for its nightlife needs at least one place serving comfort food around the clock. The familiar glow of Orphan Andy's windows and the sizzle of steaks, burgers and breakfast on the griddle are perfect for restoring morale after a long night out, or for building up your strength before you head back into the fray on the main Castro drag.

Samovar

498 Sanchez Street, at 18th Street (1-415 626 4700, www.samovartea.com). Metro to Castro/streetcar F/bus 24, 33, 35. **Open** 11am-10pm daily. **Main courses** $12-$24. **Map** p316 H10.

Destino.

The Castro's only tearoom, this tranquil spot, serving more than 100 teas, is a hit with locals searching out a Zen-like refuge. The food menu includes rice bowls, salads, sandwiches or tea and small plate pairings with international themes, such as the Russian Tea Service (with smoked salmon and beets), Japanese (with seaweed salad and duck or tempeh) or Indian style (with yellow curry).

Other locations Yerba Buena Gardens, Upper Terrace, 730 Howard Street, SoMa (1-415 227 9400); 411 Valencia Street, at 15th Street, Mission (1-415 553 6887).

Other neighbourhoods

★ AsiaSF

201 9th Street, at Howard Street, SoMa (1-415 255 2742, www.asiasf.com). BART & Metro to Civic Center/streetcar F/bus 6, 7, 9, 12, 14, 19, 27, 47, 90. **Open** *Restaurant* 7.15-11pm Wed, Thur, Sun; 7.15pm-2am Fri; 5pm-2am Sat. *Shows* 7.15pm Wed-Thur, Sun; 7.15pm, 9.15pm Fri; 5pm, 7.15pm, 9.15pm Sat. **Dinner shows** $39-$75. **Map** p316 L8.

Those women who serve you? They're not, nor are they drag queens. The gorgeous creatures who bring the food and dance seductively atop the long red bar are 'gender illusionists'. The food is inventive Cal-Asian, with small plates and shareable portions. A restaurant, lounge and club all in one, AsiaSF's crowd is a compelling mix of local party-goers and wide-eyed businessmen. Reservations essential.

Destino

1815 Market Street, between Guerrero & Valencia Streets, Hayes Valley (1-415 552 4451, www. destinosf.com). Metro to Van Ness/streetcar F/bus 6, 71. **Open** 5-10pm Tue-Thur, Sun; 5-11pm Fri, Sat. **Main courses** $11-$36. **Map** p316 J9.

This casual, fun restaurant serves specialities from Central and South America in a lively neighbourhood setting. The theme is small plates meant for sharing, but à la carte options are also available. Empanadas, ceviches and other traditional dishes are all given a robust, contemporary treatment. Try the three-course prix fixe menu ($37) to take the guesswork out of ordering.

★ Just for You Café

For listings, see p175.

The original Potrero Hill version of this lesbian-owned destination café was so popular, it prompted a relocation to bigger quarters in Dogpatch. The house speciality is a Cajun-style breakfast, with superb grits, fluffy pancakes and beignets.

BARS

The Castro

440 Castro

440 Castro Street, at 18th Street (1-415 621 8732, www.the440.com). Metro to Castro/streetcar F/bus 24, 33, 35, 37. **Open** noon-2am daily. **No credit cards**. **Map** p316 H11.

Twin Peaks Tavern.

The building at 440 Castro Street has been a queer destination almost as long as the Castro itself. Once it was Bear Hollow (later just the Bear), then it became Daddy's, the Castro's reigning leather bar, and in 2005 it entered the next phase of its life as simply 440 Castro, a moderately swanky lounge still a bit beholden to the preening bear image of Castro past (not that that's a bad thing). The crowd is a mix of old-school cruisers and youthful fans of hard techno, but the drink specials are just right to smooth out the rougher edges.

Badlands

4121 18th Street, at Castro Street (1-415 626 9320, www.sfbadlands.com). Metro to Castro/ streetcar F/bus 24, 33, 35, 37. **Open** 2pm-2am daily. **No credit cards.** **Map** p316 H11.
Young suburbanites drenched in scent and sporting the latest in designer label knock-offs flock to this flashy video bar, which boasts one of the few dance floors in the Castro. The music ranges from popular hip hop to early 1990s diva favourites, and the queue outside on weekends is often a scene of its own.

IN THE KNOW JOIN THE CLUB

A great alternative to boozy nights, the **Castro Country Club** (4058 18th Street, at Hartford Street, 1-415 552 6102, www. castrocountryclub.org) is a place for the clean and sober to socialise. There's a sitting room, a coffee bar and café, a room for board games, a video theatre and a backyard patio. The front steps are Castro's central gossip parlour and cruise lookout.

★ Blackbird Bar

2124 Market Street, between 14th & 15th Streets (1-415 503 0630, www.blackbirdbar.com). Metro to Church/streetcar F/bus 22, 37. **Open** 3pm-2am Mon-Fri; 2pm-2am Sat, Sun. **Map** p316 H9.
Of all the Castro bars, Blackbird draws the most diverse crowd. Men, women, young and old – all come for craft cocktails and quality wines befitting the handsome room. Edison bulbs hang from a ceiling of salvaged wood, and a tufted red-vinyl banquette runs the length of the place, creating cosy spots for conversation – though you may find yourself shouting to be heard above the din at peak times. The rear of the bar doubles as a games room, where friends cram into the little photo booth, between turns at the pool table. Come early or expect to stand.

Hi Tops

2247 Market Street, between 15th & 16th Streets (1-415 626 9320, www.hitopssf.com). Metro to Castro/streetcar F/bus 24, 35, 37. **Open** 4pm-midnight Mon-Wed; 4pm-2am Thur, Fri; 10am-2am Sat; 10am-midnight Sun. **Map** p316 H10.
Let's not insult anybody's intelligence by pretending that a gay sports bar is a stunning novelty. That said, it took at least this long for one to come to the Castro, so cheers to the guys at Hi Tops for finally making it a reality. Mondays are 25¢ wings and Monday Night Football, coming full circle to the Castro's roots as a blue collar working neighbourhood.

Midnight Sun

4067 18th Street, at Hartford Street (1-415 861 4186, www.midnightsunsf.com). Metro to Castro/ streetcar F/bus 24, 33, 35, 37. **Open** 2pm-2am Mon-Fri; 1pm-2am Sat, Sun. **No credit cards.** **Map** p316 H11.
The big draw at Midnight Sun is video – classic and contemporary music cross-cut with comedy clips, *The Sopranos* or *Sex and the City*. Two-for-one cocktails are on offer daily (2-7pm), and weekends are a boy fest.

Mix

4086 18th Street, at Hartford Street (1-415 431 8616, www.sfmixbar.com). Metro to Castro/ streetcar F/bus 24, 33, 35, 37. **Open** 7am-2am daily. **No credit cards.** **Map** p316 H11.
Mix is a good, old-fashioned neighbourhood bar, where you can shoot pool, catch a Niners game, and on sunny weekends smell the hot dogs and burgers grilling on the back patio. The windows face 18th Street, which make it a perfect spot for ogling.

Moby Dick

4049 18th Street, at Hartford Street (1-415 861 1199). Metro to Castro/streetcar F/bus 24, 33, 35, 37. **Open** noon-2am daily. **No credit cards.** **Map** p316 H11.
Another true neighbourhood bar, Moby Dick is exactly as it has been since the 1980s. The place is

popular with pool players (despite the fact that there's only one table) and pinball addicts (there are four machines at the back), but big windows and a prime Castro location afford ample cruising potential too. The giant aquarium hovering over the bar is a nice nod to the nautical theme (that *is* what you assumed the name referred to, right?).

Pilsner Inn

225 Church Street, at Market Street (1-415 621 7058, www.pilsnerinn.com). Metro to Church/ streetcar F/bus 22. **Open** noon-2am Mon-Fri; 10am-2am Sat, Sun. **No credit cards. Map** p316 J9.
It all happens here, especially on the heated patio at the back. The Pilsner is a local favourite among youngish beauty boys, who play pool, pinball and computer games, or chat over the sounds of the retro jukebox. There's a wide choice of draught beers, and customers can wait at the front for opening tables at ever-popular restaurant Chow (*see p171*).

Twin Peaks Tavern

401 Castro Street, at Market Street (1-415 864 9470, www.twinpeakstavern.com). Metro to Castro/streetcar F/bus 24, 33, 35, 37. **Open** noon-2am Mon-Wed; 8am-2am Thur-Sat; 10am-2am Sun. **No credit cards. Map** p316 H10.
The self-proclaimed 'Gateway to the Castro,' the snug Twin Peaks Tavern was one of the first gay bars in the US to brave the public gaze with street-level windows. Nowadays, habitués are mostly older (earning the place the nickname 'the Glass Coffin'), enjoying a quiet chat, good music, and even a game of cards. The lovely antique bar serves everything except bottled beer.

SoMa

★ Eagle Tavern

398 12th Street, at Harrison Street (www.sf-eagle. com). Bus 9, 12, 27, 47, 90. **Open** noon-2am daily. **No credit cards. Map** p316 L9.
A venerable bar offering all-male leather action, goings-on in the beer garden, occasional rock concerts or stand-up, and a chance to cosy up to gay (and straight) indie and punk rockers, including Pansy Division, Gaythiest and Enorchestra. Sunday afternoon beer busts (3-6pm) are ground zero for local alternaqueers.

Hole in the Wall

289 8th Street, between Howard & Folsom Streets (1-415 431 4695, www.holeinthewallsaloon.com). Bus 12, 14, 19, 27, 47. **Open** noon-2am daily. **No credit cards. Map** p316 L8.
This self-proclaimed 'queer bar for filthy bikers and loudmouth punks' is a veritable SoMa institution. Not only is it a magnet for the moto crowd, local leather aficionados and tourists seem to love it too. The place has a beautifully re-felted pool table, video games, pinball, rock 'n' roll oldies playing on

repeat and a bewildering array of gay memorabilia covering the walls and ceiling.

Lone Star Saloon

1354 Harrison Street, between 9th & 10th Streets (1-415 863 9999, www.lonestarsf.com). Bus 12, 19, 27, 47, 90. **Open** 2pm-2am Mon-Fri; noon-2am Sat, Sun. **No credit cards. Map** p316 L8.
Once unabashed 'bear country', the Lone Star has of late become more of a fashion show for beauty bears, though authentic rugged types can still be hunted here. The classic space has pinball machines, a pool table and a back patio for smoking.

Powerhouse

1347 Folsom Street, between 9th & 10th Streets (1-415 552 8689, www.powerhouse-sf.com). Bus 12, 14, 19, 27, 47, 90. **Open** 4pm-2am Mon-Thur, Sun; 3pm-2am Fri, Sat. **No credit cards. Map** p316 L8.
White-hot and cruisey as hell, Powerhouse is one of the city's most popular gay bars and a holdover from SoMa's true down-and-dirty past. Entertainment includes buzz-cut nights, underwear or bare-chest parties, wrestling, leather nights and S&M lessons.

Other neighbourhoods

Although it's not strictly a gay bar, **El Rio** in the Mission (3158 Mission Street, at Cesar Chavez Street, 1-415 282 3325, www.elriosf. com) draws queer types to its riotous music nights. Among them are Mango, the monthly lesbian Saturday party, and Sunday Salsa, also very queer.

Aunt Charlie's Lounge

133 Turk Street, at Taylor Street, Tenderloin (1-415 441 2922, www.auntcharlieslounge.com). BART & Metro to Powell/streetcar F/bus 27, 31, 45 & Market Street routes/cable car Powell-Hyde or Powell-Mason. **Open** noon-2am Mon-Fri; 10am-2am Sat; 10am-midnight Sun. **No credit cards. Map** p312 L6.
Warning: you have to brave one of the worst blocks in the city to get there. But Charlie's wouldn't have it any other way, and the Hot Boxxx Girls drag revues (Fridays and Saturdays) are worth it.

Cinch Saloon

1723 Polk Street, between Clay & Washington Streets, Polk Gulch (1-415 776 4162, www.cinch sf.com). Bus 1, 12, 19, 27, 47, 49, 90/cable car California. **Open** 9am-2am Mon-Fri; 6am-2am Sat, Sun. **No credit cards. Map** p312 K4.
With an ostensible Western theme, this comfortably ramshackle haunt harks back to the days when this stretch of Polk Street was a more rough-and-tumble area of hustlers, chasers and drag queens with a broken heel or two. A tiered smoking patio out back is perfect for slurred conversation.

ARTS & ENTERTAINMENT

IN THE KNOW GET PUMPED

Virtually all of San Francisco's workout spaces are queer-friendly, but if you're looking for a quintessential Castro gym, try **Alex Fitness** (2275 Market Street, between Sanchez & Noe Streets, 1-415 548 0552, www.alexfitness-sf.com), which has brand-new equipment and offers daily or weekly passes ($20 or $60 respectively).

Martuni's

4 Valencia Street, at Market Street, Hayes Valley (1-415 241 0205, www.martunis.ypguides.net). BART or Metro to Van Ness/streetcar F/bus 6, 14, 49, 71. **Open** *2pm-2am daily.* **Map** p316 J8.
Martuni's is a warm, inviting piano bar with an open mic, where surprisingly talented singers and performers live out their Broadway dreams belting out show tunes and jazz standards. The martinis are enormous and the clientele extremely diverse.

Wild Side West

424 Cortland Avenue, at Wool Street, Bernal Heights (1-415 647 3099, wildsidewest.com). Bus 14, 24, 49. **Open** *2pm-2am daily.* **No credit cards.**
Probably the longest-lived lesbian hotspot in the city, Wild Side West really sees itself as just another neighbourhood bar. The walls are a shifting art installation, the patio is perfect for live music or poetry, and the clientele is happily mixed. The ace jukebox plays Janis Joplin, Patsy Cline and – naturally – 'Walk on the Wild Side'.

CLUBS

The nightlife scene changes with bewildering rapidity, so call ahead or check websites to make sure a particular night is happening. Most clubs are 21 and over, so bring valid photo ID. For more nightclubs, *see pp212-216*. SoMa's **Mezzanine** is also a big hit with the boys.

Beaux

2344 Market Street, between Castro & Noe Streets, Castro (www.beauxsf.com). Metro to Castro/ streetcar F/bus 24, 33, 35, 37. **Open** *4pm-2am Mon-Fri; 2pm-2am Sat, Sun.* **Map** p316 H10.
This is a good place to head when you're in the mood for good, old-fashioned fun: dark bars, strong drinks, throbbing music and themed parties like the 'homo-disco circus' of Big Top Sundays. It's jut around the corner from the main Castro drag – but you might end up spending the whole night here.

The Café

2369 Market Street, at Castro Street, Castro (1-415 861 3846, www.cafesf.com). Metro to Castro/streetcar F/bus 24, 33, 35, 37. **Open** *5pm-2am Mon-Fri; 3pm-2am Sat, Sun.* **Admission** varies. **No credit cards**. **Map** p316 H10.
There's dancing every night at the Café, the Castro's largest and most popular club. Once the area's only lesbian bar, it now mainly attracts guys from outlying areas, but women show up during the day, on weeknights and (especially) on Sunday afternoons. The music blends house, hip hop and salsa. There are two bars, a dancefloor and a patio, plus pinball, pool and computer games.

★ EndUp

For listings, see p213.
When the EndUp started its infamous all-night Sunday morning dance party (revellers come in late Saturday night and don't leave) in 1980 they called it the Church. These days it's known as the T-Dance, but although a lot has changed in SoMa, the city, and the gay scene since then, it's still the same good time. The EndUp opened in 1973 and is so venerable at this point that it even 'ended up' in local writer Armistead Maupin's *Tales of the City* and played itself in the PBS movie based on the book.

★ Stud Bar

399 9th Street, at Harrison Street, SoMa (www. studsf.com). Bus 12, 19, 27, 47. **Open** *from 5pm daily, closing time varies.* **Admission** *free-$15.* **No credit cards**. **Map** p316 L8.
Opened in 1966, the Stud is one of the city's venerable gay institutions. It still has dancing all week, and the

Stud Bar.

crowd is mainly gay and male, but the club prides itself on being 'omnisexual'. Nights range from queer punk and '80s disco to house.

ENTERTAINMENT & PERFORMING ARTS

The **Castro Theatre** (*see p198*) hosts screenings of camp favourites: you haven't lived until you've seen *Valley of the Dolls* or *All About Eve* here. There are frequent *Sound of Music* and *Wizard of Oz* singalongs and, on Christmas Eve, the SF Gay Men's Chorus singing 'Home for the Holidays'. Groundbreaking gay theatre is staged at the **New Conservatory Theatre Center** (25 Van Ness Avenue, between Fell & Oak Streets, Hayes Valley, 1-415 861 8972, www.nctcsf.org).

Brava! For Women in the Arts

Theatre Center, 2781 24th Street, at York Street (1-415 641 7657, box office 1-415 647 2822, www. brava.org). BART to 24th Street Mission/bus 9, 27, 33, 48. **Tickets** vary. **Map** p317 M12.
Brava is one of few theatres that specialise in work by women of colour and lesbian playwrights.

Man Dance Company

Various venues. Box office in Human Rights Campaign Action Center & Store, 575 Castro Street, between 18th & 19th Streets (1-415 431 2200, www.mandance.org). Metro to Castro/bus 24, 35, 48 & Market Street routes. **Tickets** $35.

MDC offers ballet and dance with an (almost) all-male ensemble. Pieces tend to be about LGBT issues, with choreography designed to emphasise the gracefulness of the male physique.

★ Oasis

298 11th Street, at Folsom Street, SoMa (1-415 795 3180, sfoasis.com). Bus 9, 12, 47. **Tickets** vary. **Map** p316 L8.
Trannyshack founder Heklina, drag star D'Arcy Drollinger and singer Jason Beebout (of the Berkeley emo/punk band Samiam) all went in on a venture to zap a little life into SoMa's theatre scene with Oasis. At this bar and thespian centre, the campy, the weird and the outrageous take the stage, usually in the form of new comedy plays with a drag twist.

QComedy Showcase

Various venues (1-415 533 9133, www.qcomedy.com).
Regularly hosted by the ebullient Nick Leonard (who also performs), QComedy Showcase features such top-flight comics Heather Gold, Charlie Ballard and Aundré at spots around town.

Theatre Rhinoceros

Various venues (1-800 838 3006 www.therhino. org). **Tickets** $15-$25.
The oldest LGBT theatre company in the world, the Rhino (named for an early gay rights icon) trades off between LGBT-themed works and powerful dramas by icons like David Mamet and Noel Coward.

Nightlife

San Francisco has always been a party town. Even in the wake of the 1906 earthquake, survivors posted a sign that read: 'Eat, Drink and Be Merry, for Tomorrow We May Have to Go to Oakland.' These days, with so many young, affluent people gravitating to the city's tech industry, you'll have no trouble finding lively dancefloors, although the high male-female ratio can skew the vibe of some clubs.

The SF music scene remains as eclectic as ever. Artists, writers and musicians have been coming here for decades, melding their sounds, styles and sensibilities into a freewheeling musical panoply whose outsized cultural impact is staggering for a city this small. Whether you gravitate towards historic venues such as the Fillmore or newer avant-garde spots like the Chapel and Rickshaw Stop, you won't lack for top-notch entertainment.

Clubs

Most of San Francisco's larger clubs (including the ones that stay open later than 2am) are concentrated downtown and in SoMa. If you want to move your feet, try **Mighty**, **Public Works** and **Mezzanine**, but you'll also find (official and impromptu) dancing at many smaller venues. If you're looking to go deeper into the scene, Facebook and word of mouth are your best bets for finding underground warehouse parties that rage much longer than any club or bar can.

1015 Folsom

1015 Folsom Street, at 6th Street, SoMa (1-415 991 1015, www.1015.com). Bus 12, 19, 27, 47. **Open** 10pm-4am Fri, Sat; other nights vary. **Admission** $15-$25. **No credit cards. Map** p317 M7.

1015 has ceded its spot as San Francisco's tried-and-true dance club and lost some of the sparkle of years past, but it's always worth seeing what's on the calendar at the massive, multi-room club. It might be a house music legend, a hip hop superstar doing a DJ set or a Latin ingénue, but 1015 will always draw people who want to party and enjoy some big beats. It's one of the few real late-night spots left, partying long after most other venues have packed up.

Audio

316 11th Street, between Folsom & Harrison Streets, SoMa (1-415 481 0556, www.audiosf. com). Bus 9, 12, 27, 47, 90. **Open** 9.30pm-2am Fri, Sat. **Admission** $10-$25. **Map** p316 L9.

This weekends-only, no-dress-code spot boasts a full calendar of top underground house, techno and nu-disco talent, making it an ideal spot to work up a sweat. With its Funktion One sound system, intimate spring-loaded dancefloor, and ambience enriched by disco balls, 3D video projections and an impressive 1600 LED wall, Audio has garnered many accolades.

Basement

222 Hyde Street, between Turk & Eddy Streets, Tenderloin (1-415 742 7222, www.thebasementsf. com). BART & Metro to Civic Center/streetcar F/ bus 6, 7, 9. **Open** 6pm-midnight Tue-Fri; 7pm-2am Sat. **Admission** free. **Map** p312 L6.

In the 2000s, this space was known as 222 Hyde, which ruled the underground Tenderloin club scene. It's now the Basement, a downstairs lounge and comedy club, with house, techno and soul DJs every Friday and Saturday night. Inside the candle-lit, brick-walled space, the bartenders get creative with a fun menu of cocktails that pay homage to the space's Tenderloin locale (think Crackhead's Delirium or Crystal's Meth Corner), while also offering craft beer and wine.

Beatbox

314 11th Street, between Folsom & Harrison Streets, SoMa (1-415 500 2675, www.beatboxsf. com). Bus 12. **Open** 10pm-2am daily. **Admission** varies. **Map** p316 L9.

This is a gorgeous space in a historic building, with exposed brick walls, large street-facing windows, a glittering, oversized bar and a wooden dancefloor. In addition to the DJ talent, Beatbox hosts bands and burlesque shows. But no matter what kind of artist takes to the stage, it's guaranteed to sound epic thanks to the club's Danley Sound Labs audio system, the only one in the West.

EndUp

401 6th Street, at Harrison Street, SoMa (1-415 646 0999, www.theendup.com). Bus 9, 14, 19, 27. **Open** 11pm-8am Fri; 10pm-noon Sat; 2-10pm Sun. **Admission** varies. **Map** p317 M8.

A fixture since 1973, the EndUp boasts all-night house and techno madness on the weekends, plus a Saturday morning party from 6am and the legendary T-Dance from 6am on Sundays, which sees drag queens and straight ravers partying together. Honey, it's called the EndUp for a reason: you end up there when you want – nay, need – to keep the party going. Keep in mind this opens up the club's clientele quite a bit to those who have used any means necessary to stay up all night. Don't forget those shades for a boogie in the backyard.

F8 Nightclub & Bar

1192 Folsom Street, at 8th Street, SoMa (1-415 857 1192, www.feightsf.com). Bus 12. **Open** 8pm-1am Tue; 5pm-2am Wed, Thur; 5pm-3am Fri; 10pm-3am Sat; 10pm-2am Sun. **Admission** varies. **Map** p316 L8.

This two-room space isn't just a lively SoMa spot to dance to music blasting from a custom-made sound system; it also offers the chance to take in some art and fuel up with fresh snacks made by the chefs at local favourite Citizen's Band. The lounge has popular nights such as Housepitality (Wed) and drum 'n' bass-infused Stamina Sunday, as well as rotating DJ talent lighting up the dancefloor six nights a week. Drinks are a bit pricey, but the staff are friendly and the welcoming bouncers create an unpretentious vibe.

Infusion Lounge

124 Ellis Street, between Powell & Cyril Magnin Streets, Downtown (1-415 421 8700, www.sf. infusionlounge.com). BART & Metro to Powell Street. **Open** 6pm-2am Tue-Sat. **Admission** varies. **Map** p313 M6.

One of the few true upscale nightclub experiences in San Francisco, this place attracts a dressed-up crowd who emerge from their Uber town cars to dance to EDM and hip hop, order small plates with their cocktails, and splash out on bottle service if they're feeling fancy. Slick, geometric-grill panelling and leather sofas serve as a backdrop and go-go dancers get the crowd moving. The club's proximity to Union Square makes it attractive to tourists, bridge-and-tunnellers, and lively bachelorette parties. Prepare for a crowded dancefloor on weekends.

Infusion Lounge.

ARTS & ENTERTAINMENT

Mercer.

Mercer

255 Rhode Island Street, at 15th Street, SoMa (1-415 691 4850, mercer-sf.com). Bus 22. **Open** 5-9pm Tue-Thur; 5pm-2am Fri; 9pm-2am Sat. **Admission** from $10. **Map** p317 N9.

Little sister to nearby Mighty (*see right*), Mercer's intimate, casual space draws an attitude-free crowd. And since it inherited a prized sound system from defunct techno club 222, the sound quality is top-notch too. From Tuesday to Friday, it fills with the after-work happy-hour crowd, filling a huge void in the surrounding Design District. It's also open for select after-dark events, when DJs spin disco, house, hip hop and sometimes, as in the name of a popular recurring party, All of the Above.

Mezzanine

444 Jessie Street, at 6th Street, SoMa (1-415 625 8880, www.mezzaninesf.com). BART & Metro to Powell/bus 14, 27 & Market Street routes. **Open** 9pm-2am Fri; 9pm-7am Sat; other nights vary. **Admission** free-$30. **No credit cards**. **Map** p317 M7.

Local, national and international DJs and acts hold court on the main stage of this 900-capacity club, which has two long bars bordering the ample dancefloor and a lofty space upstairs. While it's become an increasingly hip hop-friendly place over the years, Mezzanine is still the definition of a multipurpose club and you never know what might be happening on any given night. You could catch a throwback act such as Boyz II Men, the latest electronic sensation or a rap act. Its size and multi-level layout make it a prime pick-up and people-watching spot too.

★ Mighty

119 Utah Street, at 15th Street, SoMa (1-415 626 7001, www.mighty119.com). Bus 9, 10, 19, 22, 27, 33, 90. **Open** 10pm-4am Thur-Sat; other nights vary. **Admission** free-$20. **No credit cards**. **Map** p317 M9.

The location may be inconvenient (especially for out-of-towners who don't know their way around), but Mighty is the place for eclectic after-dark action, whatever sounds you're into – a massive main room and a smaller back area usually mean you'll hear different styles in a single night. This is also one of the only clubs in town that takes the party outside into the street (not a well-manicured backyard, mind you) for special events such as the annual Breakfast of Champions, a 12-hour New Year's Day block party that always sells out.

Monarch

101 6th Street, at Mission Street, SoMa (1-415 284 9774, monarchsf.com). BART Civic Center/bus 14. **Open** 5.30pm-2am Tue-Fri; 9pm-2am Sat. **Shows** 9pm or 10pm. **Admission** $5-$20. **Map** p317 M7.

Headquarters of the weekly Housepitality party and a venue of choice for international house and techno DJs, Monarch is a beacon of friendly dance vibes on the still-tense corner of Sixth and Mission Streets in SoMa. The club opened in 2011 and has since been reimagined to incorporate a newer upstairs craft cocktail bar area called Emperor's Drawing Room, a hideaway that has a sliding wall for privacy. The custom Void Acoustics sound system is considered one of the best in San Francisco – and it's appropriately plated in gold.

ARTS & ENTERTAINMENT

★ Public Works

161 Erie Street, off Mission Street, Mission (1-415 496 6738, www.publicsf.com). BART to 16th Street Mission/bus 14, 49. **Open** 10pm-2am Wed, Thur; 10pm-4am Fri, Sat. **Admission** varies. **No credit cards. Map** p316 K9.

A great place to sample the pulse of the local and international underground scene. What's now a staple of SF nightlife opened in 2010 with a mission to 'give the people what they want', bringing in springy dancefloors, a top-notch sound system by Funktion-One, an occasional art gallery, great drinks with or without alcohol, and an upstairs loft for a party within a party. Top DJs are often invited to spin marathon sets here. The venue has also become the annual home for the Noise Pop Festival's Culture Club events.

Ruby Skye

420 Mason Street, between Geary & Post Streets, Downtown (1-415 693 0777, www.rubyskye.com). BART & Metro to Powell/bus 2, 3, 27, 30, 31, 38, 45, 76, 91/cable car Powell-Hyde or Powell-Mason. **Open** 7pm-2am Thur; 7pm-4am Fri, Sat. **Admission** $10-$30. **Map** p312 L5.

Converted from an elegant 1890s theatre, Ruby Skye has retained plenty of ornate Victorian touches, while gaining up-to-date sound and lighting systems. With its huge dancefloor and parade of surgically enhanced women, the scene feels like it's been imported from LA. Not surprisingly, it's a second home for famous EDM DJs from America and Europe. Ruby Skye is the closest you'll get to the classic big-room nightclub experience in San Francisco, complete with VIP room and bottle service. Though the area around the club has declined and can sometimes feel a bit dodgy, you'll feel transported once inside.

Temple SF

540 Howard Street, between 1st & 2nd Streets, SoMa (1-415 312 3668, www.templesf.com). BART & Metro to Montgomery/bus 10, 12, 14, 76, 108. **Open** 10pm-3am Thur; 10pm-4am Fri, Sat; other nights vary. **Admission** $20-$30. **Map** p313 N5.

A recent redesign has transformed this formerly Eastern-inflected superclub into a more futuristic dance destination. Spread across 15,000 square feet, the tri-level space offers different EDM sounds on each floor, courtesy of big-name US artists such as DJ Vice and 3LAU, and a crystal-clear Void Air Motion sound system. After hitting one of several dancefloors, chill out in a 'sky box' booth on the mezzanine while 50,000 LEDs pulse hypnotically to the beat below.

Underground SF

424 Haight Street, between Fillmore & Webster Streets, Lower Haight (1-415 864 7386, undergroundsf.com). Bus 33, 37, 43, 71. **Open** 9pm-2am daily. **Admission** free-$10. **Map** p316 H8.

On a somewhat sketchy stretch of Lower Haight, this club is little more than a converted dive with a smallish dancefloor. But set the Underground's looks aside and pay attention with your ears instead: it has a deserved reputation as a centre for turntable culture, and is a favourite spot with more discerning queers who love disco-funk but hate ABBA.

Wish

1539 Folsom Street, between 11th & 12th Streets, SoMa (1-415 431 1661, www.wishsf.com). Metro to Van Ness/bus 9, 12, 27, 47, 90. **Open** 5pm-2am Tue-Fri; 7pm-2am Sat. **Admission** varies. **Map** p316 L9.

A meat market on most nights, albeit a comfortable one, Wish plays some of the best down-tempo house and lounge music in the city and has incredibly friendly staff. This is the place to hit on weeknights for a fancy cocktail with friends or to flirt with locals while soaking up the bubbly tunes on tap. On weekends, Wish is swarming with tipsy lookers eager to suck face and talk your ear off – perfect if that's what you're looking for.

Comedy

Cobb's Comedy Club

915 Columbus Avenue, between Lombard & Taylor Streets, North Beach (1-415 928 4320, cobbscomedy.com). Bus 30. **Open** 1-6pm Wed; 4-9pm Thur; 4-10.30pm Fri, Sat; 4-9pm Sun. **Admission** varies. **Map** p312 L2.

Much like its sister club, Punch Line, Cobb's has been on the scene for decades – since 1982 – giving touring and local comedians a place to bust guts and make their name. The 400-seat venue offers a full dinner menu and bar, making it an ideal one-stop shop for a night out in this charming North Beach locale. Similar to Punch Line, the calibre of comedy is high: Dana Carvey, Dave Chappelle, Dave Attell, Bill Burr and Louis CK have all performed at Cobb's, and the roster always showcases comedians who are stars of the small screen.

Cobb's Comedy Club.

Punch Line Comedy Club

444 Battery Street, between Merchant & Washington Streets, Financial District (1-415 397 7573, www.punchlinecomedyclub.com). BART Embarcadero/bus 14. **Open** 7-10pm Tue-Thur; 7pm-midnight Fri, Sat; 7-11pm Sun. **Admission** varies. **Map** p313 N4.

As the city's longest-running comedy club (it opened in 1978), the Punch Line's list of headliners reads like a who's who of A-list comedy stars – and it shows no signs of slowing down. Comedians who have made history here include Robin Williams, Chris Rock, Dana Carvey, Rosie O'Donnell and Ellen DeGeneres. Current crowd-pullers include Margaret Cho, Dave Chappelle and George Lopez, as well as don't-miss rising stars Brendon Walsh and Mo Mandel.

Music

San Francisco's buzzing music scene can be chalked up to a cross-genre cadre of youthful musicians and forward-thinking bookers and promoters who continue to form bands and fill

ARTS & ENTERTAINMENT

stages all over: at clubs and other music events, sure, but also at galleries and warehouses.

The city has one of the most exciting underground scenes in the US. It has spawned international names such as Devendra Banhart and Joanna Newsom (both of whom have since left the city limits); kicked off the clicks, whizzes and synths of E-40, the Federation, Turf Talk and the rest of the hyphy movement; nurtured rockers such as Wooden Shjips, Film School, Vetiver, Citay and Rogue Wave, who've all landed on respected indie labels; and inspired the likes of hip hoppers Lyrics Born and the Coup, rap experimentalists Anticon, and electronica terrorist Kid 606 to make it on their own imprints.

Music lovers may consider timing their visit with a major festival, such as **Hardly Strictly Bluegrass** (*see p33*) in early October or rock extravaganza **Outside Lands** (*see p31*) in August; both are held in Golden Gate Park. **Noise Pop** (*see p35*), a week-long, citywide series of indie music, arts and film in February, is your best bet for seeing emerging artists who'll go on to be the next big thing, while September's **San Francisco Electronic Music Festival** (www. sfemf.org) acts as a public forum for electronic composers and sound artists in the Bay Area.

TICKETS

For larger concerts – pretty much anything at the 'major venues' below – it's worth buying tickets in advance. Where possible, buy from the venue's own box office to avoid the booking fees levied by the likes of Ticketmaster or Live Nation. Advance purchase isn't always necessary for 'other venues', but it's never a bad idea. Always call ahead or look at venue websites before making a special trip.

MAJOR VENUES

The venues detailed here all host concerts on a regular basis. In addition, a handful of larger arenas stage the occasional show. In San Francisco, these include **AT&T Park** (*see p77*) and the **Palace of Fine Arts** (*see p123*). Other venues include the **Oracle Arena** in Oakland (1-510 569 2121, www.oracle arena.com) and the **Greek Theatre** (1-510 642 9988, www.calperfs.berkeley.edu) in Berkeley. A bit further out, the **Shoreline Amphitheatre** in Mountain View (1-650 967 4040, www.the shorelineamphitheatre.com), the **Concord Pavilion** (1-925 363 5701, www.chronicle pavilion.com), and the **SAP Center** at San Jose (1-408 287 7070, www.sapcenter.com) also attract big-name performers, especially during the summer months. Check venue websites, **Ticketmaster** (www.ticketmaster. com) or **Live Nation** (www.livenation.com) for tickets.

Bill Graham Civic Center Auditorium

99 Grove Street, between Polk Street & Dr Carlton B Goodlett Place, Civic Center (1-415 624 8900, apeconcerts.com). BART & Metro Civic Center/ bus 19, 47, 49. **Open** during performances only. **Admission** varies. **Map** p316 K7.

Originally constructed for the Panama-Pacific International Exposition in 1915, the Bill Graham Civic Auditorium is one of the monumental buildings surrounding Civic Center Plaza. Its size dictates the kinds of acts who play here: the Weeknd, Lana Del Rey, New Order, even rave wizards such as Zedd and deadmau5. Three floors means short toilet queues (key when audiences can reach up to 7,000), and with a location in the heart of the city, there's plenty of public transport to get you to the door.

Bimbo's 365 Club

1025 Columbus Avenue, at Chestnut Street, North Beach (1-415 474 0365, www.bimbos365club.com). Bus 30, 39, 47, 91/cable car Powell-Mason. **Box office** 10am-4pm Mon-Fri. **Admission** $18-$75. **Map** p312 L2.

Bimbo's began life as a Market Street speakeasy in 1931, moving to North Beach two decades later. The venue is still owned by the descendants of Agostino 'Bimbo' Giuntoli, one of its original proprietors, and has been well preserved, with a classy mermaid theme running throughout. It's one of the most elegant places to see a show without an orchestra or opera singers present. Rita Hayworth once appeared here as a dancer, but these days you're more likely to see edgy acts such as Zola Jesus, Ariel Pink, international pop heroes like the Raveonettes, and tribute bands such as Tainted Love or Super Diamond working up the crowd.

Brick & Mortar Music Hall

1710 Mission Street, at Duboce Avenue, Mission (1-415 800 8782, brickandmortarmusic.com). BART 16th Street Mission/bus 14, 49. **Open** 2pm-2am daily. **Shows** 8pm or 9pm daily. **Admission** varies. **Map** p316 K9.

The 250-capacity venue, which opened in 2011 in the former Coda jazz club space, has quickly become one of the city's essential venues for an eclectic array of live music. Brick & Mortar is an intimate yet lively spot where you can take in a New Orleans-style brass band, an emerging indie rock act or a Bay Area-style street rapper, depending on the night. During the day, the place is home to excellent Vietnamese pop-up Rice Paper Scissors for weekday lunch.

★ Chapel

777 Valencia Street, between 18th & 19th Streets, Mission (1-415 551 5157, thechapelsf.com). BART 16th Street Mission/bus 14, 49. **Open** 7pm-2am daily. **Shows** 8pm or 9pm daily. **Admission** varies. **Map** p316 K11.

The owners of New Orleans' legendary Preservation Hall opened this West Coast counterpart in 2012 and

Rickshaw Stop.

the Preservation Hall Jazz Band performs several times a year as part of a diverse line-up. An open-minded booking policy means you might catch indie or garage rock just as swiftly as something from down South. The venue also houses Vestry, a restaurant focused on French, Italian and Mediterranean food that's open six nights a week for dinner, plus weekend brunch; and the Chapel Bar, a neighbourhood watering hole worth hitting whether or not you're attending a show (it's open seven nights a week regardless of what's on the calendar).

★ Fillmore

1805 Geary Boulevard, at Fillmore Street, Fillmore (1-415 346 3000, www.thefillmore.com). Bus 2, 3, 22, 31, 38. **Box office** 10am-4pm Sun; 7.30-10pm show nights. **Admission** $20-$50. **Map** p312 H6.
The 1,200-capacity Fillmore was built in 1912, but is better known as the stage from which Bill Graham launched his rock-promotion empire and the 1960s 'San Francisco Sound', with bands such as the Grateful Dead, Jefferson Airplane, Santana, Quicksilver Messenger Service, and Big Brother & the Holding Company. The venue later changed hands several times. It became a punk spot in the 1970s and '80s, before reopening in the '90s and establishing itself as the powerhouse it is today. The performers who play here tend to be on the verge of

megastardom – or already at its apex and reaching back for the intimacy that this legendary room can provide. After most sold-out shows, concert-goers receive a commemorative poster of that night's show, free of charge.

★ Great American Music Hall

859 O'Farrell Street, between Polk & Larkin Streets, Tenderloin (1-415 885 0750, www. slimspresents.com). Bus 2, 3, 4, 19, 27, 31, 38, 47, 49, 90. **Box office** 10.30am-6pm Mon-Fri; 1hr before show Sat, Sun. **Admission** $15-$40. **Map** p312 K6.
Originally a bordello and gambling establishment called Blanco's when it opened in 1907, then a high-falutin nightclub called the Music Box operated by notorious fan dancer Sally Rand, the grande dame of the city's live venues is as beautiful today as at any point in its century-long history. The lavish room, done out with enormous mirrors, rococo woodwork and gold-leaf trim, became the Great American in 1972 and has seen performances by the likes of Sarah Vaughan, Count Basie, Van Morrison, the Grateful Dead and Arcade Fire. These days, it's run by the owners of Slim's and presents a cutting-edge roster of well-regarded local and touring musicians (many of the indie-rock ilk). Try to snag one of the coveted seats on the upper balcony.

architecture. Built in 1958 and once a Freemasons' temple, it underwent a major overhaul in 2014 and emerged with a brand new stage, state-of-the-art sound system and more general-admission tiers. Acts include venerable contemporary and legendary names of rock and pop – My Morning Jacket, Ryan Adams, Ringo Starr – plus comedians such as Nick Swardson and Wanda Sykes. The 3,300-capacity venue also has a dedicated parking garage – a rarity in this dense city.

Regency Ballroom

1290 Sutter Street, at Van Ness Avenue, Tenderloin (1-800 745 3000, www.theregencyballroom.com). Bus 2, 3, 19, 38, 47, 49, 90. **Box office** 1hr before show. **Admission** varies. **Map** p312 K5.
Formerly a Masonic temple, a dance studio, a Polish arts foundation and a movie theatre, this gorgeous beaux arts-style ballroom, with its horseshoe-shaped balcony, hardwood floors and fin-de-siècle teardrop chandeliers, now stages everything from opera to rock and jazz gigs to dance events. The landmark 1909 building incorporates the legendary Avalon Ballroom (now the Grand), which once hosted shows by the likes of Janis Joplin and Country Joe & the Fish.

Rickshaw Stop

155 Fell Street, at Franklin Street, Hayes Valley (1-415 861 2011, www.rickshawstop.com). Metro to Van Ness/bus 21, 47, 49 & Market Street routes. **Open** 7pm-2am Wed-Sat. **Shows** vary. **Admission** $5-$25. **Map** p316 K8.
Since 2004, the Rickshaw has brought life and fun to an otherwise desolate strip near Civic Center – it's a place to discover new music and movements along the indie/dance spectrum and beyond. A crash-pad decor of mod plastic loungers, foosball table and novelty lighting gives it a collegiate/rec room vibe, but the venue serves as a gathering point for different generations. It's now home to the long-running 18s-and-over Popscene dance party, LGBT gathering Cockblock and retro party Club 1994, in addition to several all-ages shows and regular 21-plus events.

Slim's

333 11th Street, between Folsom & Harrison Streets, SoMa (1-415 255 0333, www.slims-sf.com). Bus 9, 12, 27, 47, 90. **Box office** 10.30am-6pm Mon-Fri. **Admission** $14-$24. **Map** p316 L9.
The 550-capacity Slim's isn't one of San Francisco's most comfortable venues. Most patrons have to stand, sightlines are compromised by the floor-to-ceiling pillars, and on busy nights it gets pretty steamy. Still, it's one of the few places in the city for all ages (well, six and up) to enjoy a gig and therefore remains a rite of passage for local music fans. The schedule is mostly made up of rock bands, who play alongside a smattering of hip hop acts, reggae groups and rootsy singer/songwriters.

Independent

628 Divisadero Street, at Hayes Street, Western Addition (1-415 771 1421, www.theindependent sf.com). Bus 5, 21, 24. **Box office** 11am-6pm Mon-Fri; 1hr before show. **Admission** $18-$30. **Map** p315 G8.
There are no frills at this venerable black box apart from a stellar sound and lighting system – it's all about the music here. The Independent has always showcased a wide variety of sounds from self-made artists; the calendar is filled with a mix of touring rock, pop, metal, rap, jazz, Americana, jam and otherwise undefinable acts such as Madlib, Sunn O))), the Boredoms, Fiery Furnaces, High on Fire and Lyrics Born. The line-ups and genres are unpredictable and change from night to night, but you'll always have a prime view of the stage at this intimate 500-person venue.

Masonic

1111 California Street, between Jones & Taylor Streets, Nob Hill (1-415 776 7457, sfmasonic.com). BART Embarcadero/ bus 1/cable car California Street. **Open** during performances only. **Admission** varies. **Map** p312 L5.
Set atop the city on the same majestic hill that holds the Fairmont Hotel and Grace Cathedral, the Masonic is a regal marvel of midcentury modernist

ARTS & ENTERTAINMENT

Warfield

982 Market Street, at Mason Street, Tenderloin
(1-888 929 7849, www.thewarfieldtheatre.com).
BART & Metro to Powell/bus 14, 27, 31 & Market
Street routes/cable car Powell-Hyde or Powell-
Mason. **Box office** 10am-4pm Sun; 7.30-10pm
show nights. **Admission** $20-$50. **Map** p313 M6.
Opened in 1922 as a vaudeville theatre, the Warfield
has operated in its current incarnation since the
1980s. The ornate room, which has an 1,800-seat
balcony and an overall capacity for 2,300, retains
its original splendour and showcases a variety of
musical genres, from titans of rock revisiting classic
releases to rap artists touching the stage for the first
time. Even the back balcony seats have good views
of the stage in the well-designed space. Those lucky
enough to get backstage may also get a glimpse of
a portion of the underground speakeasy once operated by Al Capone, who had an office in the building.

OTHER VENUES

Amnesia

853 Valencia Street, between 19th & 20th Streets,
Mission (1-415 970 0012, www.amnesiathebar.com).
Bus 14, 33, 49. **Open** 6pm-2am daily. **Admission**
free-$10. **No credit cards.** **Map** p316 K11.
Amnesia is still resisting the party-hearty armies
that take over most of this stretch of the Mission
on weekends. Instead, it draws a diverse, friendly,
multi-ethnic crowd, and the DJ spins suitably eclectic tunes. During the week, you'll hear the sounds of
bluegrass, jazz and comedy. With a nice selection of
Belgian brews and friendly staff to boot, the patrons
at the bar are as likely to be neighbourhood regulars
as they are curious tourists checking out the action.

★ Bottom of the Hill

1233 17th Street, at Missouri Street, Potrero Hill
(1-415 626 4455, www.bottomofthehill.com).
Bus 10, 22. **Open** 8.30pm-2am Mon, Tue, Sat,
Sun; 4pm-2am Wed-Fri. **Shows** usually 9pm
daily. **Admission** $12-$25. **Map** p317 N10.
This little club, wedged among warehouses at the
base of Potrero Hill, has long been a favourite with
the indie-rock crowd. It features local and touring
acts most nights, as well as occasional arena acts
such as Green Day hankering to play an intimate
show. Underground bands that play here one year
may become cult sensations or even major stars the
next. The decor is classic dive, with quirky touches.

DNA Lounge

375 11th Street, between Folsom & Harrison Streets,
SoMa (1-415 626 1409, www.dnalounge.com).
Bus 9, 12, 27, 47, 90. **Open** 9pm-2am Mon-Thur;
9pm-4am Fri, Sat; hours vary Sun. **Admission**
$5-$25. **No credit cards.** **Map** p316 L9.
Goth kids have flocked to SoMa for all manner of
musical fetishes and countercultural indulgences over
the years. And no night is complete without a stop at

longtime fixture DNA Lounge, the home of leading
goth/industrial synthpop night Death Guild. But this
isn't a place where darkness reigns – it's also home to
the playful, long-running mashup Bootie, where the
partygoers' outfits are as creative (and incongruous)
as the sounds. The wonderful stage set-up, which can
be viewed from both the dancefloor and the recessed
mezzanine, has turned even hip hop acts on to this
gem of a nightspot. And the upstairs lounge has its
own dark, sexy and intimate area for dancing.

Elbo Room

647 Valencia Street, between 17th & 18th Streets,
Mission (1-415 552 7788, www.elbo.com). BART
16th Street Mission/bus 14, 22, 33, 49. **Open**
5pm-2am daily. **Shows** 9pm or 10pm daily.
Admission free-$12. **Map** p316 K10.
Although the Elbo has been commandeered by yuppies, it continues to be a place to hear good music
on a lively stretch of Valencia Street. You're likely
to hear jazz (usually with a beat-driven edge), pure
funk, soul or Latin jazz in the open-raftered space
upstairs, but also hip hop, hard rock, metal and random whacked-out experimentalism. On Sundays,
it's the legendary Dub Mission DJ night, a reggae
revival that recently celebrated its 15th anniversary.

El Rio

3158 Mission Street, at Precita Street, Mission
(1-415 282 3325, www.elriosf.com). BART 24th
Street Mission/bus 12, 14, 27, 36, 49. **Open**
5pm-2am Mon-Thur; 4pm-2am Fri; 1pm-2am Sat,
Sun (5pm-2am Sat, Sun Dec-Feb). **Shows** vary.
Admission free-$10.
Head to El Rio on a Sunday afternoon and make
your way to the garden, where you'll find San
Francisco's liveliest, most diverse salsa party: a
local tradition for more than 25 years and now taking place year-round. There's an outdoor barbecue,
dancing lessons, decent margaritas and a friendly
crowd of straights and queers. Other nights you
might encounter experimental rock, DJs or the odd
home-grown film festival. Don't miss OMG! Karaoke
Wednesdays, where patrons sing their hearts out in
front of local karaoke wizard KJ Paul.

Hemlock Tavern

1131 Polk Street, at Post Street, Polk Gulch
(1-415 923 0923, www.hemlocktavern.com).
Bus 2, 3, 19, 38, 47, 49, 90. **Open** 4pm-2am
daily. **Shows** 9.30pm daily. **Admission** free-$10.
Map p312 K6.
Out front, the Hemlock looks like a capacious, matey
watering hole, a lively mix of young tastemakers,
art snobs and yuppies playing pool, yapping at the
central bar or puffing in the open-air smoking 'room'.
At the back, however, an intimate stage hosts some
of the most edgy and intelligent musical programming in the city. The roster is built around hipster-
friendly artists such as Kurt Vile and Wolf Eyes,
plus regular shows by local up-and-coming acts.

ESSENTIAL SAN FRANCISCO ALBUMS

Sounds of the city.

SURREALISTIC PILLOW
JEFFERSON AIRPLANE (1967)

The album that introduced Grace Slick's commanding contralto and one of the best examples of the feral energy and flower-child idealism of the 1960s counterculture movement. It's a folk-tinged, psychedelic masterpiece that helped put the San Francisco Sound on the map.

KILL 'EM ALL
METALLICA (1983)

It's hard to believe the technical prowess and sheer force of *Kill 'Em All* came from a quartet of drunk 21-year-olds. Fusing searing hardcore punk tempos with heavy metal guitars, this thrash metal LP reminded everyone that San Francisco wasn't peace signs and smiles all the time.

ESCAPE
JOURNEY (1981)

Although Journey's paean to its home turf – 'Lights' – appeared on the 1978 album *Infinity*, it was 1981's *Escape* that made the San Francisco band synonymous with teenage backseat makeout sessions and FM radio ubiquity. Contains massive, sing-along tracks such as 'Don't Stop Believin'.

AMERICAN BEAUTY
GRATEFUL DEAD (1970)

Diehard fans will always opt for their blissed-out live performances, but the band took its oeuvre one step further with this studio album. The work gorgeously blends country with bluegrass, folk and rock, and captures the Dead's unique chemistry in melodies such as 'Truckin'' and 'Sugar Magnolia'.

FRESH FRUIT FOR
ROTTING VEGETABLES
DEAD KENNEDYS (1980)

True to SF's 1960s legacy, the Dead Kennedys combined that fierce sense of rebellion with the acidic wit and political commentary of '80s hardcore punk. Throwing surf, psych and garage influences into the mix, they topped it off with Jello Biafra's satirical lyrics and morbid sense of humour.

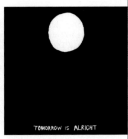

TOMORROW IS ALRIGHT
SONNY & THE SUNSETS (2009)

Released in the middle of the city's noisy garage rock explosion, Sonny & the Sunsets' debut stands as a soulful, whimsical collection of storytelling songs. The album blends psychedelia, garage and folk with a who's who of borrowed bandmates from other seminal SF bands.

Hotel Utah

500 4th Street, at Bryant Street, SoMa (1-415 546 6300, www.thehotelutah.com). Bus 10, 12, 30, 45, 47, 91. **Open** *11.30am-2am Mon-Fri; 11am-2am Sat, Sun.* **Shows** *usually 9pm daily.* **Admission** *$6-$10.* **Map** p317 N7.

The down-and-dirty days of the Barbary Coast are ingrained in the timbers of this 1908 watering hole, which has welcomed the likes of Marilyn Monroe, Bing Crosby and an assortment of gangsters and beatniks. Now gaining a fresh lease of life, the Utah is both a characterful bar and a cosy music room, hosting indie rockers, singer-songwriters and the occasional more eclectic curiosity. If you're an aspiring performer, be sure to hit up the well-attended open mic nights for a shot in the spotlight.

Knockout

3223 Mission Street, at Valencia Street, Mission (1-415 550 6994, www.theknockoutsf.com). Bus 12, 14, 24, 27, 36, 49. **Open** *5pm-2am daily.* **Shows** *usually 9pm or 10pm daily.* **Admission** *free-$8.*

This shoebox of a club recently celebrated its ten-year anniversary – no small feat on the ever-changing Mission scene. Its dark and divey vibe is punctuated by a small stage in the back, karaoke happy hours, late-night instalments of beer-sodden bingo and other quirky diversions. Catch indie-rock combos such as Imperial Teen spin-off Hey Willpower and punk act Terry Malts, as well as hugely popular monthly DJ nights such as Booty Bassment and Teenage Dance Craze.

Makeout Room

3225 22nd Street, between Bartlett & Mission Streets, Mission (1-415 647 2888, www.makeout room.com). BART 24th Street Mission/bus 12, 14, 48, 49, 67. **Open** *6pm-2am daily.* **Shows** *9pm daily.* **Admission** *$5-$10.* **Map** p316 K12.

One of the best places in town to see smallish bands, the Makeout Room attracts a laid-back, alternative, youthful crowd on its weekend live music nights. The decor lives up to the name: there's a bearskin rug on one wall and a stag's head on another, with metallic streamers and cosy booths to give it a 1960s high-school dance vibe. The atmosphere, as with many Mission bars, is that of a welcoming but hip dive.

Milk Bar

1840 Haight Street, between Shrader & Stanyan Streets, Haight-Ashbury (1-415 387 6455, www. milksf.com). Bus 6, 7, 33, 43, 71. **Open** *9pm-2am daily.* **Admission** *free-$10.* **No credit cards.* **Map** p315 E9.

For years, the Haight-Ashbury district was ground zero for the city's rock scene, but these days hip hop is creeping in and proving itself a Haight Street mainstay, due in no small part to Milk's hip hop- and R&B-friendly bookers – with splashes of rock and metal thrown into the mix. Slick, cream-coloured banquettes; large, politically provocative art; and a decent-sized dancefloor characterise the space. Big-name guests such as DJ Shadow have been known to drop in.

Neck of the Woods

406 Clement Street, between 5th & 6th Avenues, Inner Richmond (1-415 387-6343, neckofthewoods sf.com). Bus 1, 37. **Open** *6pm-2am daily.* **Shows** *9pm daily.* **Admission** *varies.* **Map** p310 C6.

What used to be known as the Rockit Room is now Neck of the Woods. The venue has hosted thousands of rock, indie, DJ, hip hop and burlesque acts since it opened in 1973 in not-so-central Inner Richmond, including venerable names such as Otis Redding, Etta James and Third Eye Blind. You can get in on the act during Wednesday's open-mic nights, and there are salsa dancing lessons every Monday. The venue even pays homage to its neighbourhood's ethnic roots by rolling out Russian karaoke once a month.

Thee Parkside

1600 17th Street, at Wisconsin Street, Potrero Hill (1-415 252 1330, www.theeparkside.com). Bus 10, 19, 22. **Open** *2pm-2am daily.* **Shows** *usually 9pm, earlier at weekends.* **Admission** *free-$15.* **Map** p317 N10.

This roadhouse started out as a lunch spot for dot-com 'cube farmers'. When the pink slips began to flutter in the early noughties, Thee Parkside found new life as a rowdy joint specialising in roots, punk, country and garage rock. Things get sweaty in the main room, where the so-called 'stage' abuts the door. In the tiki patio out the back, beer guzzlers heat up with a bit of ping-pong and pub grub.

JAZZ, BLUES, FOLK & WORLD

San Francisco's reputation as a jazz mecca goes back to the days when its bustling Fillmore District was considered a West Coast counterpart to the Harlem Renaissance. Several classic albums were recorded here, from Miles Davis's *In Person at the Blackhawk* and Thelonious Monk's *Alone in San Francisco* to *Friday Night in San Francisco*, a three-way throwdown between guitar virtuosos Al Di Meola, Paco de Lucia and John McLaughlin.

The opening of the state-of-the-art **SF JAZZ Center** in 2013 has reinvigorated an already robust scene. In addition, the **Fillmore** (*see p218*), **Hemlock Tavern** (*see p220*) and **Great American Music Hall** (*see p218*) stage sporadic jazz shows. In the Haight, **Club Deluxe** (1511 Haight Street, between Ashbury & Clayton Streets, 1-415 552 6949, www.clubdeluxe.co) offers jazzy jam sessions and a cool, vintage vibe complete with greyhound cocktails and gourmet pizza; and in North Beach, live jazz is the perfect backdrop to cocktails on the outdoor patio at **Savoy Tivoli** (*see p103*).

Boom Boom Room

1601 Fillmore Street, at Geary Boulevard, Fillmore (1-415 673 8000, www.boomboomblues.com). Bus 2, 3, 22, 31, 38. **Open** 4pm-2am Tue-Thur, Sun; 4pm-3am Fri, Sat. **Shows** 9pm. **Admission** $5-$20. **Map** p311 H6.

Opened round the corner in 1933 as Jack's Tavern, this blues bar has been a musical staple of the Fillmore District for more than 60 years. In the 1990s, it was remade into a classy blues joint with frequent resident John Lee Hooker lending it the name Boom Boom Room after his signature song. The bluesman held court at a booth up front until his death in 2001. These days, the venue attracts solid blues, roots, funk, R&B and groove-oriented acts, with an occasional surprise rock star dropping in.

Feinstein's at the Nikko

Hotel Nikko, 222 Mason Street, between Ellis & O'Farrell Streets, Tenderloin (1-415 394 1111, www.hotelnikkosf.com/feinsteins.aspx). BART & Metro to Powell/bus 2, 3, 4, 30, 45, 76 & Market Street routes/cable car Powell-Hyde or Powell-Mason. **Open** 2pm-1.30am daily. **Admission** $30-$55. **Map** p313 M6.

Feinstein's replaced the Rrazz Room in 2013, and has been on a solid roll since. The 140-seat cabaret delights guests with performances by pianist Michael Feinstein himself, Tony Award-winner Sutton Foster, and multi-talented performers such as Tony Danza, Jeff Goldblum's Mildred Snitzer Orchestra and Minnie Driver. Speciality cocktails are all top-notch, and this being cabaret, dinner or just a bite to eat are part of the fun. Feinstein's thrives on being attached to Restaurant Anzu, an upscale Japanese-Californian fusion eaterie offering steak and sushi.

Saloon

1232 Grant Avenue, at Columbus Avenue, North Beach (1-415 989 7666, www.sfblues.net/Saloon.html). Bus 10, 12, 30, 39, 41, 45, 91. **Open** noon-2am daily. **Shows** 9pm Mon-Thur; 4pm Fri-Sun. **Admission** free-$5. **Map** p313 M3.

A beer hall that scandalised the neighbourhood when it was established back in 1861 (it's now the oldest continuously operating bar in San Francisco), the Saloon has survived earthquakes and shifting musical tastes, and still remains a no-nonsense, rough-edged joint with a busy, bluesy calendar. Psychedelic-era rockers gracing the stage might include former members of Jefferson Airplane or Country Joe & the Fish.

★ SFJAZZ Center

201 Franklin Street, at Fell Street, Hayes Valley (1-415 788 7353, www.sfjazz.org/center). Metro to Van Ness/bus 6, 16X, 21, 47, 49, 71, 90. **Shows** varies. **Tickets** $30-$155. **Map** p316 K8.

San Francisco finally got the jazz hub it deserved with the 2013 opening of this $64 million centre, the first standalone venue in America built with the musical genre in mind. The SFJAZZ Center comes complete with state-of-the-art sound designed by Meyer Sound Laboratories and a rustic Mexican restaurant, South, from acclaimed chef/restaurateur Charles Phan. Now SFJAZZ has an appropriately majestic headquarters for the annual music festival it has produced since 1983, as well as a home for world-class performances not only in the jazz realm, but also global music in its many forms.

Sheba Piano Lounge

1419 Fillmore Street, between Ellis & O'Farrell Streets, Western Addition (1-415 440 7414, shebapianolounge.com). Bus 22, 24. **Open** 5pm-1am or 2am daily. **Shows** 5pm daily. **Admission** free. **Map** p312 J6.

Only in San Francisco will you find an Ethiopian-restaurant-bar-jazz lounge mashup, and that mix is exactly what attracts music lovers to Sheba. The ambience is intimate, with soft lighting, comfy sofas and even a roaring fire to make you feel at home while Latin, R&B, jazz, blues and world music performers serenade you. Ethiopian-inspired cocktails, a robust wine selection and authentic Ethiopian cuisine round out Sheba's offerings.

Boom Boom Room.

ARTS & ENTERTAINMENT

Performing Arts

Due in part to the geographical constraints of seven-by-seven-mile San Francisco, performances take place in every corner of the city, not just in conventional venues, but also bars and even the very urban infrastructure itself, using buildings as a backdrop. Major companies are always on the lookout for space – any space – to grow. The American Conservatory Theater recently transformed the derelict Strand movie house into a gorgeous stage, while the San Francisco Opera just cut the ribbon on a satellite.

On the big stages, it's all about the prestige projects: new shows bound for Broadway and tours of East Coast shows roaring triumphantly into town, as well as stagings of the classics. But off the beaten track, the weirder the better. At boundary-pushing venues like Yerba Buena Center for the Arts and SFJAZZ Center, you can catch such inventive hybrids as video art combined with shadow puppetry, or skateboarding accompanied by jazz.

Classical Music & Opera

San Francisco's deep-seated experimental culture is reflected in its major performing arts institutions: the symphony and the opera are both renowned for their challenging projects, while a number of the city's smaller ensembles have built their reputations on contemporary music without relinquishing familiar repertoire. Virtuosic performances are presented at fair prices in venues ranging from the modern (**Louise M Davies Symphony Hall**) to the historic (**Old St Mary's Cathedral**).

INFORMATION & TICKETS

San Francisco Classical Voice (www.sfcv.org) is the best source for information and events covering the Bay Area's classical music scene. Indie paper *SF Weekly* (www.sfweekly.com) also lists classical concerts and performances.

San Francisco Opera and Symphony tickets can be purchased directly at venues, online at www.sfopera.com and www.sfsymphony.org,

or at the **TIX Bay Area kiosk** in Union Square (350 Powell Street, between Geary & Post Streets, 1-415 433 7827, http://tixbayarea.org). Discounted standing room and student rush opera tickets are sold at the box office (301 Van Ness Avenue at Grove Street) starting at 10am and 11am on the day of performance. Some companies, including the San Francisco Opera, sell tickets via subscription packages, and the most popular shows do sell out. However, even on nights listed as sell-outs, there are usually a few seats available on the evening of performance.

MAJOR VENUES

★ Louise M Davies Symphony Hall

201 Van Ness Avenue, at Hayes Street, Civic Center (1-415 864 6000, www.sfsymphony.org). BART & Metro to Civic Center/Metro to Van Ness/ bus 5, 19, 21, 47, 49 & Market Street routes. **Box office** 10am-6pm Mon-Fri; noon-6pm Sat; 2hrs before concert Sun. **Tickets** $20-$150. **Map** p316 K7.

Formed to boost public morale after the 1906 earthquake and fire, the San Francisco Symphony performed its first concert in 1911. Today, under the direction of Michael Tilson Thomas, the orchestra has won multiple Grammy awards and international acclaim; it's particularly noted for its in-depth study of Mahler. MTT, as he's known, is the symphony's longest serving director, holding the position since 1995. The orchestra's home base, Louise M Davies Symphony Hall is a striking, multi-tiered curved-glass edifice with flawless acoustics and clear sightlines. There isn't a bad seat in the house, and that includes the 40 in the Center Terrace section behind the orchestra that sell for as little as $15-$20 two hours before most performances (call for details). In addition to SF Symphony concerts, look out for events in the Great Performers series, which imports world-renowned soloists, conductors and ensembles for one-nighters. *Photo p226.*

San Francisco Performances

Various venues. Box office: Suite 100, 180 Redwood Street, Civic Center (1-415 392 2545, www.performances.org). BART & Metro to Civic Center/Metro to Van Ness/bus 5, 19, 21, 47, 49 & Market Street routes. **Box office** 9.30am-5.30pm Mon-Fri. **Tickets** vary.

Since 1979, this independent promoter has brought concerts and recitals in every style and genre to San Francisco, from Beethoven to modern ballet and contemporary jazz, totalling over 200 performances each year. Most performances are held at the Herbst Theatre (*see p231*), the Yerba Buena Center for the Arts Theater, Davies Symphony Hall, and the SFJAZZ Center (*see p223*), but there are also events at the Hotel Rex (*see p275*).

War Memorial Opera House

301 Van Ness Avenue, at Grove Street, Civic Center (1-415 864 3330, www.sfopera.com). BART & Metro to Civic Center/Metro to Van Ness/bus 5, 19, 21, 47, 49 & Market Street routes. **Box office** 10am-5pm Mon; 10am-6pm Tue-Sat. **Tickets** $30-$300. **Map** p316 K7.

Inaugurated in 1923, the San Francisco Opera is renowned both for audacious stagings of classics like *The Magic Flute, The Marriage of Figaro* and *La Boheme* (the company opened with it in 1923 and has since performed it over 85 times), as well as contemporary fare and original commissions such as *Nixon in China, I Am Harvey Milk* (about the murdered SF gay rights activist and politician) and *Dream of the Red Chamber* by noted Chinese-American composer Bright Sheng. The beautiful War Memorial Opera house, designed in part by Arthur Brown Jr, creator of the nearby City Hall and Orpheum Theatre, was built as a memorial to the soldiers who fought in World War I. It's is also home to the San Francisco Ballet. In early 2016, the SF Opera opens the 300-seat Diane B Wilsey Center for the Opera in the nearby Veterans Building, to accommodate more intimate, up-close performances. *Photo p227.*

Yerba Buena Center for the Arts Theater

701 Mission Street, at 3rd Street, SoMa (1-415 978 2700, www.ybca.org). BART & Metro to Montgomery/bus 10, 12, 14, 30, 45 & Market Street routes. **Box office** noon-6pm Tue-Sun. **Tickets** vary. **Map** p317 N6.

This 757-seat auditorium hosts some of the most exciting contemporary music and dance in the country, including acclaimed string ensemble the Kronos Quartet, the Smuin Ballet and the experimental dance collective ODC Dance. Designed by modernist architect James Stewart Polshek, the exterior of the cube-shaped theatre is covered in aluminium panels that catch the sparkling San Francisco light. One of the city's most striking performance spaces, it boasts a wide variety of events, ranging from the Afro Solo Festival to fringe theatre productions and the holiday season stalwart *Velveteen Rabbit.*

LOCAL ENSEMBLES & COMPANIES

The **Philharmonia Baroque Orchestra** (1-415 252 1288, www.philharmonia.org) offers a six-programme season of baroque and classical repertoire which they 'tour' October through April to the **Herbst Theatre** (*see p231*) and Berkeley's **First Congregational Church** (2345 Channing Way, 1-510 848 3696, www.fccb.org), plus locations in Palo Alto and Contra Costa County. The **New Century Chamber Orchestra** (1-415 357 1111, www.ncco.org) has a similar set-up, playing a four-programme season in San Francisco, San Rafael, Palo Alto and Berkeley.

The famed **Kronos Quartet** (1-415 731 3533, www.kronosquartet.org) is in demand around the world for its startling string symphonies, but calls San Francisco home. The **San Francisco Contemporary Music Players** (1-415 278 9566, www.sfcmp.org) have racked up 200 commissions and more than 1,200 regional or world premieres since 1970, including collaborations with Frank Zappa and Grace Slick. Grammy-winning all-male a cappella group **Chanticleer** (1-415 252 8589, www.chanticleer.org) is less challenging, but no less accomplished and has a terrific Christmas programme. All three ensembles tour for much of the year but play in the Bay Area regularly: Kronos and the SFCMP at the **Yerba Buena Center for the Arts**, and Chanticleer at a wide variety of venues, including St Ignatius Church (650 Parker Street, Western Addition).

Pocket Opera (1-415 972 8930, www.pocketopera.org) presents works translated into English at the Legion of Honor (*see p185*), and gives SF Opera some small run for its money. The long-established **Lamplighters Musical Theatre** (1-415 227 4797, www.lamplighters.org)

Louise M Davies Symphony Hall.
See p224.

ARTS & ENTERTAINMENT

stages lighter works – mostly Gilbert and Sullivan – at various venues. The **San Francisco Conservatory of Music** (50 Oak Street, between Franklin Street & Van Ness Avenue, 1-415 864 7326, www.sfcm.edu) showcases exceptional student talent a couple of blocks from the Davies, while **Cal Performances** at Berkeley's Zellerbach Hall attracts luminaries of the calibre of diva Renée Fleming.

CHURCH VENUES

A number of the city's churches host recitals and chamber concerts, often featuring local young musicians and frequently free of charge. Among them are the **Old First Presbyterian Church** (1751 Sacramento Street, between Polk Street & Van Ness Avenue, 1-415 776 5552, www.oldfirst. org) on the edge of Pacific Heights; the **First Unitarian Universalist Church** (1187 Franklin Street, at Geary Street, 1-415 776 4580, www.uusf.org) near the Civic Center, famous for its Bartók birthday concert on the third Sunday in March; and Nob Hill's **Grace Cathedral** (*see p87*). Old **St Mary's Cathedral** (660 California Street) hosts concerts at 12.30pm every Tuesday (www.noontimeconcerts.org).

For a very different kind of devotional music and an 'only in San Francisco' experience, there's the **St John Coltrane African Orthodox Church** (1286 Fillmore Street, 1-415 673 7144, www.coltranechurch.org). Dedicated to the belief that the divine spoke through jazz saxophone

legend John Coltrane and, in particular, his composition *A Love Supreme*, the church holds a mass/jam session every Sunday at noon.

Dance

The city's vibrant modern dance scene takes in everything from the world-class **San Francisco Ballet** (*see p229*) to ethnic ensembles and experimental hybrid performances. In addition to the companies listed below, also consider the **Lily Cai Chinese Dance Company** (1-415 474 4829, www.lilycaidance.org), which has been blending ancient forms with modern dance since 1988; **Chitresh Das Dance Company** (1-415 333 9000, www.kathak.org), which performs the narrative-based Indian classical dance form Kathak; and Carolena Nericcio-Bohlman's **Fat Chance Belly Dance** (1-415 431 4322, www. fcbd.com), which offers 'American Tribal' styles of traditional Middle Eastern dancing.

COMPANIES & VENUES

Alonzo King's Lines
Information 1-415 863 3040, tickets 1-415 978 2787, www.linesballet.org. **Tickets** $30-$100.
This fine contemporary and eclectic ballet company stages mainly new works, and tours extensively both at home and abroad. A staple of the SF dance scene, it performs twice a year at Yerba Buena Center for the Arts.

The San Francisco Opera at the **War Memorial Opera House**. *See p225*.

Cal Performances

Zellerbach Hall, UC Berkeley campus, Berkeley (1-510 642 9988, www.calperfs.berkeley.edu). BART to Downtown Berkeley. **Tickets** $10-$250.
An adjunct of UC Berkeley, Cal Performances offers a smattering of everything: dance, music and drama. In the former category, it regularly presents companies from around the country and the globe, such as Alvin Ailey, Twyla Tharp and Mark Morris.

Erika Chong Shuch Performance (ESP) Project

Various venues (1-415 626 2787 ext 112, www.erikachongshuch.org). **Tickets** $10-$30.
Dancer and choreographer Shuch's eponymous project offers multi-disciplinary (dance, poetry, visual art) pieces on such out-there topics as the search for alien life, living in prison and ponderings on the abstract symbolism of a window.

Footloose

1 Grove Street, at Hyde Street, Civic Center (1-510 658 3530, tickets 1-800 838 3006, www.ftloose. org). BART & Metro to Civic Center/bus Market Street routes. **Tickets** $15-$20. **Map** p316 K11.
The emphasis here is on works by women, culminating in the annual Women on the Way Festival of up-and-coming artists.

FREE Flyaway Productions

Various outdoor locations throughout the city (1-415 672 4111, www.flyawayproductions.com). **Tickets** free.

Check the website for dates and locations of these gravity-defying outdoor performances. Dancers twirl up and down the sides of buildings, taking daring plunges off rooftops, fire escapes and other structures against an urban backdrop. The one-of-a-kind spectacles highlight social issues (not to mention the importance of very strong rope).

Joe Goode Performance Group

Information 1-415 561 6565, tickets 1-415 978 2787, www.joegoode.org. **Tickets** $19-$49.
The JGPG pushes modern dance to new theatrical heights, exploring contemporary issues from gender to AIDS. The company also holds workshops for community groups, including at-risk youth and battered women. It performs at the Yerba Buena Center for the Arts (*see p225*) every June.

★ ODC Theater

3153 17th Street, between Shotwell Street & Van Ness Avenue, Mission (1-415 863 9833, www.odcdance.org). BART to 16th Street Mission/ bus 12, 14, 22, 33, 49. **Tickets** $18-$30. **Map** p316 K10.
Founded in 1971, the Oberlin Dance Collective is the gold standard for modern dance on the West Coast. ODC has its own school and gallery, and was the first modern dance company in America to build its own facility. The main theatre is augmented by ODC Dance Commons, a 33,000-square-foot performance space around the corner. Over the years, ODC has raked in seven Isadora Duncan awards, a Guggenheim – and a general reputation for audacity.

THE WORLD CAN BE AN UNJUST AND TREACHEROUS PLACE, BUT THERE ARE THOSE WHO STRIVE TO MAKE IT SAFE FOR EVERYONE.

© 2003 Human Rights Watch; © 2009 Andrew Parsons

Operating in some of the world's most dangerous and oppressed countries, **Human Rights Watch** conducts rigorous investigations to bring those who have been targets of abuse to the world's attention. We use strategic advocacy to push people in power to end their repressive practices. And we work for as long as it takes to see that oppressors are held accountable for their crimes.

© 2009 Susan Meiselas/Magnum; © 2008 Human Rights Watch

KNOWLEDGE IS POWER.
LEARN ABOUT LIFE-CHANGING EVENTS IN YOUR WORLD THAT DON'T ALWAYS MAKE THE HEADLINES AND HOW YOU CAN HELP EFFECT POSITIVE CHANGE.

Stay informed, visit HRW.org

HUMAN RIGHTS WATCH

Robert Moses' Kin

Various venues (1-415 252 8384, www. robertmoseskin.org). **Tickets** $20-$60.
Consistently breaking new ground since it was founded in 1995, the choreographer's 11-person group collaborates with everyone from sculptors and poets to musicians and designers. Pieces tend to focus on the realities of race, class, gender and the conflicts that come with them. In addition to national tours, the company presents an annual home season, usually in the autumn.

★ San Francisco Ballet

War Memorial Opera House, see p225.
Tickets $20-$150. **Map** p316 K7.
Founded in 1933, the San Francisco Ballet is the longest-running professional ballet company in the US, responsible for the first full-length American production of *Coppélia* and the country's first complete *Swan Lake*. The company is based in the War Memorial Opera House (*see p225*), and its annual season (Feb-May) offers a blend of traditional pieces and new works by the likes of Royal Ballet wunderkind Liam Scarlett.

Smuin Ballet

Information 1-415 495 2234, tickets 1-415 978 2787, www.smuinballet.org. **Tickets** $20-$62.
A former principal dancer and director of the San Francisco Ballet who also worked on Broadway and in film and television, Michael Smuin left a national legacy of bold, dancer-driven works melding classical and modern techniques. Even following Smuin's death in 2007, the company bearing his name offers technically rigorous and inventive winter, spring and holiday programmes of classics and world premieres alike. In San Francisco, the company performs at Yerba Buena Center for the Arts (*see p225*).

Smuin Ballet.

Theatre

Though small in size, San Francisco proves time and again it can deliver as much cultural capital as the biggest and best of 'em. Broadway-bound mega-budget musicals such as *Wicked* and *Beautiful: The Carole King Musical* flourish alongside extraordinary solo works from emerging actor-playwrights and avant-garde amalgamations of music, poetry and performance. San Francisco's discriminating audiences, excellent venues and fine pool of artistic talent make it an ideal launch pad for the rest of the country.

INFORMATION AND TICKETS

The *Chronicle*'s Sunday 'Datebook' section, accessible online at www.sfgate.com, has extensive listings. For additional reviews and listings, try *SF Weekly* (www.sfweekly.com).

Prices vary wildly: tickets for some fringe shows are just $5, but you could pay 30 times that for a blockbuster. To avoid booking fees, call the theatre's own box office or book on its website. And visiting the box office in person can save you money on 'convenience' fees. If you're willing to take a chance, the **TIX Bay Area kiosk** in Union Square (*see p224*) sells half-price tickets for many shows on the day of performance. Some venues also sell through

---

IN THE KNOW FREE CULTURE

From April to October, you can catch free weekend classical, jazz, and world music and dance performances, Thursday lunchtime concerts, and children's shows at Yerba Buena Gardens as part of the **Yerba Buena Gardens Festival** (www. ybgf.org). Most shows are held on the esplanade lawn next to Yerba Buena Center for the Arts (see p225).

SECOND ACT

A faded movie palace is reprised as the city's red-hot new stage.

The revival of the Strand Theatre is a tale of the destructive and redemptive powers of progress. Opened as a cinema called the Jewel in 1917, it stood shoulder-to-shoulder with the city's other grand movie palaces during Hollywood's golden age. But with the advent of television, the theatre fell on hard times, first offering triple features to its dwindling customers, then throwing in nightly bingo games as an added enticement. Its star briefly rose again in the 1970s as a revival house popular for midnight showings of the cult film, *The Rocky Horror Picture Show*, before descending into debauchery as a sleazy porn theatre and hotbed of drug dealing.

The Strand faded to black in 2003, its boarded-up derelict shell haunting Civic Center for years, as the neighbourhood itself became an embarrassing blight in the heart of the city. Then in 2013, the **American Conservatory Theater (ACT)** (*see p231*), long hankering for a new mid-sized stage that would let the company expand its annual season, decided there was life in the old girl yet. The ACT spent two years and more than $30 million renovating the space, part of a wider, largely tech-fuelled trend towards rehabilitating the area around Civic Center and mid-Market Street as a whole.

The new, 238-seat Strand Theatre reopened to a fanfare in 2015 with an acclaimed production of English playwright Caryl Churchill's *Love & Information*. Architects at Skidmore, Owings & Merrill preserved the distinctive slat row windows on the top half of the theatre's face but opened up the bottom half with enormous windows to show off the floating LED screen in the lobby – a surreal but gorgeous reminder of the building's movie-house past. As a finishing touch, the whole place was painted eye-popping red inside and out – a sparkling reminder that it's always been the jewel it was originally intended to be.

ticket agencies such as **City Box Office** (1-415 392 4400, www.cityboxoffice.com).

MAJOR THEATRES

A handful of San Francisco's theatres host major touring shows. Entertainment company SHN (www.shnsf.com) imports hit Broadway musicals and other productions to the grand **Orpheum** (1192 Market Street, at Hyde Street, Civic Center) and the 2,300-seat art deco **Golden Gate Theatre** (1 Taylor Street, at Golden Gate Avenue, Tenderloin). For further information, call 1-415 551 2000; to purchase tickets, which typically run from $35 to $200, use **Ticketmaster** (1-800 745 3000, www.ticketmaster.com).

The **Herbst Theatre** (401 Van Ness Avenue, at Grove Street, Civic Center, 1-415 392 4400), due to reopen following renovation by publication of this guide, hosts local and out-of-town guests, many as part of the San Francisco Performances series (*see p225*). The 1926 **Marines' Memorial Theatre** (609 Sutter Street, at Mason Street, Tenderloin, 1-415 771 6900, www.marines memorialtheatre.com) presents off-Broadway, regional and local productions.

★ American Conservatory Theater (ACT)

Geary Theater, 415 Geary Street, between Mason & Taylor Streets, Tenderloin; Strand Theater, 1127 Market Street, between 7th & 8th Streets, Civic Center (information 1-415 834 3200, box office 1-415 749 2228, www.act-sf.org). Bus 2, 3, 27, 30, 31, 38, 45, 91/cable car Powell-Hyde or Powell-Mason. **Tickets** $20-$115. **Map** p312 L6.

The city's masthead company, ACT has been staging modern classics and new works by the likes of David Mamet and Tom Stoppard since 1967. Its annual production of *A Christmas Carol* is almost as popular a tradition as Christmas itself in San Francisco. It's also known for its fine conservatory, whose alumni include Annette Bening, Denzel Washington, Nicolas Cage and Danny Glover. In 2015, ACT converted the remains of an old-time movie palace into the gorgeous 238-seat Strand Theatre near Civic Center (*see p230*).

Magic Theatre

Building D, Fort Mason, Marina Boulevard, at Buchanan Street, Marina (1-415 441 8822, www. magictheatre.org). Bus 22, 28/cable car Powell-Hyde. **Tickets** $30-$60. **Map** p312 H2.

Drawing its name from a line in Hermann Hesse's *Steppenwolf*, the Magic Theatre has impressed throughout its nearly 50-year history with groundbreaking works by the likes of former resident playwright Sam Shepard. The two 150-seat houses, overlooking the Golden Gate Bridge, offer an intriguing mix of new works by both emerging playwrights and leading lights.

FRINGE THEATRES & COMPANIES

For gay theatre and cabaret, *see p211*. For the **Yerba Buena Center for the Arts Theater**, *see p225*.

Asian American Theater Company

Various venues (tickets 1-800 838 3006, www. asianamericantheater.org). **Tickets** $10-$25.

Started by ACT in 1973, the AATC fosters work that speaks to the experience of Americans of Asian and Pacific Island descent. Phillip Kan Gotanda and David Henry Hwang are among the exceptional talents nurtured in its first 30 years; both have recently returned to collaborate with the next generation. The emphasis is on new work, and the quality can vary wildly.

★ Beach Blanket Babylon

Club Fugazi, 678 Green Street, between Columbus Avenue & Powell Street, North Beach (1-415 421 4222, www.beachblanketbabylon.com). Bus 10, 12, 30, 39, 41, 45, 91/cable car Powell-Mason. **Tickets** $25-$120. **Map** p312 L3.

The longest-running musical revue in theatrical history and an inescapable piece of San Francisco camp culture, *Beach Blanket Babylon* sells its blend of parody songs, puns and outrageous headgear with such irresistible conviction that it's become an institution. Now well over 40 years old (although she doesn't look a day over 25), *BBB* takes Snow White on a whirlwind tour of America and pop culture (the script is constantly being updated with topical themes and characters) in search of her Happily Ever After ending. Evening performances are for over-21s only.

Custom Made Theatre Company

533 Sutter Street at Powell Street (1-415 798 2682, www.custommade.org). Bus 2,3,76/cable car Powell-Hyde or Powell-Mason. **Tickets** $20-$28 **Map** p312 J5.

The Custom Made Theatre Company produces five full-length shows each year, as well as additional performances and workshops. Past productions include the world premiere of *Candide of California* by Brian Katz and a play by David and Amy Sedaris, *The Book of Liz.*

EXIT Theatre

156 Eddy Street, between Mason & Taylor Streets, Tenderloin (1-415 673 3847, tickets 1-800 838 3006, www.theexit.org). BART & Metro to Powell/ bus 27, 31, 38, 45 & Market Street routes/cable car Powell-Hyde or Powell-Mason. **Tickets** $15-$25. **Map** p312 L6.

This three-stage set-up offers eclectic, provocative shows, from new one-acts to work by well-known authors. The Exit also hosts the annual San Francisco Fringe Festival of non-censored and

ARTS & ENTERTAINMENT

Hypnodrome.

IN THE KNOW BACKSTAGE TOURS

During opera season, you can get a glimpse behind the scenes of the **War Memorial Opera House** (see p225) on a backstage tour (1-415 551 6353, $20) with guild volunteers. Tours take in dressing rooms, wardrobe department and makeup areas, and explore the architecture and history of the building (reservations required). During the off-season, combined tours of the symphony hall and opera house are offered on Mondays, hourly 10am-2pm (1-415 552 8338, $5-$7).

non-curated works every September. A fourth stage (Exit on Taylor) lies just around the corner at 277 Taylor Street and hosts Cutting Ball Theatre, the city's self-styled theatrical avant-garde, offering weird and wild new works by resident playwright Andrew Saito as well as experimental takes on classics from Sophocles to Alfred Jarry.

Hypnodrome

575 10th Street, at Division Street, SoMa (1-415 377 4202, www.thrillpeddlers.com). Bus 9, 12, 27, 47. **Tickets** $25-$35. **Map** p317 M9.

The Hypnodrome is the home of Thrillpeddlers, the city's most tasteless theatrical tastemakers. Every autumn the troupe offers Shocktoberfest, a Halloweenwish cocktail of authentic Grand Guignol theatre (classic French horror plays that are rarely translated into English), and the rest of the year is devoted to 'theatre of the absurd', which usually means drag, camp, parody and the music of Scrumbly Koldewyn (composer for the original Cockettes). If *Beach Blanket Babylon* is a bit too polished for you, this is your only-in-San Francisco theatre experience.

Lorraine Hansberry Theatre

Multiple venues (1-415 474 8800, www.lhtsf.com). **Tickets** $16-$35.

The foremost African-American theatre company in the Bay Area produces four or five plays each year, by black playwrights or dealing with issues affecting African-Americans. The schedule usually includes a musical Christmas offering, such as Langston Hughes's *Black Nativity*.

★ The Marsh

1062 Valencia Street, at 22nd Street, Mission (information 1-415 641 0235, tickets 1-415 282 3055, www.themarsh.org). BART to 24th Street Mission/bus 14, 49. **Tickets** $8-$35. **Map** p316 K12.

The Marsh presents original solo plays by local and visiting artists. Locally acclaimed pieces, such as

Josh Kornbluth's *Red Diaper Baby* (about growing up the child of New York communists), Brian Copeland's *Not a Genuine Black Man* (the longest running one-man show in San Francisco history) and Geoff Hoyle's *The Real Americans* (about a sometimes uncomfortable road trip meeting people coast to coast), move on to larger venues in the Bay Area or countrywide, while seasoned pros like Merle Kessler (aka Ian Shoales) and John O'Keefe alight here as well.

Project Artaud Theater

499 Alabama Street, at Mariposa Street, Mission (1-415 621 4240, www.projectartaud.org). Bus 33, 27. **Tickets** $5-$30. **Map** p316 L10.

This non-profit theatre stages boundary-pushing new works, from monologues and modern dance to provocative aerial circus theatre. The Theatre of Yugen/Noh Space, which specialises in Eastern-influenced theatre, Butoh and performance art, shares the space.

FREE SF Mime Troupe

Various venues (1-415 285 1717, www.sfmt.org). **Tickets** free.

No, it's not that kind of mime. The performers in the so-called SF Mime Troupe are the city's premier political satirists, who have offered free summer shows in various Bay Area parks since the early 1960s and count counterculture icon Peter Coyote among their alumni (he starred in the 1967 satire of the Vietnam war that cinched the troupe's radical reputation). Decidedly left wing and always painfully

contemporary, the SF Mime Troupe is a constant source of amusement – provided you're not one of the Powers That Be who are getting skewered.

SF Playhouse

450 Post Street, between Mason & Powell Streets, Union Square (1-415 677 9596, www.sfplayhouse.org). Bus 2, 3, 27, 38, 76/cable car Powell-Hyde or Powell-Mason. **Tickets** $30-$100. **Map** p313 M5.

A modest-sized repertory house and probably the most reliably creative company in the city, SF Playhouse presents musicals like Sondheim's *Company* and *Into the Woods*, jaw-dropping satire like Aaron Posner's *Stupid F#!cking Bird* (a tribute to and send-up of Chekhov's *The Seagull*) and brash premieres, including the first and (so far) only American production of Jez Butterworth's *Jerusalem*, all from a lofty perch on the second floor of the Kensington Park Hotel.

FREE Theater Pub

Various venues (www.sftheaterpub.wordpress.com). **Tickets** free.

What could be more fundamentally San Franciscan than classic theatre performed in the dark recesses of a working bar? Theater Pub brings Shakespeare (and sometimes other classic playwrights, as well as occasional original works) back to its roots as popular entertainment for the masses by enacting plays such as *Richard III* and *The Taming of the Shrew* smack dab in the middle of a local tavern. Wait staff simply walk around the show to continue serving customers, some of whom wander in with no idea that there's a play on. Every second Saturday, Theater Pub hosts Saturday *Write Fever* at the EXIT Theatre's café, where playwrights ad-lib on-the-spot 'flash-fried' scripts for brave actors who must then perform them for the eager café audience.

Thick House

1695 18th Street, at Carolina Street, Potrero Hill (www.thickhouse.org). Bus 10, 19, 22. **Tickets** vary. **Map** p317 N10.

Home to the likes of Crowded Fire Theatre, which produces new plays by West Coast artists, and 3Girls Theatre, dedicated to showcasing female playwrights, Thick House offers contemporary and cutting-edge drama that is funny, provoking and occasionally even a little shocking.

Z Space

450 Florida Street, between 17th & Mariposa Streets, Mission (1-415 626 0453, box office 1-866 811 4111, www.zspace.org). Bus 27, 33. **Tickets** vary. **Map** p316 L10.

A small venue in a huge space (a mere 229 seats occupying 13,000 square feet), this warehouse-style theatre tucked low in the Mission hosts Word for Word. The well-read performing arts company 'brings literature to its feet' with adaptations of acclaimed short stories by the likes of Tobias Wolff and Emma Donoghue. The thrilling inventiveness and talent brought to bear on such pop-up book productions has earned it acclaim from both literature lovers and lazy readers.

Escapes & Excursions

Escapes & Excursions

R eady to take a break from the city fog?
One of the beauties of San Francisco's hilly
geography is that heading a few miles in any
direction takes you to warmer climes and wide-
open spaces. Head north over the Golden Gate
Bridge and you'll find miles of sunny beaches
along the Marin coastline and groves of ancient
redwoods in Muir Woods. Meander south down
scenic Highway One to the surfers' turf of
Half Moon Bay and Santa Cruz. Or drive east
across the Bay Bridge to the intellectual and
culinary hot zones of Berkeley and Oakland.
Most of these escapes are accessible on
public transport, so you can avoid both rental-
car expenses and sitting in (perpetually)
gridlocked traffic.

East Bay cities

OAKLAND

Across the Bay Bridge, Oakland was once
the western terminus of the 3,000-mile
transcontinental railway and is still ranked in
the top ten of the West Coast's busiest ports.
This constant influx of imports (both goods
and people) imbued the city with a diverse
populace that hasn't always seen eye to eye with
mainstream America. In the 1960s, it was the
scene of violence and social change, with the
once-notorious activist Black Panthers leaving
their imprint, along with hippies, yippies,
Merry Pranksters and mob-handed Hell's
Angels. Today, parts of Oakland (specifically
the more industrial regions of West Oakland)
still have a high crime rate, but much of the city
is experiencing a renaissance – the high rents and
home prices of San Francisco creating a vacuum
of artists and other working- and middle-class
folk that Oakland was only too happy to fill.
Today, the city's modest bungalows sit alongside

luxurious hillside mansions, swanky live-work
lofts, hip shopping districts and a restaurant
scene that rivals San Francisco's.

On the waterfront lies one of Oakland's main
tourist hives: **Jack London Square** (Broadway
& Embarcadero), named after the noted local
author who used to carouse at **Heinold's First
& Last Chance** (48 Webster Street, 1-510 839
6761, www.heinolds.com), a funky bar in a little
wooden shack built from the timbers of a whaling
ship. The square also offers a weekly farmers'
market (9am-2pm Sundays), and Franklin Delano
Roosevelt's 'floating White House', the USS
Potomac (540 Water Street, 1-510 627 1215,
www.usspotomac.org); its visitors' centre arranges
tours and Bay cruises. At night, the lowing of the
foghorns across the Bay provides a counterpoint to
the beat at **Yoshi's** (510 Embarcadero West, 1-510
238 9200, www.yoshis.com), a world-renowned
jazz club that has been drawing top names to the
Oakland waterfront for more than 40 years.

Chinatown, which covers the few blocks
south of Broadway around 7th, 8th and 9th
Streets, is less tourist-focused than its San

Francisco counterpart, but still packed with places to eat and shop. Grab a Vietnamese sandwich, some dim sum or Thai barbecue, then head across Broadway and check out **Swan's Marketplace** (538 9th Street, www.swans market.tumblr.com), a renovated 1917 brick building filled with local food and wine vendors. The **Oakland Museum of California** (1000 Oak Street, 1-510 318 8400, www.museum ca.org) is a great place to learn about the state's history, art and culture; it's also well worth a quick detour to pretty Lake Merritt, where you can catch a ride in a Venetian-style gondola at the end of Bellevue Avenue (1-510 663 6603, www.gondolaservizio.com). Down the road is the charming **Children's Fairyland** (699 Bellevue Avenue, 1-510 452 2259, www.fairyland. org), full of sets and characters from classic nursery rhymes; Walt Disney allegedly used it as inspiration for Disneyland.

West of Lake Merritt is the **Paramount Theatre** (2025 Broadway, between 20th & 21st Streets, 1-510 465 6400, www.paramounttheatre. com), a fabulous 1931 art deco movie house designed by renowned Bay Area architect Timothy L Pflueger. Complete with a Mighty Wurlitzer organ and full bar in the lobby, the theatre is home to the Oakland East Bay Symphony (1-510 444 0801, www.oebs.org), and also features rock, blues, soul and comedy shows. The beautifully restored **Fox Theater** (1807 Telegraph Avenue, 1-510 302 2250, www.thefoxoakland.com) draws some of the top names in the indie music scene.

The best corner for shoppers is the stretch of College Avenue in the ritzy Rockridge district to the north (served by its own BART station). As well as high-end home accessories, pricey children's boutiques and French bistros, you'll find **Market Hall** (5665 College Avenue, 1-510 250 6000, www.rockridgemarkethall.com), with a butcher, fishmonger, wine shop, bakery, pasta shop, cheese shop, florist and café. In the Temescal district, a weekly farmers' market (5300 Claremont Avenue, at Telegraph Avenue, 1-510 745 7100, www.urban villageonline.com, 9am-1pm Sun) is a major draw. A bit further down Telegraph, Oakland's **Koreatown** is known for its restaurants.

Where to eat & drink

Impeccably sourced and exquisitely crafted California cuisine at Michelin-starred **Commis** (3859 Piedmont Avenue, 1-510 653 3902, www. commisrestaurant.com) has made chef/owner James Syhabout a household name. A few blocks away, **Adesso** (4395 Piedmont Avenue, 1-510 601 0305, www.dopoadesso.com) boasts one of the region's best happy hours and a minimum of 30 – yes, 30 – kinds of house-made salumi and charcuterie. San Francisco star chef Daniel Patterson, who gained acclaim with his two

Michelin-starred Coi in San Francisco's North Beach, added **Plum** (2216 Broadway, 1-510 444 7586, www.plumoakland.com), an upscale American comfort food spot to the Uptown District in 2010. Also in the Uptown District is **Flora** (1900 Telegraph Avenue, 1-510 286 0100, www.floraoakland.com), housed in a stunning art deco building and boasting some of the Bay's best cocktails (try a Carter Beats the Devil), as well as a wide-ranging American classic menu. Upscale sushi and Japanese cuisine complement one of the region's most well-tended saké lists at the Oakland outpost of **Ozumo** (2251 Broadway, 1-510 286 9866, www.ozumo.com), while next door, **Pican** (2295 Broadway, 1-510 834 1000, www.pican restaurant.com) offers gourmet Southern fare (don't miss the fried chicken with truffle-honey drizzle) paired with the best bourbon and rye whiskey selections this side of the Mississippi.

The Temescal district is home to Chez Panisse alumnus Charlie Hallowell's **Pizzaiolo** (5008 Telegraph Avenue, 1-510 652 4888, www. pizzaiolooakland.com), where the wood oven-baked pizza Napoletano is topped with fresh, seasonal ingredients and house-made charcuterie. The Lakeshore District's justly acclaimed **Camino** (3917 Grand Avenue, 1-510 547 5035, www.caminorestaurant.com) focuses on dishes cooked in a massive, open fireplace at the rear of the restaurant. Nearby, the **Lake Chalet** (1520 Lakeside Drive, 1-510 208 5253, www.thelake chalet.com) offers visitors a chance to enjoy the sunny East Bay weather, along with burgers and seafood, on a pier extending over Lake Merritt.

In the smart Rockridge neighbourhood, just steps from the BART station, is the granddaddy of Oakland's fine dining scene, **Oliveto** (5655 College Avenue, 1-510 547 5356, www.oliveto. com). Its house-made pastas, salumi, and whole hog dinners have made it a destination dining spot since the mid-1980s.

Getting there

Oakland is easily accessible from San Francisco. At off-peak times it's a 20-minute drive over the Bay Bridge or a BART (*see p291*) ride to City Center/12th Street or 19th Street, both handy for central Oakland. Regular ferry service runs from the Ferry Building (Market Street and Embarcadero) to Oakland's Jack London Square Terminal (1-510 522 3300, www. sanfranciscobayferry.com).

BERKELEY

Berkeley has worked hard to earn its reputation for avant-garde arts, leftist politics and marvellous food. Over the decades, it has shown proper dedication to maintaining all three. It remains a fascinating and wonderfully contradictory place, where gourmet eating is accepted as a form of radical liberalism.

At its heart is the thriving campus of the **University of California**. To suggest that Berkeley is slightly in thrall to its university is like hinting that San Francisco gets a little foggy from time to time – 'Cal' is the straw that stirs the Berkeley cocktail, and it has lent the place a nationwide reputation for erudite, progressive liberalism. The university was the birthplace of the Free Speech Movement in the 1960s, with student protests against campus rules and the Vietnam War inspiring a nation of rebels. Head up to the 200-foot observation deck of the Sather Tower, known as 'the Campanile' (open 10am-3.45pm Mon-Fri;10am-4.45pm Sat; 10am-1.30pm, 3-4.45pm Sun) for great views of the campus and the surrounding area. Elsewhere on campus are museums dedicated to art, anthropology, palaeontology and more. On the peak above the campus, but still run by the university, is the **Lawrence Hall of Science** (1 Centennial Drive, 1-510 642 5132, www.lawrencehallof science.org), a fascinating hands-on science museum aimed at children, with views over the entire Bay Area. For more information, drop in on the campus **visitors' centre** (University Hall, 2200 University Avenue, 1-510 642 5215, www. berkeley.edu/visitors), which is also the starting point for a 90-minute campus tour (10am Mon-Sat, 1pm Sun from the Campanile).

Spiking southwards from the university, **Telegraph Avenue** provides a home for street-vendor jewellery, crafts stands and hippyish clothes shops. Bibliophiles should check out **Moe's** (no.2476, between Dwight Way & Haste Street, 1-510 849 2087, www.moesbooks.com) for a huge selection of both new and used books. Further south along Telegraph are two huge music stores: **Rasputin** (no.2401, at Channing Way, 1-510 704 1146, www. rasputinmusic.com) and the superior **Amoeba Records** (No.2455, at Haste Street, 1-510 549 1125, www.amoebamusic.com).

In the downtown arts district, the **Berkeley Art Museum/Pacific Film Archive** (*see p193*), a treasure trove of 20th-century art and archival cinematic works, has reopened in a spectacular new building designed by New York firm Diller Scofidio + Renfro. A few blocks away, the **Berkeley Repertory Theatre** (2025 Addison Street, 1-510 647 2900, www.berkeleyrep.org) is an innovative and ambitious stage with an impressive track record of producing shows that transfer to Broadway.

High above in the Berkeley hills, the lovely and wild **Tilden Regional Park** (1-510 562 7275, www.ebparks.org) covers 2,079 acres of hiking, nature trails, pony rides, a miniature steam train, a botanical garden, and Lake Anza – a great spot for a dip on hot days.

IN THE KNOW COFFEE CONNECTION

The Berkeley branch of Peet's Coffee & Tea (*see below*) on Vine Street is the shop where Jerry Baldwin, one of the founders of Starbucks, got his start – and where the chain got its beans for its first year of operation. So now you know who to blame.

Where to eat & drink

Cafés line the university's southern limit, among them the mainly outdoor **Café Strada** (2300 College Avenue, 1-510 843 5282) and Café Milano (2522 Bancroft Way, 1-510 644 3100). Northwest of campus sits the culinary hot zone known as the **Gourmet Ghetto**, which runs along Shattuck Avenue between Delaware and Rose Streets. The star of the show is undeniably **Chez Panisse** (1517 Shattuck Avenue, 1-510 548 5525, www. chezpanisse.com), opened back in 1971 by Alice Waters, the elfin leader of the California slow food revolution (she was honoured by President Obama in 2015 with a National Humanities Medal for her work). Alice's restaurant is hardly the only good option in the Ghetto, though. Next door is **Bar César** (1515 Shattuck Avenue, 1-510 985 1200, www.barcesar.com), which serves an enticing array of tapas; more or less opposite is **Cheese Board Collective** (no.1512, 1-510 549 3183, www.cheeseboardcollective.coop), an employee-owned collective bakery that offers heavenly breads, cheeses and a daily pizza. A few doors away lies the original branch of **Peet's Coffee & Tea** (2124 Vine Street, at Walnut Street, 1-510 841 0564, www.peets.com), opened in 1966.

Numerous gourmet options also entice along trendy Fourth Street, between Hearst Avenue and Virginia Street. The lines form most mornings at **Bette's Oceanview Diner** (1807 Fourth Street, 1-510 644 3230, www.bettesdiner.com) for stacks of buttermilk pancakes and lavish BLTs. Critically acclaimed **Iyasare** (1830 Fourth Street, 1-510 845 8100, www.iyasare-berkeley.com) features the regional Japanese cooking of chef Shotaro Kamio. There's also great fish and a boisterous bar at century-old Spenger's **Fresh Fish Grotto** (1919 4th Street, 1-510 845 7771, www.mccormickandschmicks.com).

Getting there

Berkeley is about a 30-minute drive over the Bay Bridge, though traffic can double your drive time. Much more expedient is taking BART (*see p198*) to Ashby Street or Downtown Berkeley. The Richmond train offers direct service from SF, except on Sundays (transfer at 19th Street Oakland).

Sun, Sand & Surf

The Northern California coastline encompasses everything from well-heeled hamlets to wild, windswept landscapes – all an easy day drive from San Francisco. The harbour town of Sausalito, about a 20-minute drive or a ferry ride away, is the most accessible. At the southern end, the laid-back town of Santa Cruz is home to surfers, sunny beaches, a seaside amusement park, and a top campus of the University of California.

SAUSALITO

Tucked just across the Golden Gate Bridge in the wealthy northern suburbs of Marin County, Sausalito is a postcard of a quaint seaside village, its maze of tiny streets meandering from the shoreline up the steep hillside. Originally a fishing village, the town is now a bastion for not-so-starving artists who live in haute hilltop villas and houseboats anchored in Richardson Bay. Spend a day shopping, gallery hopping, admiring views and dining or drinking at one of the waterfront bars or restaurants.

Off North Bridgeway, the free **San Francisco Bay Model Visitor Center** (2100 Bridgeway, 1-415 332 3871, www.spn.usace.army.mil, closed Mon, Sun) lets you experience a complete full tide cycle of the San Francisco Bay in under 15 minutes, via a two-acre hydraulic model.

At Sausalito harbour, the elaborately bedecked houseboats docked at the end of Gate 5 and Gate 6 Roads haven't budged in decades. The floating homes provide a snapshot of how this seaside community has changed over the years. Once the arty crashpads of hippies, the houseboats were considered a blight by rich hill dwellers back in the '60s. Nowadays, homeowners pay a premium for the privilege of living on the water.

Take Alexander Avenue to the southern end of town to check out the **Bay Area Discovery Museum** (*see p193*), an interactive museum geared towards youngsters, snuggled at the foot of the Golden Gate Bridge. Head through the tunnel toward the Marin Headlands and Rodeo Beach to visit the **Marine Mammal Center** (1-415 289 7325, www.marinemammalcenter.org), a sanctuary for injured marine mammals.

Where to eat, drink & stay

Poggio (777 Bridgeway, 1-415 332 7771, www.poggiotrattoria.com), an Italian trattoria overlooking the harbour, features a daily-changing menu of northern Italian classics made with local ingredients and organic herbs and vegetables from the restaurant's own garden. **Scoma's** (588 Bridgeway, 1-415 332 9551,

Sausalito.

Santa Cruz. See p242.

www.scomassausalito.com), the dockside Marin branch of the Fisherman's Wharf institution, serves fresh (and pricey) seafood specialities such as cioppino with unobstructed views of the bay.

Cavallo Point Lodge (601 Murray Circle, Fort Baker, 1-888 651 2003, www.cavallopoint.com) is a luxe eco-hotel, spa and restaurant housed in beautifully refurbished military barracks at Fort Baker, below the base of the Golden Gate Bridge. Perched on the hillside above the harbour, Casa Madrona (801 Bridgeway, 1-415 332 0502, www. casamadrona.com) has romantic bay views and fireplaces in its guest rooms and cottages.

Getting there

Eight miles from San Francisco, Sausalito is easily reached by car or ferry. Take US 101 across the Golden Gate Bridge to the Alexander Avenue or Spencer Avenue exit. Golden Gate Transit ferries (www.goldengatetransit.org) run from the Ferry Building at the bottom of Market Street on the Embarcadero to Sausalito. Blue & Gold Fleet (www.blueandgoldfleet.com) sails to Sausalito and Angel Island from Pier 41 at Fisherman's Wharf.

Further information

Sausalito Visitor Center & Historical Exhibit
780 Bridgeway (1-415 332 0505, www.sausalito. org). **Open** 11.30am-4pm Tue-Sun.

POINT REYES NATIONAL SEASHORE

About an hour north of San Francisco on Highway 1, Point Reyes National Seashore (1-415 464 5100, www.nps.gov/pore/index.htm) is a vast,

extraordinary wildlife refuge, with trails, waterfalls and miles of unspoilt beaches. Make your first stop the **Bear Valley Visitor Center** near Olema, which has maps and exhibits about the area. From here, you can either head west towards the coast for **Drake's Beach**, or go north via Inverness to the tip of the peninsula: **Point Reyes Lighthouse** (1-415 669 1534, closed Tue & Wed) is a perfect lookout for whale-watching. Several trails also start here, including the popular **Chimney Rock**. Tiny **Point Reyes Station** bustles with energy along its three-block downtown; a hub for organic farmers and ranchers, as well as locla artisanal cheesemakers, including **Cowgirl Creamery** (80 4th Street, 1-415 663 9335, www.cowgirlcreamery. com), where you can try excellent local cheeses and charcuterie, and picnic at indoor and outdoor tables.

Stop in at **Toby's Feed Barn** (11250 Hwy 1, 1-415 663 1223, www.tobysfeedbarn.com), a family-owned community centre that includes a general store, a farmers' market, a yoga studio, a coffee bar and an art gallery.

Where to eat, drink & stay

In Point Reyes Station, the **Station House Café** (Main Street, 1-415 663 1515, www.stationhouse cafe.com, closed Wed) is a mellow place that serves California cuisine. In nearby Olema, renowned Manka's Inverness Lodge chef-owners Margaret Grade and Daniel DeLong took over a 19th-century inn and transformed it into destination dining spot, **Sir & Star** (10000 Sir Francis Drake Boulevard, 1-415 663 1034, www.sirandstar.com).

Up the coast about 20 minutes north, **Nick's Cove** (23240 State Route 1, 1-415 663 1033, www.nickscove.com) is a rustic retreat over Tomales Bay, featuring former fishing cabins

transformed into luxurious cottages. The restaurant is also top-notch.

In Point Reyes, try art-heavy **Abalone Inn** (12355 Sir Francis Drake Boulevard, 1-415 663 9149, 1-877 416 0458, www.abaloneinn.com) or **Knob Hill** (40 Knob Hill Road, 663 1784, www.knobhill.com).

Getting there

Point Reyes is 32 miles from SF. Take US 101 across the Golden Gate Bridge, then Highway 1. The West Marin Stagecoach 68 bus (www.marintransit.org) runs from San Rafael Transit Center to Point Reyes five days a week.

Further information

Point Reyes National Seashore Bear Valley Visitor Center *1 Bear Valley Road (1-415 464 5100).* **Open** 10am-4.30pm Mon-Fri; 9am-4.30pm Sat, Sun (see website for extended spring and summer hours).

Point Reyes Lighthouse Visitor Center *(1-415 669 1534).* **Open** 10am-4.30pm Mon, Fri-Sun, weather permitting (see website for extended spring and summer hours).

HALF MOON BAY

Half Moon Bay is a small, easy-going seaside town. Quaint Main Street is good for a wander, with bookstores, antiques shops, cafés and restaurants – the town is famous for its fresh seafood.

At Half Moon Bay and Highway 1, **Sea Horse & Friendly Acres Ranch** (1-650 726 9903, www.seahorseranch.org) offers beach horseback

rides. Some of the coast's richest tidal rock pools, populated with a variety of colourful marine creatures, lie about 15 minutes up the road at **James V Fitzgerald Marine Reserve** in Moss Beach. Then there's **Mavericks**: right in the middle of Half Moon Bay itself, and about half a mile offshore from the charming harbour village of Princeton-by-the-Sea, it's one of the gnarliest big-wave surf spots in the world.

Where to eat, drink & stay

In Half Moon Bay, cosy **Pasta Moon** (315 Main Street, 1-650 726 5125, www.pastamoon.com) serves elegant house-made pasta dishes. Old-school **Main Street Grill** (547 Main Street, 1-650 726 5300, www.mainstgrillhmb.com, closed evenings) offers hearty breakfast and lunch. **Half Moon Bay Brewing Company** (390 Capistrano Road, 1-650 728 2739, www.hmbbrewingco.com) boasts views of the harbour from its sunny outdoor patio, along with crab rolls, excellent burgers and house-brewed beer. With spectacular ocean views and an outdoor deck, **Sam's Chowder House** (4210 North Cabrillo Highway, 1-650 712 0245, www.samschowderhouse.com) is a wildly popular spot for platters of fresh seafood, lobster rolls, and of course, chowder. If the line is too long, head to local favourite **Barbara's Fishtrap** (281 Capistrano Road, 1-650 728 7049, www.barbarasfishtrap.com) for what many think is the coast's best clam chowder.

There's no shortage of places to stay in and around Half Moon Bay. The grandest is the **Ritz-Carlton** (1 Miramontes Point Road, 1-650 712 7000, www.ritzcarlton.com), set on a spectacular bluff overlooking the rugged coastline with two golf courses and a spa. About 25 miles south of here, **Costanoa** (2001 Rossi Road, 1-650 879 1100, www.costanoa.com) is part rustic resort, part campground; there are wooden cabins and a 40-room lodge, but you can also pitch a tent.

Getting there

Half Moon Bay is 30 miles south of San Francisco on Highway 1. It's about a 45-minute drive, but the BART (*see p291*) to Daly City is only 15mins. Pick up SamTrans bus 110 to Linda Mar and transfer to bus 17 for Half Moon Bay.

Further information

Half Moon Bay *Coastside Chamber of Commerce, 235 Main Street (1-650 726 8380, www. hmbchamber.com)*. **Open** 9am-5pm Mon-Fri.

SANTA CRUZ

Established as a mission at the end of the 18th century, Santa Cruz is now a beach town well known for being easy-going and politically progressive. The University of California at Santa Cruz takes the lead; its students can often be found down at robustly independent **Bookshop Santa Cruz** (1520 Pacific Avenue, 1-831 423 0900, www.bookshopsantacruz.com).

All that remains of Misión la Exaltación de la Santa Cruz is the Neary-Rodriguez Adobe in **Santa Cruz Mission State Historic Park**; commonly known as **Mission Adobe** (1-831 425 5849, www.parks.ca.gov, closed Mon-Wed in winter), it once housed the mission's Native American population. Down the street is **Mission Plaza** (1-831 426 5686, closed Mon), a complete 1930s replica. The **Santa Cruz Museum of Natural History** (1305 East Cliff Drive, 1-831 420 6115, www.santacruzmuseums.org, closed Mon) contains information about the Ohlone people who once populated the area. The culturally inclined can visit the **Santa Cruz Museum of Art & History** (705 Front Street, 1-831 429 1964, www. santacruzmah.org), while those with a penchant for paranormal phenomena and kitsch roadside attractions will be unable to resist the **Mystery Spot** (465 Mystery Spot Road, 1-831 423 8897, www.mysteryspot.com). A few miles north of the city in the woods off Highway 17, it's a 150-foot-diameter patch of earth that appears to confound the laws of physics and gravity.

Directly on the beach, the **Santa Cruz Beach Boardwalk** (400 Beach Street, 1-831 423 5590, www.beachboardwalk.com) is an old-fashioned seaside amusement park that contains, among other things, a vintage carousel and a classic wooden rollercoaster.

Continuing the beach theme, the Mark Abbott Memorial Lighthouse contains the engaging, free **Surfing Museum** (West Cliff Drive,

1-831 420 6289, www.santacruzsurfingmuseum. org, open 10am-5pm Mon, Wed-Sun, hours vary in winter), while outside the lighthouse is **Steamer Lane**, one of the best surfing spots in the state.

Fans of towering redwoods should head north into the Santa Cruz Mountains to **Big Basin Redwoods State Park** (21600 Big Basin Way, Boulder Creek, 1-831 338 8860, www.parks. ca.gov), or **Henry Cowell Redwoods State Park** (101 North Big Trees Park Road, Felton, 1-831 335 4598, www.parks.ca.gov), which has a tree you can drive through.

Some 50 wineries are scattered across the area, most open to the public. Two good choices are **Santa Cruz Mountain Vineyard** (334A Ingalls Street, 1-831 426 6209, www.santacruzmountainvineyard. com), and the award-winning **Storrs** (303 Potrero Street, 1-831 458 5030, www.storrswine.com).

Where to eat, drink & stay

High above Santa Cruz Yacht Harbor, the **Crow's Nest** (2218 East Cliff Drive, 1-831 476 4560, www.crowsnest-santacruz.com) offers magnificent views and great seafood. Downtown has a whole world of options, among them the hip **Mobo Sushi** (105 S River Street, 1-831 425 1700, www.mobosushirestaurant.com) and premier Mexican **El Palomar** (1336 Pacific Avenue, 1-831 425 7575, www.elpalomarsantacruz.com). On the Eastside, there's fabulous wood-fired pizza to be had at **Engfer Pizza Works** (537 Seabright Avenue, 1-831 429 1856, www.engferpizzaworks. com, closed Mon), as well as a ping-pong table and an exotic array of old-time sodas. You're also spoiled for cheap choices. One of the best is the **Saturn Café** (145 Laurel Street, 1-831 429 8505, www.saturncafe.com), a vegetarian/vegan diner.

Santa Cruz has many dreary motels, but there are some charming spots too. The **Babbling Brook Inn** (1025 Laurel Street, 1-831 427 2437, www.babblingbrookinn.com) is surrounded by leafy gardens with tall redwood trees. The smart, retro **Dream Inn** (175 West Cliff Drive, 1-831 426 4330, www.jdvhotels.com) has an enviable address on the site of Jack O'Neill's first surf shop overlooking the beach and Monterey Bay.

Getting there

Santa Cruz is 74 miles south of San Francisco; take I-280 south to I-85 to Highway 17. Greyhound buses (*see p290*) leave San Francisco for Santa Cruz about four times a day.

Further information

Santa Cruz County Conference & Visitors Council *Suite 100, 303 Water Street (1-800 833 3494, 1-831 425 1234, www.santacruz.org)*. **Open** 9am-5pm Mon-Fri; 10am-4pm Sat, Sun.

Wine Country

About an hour's drive from San Francisco and separated by the Mayacamas Mountains, the Napa and Sonoma wine valleys are a prime destination for visitors around the world, sometimes eclipsing the city itself. Of the two, Napa is the largest, the most famous and the most popular, though Sonoma's smaller, often family-run wineries are catching up, partly due to their appealing lack of attitude. Most charge for tastings these days, but many let you apply the fee to purchase.

Dining is as important as wining here. Many wineries have picnic areas, but it's courteous to buy a bottle to enjoy with your feast. Plenty of restaurants allow BYOB: check the corkage fee when booking, and do purchase something from the wine list if you're planning to consume more than one bottle.

A classic route winds through both valleys. In Napa, drive up Highway 29 to **Calistoga**, hitting the towns of **Napa**, **Yountville**, **Oakville**, **Rutherford** and **St Helena**. From Calistoga, head west on Petrified Forest Road for 12 miles towards **Fulton**, then drive a few miles south on Highway 101 to **Santa Rosa**, where you can pick up Route 12, which takes you south through the Sonoma Valley.

NAPA VALLEY

The 30-mile-long Napa Valley, on the east side of the Mayacamas Mountains, was originally settled by the Wappo Indian tribe several centuries ago. The Gold Rush of the 1850s saw its population grow, with Europeans and migrant Californians. Prussian immigrant Charles Krug introduced grapes here in 1861.

The valley, bisected by the Napa River, runs from the San Pablo Bay's fertile Carneros region north to the geothermal area in Calistoga. There are now more than 250 commercial vineyards here, along with smaller boutique wineries. Many are situated on the often-busy Highway 29 (aka the St Helena Highway), which runs up the centre of the valley; along the way, towns and villages have plenty of shopping and dining opportunities. Smaller wineries are found mostly on the **Silverado Trail**, a more scenic and less cramped artery to the east, or on the lanes that criss-cross the valley. Alternatively, take the **Wine Train** (1-800 427 4124, 1-707 253 2111, www.winetrain.com), which offers dining and wine tasting in vintage railcars that run between Napa and St Helena or Rutherford.

The tidy towns of **Rutherford** and **Oakville** are both dominated by the wineries that surround them, but **St Helena**, further north, has real small-town American charm. Worth a visit is the free **Robert Louis Stevenson Museum** (1490 Library Lane, St. Helena, 1-707 963 3757, www.silveradomuseum.org), which chronicles the writer's residence in the area in the 1880s through manuscripts, personal scrapbooks, photographs, furnishings and memorabilia.

Further north in **Calistoga**, geothermal springs and mud baths, not wineries, bring in the majority of visitors. The town is awash with spas offering treatments from dips in mineral pools to baths in volcanic ash, among them **Dr Wilkinson's Hot Springs Resort** (1507 Lincoln Avenue, 1-707 942 4102, www.drwilkinson.com) and historic **Indian Springs** (1712 Lincoln Avenue, 1-707 942 4913, www.indianspringscalistoga.com), site of town founder Sam Brannan's original hot springs resort. The town's other draw is the **Old Faithful Geyser** (www.oldfaithfulgeyser.com), one of only three geysers on earth that blast out water and steam at regular intervals – around every 30 to 40 minutes – to heights from 60 to 100 feet.

Wineries

Depending on the traffic, which can get pretty bad at peak times, you're rarely more than a ten-minute drive from a winery in the Napa Valley. Napa offers a number of fine tasting rooms, led by the fabulously curated selection at **Back Room Wines** (1000 Main Street, Suite 120, 1-707 226 1378, www.backroomwines.com) and the **Vintner's Collective** (1245 Main Street, 1-707 255 7150, www.vintnerscollective.com). Notable wineries southwest of town, along or off the Carneros Highway towards Sonoma, include **Domaine Carneros** (1240 Duhig Road, 1-707 257 0101, www.domaine.com, *photo p244*), where the pinot you'll be sipping is sparkling: the winery is owned by Taittinger. The views are spectacular, as they are from the terrace at off-the-beaten-track **Artesa Vineyards & Winery** (1345 Henry Road, 1-707 224 1668, www.artesawinery.com). North of Napa on the Silverado Trail is **Black Stallion** (no.4089, 1-888 200 9756, www.black stallionwinery.com), which opened on the site of an historic equestrian centre (the horse stalls are still part of the production room), and is known for full-bodied and well-priced cabernet sauvignons.

Near Yountville is **Domaine Chandon** (1 California Drive, 1-888 242 6366, www.chandon.com), which offers an excellent tour introducing visitors to its interpretation of *méthode champenoise*. Oakville is home to the granddaddy of wine estates, **Robert Mondavi** (7801 St Helena Highway, 1-888 766 6328, www.robertmondavi.com, reservations recommended), a good bet for first-timers, and the unstuffy **PlumpJack** (620 Oakville Crossroad, 1-707 945 1220, www.plumpjackwinery.com).

Another cluster of wineries draws oenophiles to Rutherford. **Mumm** (8445 Silverado Trail, 1-707 967 7700, www.mummnapa.com) has a collection of Ansel Adams photographs, while

Francis Ford Coppola's historic **Inglenook Vineyard** (1991 St Helena Highway, 1-707 968 1100, www.inglenook.com), lovingly restored over the course of more than 30 years, features an outdoor dining terrace overlooking a reflecting pool where kids can sail model boats.

The list of wineries in St Helena is led by historic **Beringer** (2000 Main Street, 1-707 302 7592, www.beringer.com), where events run from wine and cheese tastings to a cave tour. **Charles Krug** (2800 Main Street, 1-800 682 5784, www.charleskrug.com), founded in 1861, enhances its wines with summer chocolate tastings. Two unique St Helena offerings are **Prager** (1281 Lewelling Lane, 1-707 963 7678, www.pragerport.com), where the speciality is port, and **Charbay Distillery & Winery** (4001 Spring Mountain Road, 1-707 963 9327, www.charbay.com), which handcrafts its brandy from an alambic pot still.

Up the road in Calistoga, check out **Clos Pegase** (1060 Dunaweal Lane, 1-707 942 4981, www.clospegase.com) both for the Michael Graves architecture and the cabernets and chardonnays.

Where to eat & drink

Once a blue-collar town, **Napa** has grown increasingly sophisticated over the last few years, and now boasts a number of top-rated restaurants, wine shops and theatres. Most of the changes have centred on its historic downtown riverfront. Opened in 2008, the **Oxbow Public Market** (610 First Street, 1-415 277-6836, www.oxbowpublicmarket.com) houses gourmet food and wine vendors, as well as a farmers' market, and is a great spot to pick up picnic supplies. Dining options include Iron Chef Masaharu Morimoto's acclaimed namesake Japanese restaurant, **Morimoto Napa** (610 Main Street, 1-707 252 1600, www.morimotonapa.com), and prominent local chef Greg Cole's **Celadon** (500 Main Street, Suite G, 1-707 254 9690, www.celadonnapa.com), serving 'global comfort food' along the lines of flash-fried calamari with spicy chipotle chilli glaze. **Angèle** (540 Main Street, 1-707 252 8115, www.angelerestaurant.com) is a popular spot for terrace drinks and French country cooking. The river patio of the **Napa General Store** (540 Main Street, 1-707 259 0762, www.napageneralstore.com) is good for sandwiches, salads and thin pizzas. House-made focaccia, pasta, pizza and an outdoor patio overlooking vineyards and a culinary garden are the big draws at Italian **Bistro Don Giovanni** (4100 Howard Lane, 1-707 224 3300, www.bistrodongiovanni.com), which has topped critics' lists for more than 20 years.

North of here, the town of **Yountville** is renowned around the world as the home of the Michelin three-star **French Laundry** (6640 Washington Street, 1-707 944 2380,

Domaine Carneros. See p243.

www.thomaskeller.com). Prices are high to say the least, and you'll have to book two months in advance, but you'll get a world-class meal. Thomas Keller, lord of the Laundry, also runs urbane **Bouchon** (6534 Washington Street, 1-707 944 8037), where the French bistro menu (steak frites, croque madame) is more moderately priced. Its chic next-door bakery offers posh picnic fare. Philippe Jeanty is the other big name around these parts, and the casual **Bistro Jeanty** (6510 Washington Street, 1-707 944 0103, www.bistrojeanty.com) is his signature spot.

In St Helena, **Model Bakery** (1357 Main Street, 1-707 963 8192, www.themodelbakery.com) is famed for its pastries, cakes, breads and delectable English muffins; for lunch, there's **Ana's Cantina** (1205 Main Street, 1-707 963 4921) or Gott's Roadside (933 Main Street, 1-707 963 3486, www.gotts.com), offering terrific 1950s-style burgers and shakes that you can wash down with a vintage Napa cabernet. Along Main Street, don't miss **Woodhouse Chocolate** (no.1367, 1-800 966 3468, 1-707 963 8413, www.woodhousechocolate.com), and **Olivier Napa Valley** (no.1375, 1-707 967 8777, www.oliviernapavalley.com) for olive oils, condiments and more. Just south of town, on Highway 29, posh deli and wine store **Dean & Deluca** (607 South St Helena Highway, 1-707 967 9980, www.deandeluca.com) has a coffee and pastry bar.

Calistoga's restaurants are concentrated mainly on Lincoln Avenue: sturdy American

Napa Valley.

classics dominate at **Brannan's** (no.1374, 1-707 942 2233, www.brannansgrill.com) and farm-to-table cuisine at **JoLe** (no.1457, 1-707 942 5938, www.jolerestaurant.com).

Where to stay

Lodgings around Napa run the gamut from quaint Queen Anne-style B&Bs to full resorts. The sleek and luxurious **Carneros Inn** (4048 Sonoma Highway, 1-707 299 4900, www. thecarnerosinn.com), just southwest of Napa, fits into the latter category: its 86 ultra-modern cottages have fireplaces, flatscreen televisions and outdoor showers. In the restored Napa Mill, you'll find the deluxe, 66-room **Napa River Inn** (500 Main Street, 1-877 251 8500, 1-707 251 8500, www.napariverinn.com). **The Oak Knoll Inn** (2200 E Oak Knoll Avenue, 1-707 255 2200, www.oakknollinn.com) is one of the valley's most luxurious B&Bs; and if you've had enough of all things quaint, the **Napa Winery Inn** (1998 Trower Avenue, 1-707 257 7220, www. napawineryinn.com) is an above-par motel.

There are fewer budget options in Yountville, but the high-class **Villagio Inn & Spa** (6481 Washington Street, 1-800 351 1133, 1-707 944 8877, www.villagio.com) is one of several deluxe hotels. In Rutherford, you'll need to spend a lot of cash for a night at the **Auberge du Soleil** (180 Rutherford Hill Road, 1-800 348 5406, 1-707 963 1211, www.aubergedusoleil.com) – one for special occasions.

Along St Helena's Main Street, try the luxurious **Southbridge Napa Valley** (no.1020, 1-800 520 6800, 1-707 967 9400, www.southbridge napavalley.com), or the delightful **El Bonita Motel** (no.195, 1-800 541 3284, 1-707 963 3216, www.elbonita.com), an aesthetic mix of art deco and French colonial that's a bargain by St Helena standards. Outside town, **Meadowood** (900 Meadowood Lane, 1-877 963 3646, www. meadowood.com) comprises a resort hotel, separate cottages and a three Michelin-starred restaurant, as well as a golf course and swanky spa. At the high end of the valley and the rate scale is the breathtaking **Calistoga Ranch**, with 46 deluxe lodges, a splendid spa and a lake (580 Lommel Road, 1-855 942 4220, www.calistoga ranch.com), tucked into a private canyon.

Wherever you want to stay in the area, book well in advance, especially in summer. If you do get stuck, try **Napa Valley Reservations** (1-800 251 6272, www.napavalleyreservations.com).

IN THE KNOW TASTING NOTE

Napa Valley's **Chateau Montelena** (1429 Tubbs Lane, 1-707 942 5105, www.montelena.com) was the winery that put California on the map in 1976 when it beat out the French burgundies in a blind tasting at the now-infamous Judgment of Paris competition.

Getting there

Napa Valley is about an hour north of San Francisco by car. Two routes will get you there: take the Bay Bridge/Hwy 80 East to Vallejo exit and Hwy 37 west. Turn onto Hwy 29 north to Napa. Alternatively, from the Golden Gate Bridge, take Highway 37 east to Highway 29 north.

Further information

Napa Valley Welcome Center *600 Main Street, Napa (1-707 251 5895, www.visitnapavalley.com).* **Open** 9am-5pm daily.

St Helena Chamber of Commerce *1010 Main Street (1-707 963 4456, www.sthelena.com).* **Open** 10am-5pm Mon-Fri; 11am-3pm Sat.

Yountville Chamber of Commerce *6484 Washington Street (1-707 944 0904, www. yountville.com).* **Open** 10am-5pm daily.

Calistoga Visitors Center *1133 Washington Street (1-707 942 6333, www.visitcalistoga.com).* **Open** 8am-5pm Mon-Sat; 8am-4pm Sun.

SONOMA VALLEY

The Sonoma Valley, which runs around 23 miles north from San Pablo Bay, is home to more than 200 growers and wineries. However, the main attraction of a Sonoma tour is the landscape. The topography is diverse, from beaches to redwood forests and rolling hills. It's also agriculturally rich, and the areas around towns such as Glen Ellen and Sebastopol brim with farms.

The town of **Sonoma** retains a feel of old California, built around a central square now ringed by restaurants, shops, wine tasting rooms and a cinema (the delightful Sebastiani Theatre, built in 1933). The town was founded in 1823 as the **Mission San Francisco Solano** (114 East Spain Street, 1-707 938 9560); today, the mission is part of the loose affiliation of atmospheric sites known as Sonoma State Historic Park. The town hall and Bear Flag Monument on the plaza mark the site where the Californian Bear Flag first flew:

for 25 days during the riotous Bear Flag Revolt in 1846, this was the capital of the independent Republic of California. Fast-forward more than 160 years and the plaza is home to the town's Tuesday evening farmers' market (May-Oct).

Just north of Sonoma, the small town of **Glen Ellen** was once the home of Jack London, adventurer, farmer, autodidact and author; **Jack London State Historic Park** (www.jack londonpark.com) contains the charred remains of Wolf House, the author's home, and a museum housing first-edition books and mementos.

Though it has twice the population of the city of Napa, **Santa Rosa** at the north end of the valley, still manages to retain a low-key appeal. Historic Railroad Square is the city's downtown area, but the real visitor attraction is the park on the corner of Santa Rosa and Sonoma Avenues: **Luther Burbank Home & Gardens** (www. lutherburbank.org), where horticulturalist Burbank lived for nearly 50 years. Also here is the **Charles M Schulz Museum** (2301 Hardies Lane, 1-707 579 4452, www.schulzmuseum.org), commemorating the man who created Snoopy, Charlie Brown and the *Peanuts* gang.

Further north is **Healdsburg**, a picture-postcard boutique town where Bay Area boomers come to drop some serious cash. Gourmet food stores, artisan bakeries and sleek eateries bring in the herds – as does the annual jazz fest every June (www.healdsburgjazzfestival.org). The town's old-fashioned central square is a lovely place to stroll, and hosts a Wednesday farmers' market (June-Oct) as well as a Saturday one (May-Nov).

Wineries

Sonoma County's quaint, family-owned wineries are more secluded than many of their Napa neighbours. Its history is intertwined with that of the California wine industry, which began at the **Buena Vista Winery** (18000 Old Winery Road, 1-800 926 1266, www.buenavistawinery. com) in 1857 with the planting of the first vines by 'Count' Agoston Haraszthy, a Hungarian immigrant who is credited with introducing zinfandel to California. Of the nearly 40 wineries in the valley, several are near the city's main plaza. **Bartholomew Park Winery** (1000 Vineyard Lane, 1-707 939 3026, www.bartpark.com) is great for picnics; **Sebastiani Vineyards** (389 Fourth Street East, 1-707 933 3230, www.sebastiani.com) may not be the region's most charming winery, but it gives another perspective on the ubiquitous wine family and offers a plethora of picnic spots.

The **Carneros** region includes southern Sonoma as well as Napa; wineries take advantage of the cooler climate to produce excellent pinot noir grapes and sparkling wines. Fans of sparkling wines should try a tasting at **Gloria Ferrer Champagne Caves** (23555 Arnold

IN THE KNOW QUAKESPOTTING

The Earthquake Trail that leads from the Bear Valley Visitor Center in Point Reyes (see p241) takes you to a broken fence line directly atop the San Andreas Fault, epicentre of the 1906 earthquake. When the temblor struck, the once-contiguous fence jumped 20 feet. It's been moving incrementally north ever since.

Drive, 1-707 933 1917, www.gloriaferrer.com). Further south, the **Viansa Winery** (25200 Arnold Drive, 1-800 995 4740, www.viansa.com), a Tuscan-style winery situated on a knoll, offers informal tastings and has a large Italian-style deli.

The pick of the viticulture in and around Glen Ellen includes the **Arrowood Vineyards & Winery** (14347 Sonoma Highway, 1-800 938 5170, 1-707 935 2600, www.arrowoodvineyards. com) and the **Benziger Family Winery** (1883 London Ranch Road, 1-888 490 2739, www.benziger.com), which makes its wines using biodynamic farming methods devised in the 1920s by Rudolf Steiner.

Nearby **Kenwood** is synonymous with the **Kenwood Vineyards** (9592 Sonoma Highway, 1-707 833 5891, www.kenwoodvineyards.com), known for wine made from grapes grown on Jack London's former ranch (novelist Haruki Murakami drinks a bottle from here on his birthday each year). The original barn, now the tasting room and shop, dates from before Prohibition.

The area around Santa Rosa boasts several fine wineries, including **Kendall-Jackson Wine Center** (5007 Fulton Road, 1-800 769 3649, www.kj.com), which has an expansive tasting room, education centre, and sensory and culinary gardens (tours offered daily).

Where to eat & drink

In Sonoma, the **Girl & the Fig** (110 West Spain Street, 1-707 933 3000, www.thegirlandthefig.com), inside the landmark Sonoma Hotel (*see right*), has a reputation for garden-fresh dishes including salads, steaks and cheese plates. Small but characterful **Café La Haye** (140 E Napa Street, 1-707 935 5994, www.cafelahaye.com) is another winner, although it's open for dinner only (Tue-Sat). Picnickers get supplies from the **Sonoma Cheese Factory** (2 Spain Street, 1-707 996 1931, www.sonomacheesefactory.com), which has a full deli and BBQ patio, as well as the fantastic **Vella Cheese Company** (315 Second Street East, 1-707 938 3232, www.vellacheese.com) and **Sonoma Market** (500 W Napa Street, 1-707 996 3411).

In Santa Rosa, try **Willi's Wine Bar** (4404 Old Redwood Highway, 1-707 526 3096, www.starkrestaurants.com) for small plates ranging from foie gras 'poppers' to calamari salad and wines by the glass.

Healdsburg has plenty of appealing options, both pricey and wallet-friendly. The Hotel Healdsburg (*see right*) is home to award-winning chef Charlie Palmer's **Dry Creek Kitchen** (317 Healdsburg Avenue, 1-707 431 0330, www.drycreekkitchen.com), where the changing menus are based on local, fresh seasonal ingredients. Cosy Italian bistro **Scopa** (109A Plaza Street, 1-707 433 5282, www.scopahealdsburg.com) offers inventive pizzas, house-made pastas and a nice selection of

local wines. DIY options include the gourmet **Oakville Grocery** (124 Matheson Street, 1-707 433 3200, www.oakvillegrocery.com), which has a patio where you can eat goodies purchased inside.

Where to stay

The **Sonoma Hotel** (110 West Spain Street, 1-800 468 6016, 1-707 996 2996, www.sonomahotel.com), built in 1872, has period details such as clapboard ceilings and claw foot bathtubs. Also in Sonoma, the country-chic **El Dorado Hotel** (405 First Street West, 1-707 996 3030, www.eldorado sonoma.com), located on the plaza, features a farm-to-table restaurant and a solar-heated pool out back. The **Ledson Hotel** (480 First Street East, 1-707 996 9779, www.ledsonhotel.com) has six ultra-deluxe rooms, but if you want to take pampering to the max it has to be the stunning **Fairmont Sonoma Mission Inn & Spa** (100 Boyes Boulevard, 1-707 938 9000, www.fairmont. com), a few miles north in Boyes Hot Springs, where you can soak in natural mineral hot springs while sipping premium Sonoma wines.

In Kenwood, you'll likely be tempted by the luxurious Mediterranean-style **Kenwood Inn & Spa** (10400 Sonoma Highway, 1-800 353 6966, 1-707 833 1293, www.kenwoodinn.com). Glen Ellen, meanwhile, is home to the **Jack London Lodge** (13740 Arnold Drive, 1-707 938 8510, www.jacklondonlodge.com), a straightforward motel, and **Gaige House** (13540 Arnold Drive, 1-800 935 0237, 1-707 935 0237, www.gaige.com), a luxe B&B complete with spa, pool and hot tubs.

Santa Rosa's nicest option is the 44-room **Vintners Inn** (4350 Barnes Road, 1-707 575 7350, www.vintnersinn.com), a prime place to stay for some proper Wine Country relaxation.

In Healdsburg, a number of decent motels off the freeway will serve as a good base if you don't want to blow your entire budget on accommodation, but for high-flyers, the trendy **Hotel Healdsburg** (25 Matheson Street, 1-707 431 2800, www.hotel healdsburg.com), and the posh French-style **Hôtel Les Mars** (27 North Street, 1-877 431 1700, www. hotellesmars.com), are pure luxury.

Getting there

Sonoma is 44 miles north of San Francisco, about an hour's drive over the Golden Gate Bridge and along US 101. Turn east at Ignacio to Highway 37 and take Highway 121 north. From here, Highway 12 follows the Sonoma Valley.

Further information

Sonoma Valley Visitors Bureau *453 First Street East (1-866 996 1090, www.sonomavalley.com).* **Open** 9am-5pm Mon-Sat; 10am-5pm Sun.

Healdsburg Chamber of Commerce & Visitors Bureau *217 Healdsburg Avenue (1-707 433 6935, www.healdsburg.org)*. **Open** 9am-5pm Mon-Fri; 9am-3pm Sat; 10am-2pm Sun.

California Welcome Center – Santa Rosa
9 Fourth Street (1-800 404 7673, 1-707 577 8674, www.visitsantarosa.com). **Open** 9am-5pm Mon-Sat; 10am-5pm Sun.

Peaks & Valleys

YOSEMITE NATIONAL PARK

Located approximately four hours southeast of San Francisco and covering some 1,100 square miles of forest, alpine meadows, sheer granite cliffs, lush waterfalls and wildlife, Yosemite National Park is a must-see for any visitor to Northern California with a couple of days to spare. With park elevations that range from 2,000 feet to over 13,000 feet, Yosemite offers breathtaking views. As you drive into the valley, the dramatic countenance of El Capitan greets you – a sheer rock wall that rises 3,000 feet straight up. Look closely and you'll see intrepid climbers scaling its face.

Highway 120 runs east–west for the entire length of the park, climbing to 9,945 feet at Tioga Pass, the highest automobile pass in California (closed in winter). Though the roads are engineered as scenic drives, the best way to experience the park and properly commune with nature is on foot. In spring, the wildflowers are in bloom; in winter, snow-capped peaks are majestic; in autumn, the quietest season, warm days and fiery colours offer a prime hiking experience. In summer, Yosemite Valley attracts tour buses, but you can escape the crowds the along the trails, in meadows and beneath waterfalls. You don't need reservations to visit the park (although you should certainly book lodgings in advance); the $25 to $30 entrance fee (it's cheaper from November to March) per vehicle is good for seven days.

Most people head for seven-mile-long **Yosemite Valley**, where most of the lodgings and services are located. Though there's plenty to do – hikes, glorious vistas, ice-skating in winter, and the park's best dining – keep in mind that the Valley makes up less than one per cent of the park. For non-Valley sites, head to **Tuolumne Meadows** (via Highway 120), stunning Glacier Point, the Hetch Hetchy Reservoir (north of Big Oak Flat) and **Tunnel View** at the eastern end of the Wawona tunnel on Highway 41. Free shuttle service (highly recommended) is available in several areas of the park, including the valley floor and Tuolemne Meadows.

For hiking, the **Mist Trail** is the most popular: three miles from Happy Isles to Vernal Falls and back, or a seven-mile round trip to Nevada Falls. The trek to **Glacier Point** is just as challenging, but you can cheat by driving there instead. Experienced hikers may want to tackle **Half Dome** (16-mile round trip), but reservations are required and you have to cling to cables anchored into a sheer rockface for the last half mile. For more information on trails, see www.nps.gov.

Where to eat, drink & stay

To refuel, head to one of three main areas of the Valley: Yosemite Lodge, Yosemite Village and Curry Village. **Mountain Room** is the best of the handful of restaurants at Yosemite Lodge. In Yosemite Village, **Degnan's Deli** is busy at lunchtime, with sandwiches, salads and soups. Curry Village also has a variety of options, from Mexican and pizza to the grand WPA-built Ahwahnee Hotel, which serves a legendary Sunday brunch.

There are seven lodgings inside the park, running the gamut from grungy to extravagant; call 1-801 559-4884 or book online at www. yosemitepark.com. The 260-room **Yosemite Lodge at the Falls** has all the charm of a chain motel, but is unbeatable for its central location. Those with money to blow should consider the **Ahwahnee Hotel**, a National Historic Landmark built in 1927 of huge timbers and river rock, its grand wood-beamed dining room replete with enormous windows that perfectly frame Yosemite Falls, Half Dome and Glacier Point. In a tranquil spot outside the Valley is the whitewashed Victorian **Wawona Hotel**. Just outside the park and booked independently, the modern, fairly upscale **Tenaya Lodge** (1-888 514 2167, www.tenayalodge.com) has a 10,000-square-foot spa.

Getting there

Yosemite is 195 miles southeast of San Francisco. By car, take I-580 east to I-205 east to Highway 120 east (Manteca) or Highway 140 east (Merced) into the park. Amtrak (*see p290*) runs a combination of train and bus service to Yosemite Valley.

Further information

National Park Service information *1-209 372 0200, www.nps.gov/yose*

MUIR WOODS & MOUNT TAMALPAIS

The spectacular swathe of coastal redwoods that makes up Muir Woods **National Monument** was established on 9 January 1908, after President Theodore Roosevelt stepped in to prevent a local water company from turning it into a reservoir. The forest contains majestic groves of old-growth redwoods, ranging in age from 600 to 1,200 years, and reaching as high as 258 feet. You'll find several miles of trails here; those along the valley floor are boardwalked, offering easy access for strollers and wheelchairs. Self-guided trail maps, available at the visitor centre, take you past historic tree stands, through quiet fern canyons, and across creeks that are host every winter to one of the last remaining native runs of coho salmon and steelhead trout. Many trails also connect to surrounding Mount Tamalpais State Park. To avoid crowds, visit on weekday mornings and late afternoons.

Visible from as far away as Sonoma, **Mount Tamalpais State Park** covers ten square miles around the western and southern slopes of the iconic peak. The mountain itself soars to nearly 2,600 feet, but its rise is so steep it seems far taller. It gets its name from the Miwok Indian phrase for 'west hill', Beautiful at any time of day, it's magnificent at sunset. The roads that snake over Mount Tam, while challenging, are great for hiking and mountain biking; indeed, it is considered by many to be mountain biking's birthplace. A gorgeous, paved rim trail, a visitor centre and snack bar (open weekends) and exhibits about the **Mount Tamalpais Railway lie at the top of** the East Peak. On the southern side of the mountain, the Mountain Play (https://mountainplay.org) at Cushing Memorial Amphitheatre has been staging open-air Broadway musicals every summer since 1913.

Where to eat, drink & stay

The restaurant at the English-style **Pelican Inn** (10 Pacific Way, 1-415 383 6000, www.pelicaninn.com) offers pub staples such as beef Wellington, bangers and mash, and shepherd's pie a seashell's throw from Muir Beach. It's also a fine hotel: quaint rooms have canopied beds, balconies and private bathrooms. Rugged travellers may want to opt for the century-old **West Point Inn** (1-415 388 9955, www.westpointinn.com), a collection of five rustic cabins that's a two-mile hike up Mount Tam from **Pantoll Ranger Station** (1-415 388 2070). Guests bring their own sleeping bags and cook grub in a communal kitchen. There's no electricity, but nothing beats the views.

Getting there

Muir Woods is a 15-mile drive from San Francisco. Take US 101 across the Golden Gate Bridge, then turn on to Highway 1. A free shuttle bus, no.66, runs from Marin City to Muir Woods on weekends and holidays from April through October, with extended daily service in summer.

Further information

Muir Woods Visitor Center *1-415 388 2595, www.nps.gov/muwo*. **Open** 8am-sunset daily. **Admission** $7; free under-16s.

Mount Tamalpais State Park *(1-415 388 2070, www.parks.ca.gov)*. **Open** 7am-sunset daily.

Yosemite National Park.

History

The (sometimes seismic) events that shaped a free-spirited, innovative hub.

TEXT: MICHAEL ANSALDO

When excavation began in 1969 for BART's Civic Center station, workers uncovered the body of a young woman. Experts dated the remains to approximately 2,950 BC, offering a glimpse into the rich indigenous culture of the Bay Area. During the last Ice Age, 15,000 years ago, nomadic tribes migrated across the Bering Strait from Asia and eventually settled along the shores of the Bay, which despite its name, is actually an estuary that mixes the Pacific Ocean with fresh Sierra Nevada snowmelt from the San Joaquin and Sacramento rivers. Ringed by hills and covered with pastures, the Bay Area sustained more than 10,000 Northern Californian natives. At first, the Ohlone tribes lived in harmony with their Coast Miwok neighbours in this land of 'inexpressible fertility', to quote 18th-century French explorer Jean-François de La Pérouse. The arrival of Spanish missionaries, however, brought the dubious gifts of Christianity, hard labour and diseases such as smallpox, which eventually annihilated half the native population.

Mission Dolores

THEY CAME, THEY SAW

Looking at the Golden Gate today, it's not hard to imagine how early navigators missed the mile-wide opening. The Bay and its native peoples were hidden by 'stynkinge fogges' (as Francis Drake called them), which prevented numerous explorers from discovering the harbour entrance for 200 years after the first Europeans ventured into the region.

An early series of Spanish expeditions sent up the coast by Hernán Cortés, notorious conqueror of Mexico and the Aztecs, never got as far as Upper California. In 1542, under the flag of the new Spanish viceroy Antonio de Mendoza, Portuguese explorer Juan Rodríguez Cabrillo became the first European to visit the area. Inspired by a popular 16th-century novel, the Spanish named their new land California. Cabrillo passed the Bay's entrance on his way north and on his way back again, but failed to discover its large natural harbour.

An Englishman got even closer, yet still managed to miss it. In 1579, during a foraging and spoiling mission in the name of Elizabeth I, the as-yet-unknighted Francis Drake landed the Golden Hind in Miwok Indian territory just north of the Bay. With a crew in dire need of rest and recreation, he put in for a six-week

berth on the Marin coastline, probably near Point Reyes. Long before the Pilgrims landed at Plymouth Rock or the English settled Cupid's Cove at Newfoundland, Drake claimed California for Elizabeth I as 'Nova Albion' or 'New Britain'.

It would be 190 years before another European set eyes on the Bay. Spurred on by the pressure of British colonial ambitions in America, the Spanish sent northbound parties to stake out their own territories, intent on converting the indigenous people and claiming land for the Spanish crown. Sailing under the Spanish flag in 1595, Portuguese explorer Sebastian Rodríguez Cermeno was shipwrecked just north of the Golden Gate at what is now known as Drake's Bay. Before he made his way back to Mexico in a small boat saved from the ship, he named the protected cove Bahia de San Francisco.

In 1769 came the 'sacred expedition' of Gaspar de Pórtola, a Spanish aristocrat who would later become the first governor of California, and the Franciscan priest Father Junípero Serra, who set off with six men on a gruelling march across the Mexican desert with the aim of establishing a mission at San Diego. Once they'd done so, the party worked

IN CONTEXT

its way north toward Monterey, building missions and baptising Indians as they went. The expedition actually overshot Monterey, trekking up through Santa Cruz and to the San Francisco Bay before realising their mistake and turning back.

Finally, in August 1775, the *San Carlos*, a Spanish supply vessel, became the first ship to sail into the Bay. At the same time, a mission set off to establish a safer land route to what would eventually become San Francisco. Roughly concurrent with the signing of the American Declaration of Independence, Captain Juan Bautista de Anza led an advance party to the southern point of the Golden Gate, which he declared a perfect location for a Spanish military garrison, or *presidio*. Three miles inland to the southeast, a suitable site was found for a mission. Before the year was out, the Presidio was erected, and the mission – Misión San Francisco de Asís (popularly known as Mission Dolores) – was established by the indefatigable Serra.

FOLLOW THE BEAR

A mix of favouritism, authoritarianism and religious fervour eventually helped sow the seeds of resentment and resistance in territories colonised by Spain. The country's hold on its American empires first began to crumble in Mexico, which declared itself a republic in 1821. The Mexican annexation of California in the same year opened up the area to foreign settlers, among them American pioneers like fur trapper Jedediah Smith, who in 1827 became the first non-native American to cross the Sierra Nevada mountain range. His feat was impressive, but a more sedate arrival by a whaler ship had more lasting impact. Englishman Captain William Richardson, who in 1835 built the first dwelling on the site of the future San Francisco, is credited with giving the city its first name: Yerba Buena, named after the sweet mint (literally 'good herb') the Spanish used for tea.

That same year, the US tried unsuccessfully to buy the whole of the Bay Area from the Mexicans. In the end, they got California for free: the declaration of independence by the Texas territory, and its subsequent annexation by the US, triggered the Mexican-American war in June 1846. The resulting Treaty of Guadalupe-Hidalgo in 1848 officially granted the Union all the land from Texas to California

and from the Rio Grande to Oregon. But before the treaty could be nailed down, a few hotheads decided to 'liberate' the territory from Mexico themselves.

The short-lived Mexican rule of California coincided with the era of idealistic frontiersmen Kit Carson and Captain John Fremont who, in June 1846, convinced a motley crew to take over the abandoned *presidio* to the north of Yerba Buena in Sonoma. Fremont proclaimed his new state the 'Bear Flag Republic', after the ragged banner he raised over Sonoma's square (the design was eventually adopted as the state flag), and he named the mouth of San Francisco Bay the 'Golden Gate' after Istanbul's Golden Horn. A few weeks after the Bear Flaggers annexed Sonoma, the US Navy captured Yerba Buena without a struggle and the whole of California became US territory.

The infant Yerba Buena was a sleepy trading post of 500 people. The newly appointed mayor, Lieutenant Washington A Bartlett, officially renamed it San Francisco on 30 January 1847. But unbeknownst to its residents, the tiny settlement was about to change dramatically.

ALL THAT GLITTERS

Californians have the eagle eye of one James Marshall to thank for their current prosperity. While building a mill on the American River near Sacramento in January 1848, Marshall spotted gold in a sawmill ditch. Along with John Sutter, the Swiss-born rancher who was Marshall's landlord, he attempted to keep his findings secret, but when newspaper publisher Sam Brannan got word, he marched down to San Francisco's Portsmouth Square, waved a bottle of gold dust, and the Gold Rush was on.

The news brought droves of drifters and fortune-seekers to the Bay Area, their fever fanned by people like Brannan, whose *California Star* newspaper told of men digging up a fortune in an hour. Many never made it: by land, the journey meant months of exposure to blizzards, mountains, deserts and hostile tribes; by sea, they faced disease, starvation and brutal weather.

Still, more than 90,000 prospectors appeared in California in the first two years after gold was discovered, and 300,000 had arrived in the state by 1854 – one out of every 76 people then living in the US. Though they called themselves the Argonauts (after the

IN CONTEXT

mythical sailors who accompanied Jason in search of the Golden Fleece), locals named them after the year the Rush began: the Forty-Niners.

The port town in which they arrived was one without structure, government, or even a name (to many, it was still Yerba Buena). They found more hardship than gold: on their way to the mines, predatory merchants fleeced them; when they returned, broke, they were left to grub mean existences from the city streets, seeking refuge in brothels, gambling dens and bars. Within two years of Marshall's discovery, nearly 100,000 men had passed through the city; the population grew from 600 in 1848 to 25,000 in 1849, swelling the tiny community into a giant, muddy campsite. Despite a fire that levelled the settlement on Christmas Eve 1849, a new town rose up to take its place and the population exploded. Lawlessness and arson ruled; frontier justice was common.

'Naive newcomers and drunken sailors were seen as fair game by gamblers and hoods.'

The opening of a post office marked the city's first optimistic stab at improving links with the rest of the continent. John White Geary, appointed postmaster by President James K Polk, rented a room at the corner of Montgomery and Washington Streets, where he marked out a series of squares for each letter of the alphabet and began filing letters. This crude set-up was San Francisco's first postal system. In April 1850, the year California became the Union's 31st state, San Francisco's city charter was approved; the city elected Geary its first mayor.

Geary's council later bought the ship *Euphemia* to serve as San Francisco's first jail. It proved a sound investment. Gangs of hoodlums controlled certain districts: the Ducks, led by Australian convicts, lived at a spot known as Sydney Town and, together with New York toughs the Hounds, roamed Telegraph Hill, raping and pillaging the orderly community of Chilean merchants who occupied Little Chile. Eventually,

'right-minded' citizens decided to take the law into their own hands. Whipped into a fury by rabble-rouser Brannan, vigilantes lynched their first victim, John Jenkins, at Portsmouth Square in June 1851. They strung up three more thieves during the following weeks; the other Ducks and Hounds wisely cut out for the Sierras. By 1853, the riverbed gold started running dry and boom had turned to bust. The resulting depression set a cyclical pattern often repeated through the city's history. Then, in 1859, a second boom arrived. Henry Comstock's discovery of a rich blue vein of silver (the 'Comstock Lode') in western Nevada triggered another invasion by fortune-seekers, nicknamed the Silver Rush. This time the ore's nature demanded more elaborate methods of extraction, with high yields going to a small number of companies and tycoons rather than individual prospectors. Before the supply had been exhausted, silver barons had made enough money to transform San Francisco, establishing a nouveau riche neighbourhood atop Nob Hill (the name was adapted from the word 'nabob').

If the nabobs took the geographical and moral high ground, those on the waterfront were busy legitimising their reputation as occupants of the 'Barbary Coast'. Naive newcomers and drunken sailors were seen as fair game by gamblers and hoods waiting to 'shanghai' them (shanghai, like 'hoodlum', is a San Francisco expression), as were the immigrant women who found themselves trapped into lives of prostitution or slavery. At one low point, the female population numbered just 22; many a madam made fortune enough to buy her way on to Nob Hill.

COME ONE, COME ALL

The seeds of San Francisco's present-day multiculturalism were sown during this period, when a deluge of immigrants poured in from all over the world. French immigrants vying with Italians to make the best bread started baking sourdough in North Beach. A young German garment-maker named Levi Strauss started using rivets to strengthen the jeans he made for miners. In Chinatown, criminal tongs (Mafia-like gangs) controlled the opium dens and other rackets, while a Chinese immigrant named Wah Lee opened the city's first laundry. The building of the transcontinental railroad in the 1860s employed thousands of Chinese labourers at low pay rates, which led to further expansion of Chinatown. Still, despite their usefulness as cheap labour, the Chinese were targets of racist anti-immigrant activity. Indeed, proscriptive anti-Chinese legislation persisted until 1943.

Even in those days, entertainment was high on the agenda for San Franciscans. By 1853, the city boasted five theatres and some 600 saloons and taverns serving 42,000 customers. Locals downed seven bottles of champagne for every bottle swallowed in Boston (as the third-biggest consumer of alcohol per capita in the US, San Francisco maintains its high-living reputation). Arriving on a paddle steamer from Panama in 1853, Lola Montez, entertainer to European monarchs and thieves, made her 'spider dance' an instant hit at the American Theater.

San Francisco's relative isolation from the rest of the continent meant the city was hardly affected by the Civil War that devastated the American South in the early 1860s. The rest of the country seemed remote; mail sometimes took six months to arrive. But communications were slowly improving. Telegraph wires were being strung across the continent; where telegraph poles ran out, the Pony Express picked up messages, relaying up to 75 riders across the West to the Pacific coast.

The completion of the Central Pacific Railroad in 1869 was the signal for runaway consumption in the city. The biggest spenders were the 'Big Four' – Charles Crocker, Collis P Huntington, Mark Hopkins and Leland Stanford – brutally competitive millionaires who were the powerful principal investors behind the Central Pacific. Their eagerness to impress the West with their flamboyantly successful business practices manifested itself in the mansions they built on Nob Hill. By 1871, 121 businessmen controlled $146 million, according to one newspaper, but others got in on the act. In particular four Irishmen – 'Bonanza Kings' James Flood, William O'Brien, James Fair and John Mackay – made the ascent to Nob Hill, having started out as rough-hewn miners and bartenders chipping out their fortunes from the Comstock Lode.

A Scottish-Irish banker, William Ralston, opened the Bank of California on Sansome Street in 1864. Partnered with Prussian engineer Adolph Sutro, later famous for building the Cliff House and the Sutro Baths, Ralston was determined to extract every last ounce of silver from the Comstock's Sun Mountain. Unfortunately, he did so too quickly: the ore ran out before he could recoup his investment, and his bank collapsed. Ralston drowned himself, leaving behind the luxurious Palace Hotel and a lasting contribution towards San Francisco's new civic pride: Golden Gate Park. Ralston's company provided the water for William Hammond Hall's audacious project, which transformed a barren area of sand dunes into a magnificent expanse of trees, flowers and lakes.

THE BIG ONE

The city continued to grow, and by 1900 its population had reached more than a third of a million, making it the ninth-largest city in the Union. But shortly after 5am on 18 April 1906, dogs began howling and horses whinnying – noises that, along with glasses tinkling and windows rattling, marked the unnerving moments before an earthquake.

When the quake hit – a rending in the tectonic plates five miles beneath the ocean bed that triggered the shifting of billions of tons of rock – it generated more energy than all the explosives used in World War II. The rift snaked inland, along the crack now known as the San Andreas Fault and down the coastline. Cliffs appeared from nowhere, cracks yawned, ancient redwoods toppled and part of the newly built City Hall tumbled down. A second tremor struck, ripping the walls out of buildings and disrupting the water pipes that fed the fire hydrants, leaving the city's

IN CONTEXT

Lola Montez.

Relief services after the 1906 earthquake.

firefighters helpless. The blaze that followed did most of the damage. In desperation, Mayor Eugene Schmitz and General Frederick Funston blew up the mansions along Van Ness Avenue in an attempt to create fire breaks.

The earthquake and three-day inferno killed several thousand. Around 250,000 people were left homeless and thousands of acres of buildings were destroyed. On Schmitz's orders, anyone suspected of looting in the ensuing chaos was shot dead. On the third day of the catastrophe, the wind changed direction, bringing rain. By 21 April, the fire was out.

ONWARDS AND UPWARDS

The citizens of San Francisco were undaunted. They set about rebuilding, and within ten years, San Francisco had risen from the ruins. Some claimed that in the rush to rebuild, planners passed up the chance to replace the city's grid street system with a more sensible one that followed the area's natural contours. But there's no doubt San Francisco was reborn as a cleaner, more attractive city – within three years of the fire, it could boast half of the nation's concrete and steel buildings. Such statistical pride was not out of keeping with the boosterism that accelerated San Francisco's post-Gold Rush growth into a large, modern city. The most potent symbol of restored civic pride was the new City Hall, the construction of which was secured by an $8 million city bond. Completed in 1915, it rose 14 inches higher than its model, the US Capitol in Washington, DC.

In the years following the catastrophe, two waterways opened that would prove critical to California's economic vitality. The Los Angeles aqueduct was completed in 1913, and in 1915, the opening of the Panama Canal considerably shortened shipping times between the Atlantic and Pacific coasts, an achievement celebrated in San Francisco by the Panama-Pacific Exposition. Not even the outbreak of World War I in Europe could dampen the city's high spirits. Its optimism was well founded: the war stimulated California's mining and manufacturing industries. But, as elsewhere in America, the good times were quickly swallowed up by the Wall Street Crash of 1929 and the Great Depression.

The crisis hit the port of San Francisco especially badly – half the workforce was laid off. On 9 May 1934, under the leadership of Harry Bridges, the International Longshoremen's Association declared a coast-wide strike. Other unions, including the powerful Teamsters, came out in sympathy, shutting down West Coast ports for three months. Blackleg workers managed to break through the picket on 5 July – Bloody Thursday – but with disastrous results. As violence escalated, police opened fire, killing two strikers and wounding 64. A general strike was called for 14 July, when 150,000 people stopped work and brought San Francisco to a standstill for four days. The strike fizzled out, but the action wasn't completely futile: the longshoremen won a wage increase and control of the hiring halls.

MARK HIS WORDS

San Francisco's most famous literary resident had a lot to say about the city.

When Samuel Clemens arrived in San Francisco in May 1864, he'd been 'Mark Twain' for a little over a year. He first adopted the pseudonym in Virginia City, Nevada, where he worked as city editor on the local newspaper. But it wasn't until he settled in San Francisco that Twain began to treat that name as if it were his own. Twain found a room on California Street and a job as a reporter on the *Call*. He was dazzled by the city, which was then in the grip of an extraordinary share-dealing boom. San Francisco was a 'gambling carnival', Twain wrote, simply the 'liveliest, heartiest community on our continent' – compensation, it seems, for the frequent earthquakes, which he never got used to. He complained that when he 'contracted to report for this newspaper, the important matter of two earthquakes a month was not considered in the salary'.

He needn't have worried: the job on the *Call* didn't last long. Twain was soon contributing essays, criticism and society gossip to a number of other publications. Indeed, it was in San Francisco that Twain first properly acknowledged that his vocation was writing. And it wasn't long before he was at the centre of a literary circle known as the 'Bohemians'.

Twain wrote vividly about the city, not least about earthquakes. The most powerful struck on 8 October 1865, with Twain noting that 'such another destruction of mantel ornaments and toilet bottles as the earthquake created, San Francisco never saw before'.

He left San Francisco in December 1866. In the last piece he ever wrote in the city, Twain looked to the future. 'This straggling town shall be a vast metropolis: this sparsely populated land shall become a crowded hive of busy men. Its estate will be brighter, happier and prouder a hundred fold than it is this day. This is its destiny, and in all sincerity I can say, So mote it be!'

Prophetic words indeed. However, it's doubtful that Mark Twain really uttered his often-quoted comment on the city's weather: 'The coldest winter I ever spent was summer in San Francisco'.

IN CONTEXT

Janis Joplin.

Despite all the turmoil, San Francisco managed to complete an amazing amount of construction. The Opera House opened in 1932; the following year, the island of Alcatraz was transferred from the army to the Federal Bureau of Prisons, which set about building a high-security lock-up. The San Francisco Museum of Modern Art, the first West Coast museum to feature exclusively 20th century works, opened in 1935. The same decade saw the completion of the San Francisco–Oakland Bay Bridge – six months before work started on the Golden Gate Bridge's revolutionary design. In 1939, on man-made Treasure Island, the city hosted another fair: the Golden Gate International Exposition, described as a 'pageant of the Pacific'. It was to be San Francisco's last big celebration for a while: in 1941 the Japanese attacked Pearl Harbor, and America entered World War II.

The war changed the city almost as much as the Gold Rush or the Great Quake. More than 1.5 million men and 23.5 million tons of materials were shipped to the Pacific from the Presidio, Travis Air Force Base and Treasure Island. Between 1941 and 1945, almost the entire Pacific war effort passed under the Golden Gate. The massed ranks of troops,

not to mention half a million civilian workers who flooded into San Francisco, turned the city into a milling party town hell-bent on sending its boys into battle with smiles on their faces.

In April 1945, representatives of 50 nations met at the San Francisco Opera House to draft the United Nations Charter. It was signed on 26 June 1945 and formally ratified in October at the General Organisation of the United Nations in London. Many people felt that San Francisco would be the ideal location for the UN's headquarters, but the British and French thought it too far to travel. To the city's great disappointment, the UN moved to New York.

BEATNIK BLUES AND HIPPIE HIGHS

The immediate post-war period was coloured by the return of the demobilised GIs, among them Lawrence Ferlinghetti. While studying at the Sorbonne in the early 1950s, the poet had discovered Penguin paperbacks, which inspired him to open his tiny, wedge-shaped bookshop at 261 Columbus Avenue. Called City Lights, the shop became a mecca for the bohemians and poets later dubbed the Beat Generation by Jack Kerouac.

The beats reflected the angst and ambition of a post-war generation attempting to escape both the shadow of the Bomb and the rampant consumerism of ultra-conformist 1950s America. In Kerouac's definition, beat could stand for either beatific or beat – exhausted. The condition is best explained in his novel *On the Road*, which charts the coast-to-coast odysseys of San Francisco-based beat saint Neal Cassady (thinly disguised as Dean Moriarty), poet Allen Ginsberg and Kerouac himself (named Sal Paradise).

'The emergence of the Beat Generation made North Beach the literary centre of San Francisco and nurtured a new vision that would spread far beyond its bounds,' reflected Ferlinghetti 40 years on. 'The beats prefigured the New Left evolution and the impulse for change that swept eastward from San Francisco.'

The media exposure received by Kerouac and Ginsberg established the Bay Area as a centre for the burgeoning counterculture, generating mainstream America's suspicions that San Francisco was the noncomformist capital of the US. Its fears were about to be confirmed by the hippie explosion of the 1960s. The beats and hippies might have shared a love of marijuana and a common distaste for 'the system', but Kerouac abhorred what he saw as the hippies' anti-Americanism. (It was, in fact, the beats who coined the term 'hippie' to refer to those they saw as second-rate, lightweight hipsters.) Kerouac's distaste for these new bohemians was shared by John Steinbeck, who shied away from the recognition he received in the streets.

The original beats had no interest in political action, but the newer generation embraced it. A sit-in protest against a closed session of the House of Representatives Un-American Activities Committee (HUAC) at City Hall in 1960 drew protesters from San Francisco State University and the University of California's Berkeley campus. Police turned their hoses on the crowd and it quickly degenerated into a riot, establishing the pattern for later protests and police responses. In 1964, Berkeley students, returning from a summer of civil rights protests in the South, butted heads with university officials over the right to use campus facilities for their campaigns. The conflict signalled the beginning of the Free Speech Movement, led by student activist Mario Savio, and firmly marked the split between the politically conscious and those who chose to opt out of the system

altogether. America's escalating involvement in the Vietnam War added urgency to the voices of dissent; Berkeley students remained at the forefront of campus protests around the country.

In San Francisco, the availability of LSD, its popularity boosted by such events as the Human Be-In and the Acid Tests overseen by Ken Kesey and Owsley Stanley and accompanied by Grateful Dead concerts, helped draw an estimated 8,000 hippies to the city from across America. More than half stayed, occupying the cheap Victorian houses around the Haight-Ashbury district (dubbed 'the Hashbury'). Combined with the sun, drugs and a psychedelic music explosion, the local *laissez-faire* attitude gave rise to the famous Summer of Love. By 1968, however, the spread of hard drugs, notably heroin, had taken the shine off the hippie movement. The fatal stabbing by Hells Angels of a Rolling Stones fan at the Altamont Speedway during the band's 1969 concert there signalled that darker times were ahead.

Like its drugs, the city's politics were getting harder. Members of the Black Panther movement, a radical black organisation founded across the Bay in Oakland by Huey Newton and Bobby Seale, asked themselves why they should ship out to shoot the Vietnamese when the real enemy was at home. Around Oakland, the Panthers took to exercising the American right to bear arms. Gunfights inevitably followed: Panther leader Eldridge Cleaver was wounded and 17-year-old Bobby Hutton killed in a shoot-out with Oakland police in April 1968. The Black Panther movement had petered out by the early 1970s, its leaders either dead, imprisoned or, like Cleaver, on the run. The kidnapping in 1974 of Patty Hearst, heir to the Hearst newspaper fortune, was the point at which the 1960s revolution turned into deadly farce. When she was recaptured, along with the other members of the tiny Symbionese Liberation Army, Hearst seemed to have been brainwashed into joining the cause.

Despite the violence, radicalism, and failed revolutions, the enduring memory of 1960s San Francisco is as host city to the Summer of Love. The music of the Grateful Dead, Janis Joplin, Country Joe and the Fish, and Jefferson Airplane defined both the San Francisco Sound and its countercultural attitude. Berkeley student Jann Wenner founded *Rolling Stone* magazine in 1967

IN CONTEXT

THE SOCIAL NETWORK

The rise, fall and rise again of a revolutionary technology.

At its peak in 2001, the internet economy had produced what one Silicon Valley venture capitalist called 'the largest legal accumulation of wealth in the history of the world'. Two years later it tanked. Companies such as San Francisco's Pets.com, which went from an IPO (Initial Public Offering) on the stock exchange to liquidation in just 268 days – in between spending an estimated $1.2 million to feature its sock puppet in a 2000 Super Bowl ad – seemed like a textbook example of hubris. Many looked on the much-ballyhooed Death of the Internet with no small amount of glee. Yet, while there was no shortage of Pets.coms, reports of the web's demise were greatly exaggerated. The people that had built the true internet, the young tinkerers and coders in dorm rooms, garages and their parents' basements, apparently failed to heed the voices of doom.

One year to the month after the NASDAQ stock index bottomed out, the man who would become the world's youngest billionaire began a small internet group called Facemash. Nineteen-year-old Harvard University freshman Mark Zuckerberg and his company, Facebook, would eventually count more than 1.49 billion users worldwide.

The speed with which these mega companies have been created, and their technologies universally adopted, is as surprising as the relative proximity of their headquarters from each other. The top three most trafficked internet sites in the world – Google (located in nearby Mountain View), Palo Alto's Facebook, and San Bruno-based YouTube – are all located within 30 miles of each other. Add in networking, software, and chip-making powerhouses Cisco, Oracle and Intel, ecommerce giant eBay, app-based car service Uber and Apple Computers, and one quickly realises that the Bay Area hasn't missed a step in maintaining its status as the nexus of the information age.

In San Francisco, a stroll through the former urban wasteland along Market Street, between 6th and 10th Streets, is all the visual proof you'll need of Web 2.0's skyrocketing resurgence. Encouraged by city tax breaks, companies such as Twitter, One King's Lane, Spotify, Yammer, Dolby, Square and Zendesk have moved into vacant and dilapidated buildings and are starting to transform one of San Francisco's grittiest quadrants into a slick corridor of high-end office towers and glossy restaurants and bars. At the time of writing, half a dozen top-dollar luxury condo/apartment buildings, a new theatre and a foodie marketplace had already opened, with 5,500 additional residential units, arts venues and a 250,000-square-foot retail development in the works.

to explain and advance the cause, helping to invent the New Journalism in the process.

THE RAINBOW REVOLUTION

San Francisco's radical baton was taken up in the 1970s by the gay liberation movement. Local activists insisted that gay traditions had always existed in the city, first among the Ohlone and later during the 1849 Gold Rush, when women in the West were more scarce than gold. Early groups such as the Daughters of Bilitis, the Mattachine Society and the Society for Individual Rights (SIR) paved the way for more radical new political movements. Gay activists made successful forays into mainstream politics in 1977: SIR's Jim Foster became the first openly gay delegate at a Democratic Convention, and Harvey Milk was elected to the city's Board of Supervisors.

Then Dan White changed everything. A former policeman, White had run for supervisor as an angry young blue-collar populist – and won. He suffered poor mental health and had to resign under the strain of office, but quickly changed his mind and asked Mayor George Moscone to reinstate him. When Moscone refused, White assassinated him along with Harvey Milk. The killings stunned the city, but the slap-on-the-wrist verdict of seven years for manslaughter outraged its citizenry, resulting in the White Night Riot. White served five years of the sentence and committed suicide not long after his release.

Gay life and politics changed radically and irrevocably with the onset of AIDS, which tore the gay community apart. There was controversy when the city's bathhouses, a symbol of gay liberation and promiscuity, closed in a panic over the spread of the disease. Gay radicals branded San Francisco Chronicle writer Randy Shilts a 'fascist Nazi, traitor and homophobe' when he criticised bathhouse owners who refused to post safe-sex warnings. However, his book, And the Band Played On, is still the definitive account of the period.

COLLAPSE AND RECOVERY

Because of its location on the San Andreas Fault, San Francisco has always lived in anticipation of a major earthquake to rival the 1906 disaster. It came in October 1989: the Loma Prieta quake, named after the ridge of mountains at its epicentre, registered 7.1 on the Richter scale (the 1906 quake was

an estimated 7.8). Part of the West Oakland Freeway collapsed, crushing drivers; the Marina district was devastated by fires; and 50 feet of the Bay Bridge's upper deck collapsed. In just 15 seconds, more than 19,000 homes were damaged or destroyed; 63 people were killed and 12,000 were displaced.

As the 1990s progressed, changes in the city reflected those in the world beyond. The end of the Cold War meant cuts in military spending, and the Presidio – which operated as a US military base for almost 150 years – was closed in 1994. As part of the Base Closure and Realignment Act, the land was transferred to the National Park Service. Over the next two decades, it would be transformed with restaurants, a campus for filmmaker George Lucas's digital arts, a Walt Disney museum, and a weekend playground for San Franciscans.

In the wake of the Loma Prieta earthquake, the Embarcadero Freeway was torn down and the city's historic bayside boulevard turned into a palm-tree-lined haven for walkers, joggers, in-line skaters and cyclists. Numerous major projects were brought to completion and others begun: in 1995, the San Francisco Museum of Modern Art moved into a new building in burgeoning SoMa, and voters voted to restore City Hall. Five years later, Pac Bell Park (now AT&T Park), the first privately funded Major League Baseball park in nearly 40 years, opened its gates.

As the 20th century rolled into the 21st, San Francisco suffered from many of the same social problems that plagued other major US cities. Homelessness was particularly severe, with up to 4,000 destitute men and women. The late '90s internet boom brought workers from around the world into an increasingly tight housing market and gentrified working-class neighbourhoods. By the end of the decade, the dotcom bubble had burst. What no one could have predicted was that within a few years there would be another tech boom. By 2008, technology companies were on the move again, followed on their heels by the phenomena of social networking. With feet firmly planted in the San Francisco area and profits soaring, Google, Facebook, YouTube and Twitter paved the way for the next gold rush. A collection of new skyscrapers, many exceeding height limits set in the previous century, are perhaps the most obvious manifestation of the once-again burgeoning economy.

IN CONTEXT

Architecture

The seven-by-seven-mile city packs in a world of styles.

TEXT: MATT MARKOVICH

Building in San Francisco has always been a challenge. Set on a tiny 47-square-mile peninsula punctuated by more than 70 hills ranging in height from 100 to 927 feet, surrounded on three sides by water, and resting atop one of the nation's most populous and seismically active earthquake faults, the city has had to rebuild more times than it cares to remember. Yet these challenges haven't prevented architects from wanting to put their stamp on the metropolis. The result is a richly textured cityscape that spans everything from the famous 'Painted Lady' Victorian row houses and only-in-San-Francisco curiosities to starchitect-conceived contemporary landmarks.

Yet, as the latest tech boom ushers in a new era of mega-skyscrapers, the prospect of towering structures that seem so antithetical to the city's overall vibe is, to put it mildly, disconcerting to many San Franciscans.

A MISSIONARY POSITION

It was the founding of **Mission Dolores** (see p157) in 1776 that initially drew settlers to the city. One of 21 missions built in California by the Spanish, the simple church is the city's oldest surviving structure, and along with a portion of walls at the Officers' Club in the Presidio, the sole piece of colonial architecture to have outlived the city's progress from hamlet to metropolis. The church has four-foot-thick adobe walls – inside, a small section is exposed so you can see they're made of clay and straw – and sits beside a cemetery where Native Americans, outlaws and the city's first Irish and Hispanic mayors are buried.

THE BOOM YEARS: PART ONE

The town inhabited by Gold Rush immigrants known as the Forty-Niners in the 1850s suffered a series of fires. The heart of the outpost was **Portsmouth Square** (see p90), in present-day Chinatown. It was incinerated by two blazes; the surrounding streets perished in the fire following the 1906 earthquake. The most impressive buildings from the Gold Rush era are in the **Jackson Square Historical District** (best viewed on Jackson between Montgomery and Sansome Streets).

Although precious metals flooded the town, the big Gold Rush money actually came from outfitting the legions of fortune-seekers. A burst of prosperity in the 19th century quickly filled San Francisco's once-empty sloping streets with what have become its signature Victorian terraced houses. Built by middle-class tradesmen in the Mission, Castro and Haight districts, and by rich merchants in Presidio Heights and around **Alamo Square**, these famous 'Painted Ladies' are the city's most characteristic architectural face. One of the most popular views is framed by a row of six painted Victorians along Steiner Street between Hayes and Grove Streets ('**Postcard Row**'), but there are more than 14,000 examples of this eye-catching vernacular, some even more fanciful.

The wooden frames and elaborate woodwork of San Francisco's Victorians come in four distinct styles: Gothic Revival, Italianate, Stick-Eastlake and Queen Anne. The earliest Gothic Revival houses have pointed arches over their windows and were often painted white, rather than in the bright colours of the later styles. The Italianate style, with tall cornices, neoclassical elements and add-on porches, are best exemplified in the Lower Haight, notably on Grove Street near Webster Street, but there are other examples at **1900 Sacramento Street** (near Lafayette Park) and at 1818 California Street (the **Lilienthal-Pratt House**, built in 1876).

Flood Mansion.

The Italianate was succeeded by the Stick-Eastlake style, named after furniture designer Charles Eastlake and characterised by square bay windows framed with angular, carved ornamentation. The 'Sticks' are the most common of the Victorian houses left in the city. A shining example is the over-the-top extravaganza at **1057 Steiner Street** on the corner of Golden Gate Avenue.

With its turrets, towers and curvaceous corner bay windows, the Queen Anne style is amply demonstrated by the left tower of the **Wormser-Coleman House** in Pacific Heights (1834 California Street, at Franklin Street). However, the most extravagant example is the **Haas-Lilienthal House** (see p115); it was built in 1886 by Bavarian grocer William Haas, who treated himself to a home with 26 rooms and seven bathrooms. Now a museum, the house is one of the few such examples of Victorian architecture open to the public.

TAKING A BATH

Engineer Adolph Sutro came to own most of the western side of the city, including the sandy wasteland on its westerly edge, which he bought in 1881 for his **Sutro Baths**. The therapeutic baths were the most elaborate in the western world, but eventually fell into disrepair. In the 1960s, the site was sold to developers for high-rise apartments that never got built after a fire in 1966 destroyed the buildings. Today, the baths are San Franciscans' favorite ruins. The adjoining **Cliff House** (see p185) burned twice and was once struck by a boat that ran aground full of dynamite. Rebuilt first in the fashion of a grand Victorian fantasy and later in neoclassical style, it underwent further cannibalisation over the years before the owners gave it an extreme makeover in 2004 that brought it back to its neoclassical roots.

Closer to downtown, San Francisco's 'Big Four' railroad barons – Mark Hopkins, Leland Stanford, Collis P Huntington and Charles Crocker – made their architectural mark in the late 19th century by building grand edifices. Their mining investments funded railroads, banks and businesses, but also paid for their baronial mansions on Nob Hill. Many were destroyed in the 1906 fire, but their sites have since been filled in suitably grand fashion. Two old mansions have been replaced by hotels: the **Stanford Court** (905 California Street, at

Powell Street) and the **InterContinental Mark Hopkins** (999 California Street, at Mason Street), while the site of the former Crocker Mansion, a Queen Anne manor built in 1888, is now occupied by Gothic **Grace Cathedral** (see p87), itself a stunning addition to San Francisco's architectural heritage.

The nearby **Flood Mansion** (1000 California Street, at Mason Street) survived the Great Earthquake and remains a brilliant example of the grandeur of the homes that once perched on Nob Hill. Believed to be the first brownstone west of the Mississippi river, the sandstone marvel was built in 1886 by silver baron James C Flood and now houses a private gentlemen's club. Another grand old survivor, albeit one that post-dates the quake, is the **Spreckels Mansion**, an impressive Beaux Arts building in Pacific Heights (2080 Washington Street, at Octavia Street). Built in 1912 for sugar baron Adolph Spreckels, it's now owned by novelist Danielle Steel.

Unsurprisingly, this most unconventional city boasts many architectural curiosities, perhaps chief among them the **Octagon House** (see p122). Built in 1861 during a citywide craze for eight-sided buildings (they were considered healthier because they let in more light), it's one of just three octagonal buildings left in the city.

Another oddity is the **Columbarium** (see p185), a neoclassical temple built in 1898 that holds the ashes of thousands of city residents. Its interior is decorated with mosaic tiling and elaborate urns in imaginatively bedecked niches. Oriental promise meets occidental vulgarity at the **Vedanta Temple** (see p122), an eccentricity built in 1905 for the Hindu Vedanta Society. Its bizarre mix of styles includes a Russian Orthodox onion-shaped dome, a Hindu cupola, castle-like crenellations and Moorish arches.

FROM BOOMTOWN TO METROPOLIS

When the growing city began to burst at its peninsula seams, a ferry network evolved to carry passengers to and from other parts of the Bay Area. Intended as a symbol of civic pride for the young city, with a clock tower inspired by the Moorish campanile of the Giralda Cathedral in Seville, Spain, the **Ferry Building** was built on the Embarcadero in 1898. Its impeccably restored Great Nave, a 660-foot-long steel-framed, two-storey

IN CONTEXT

expanse, now houses a wildly popular gourmet marketplace.

After the 1906 earthquake, a passion for engineering spurred an interest in Chicago architect Daniel Burnham's City Beautiful project. Arising from it was a proposal for a heroic new Civic Center planted below a terraced Telegraph Hill, laced with tree-lined boulevards that would trace the city's contours. The result of Burnham's two-year consultations with leading city architects Bernard Maybeck and Willis Polk (the latter designed the wonderful **Hobart Building** at Market and Montgomery Streets; the former the **Palace of Fine Arts**, see p123), the plan countered the city's impractical grid street pattern. It never came to fruition.

Under Mayor 'Sunny Jim' Rolph, the thrust of the 1915 Civic Center complex eventually came from public contests; many were won by Arthur Brown, architect of the mighty domed **City Hall** (see p64). Several other Civic Center buildings date back to this era, among them Brown's **War Memorial Opera House** (see p225), completed in 1932, and the **Bill Graham Civic Auditorium** (see p217). All reflect the Parisian Beaux Arts style, with grandiose proportions and ornamentation. The former main library, built by George Kelham in 1917, was made over by Italian architect Gae Aulenti, (best known for her transformation of Paris's Musée d'Orsay) into the **Asian Art Museum** (see p64). It was largely Rolph's idea to host the huge Panama-Pacific Exposition in 1915, for which he commissioned Bernard Maybeck to build the **Palace of Fine Arts** and its myriad pavilions. The only building left from the Exposition, the Palace was originally made of wood and plaster and rebuilt using reinforced concrete in the 1960s. It underwent a complete restoration 2011.

Passionate rebuilding continued during the Depression, with two staggering landmarks leading the way. The **Golden Gate Bridge** (see p127) opened to traffic in 1937, six months after the completion of the **San Francisco-Oakland Bay Bridge**. The latter now features a new, sparkling white suspension bridge on its eastern span that replaced the leg damaged in the 1989 earthquake.

The Works Progress Administration (WPA), part of President Roosevelt's New Deal job-creation scheme, contributed to many

structures, such as **Coit Tower** (see p101), designed by Arthur Brown in 1932, and the Bay and Golden Gate Bridges. Other examples include the Rincon Annex Post Office Building and Anton Refregier's murals, built in 1940 and now part of **Rincon Center** (see p59).

Arts and Crafts architect Julia Morgan hit her stride around this time, designing numerous buildings in the East Bay, at least when she wasn't working for San Francisco newspaper magnate William Randolph Hearst on the extravagant Hearst Castle in San Simeon. In San Francisco, she designed the old Chinese YWCA building in 1932, now home to the **Chinese Historical Society of America Museum** (see p91).

While Frank Lloyd Wright's **Marin Civic Center**, located north of the city in San Rafael and completed after his death in 1959, is his most notable civic work, there is another, often overlooked Lloyd Wright building in San Francisco, at **140 Maiden Lane**. Wright designed the edifice in 1948, originally a gift store, as a prototype Guggenheim.

CONTEMPORARY CLASSICS

The 1970s saw a small wave of construction that had a big impact on the city's image. Pietro Belluschi and Pier Luigi Nervi completed the **Cathedral of St Mary of the Assumption** (see p139) in 1971; a 255-foot concrete structure supporting a cross-shaped, stained-glass ceiling, it's a 1970s symbol of anti-quake defiance. The next year saw the completion of the 853-foot **Transamerica Pyramid** (see p52), one of San Francisco's most iconic buildings. The $34-million structure has an internal suspension system, which served to protect its 48 storeys and 212-foot spire in the 1989 quake. At first unpopular, the pyramid now has few detractors: for many it's become a symbol for the city itself.

THE BOOM YEARS: PART TWO

During the second Bay Area boom of the mid to late 1990s, there was not only a renewed interest in development, but deeper pockets to fund it. Designed by architects James Ingo Freed of Pei Cobb Freed and Cathy Simon of Simon Martin-Vegue Winkelstein & Moris, the **San Francisco Main Library** (see p64) downtown is a marriage of Beaux Arts and more recent styles, with neoclassical columns and a dramatic interior centred on a five-storey atrium below a domed skylight designed to let natural light filter throughout the building.

However, it's the **SoMa** neighbourhood that has really been transformed, kicking off with the **San Francisco Museum of Modern Art** (*see p72*). Designed by Mario Botta and opened in 1995, it features a series of stepped boxes and a black-and-white striped cylindrical façade. The museum debuts an addition by Norwegian firm Snøhetta in early 2016. The striated white edifice rises 20 storeys behind the museum, and features bands of windows, terraces, and a vertical sculpture garden.

Just west of SFMOMA, **Yerba Buena Gardens** (*see p68*) was one of the great triumphs of urban renewal, a beautiful park framed by museums, theatres and shops, and replete with lush greenery, fountains, cafés and a hyper-modern urban mall. Directly opposite is Moscone West, the latest addition to the **Moscone Convention Center** (*see p68*). Just inside the stunning glass structure sits a 101-foot-tall hand-carved California Redwood trunk (it died of natural causes and was reclaimed for the piece) added as a sculptural element by artists Hilda Shum, Po Shu Wang, and David S Gordon.

Perhaps the two most dramatic of SoMa's recent projects are the **San Francisco Federal Building** at 7th and Mission Streets and the Contemporary Jewish Museum. Designed by Thom Mayne, the Federal Building's perforated metal façade plays on the idea of government transparency and promises to reduce energy use. Daniel Libeskind's **Contemporary Jewish Museum** (*see p69*) is a strikingly modern update of a 1907 Willis Polk power substation. A blue steel cube – symbolic of the Hebrew letters for *chai* (life) – is attached to the original brick façade, marrying old and new. Nearby, in Mission Bay, Ricardo Legorreta's **UCSF Community Center** at the University of California's Mission Bay campus echoes the architect's Mexican roots with its brilliant-red clay and fuchsia-toned palette.

There has been plenty of activity across town at Golden Gate Park, too. The old **de Young Museum** (*see p184*) was replaced with an ultra-modern design by Swiss architects Herzog & de Meuron that caused huge controversy when it was unveiled in 2005. Angular in shape, the museum's helix-like

viewing tower rises high above the park; the dappled, copper façade, which will allegedly develop a patina over time (no sign of it yet), offers a dramatic focal point in the otherwise mild-mannered park setting.

Across from the de Young, the **California Academy of Sciences** (*see p182*) received a similar makeover in 2008. Architect Renzo Piano transformed the 164-year-old institution into the world's 'greenest' museum, featuring a digital planetarium, an indoor rainforest, an aquarium with an active coral reef, and a 'living' roof that recycles rainwater and provides insulation for the museum.

The Presidio has also seen action in recent years, as work continues on converting the old army properties on the site. The decision to allow filmmaker George Lucas to build the $350-million **Letterman Digital Arts Center** on a plot at the eastern edge of the park was not without controversy, but the whitewashed campus blends in seamlessly with its surroundings, and has won over most critics.

FUTURE SHOCK

The most significant new building project in the city is taking place in **Mission Bay**, the old working waterfront south of AT&T Park. A massive development of office structures, residential towers, and a recently completed 303-acre UCSF medical complex, Mission Bay is an entirely new neighbourhood – no small feat given the city's seven-by-seven-mile footprint. At completion, the area will include restaurants, marketplaces, parks, public plazas and even new streets, transforming an area that used to be home to rusted tankers and decrepit factories and warehouses.

Nearby at the foot of the Bay Bridge, **One Rincon Hill**'s south tower, built in 2008, rises 641 feet over the city, briefly giving it status as the city's tallest building, until completion of nearby Salesforce Tower. The looming 1,070-foot obelisk will sit behind a new Transbay Transit Center, replacing the old, dilapidated terminal. Dubbed the 'Grand Central Terminal of the West', the $4 billion project by Hines and Pelli Clarke Pelli Architects will connect eight Bay Area counties and the state of California through 11 transit systems. At the time of writing, Salesforce Tower will be the tallest building on the West Coast – sitting smack in the middle of the most earthquake-prone region in the country.

IN CONTEXT

Essential Information

Hotels

While San Francisco has its fair share of major chains such as Hyatt and Hilton, the lodging scene is defined by boutique hotels and historic properties. Several of the city's most iconic grandes dames – including the Westin St Francis and InterContinental Mark Hopkins – have retained their historic properties, but are now owned by mega hotel corporations. Given California's recent drought, the key word for most new and revamped properties is 'green', with sustainable and environmentally conscious features being built into every aspect. The W Hotel, Hotel Carlton and Orchard Garden Hotel are among the growing number of places that have achieved LEED certification in recent years. The Good Hotel incorporates eco-friendly practices and design into every aspect of the property – from furnishings constructed from recycled materials to bike loans and free parking for hybrid cars.

INFORMATION & PRICES

While San Francisco's hemmed-in geography tends to restrict the building of massive new hotels downtown, several major properties have been reincarnated and upgraded in the last few years with new names and fresh faces, including the **Hotel Zelos** (formerly the Palomar, www.hotelzelos.com), the **Hotel Marker San Francisco** (formerly Hotel Monaco, 501 Geary Street, 1-415 292 0100, www.themarkersanfrancisco.com), and the **Loews Regency San Francisco Hotel** (formerly the Mandarin Oriental, 222 Sansome Street, 1-415 276 9888, www.loewshotels.com/regency-san-francisco).

Financial District hotels tend to offer the best deals on Friday and Saturday nights, when business travellers have gone home. The high season runs from April to November, and rates fluctuate wildly. Demand often exceeds supply and prices can double, or even triple, during major conferences and events, such as the annual Oracle convention or LGBT Pride weekend (go to www.moscone.com to see the major convention calendar).

In general, expensive and luxury properties cost anywhere from $300 to $500 and above,

moderate hotels from $175 to $300, and budget accommodation below $200. Bear in mind, too, that rates exclude a 14 per cent room tax. Parking fees can be exorbitant ($30-$55 per day), and in-room internet charges can also add up (although there are plenty of hotels and other sites in the city with free Wi-Fi access). Many hotels offer internet-only deals and special packages, but if those prices aren't low enough, check booking sites such as www.booking.com and www.hotels.com, which include many of the properties listed here. Always ask about cancellation policies when booking, so you don't get stuck paying for a room you can't use.

Downtown

UNION SQUARE & AROUND

Expensive

Four Seasons

757 Market Street, between 3rd & 4th Streets, CA 94103 (1-415 633 3000, www.fourseasons.com). BART & Metro to Powell/bus 2, 3, 5, 6, 9, 14, 21,

*27, 30, 38, 45, 71, 91 & Market Street routes/
cable car Powell-Hyde or Powell-Mason.*
Map p313 M6.

The sleek 36-storey Four Seasons is well located on
the south side of Market Street, convenient for both
Union Square and SoMa. Its 277 rooms and suites,
142 residential condos, high-end shops and upscale
restaurant create the feeling of a city within a city.
The general design and ambience are pretty similar to other Four Seasons around the world: as you
might expect, the ample guest quarters (the small-
est are 460sq ft) are sumptuously appointed, with
no corner-cutting. The list of on-site amenities is
lengthy and all-encompassing; perhaps the jewel
is complimentary use of the Equinox Sports Club,
with spa, steam/sauna and Olympic-sized pool.

Hotel Nikko

*222 Mason Street, between Ellis & O'Farrell
Streets, CA 94102 (1-415 403 1800, www.
hotelnikkosf.com). BART & Metro to Powell/
bus 2, 3, 5, 6, 9, 21, 27, 30, 38, 45, 71, 91 &
Market Street routes/cable car Powell-Hyde or
Powell-Mason.* **Map** p313 M6.

Part of the Japan Airlines hotel chain, the 25-storey
Nikko is incredibly popular with Japanese visitors
but welcoming to all. Rooms are large, bright and
reasonably attractive, furnished with a light colour
scheme, Frette linens and pillow-top mattresses.
Elsewhere, the design is clean with Asian touches
throughout. There's an indoor pool that lets in

light through a glass ceiling, plus a gym and a
kamaburo (dry Japanese sauna). The in-house
restaurant, Anzu, specialises in sushi. Its nightclub
and cabaret, Feinstein's (*see p223*), operated in
partnership with pianist/singer Michael Feinstein,
features performances by big-name jazz, pop and
Broadway artists, plus moonlighting celebs such as
Jeff Goldblum and Tony Danza.

JW Marriott San Francisco

*515 Mason Street, at Post Street, CA 94102
(1-415 771 8600, www.marriott.com). Bus 2,
3, 4, 27, 30, 38, 45, 91/cable car Powell-Hyde
or Powell-Mason.* **Map** p312 L5.

Far enough from Union Square so guests can avoid
the crush, but close enough for the shops to be mere
steps away, the JW features a dazzling third-floor
lobby with a soaring 18-storey atrium, an in-house
coffee kiosk, and a third-floor bar and American
restaurant. Among the many plush amenities is a
24-hour personal butler service.

Taj Campton Place

*340 Stockton Street, between Post & Sutter Streets,
CA 94108 (1-415 781 5555, www.tajhotels.com).
BART & Metro to Montgomery/bus 2, 3, 30, 38,
45, 91 & Market Street routes/cable car Powell-
Hyde or Powell-Mason.* **Map** p313 M5.

San Francisco has only a handful of five-star hotels,
a ranking dependent upon a long list of amenities,
facilities and services that few can deliver. And

Hotel Rex. See p275.

ESSENTIAL INFORMATION

Palace Hotel. *See p277.*

then there's Taj Campton Place, officially a four-star thanks to its lack of a spa and swimming pool, but in every other way a bona fide luxury hotel, with service on par with the city's best. Elegant and correct in their restrained design, all 110 rooms are decked out in soothing shades of neutral ecru, with walls of pear wood and high-end furnishings, including leather-top writing desks. Beds are dressed in silky-soft Frette linens, and the limestone bathrooms are stocked with high-end products and chenille robes. Downstairs, the eponymous Michelin-starred restaurant, Campton Place, serves three meals daily, and the same kitchen provides room service to guests. Bonus: the hotel is pet-friendly ($100 fee for up to two animals).

Moderate

Hotel Carlton
1075 Sutter Street, between Larkin & Hyde Streets, CA 94109 (1-415 673 0242, www.jdvhotels.com). Bus 2, 3, 19, 27, 76X. **Map** p312 K5.

The Carlton is one of the city's best-value mid-range hotels. It had a total makeover in 2013, but because

it's just beyond the usual tourist path, rates are lower than at comparable Union Square-area hotels. This is an older building, constructed in 1920, with fire-sprinkler pipes running along the hallway ceilings. But there's nothing old-fashioned about the finish in the rooms, which include iPod docks, multiple surge-protected outlets and Keurig coffee-makers. The design aesthetic draws inspiration from Morocco, with lush jewel tones playing off white-on-white bed linens. The subway-tile bathrooms are compact, but have enough room to unpack your things. If you're a light sleeper, request a high floor and a room without a connecting door. *Photo p273.*

Hotel Diva
440 Geary Street, between Mason & Taylor Streets, CA 94102 (1-415 885 0200, www. hoteldiva.com). Bus 2, 3, 27, 30, 31, 38, 45, 91/cable car Powell-Hyde or Powell-Mason. **Map** p312 L5.

Located in the heart of the city's Theater District, just a block from Union Square, the Diva has a dressy look, with deluxe bedding (400-thread-count sheets), as well as leather sleeper sofas and stainless

ESSENTIAL INFORMATION

steel-sculpted headboards. The Little Divas suite for children (connected via a door to the parents' room) comes with a computer, Wii gaming system, karaoke machine and costume trunk. Other unique amenities include a nightly complimentary saké hour and 24-hour designer work lounges.

Hotel G

386 Geary Street, at Mason Street, CA 94102 (1-415 986 2000, www.hotelgsanfrancisco.com). Bus 2, 3, 4, 30, 38, 45/cable car Powell-Hyde or Powell-Mason. **Map** p313 M5.

The G is a boutique property housed inside a 1909 building that was once home to the Fielding Hotel. Ideally located just off Union Square, a block from theatres and shops, it combines a residential vibe with modern amenities that include 42-inch smart TVs, Nespresso coffeemakers, and guest-room interiors that include standing full-length mirrors, houndstooth carpeting, turquoise crocodile headboards and white leather couches. The street level is anchored by the French-American Three 9 Eight Brasserie, stylish Klyde wine bar, and Benjamin Cooper cocktail/oyster bar.

★ Hotel Rex

562 Sutter Street, between Powell & Mason Streets, CA 94102 (1-800 433 4434, www.jdvhotels.com). Bus 5, 6, 9, 14, 21, 27, 30, 31, 38, 45, 71, 91/ cable car Powell-Hyde or Powell-Mason. **Map** p312 L5.

Named after Kenneth Rexroth, MC for the fabled Six Gallery reading that provided a launchpad for the Beat Generation, the Rex is one of the city's most appealing small hotels. Taking 20th-century literary salons for inspiration, there are books scattered throughout and the walls are adorned with caricatures of writers with local ties. Literary events are often held in the back salon, and the modern business centre even has a few antique typewriters. Local artists' work decorates the guest rooms, and guests have discounted access to a spacious gym near the hotel. The Library Bar serves upscale bar food; there's live jazz on Friday nights.

Hotel Triton

342 Grant Avenue, between Bush & Sutter Streets, CA 94108 (1-415 394 0500, www.hoteltriton.com). Bus 1, 2, 3, 30, 38, 45, 76, 91. **Map** p313 M5.

Bags packed, milk cancelled, house raised on stilts.

You've packed the suntan lotion, the snorkel set, the stay-pressed shirts. Just one more thing left to do – your bit for climate change. In some of the world's poorest countries, changing weather patterns are destroying lives.

You can help people to deal with the extreme effects of climate change. Raising houses in flood-prone regions is just one life-saving solution.

Climate change costs lives.
Give £5 and let's sort it *Here & Now*

www.oxfam.org.uk/climate-change

Oxfam is a registered charity in England and Wales (No.202918) and Scotland (SCO039042). Oxfam GB is a member of Oxfam International.

Be Humankind Oxfam

This colourful hotel, across from the ornate Chinatown gate, succeeds in being both fun and funky. A pioneer in 'green hotel' practices, rooms have Frette linens and Earthly Beds made entirely of recycled materials; the seventh-storey Eco-Floor has special water- and air-filtration systems and water-saving devices. Also on the hotel's eclectic menu are nightly tarot readings, fresh cookies and free drinks in the lobby. Much of the joy, though, is in the design quirks: the small 'Zen Dens' have incense, daybeds and books on Buddhism, and there are celebrity suites designed by the late Jerry Garcia, Carlos Santana and even comedienne Kathy Griffin.

Mystic Hotel

417 Stockton Street, at Sutter Street, CA 94108 (1-415 400 0500, www.crescentsf.com). Bus 1, 2, 3, 30, 38, 45, 76, 91. **Map** p313 M5.

Previously the Crescent, this revamped Victorian got a new life in 2012 when celebrity Chef Charlie Palmer took it over and revamped it as the Mystic. Set in a prime Union Square location, it exudes noir charm, with exposed brick walls and porcelain sink basins. The biggest draw, though, is the speakeasy-cool Burritt Room + Tavern, offering artisan cocktails, a modern American menu, and jazz musicians in a darkwood-and-curtained-booth setting that befits its location below the spot where Miles Archer was gunned down in the hard-boiled classic, *The Maltese Falcon*.

▶ *For the Burritt Room bar, see p49.*

Sir Francis Drake Hotel

450 Powell Street, between Post & Sutter Streets, CA 94102 (1-415 392 7755, www.sirfrancisdrake. com). Bus 2, 3, 27, 30, 38, 45, 76, 91/cable car Powell-Hyde or Powell-Mason. **Map** p313 M5.

Named after the Elizabethan explorer whose near-discovery of San Francisco is celebrated in vintage murals in the lobby, this venerable 1930s hotel plays up its heritage with Beefeater-costumed doormen (its most famous, Tom Sweeney, has served four decades as a greeter here), an over-the-top ornate lobby and tours of the subterranean speakeasy that once occupied a hidden space beneath the street. The rooms are more up to date, with flatscreen TVs and smart bathrooms done out in black tiles and stainless steel. At the top, Harry Denton's glam Starlight Room draws a young crowd for its panoramic city views and dancing, while downstairs, a morning café and Scala's Bistro offer much better than average hotel dining options.

FINANCIAL DISTRICT

Two popular chain options here are the **Hyatt Regency** (5 Embarcadero Center, CA 94111, 1-866 716 8145, 1-866 788 1234, www.sanfranciscoregency.hyatt.com) and the polished **Le Méridien** (333 Battery Street, CA 94111, 1-415 296 2900, www.lemeridien.com).

Expensive

Omni San Francisco

500 California Street, at Montgomery Street, CA 94104 (1-415 677 9494, www.omni hotels.com). BART & Metro to Montgomery/ bus 1, 9X, 10, 12, 41/cable car California. **Map** p313 N4.

With a great central location right on the cable car line, this business-friendly hotel is relatively new, but feels as though it's been part of the landscape for years. That's partly because it has been built into a historic structure, with decor inspired by the 1920s and '30s, but it's also due to the exceptional service. The rooms are larger than you might expect and are appointed with comfortable amenities, including upscale bath accessories, plush robes and large work desks. The ground-floor restaurant, Bob's Steaks & Chop House, is one of the better steakhouses in town.

★ Palace Hotel

2 New Montgomery Street, at Market Street, CA 94105 (1-415 512 1111, www.sfpalace.com). BART & Metro to Montgomery/bus 2, 3, 4, 30, 45 & Market Street routes. **Map** p313 N5.

The city's most famous hotel opened in its current incarnation in 1909, and has hosted multiple presidents, including Woodrow Wilson, who gave his League of Nations speech here in 1919. Presidents no longer stay here (there's no underground security access), but still the Palace remains one of the city's grandest addresses – and one of the few with an indoor swimming pool. The Garden Court dining room is among the most beautiful in California, an 8,000sq ft space with a domed glass ceiling, 16 Italian marble columns and 20 Austrian crystal chandeliers. Walls of mahogany rise behind the reception desk, and an original Maxfield Parrish mural adorns the Pied Piper Bar. Guest rooms have high ceilings, crown mouldings and sumptuous beds, but the mass-market furniture is decidedly business class. Still, for a glimpse of San Francisco history, you can't beat the Palace. *See also p285* **Ralston's Palace**. *Photos pp274-275.*

Moderate

Galleria Park Hotel

191 Sutter Street, at Kearny Street, CA 94104 (1-415 781 3060, www.jdvhotels.com/galleria_ park). Bus 1, 9X, 30, 31, 38, 45. **Map** p313 M5.

Next to the Crocker Galleria mall, this boutique hotel was looking a bit frayed until the Joie de Vivre chain snapped it up some years ago and poured in $7 million of updates. Now its rooms provide pillow-top bedding with Frette linens, flatscreen TVs and DVD players, and free internet access and office supplies. The endearingly snug lobby, with its elegant art nouveau fireplace, and the Parisian-style brasserie Gaspar, are its biggest charms.

THE EMBARCADERO
Expensive

★ Hotel Vitale
8 Mission Street, at The Embarcadero, CA 94105 (1-415 278 3777, www.jdvhotels.com). BART & Metro to Montgomery/bus 2, 14, 31 & Market Street routes. **Map** p313 O4.

Blessed with a truly dramatic location on the Embarcadero (many of the rooms have great views of the Bay Bridge, and the spa is atop a penthouse suite), the Vitale aesthetic is hip and sexy, a play on midcentury modern design, with swoop-back chairs and low-slung sofas in a lobby of limestone and wood. Capacious rooms are decorated in a pale colour palette, all the better to reflect the light, with super-comfortable beds and excellent amenities. The huge but inviting bathrooms have a sliding door that allows some sounds to waft through. Downstairs is a bar and a restaurant (the Americano) that conform immaculately to the comfortably chic ambience, while the rooftop spa is perfect for an outdoor soak with a view.
▶ *For the Americano restaurant, see p60.*

Moderate

★ Harbor Court Hotel
165 Steuart Street, between Mission & Howard Streets, CA 94105 (1-866 792 6283, 1-415 882 1300, www.harborcourthotel.com). BART & Metro to Embarcadero/bus 12, 14, 20, 38, 41 & Market Street routes. **Map** p313 O4.

On the Embarcadero waterfront, Harbor Court is an underdiscovered treat. The stylishly cosy rooms look out to San Francisco Bay and the Bay Bridge. In addition to niceties such as bathrobes, guests enjoy freebies such as Wi-Fi and a weekday morning in-town car service, as well as use of the adjacent fitness club (a top-quality facility with pool, sauna and steam room) at a discounted fee. The on-site Japanese restaurant, Ozumo, is one of half a dozen excellent dining options on this block.

THE TENDERLOIN
Expensive

Clift Hotel
495 Steuart Street, at Taylor Street, CA 94102 (1-415 775 4700, www.clifthotel.com). Bus 2, 3, 27, 31, 38/cable car Powell-Hyde or Powell-Mason. **Map** p312 L6.

This historic hotel, which celebrated its centenary in 2015, still exudes a certain Old World glamour, although a redesign by Philippe Starck in 2001 added elements of surreal opulence – including a huge bronze Eames chair and a coffee table by Salvador Dali in the lobby. The beautifully restored art deco Redwood Room, added in 1933, features panelled walls and an elegant, carved bar believed to have come from a single redwood tree. The

Hotel Vitale.

minimalist rooms are on the right side of comfortable, with easy-on-the eye grey, tangerine and lavender decor, but standard quarters lack the 'wow' factor and the bathrooms are poky. The staff range from cooler-than-thou to ultra-friendly (thankfully, there are more of the latter).

★ Hotel Adagio

550 Geary Street, between Taylor & Jones Streets, CA 94102 (1-415 775 5000, www.hoteladagiosf. com). Bus 2, 3, 27, 31, 38/cable car Powell-Hyde or Powell-Mason. **Map** *p312 L5.*

The Adagio has been in town in one incarnation or another since 1929. Its current version is the best yet: the casual, mellow decor combines rust and cream colours with a 1920s arty feel, making the 171-room hotel feel both languidly chic and up-to-the-minute modern. Luxurious touches include 49-inch HDTVs, and there are spectacular views of the skyline from the 16th-floor suites. Downstairs, the Green Room serves farm-to-table breakfast, while the Mortimer is a chic cocktail lounge.

Moderate

Hotel Bijou

111 Mason Street, at Eddy Street, CA 94102 (1-415 771 1200, www.hotelbijou.com). BART & Metro to Powell/bus 14, 27, 30, 31, 38 & Market Street routes/cable car Powell-Hyde or Powell-Mason. **Map** *p313 M6.*

If you're happy in this slightly edgy pocket of the Tenderloin, you'll appreciate this hotel's proximity to Market Street. Cinephiles will love the cleverly executed homage to 1930s movie houses: walls are covered in black-and-white images of old cinema marquees, and local film schedules are posted on a board. Best of all, there's a mini-theatre with vintage cinema seating, in which guests can enjoy nightly viewings (albeit on a TV). All of the comfortably stylish rooms are named after a movie shot in the city. Free pastries, coffee and tea in the morning will help you to face the all-too-real world outside.

Hotel Metropolis

25 Mason Street, at Turk Street, CA 94102 (1-415 775 4600, www.hotelmetropolis.com). BART & Metro to Powell/bus 14, 27, 30, 31 & Market Street routes/cable car Powell-Hyde. **Map** *p313 M6.*

An oasis where Market Street turns dodgy (especially at night), the Metropolis is eco-friendly yin meets mid-priced yang, with each floor colour-coded in shades of olive green (earth), taupe (wind), yellow (fire) and aquamarine (water). The compact quarters have pleasantly understated furnishings: one of the suites, specially designed for kids, has bunk beds, a blackboard and toys. Cable TV and better-than-average toiletries complete the comforts. From the tenth floor, where some rooms have balconies, there are splendid views to the Oakland Hills. Facilities include a small library, tiny workout room (ask for

ESSENTIAL INFORMATION

discounted passes to a nearby gym) and small meditation space. You can expect some street noise at night, but bargain hunters will be happy.

Phoenix Hotel
601 Eddy Street, at Larkin Street, CA 94109 (1-415 776 1380, www.thephoenixhotel.com). Bus 19, 31, 38. **Map** p312 K6.
Add funky styling to affordable rates and parking for tour buses in a 'gritty' neighbourhood, and then sit back and watch the hipsters roll in. That's certainly the way things have worked at the Phoenix, which has housed a who's who of upcoming musical talent on tour – everyone from Red Hot Chili Peppers to the Killers. Rooms are bright and casual, but they're not the main draw. Moody-cool Chambers Eat + Drink serves New American-style tapas, with booths backing up to walls of vintage vinyl and sultry images of glamour girls. The heated courtyard swimming pool is a bonus, and a free continental breakfast is served poolside.

Budget

Touchstone Hotel
480 Geary Street, between Mason & Taylor Streets, CA 94102 (1-415 771 1600, www.thetouchstone. com). BART & Metro to Powell/bus 2, 3, 27, 31, 38/cable car Powell-Hyde or Powell-Mason. **Map** p312 L5.
This family-run hotel offers good-value basic accommodation in an excellent location (it's two blocks from Union Square and virtually next door to the pricier Clift). Rooms are small and come with few frills, but they're all clean and well appointed, with complimentary bottled water and organic toiletries. The Jewish deli downstairs is a local institution, popular with theatregoers for the pastrami on rye, and with guests for the made-to-order breakfasts with organic coffee.

CIVIC CENTER

Moderate

★ Inn at the Opera
333 Fulton Street, between Gough & Franklin Streets, CA 94102 (1-415 863 8400, www.shell hospitality.com/inn-at-the-opera). BART & Metro to Civic Center/bus 5, 21, 47, 49, 90. **Map** p316 J7.
Tagged by crooner Tony Bennett as the 'best romantic hotel I know', this charmer is popular with a culturally motivated older crowd, thanks to its handy location near the Opera House, Davies Symphony Hall and the shops of Hayes Valley. Framed portraits of composers hang on the walls, and the sound systems in every room are tuned to classical stations. Rooms are fairly handsome and spacious, and most have kitchenettes (a continental breakfast buffet is complimentary). The restaurant, Pläj, features Scandinavian-inspired cuisine.

Budget

Edwardian Inn
1668 Market Street, between Rose & Haight Streets, CA 94102 (1-415 864 1271, www.edwardiansf. com). Metro to Van Ness/bus 6, 9, 14, 47, 49, 71, 90. **Map** p316 K8.
This European-style hotel is one of the best bargains in the area, offering charm and tidiness for a relative song. The inn's location is a plus: it's close to various performing-arts venues and offers easy access to Market Street transportation. Some rooms are small, but all have private bathrooms (some with jetted tubs), and feature good-quality bedlinens and nice touches such as freshly cut flowers.

SoMa & South Beach

Expensive

Hotel Zetta
55 5th Street, between Mission & Market Streets (1-415 543 8555, www.viceroyhotelgroup.com). BART & Metro to Powell/bus 14, 30, 38, 45 & Market Street routes/cable car Powell-Hyde or Powell-Mason. **Map** p313 M6.
A giant Plinko board rises in the lobby of this art-filled hotel just south of Union Square, whose mezzanine games room suits the overworked Silicon Valley techies who are its target market. Built in 1903 and completely gutted in 2013 by the Viceroy Hotel Group, the 116-room property is up with all the latest gadgets. The design theme plays off salvage and rescue (which is also the name of the lobby bar), and repurposed materials are everywhere, as in the lobby's tiered chandelier of cast-off eyeglasses. Rooms are larger than average, uncluttered and whisper-quiet, with giant butcher-block architect's desks, plush beds with 500-thread-count sheets, and Bluetooth pairing to link your gadgets with the 47-inch TV and Jambox speaker. The onsite Cavalier brasserie is a top dining destination in its own right, serving stick-to-your-ribs British favourites such as fish and chips or meat pies.

St Regis Hotel
125 3rd Street, at Mission Street, CA 94103 (1-415 284 4000, www.stregis.com). BART & Metro to Montgomery/bus 12, 30, 38, 45 & Market Street routes. **Map** p313 N6.
The pinnacle of SoMa's museum district and a worthy rival to the nearby Four Seasons, this 40-storey hotel and condominium tower has redefined luxury (and how much people are willing to pay for it). Guest quarters come with butler service, limestone baths, and high-tech fixtures such as in-room scanner/copiers, and flat-screen TVs in the bathroom; rooms on the sixth floor and above have the best city views. A combination of new and old construction, the property includes sprawling spa facilities with a heated

Good Hotel.

indoor infinity pool, the Museum of the African Diaspora, and two restaurants, Ame and Vitrine, patronised by the city's foodie elite.

W Hotel

181 3rd Street, at Howard Street, CA 94103 (1-415 777 5300, www.whotels.com). BART & Metro to Montgomery/bus 12, 30, 38, 45 & Market Street routes. **Map** p313 N6.

As this trailblazing, chic-urban hotel chain continues to expand around the world, it's lost a bit of its cachet, but still manages to exude enough cool to attract trendy tech crowds and SoMa partiers. For that, full credit goes to the design, which eschews grand flourishes in favour of a modern, unobtrusive stylishness in both the guest quarters and the public spaces, and the in-house restaurant, TRACE, which offers sustainable, locally sourced cuisine in a modernist nightclubby setting. Immediately on entering the hotel, you'll find yourself in a buzzing lobby bar, crowded with visitors and after-work locals. The rooms are modern and loaded up with indulgences: 37-inch flatscreen TVs, goose-down duvets and pillow menus. The Bliss Spa includes manicures with movies, and men's and women's lounges.

Moderate

Good Hotel

112 7th Street, between Mission & Minna Streets (1-415 621 7001, www.thegoodhotel.com). BART & Metro to Civic Center/Bus 14 & Market Street routes. **Map** p316 L7.

This simple hotel plays to an under-30 demographic, with a dorm-room aesthetic and a green emphasis – repurposed-glass chandeliers, salvaged-wood bed frames and fleece bedspreads made from recycled soda bottles. The look is playful, fun and decidedly non-generic. Most rooms are in a five-storey 1911 building, converted in 2008, with multiple bed configurations, perfect for groups of friends travelling together. An adjoining two-storey 1950s-era motel has rooms with air-conditioning; these are best if you have a car and want easy access to on-site parking (free for hybrid cars). The in-between neighbourhood can be sketchy, but it's generally safe and fairly close to the Metro.

★ Mosser

54 4th Street, between Market & Mission Streets (1-415 986 4400, www.themosser.com). BART & Metro to Powell/bus 14, 30, 38, 45 & Market Street routes/cable car Powell-Hyde or Powell-Mason. **Map** p313 M6.

At this well-priced, eco-friendly hotel, a distinguished-looking Victorian lobby leads to spruced-up modern rooms that are compact, but chic and comfortable with clever use of space. The simple but effective colour scheme combines white walls with pops of bright accents. A few rooms are available with shared bathroom facilities, hence the very reasonable charges at the lower end of the price scale. The location of the Mosser is ideal: a block from Yerba Buena Center and the Westfield Shopping Centre.

Nob Hill & Chinatown

NOB HILL

The **Stanford Court** (905 California Street, CA 94108, 1-415 989 3500, www.stanfordcourt. com) and the upmarket **Mark Hopkins InterContinental** (1 Nob Hill, CA 94108, 1-415 392 3434, www.san-francisco.intercontinental. com) are also recommended.

Expensive

Fairmont San Francisco

950 Mason Street, between California & Sacramento Streets, CA 94108 (1-415 772 5000, www.fairmont.com). Bus 12, 19, 27, 47, 91, 292, 397, KX. **Map** p312 L4.

High on Nob Hill, the Fairmont is one of the city's grandest hotels, listed on the National Register of Historic Places. Tony Bennett debuted 'I Left My Heart in San Francisco' here in 1961. The main building was built in 1908 and the lobby reveals traces of the Gilded Age in polished marble floors that reflect the glow of century-old crystal chandeliers, and rows of yellow-marble Corinthian columns soaring two storeys high. The 1920s-designed Presidential Suite is the most opulent hotel room in town, covering the entire eighth floor; it even has a movable bookcase for secret escapes to the rooftop's former helipad. Service is high-end business class and rooms underwent a total make-over in 2014. Choose between the original main building or the 1960s tower. Rooms in the main building have high ceilings and crown mouldings, and feel grand for their proportions. Tower rooms are boxy with lower ceilings, but have incredible bay and city views, especially from high floors. All are furnished with sumptuous beds and marble baths. At the tiki-themed Tonga Room & Hurricane Bar, a dance band plays standards, and artificial thunderstorms rain down hourly on the floating bandstand. A classic SF experience.

Fairmont San Francisco.

Ritz-Carlton

600 Stockton Street, at California Street, CA 94108 (1-800 241 3333, 1-415 296 7465, www.ritzcarlton. com). Bus 1, 2, 3, 30, 45, 91/cable car California, Powell-Hyde or Powell-Mason. **Map** p313 M4.

The Ritz-Carlton has been the de facto choice for dignitaries and heads of state for years. As you might expect, then, the rooms and suites are sumptuously appointed and stocked with luxurious 46-inch HD TVs, Italian marble bathrooms and Frette linens. On-site amenities include an indoor spa with gym, swimming pool, whirlpool and sauna; Parallel 37, a critically acclaimed American-style restaurant; daily piano performances in the Lounge; and an armada of valets to meet your every need. Mere mortals can pop in for the lavish Sunday Jazz Brunch, held on a sunken roof terrace.

★ Scarlet Huntington

1075 California Street, at Taylor Street, CA 94108 (1-800 227 4683, 1-415 474 5400, www.thescarlet hotels.com). Bus 1, 2, 3, 27/cable car California, Powell-Hyde or Powell-Mason. **Map** p312 L5.

One of San Francisco's grande dame hotels, this Old-World property exudes understated luxury. The hotel is perched high on Nob Hill, and the well-appointed rooms and suites offer Irish linens, iPod clock radios and eye-popping views of the city. Indulge in a treatment at the lush Nob Hill Spa (1-415 345 2888), which has a small 'relaxation pool' overlooking Union Square. Of course, you'll pay for the privilege: if you have to check the rates before booking, you're probably in the wrong place. The California cable car line rattles past the front door.

Moderate

White Swan Inn

845 Bush Street, between Taylor & Mason Streets, CA 94108 (1-415 775 1755, www.whiteswaninnsf. com). Bus 2, 3, 27, 38/cable car Powell-Hyde or Powell-Mason. **Map** p312 L5.

The White Swan is essentially a Californian version of an English B&B, and how you just reacted to that sentence will be pretty much how you react to the inn itself. Some people will find it quaint and delightful, while others will take one look, throw both hands in the air, scream 'Chintz!' and walk swiftly from the premises. Either way, the evening wine receptions and breakfast buffet with freshly baked bread are nice touches , as are the fireplaces in all the rooms, and the staff are charmers. Next door, the Petite Auberge (www.petiteaubergesf.com) is a cheaper, French country version of the Swan, with many of the same amenities.

Budget

Andrews Hotel

624 Post Street, between Jones & Taylor Streets, CA 94109 (1-415 563 6877, www.andrewshotel.com).

BART & Metro to Powell/bus 2, 3, 4, 27, 38, 76/cable car Powell-Hyde or Powell-Mason. **Map** p312 L5.

This handsome 1905 Queen Anne structure, formerly the opulent Sultan Turkish Baths, offers well-priced, well-kept guest rooms that, while hardly stylish, offer their fair share of creature comforts, including down duvets, flatscreen TVs and free Wi-Fi. In the morning, coffee and complimentary fresh-baked croissants and muffins are served at stations just outside your room. Fino, the hotel's restaurant, is a pleasant spot for Italian food, and lists plenty of vegetarian options on its menu. The main drawback of the Andrews Hotel is that the walls are on the thin side – but that's true of many vintage buildings.

Golden Gate Hotel

775 Bush Street, between Powell & Mason Streets, CA 94108 (1-415 392 3702, www.goldengatehotel. com). Bus 2, 3, 27, 38/cable car Powell-Hyde or Powell-Mason. **Map** p312 L5.

This 1913 Edwardian hotel is a real charmer – a little creaky in places, certainly, but generally delightful. Rooms vary in style a fair bit, thanks to the presence throughout of one-of-a-kind antiques, but the majority are cosy and easy on the eye; many have claw-foot tubs. The welcome from owners John and Renate Kenaston, not to mention the hotel dog and cat, couldn't be warmer (or the oatmeal cookies fresher). The traffic noise from busy Bush Street isn't as bad as you might expect, but light sleepers should ask for a room in the back.

CHINATOWN

Moderate

Orchard Garden Hotel

466 Bush Street, between Grant & Kearny Streets, CA 94108 (1-415 399 9807, www.theorchard gardenhotel.com). Bus 1, 2, 3, 30, 38, 45, 91/ cable car Powell-Hyde or Powell-Market. **Map** p313 M5.

Opened in 2007, the Orchard Garden was only the fourth hotel in the world to win LEED (Leadership in Energy & Environmental Design) certification, meaning it was designed according to strict environmental standards. Chemical-free cleaning products are used in its energy-saving rooms (the lights go off when you're not there), which are large by boutique hotel standards (and surprisingly quiet); furnishings sport a pale green and light wood palette. The lobby-level restaurant relies on organic, seasonal ingredients. The fitness centre is petite, but discounted day passes are available to larger gyms nearby; the rooftop garden beckons in fair weather. A few blocks away on Bush Street, between Stockton and Powell, is its sister operation, the similarly pleasant and modern – though not as green – Orchard Hotel.

ESSENTIAL INFORMATION

North Beach & Around

NORTH BEACH

Moderate

★ Hotel Bohème

444 Columbus Avenue, between Vallejo & Green Streets, CA 94133 (1-415 433 9111, www.hotel boheme.com). Bus 10, 12, 30, 39, 41, 45, 91. **Map** p313 M3.

Built in the 1880s by an Italian immigrant family, the original hotel was dynamited in an unsuccessful attempt to create a firebreak after the 1906 earthquake. Rebuilt, it was converted in 1995 to the Hotel Bohème, which positively brims with North Beach Beat-era history. The walls are lined with smoky black-and-white photos of 1950s jazz luminaries, fragments of poetry turn up everywhere and you may even sleep in Allen Ginsberg's room (no.204): in his last years he was often seen here, looking out of the bay window, tapping away on his laptop (Wi-Fi access is free). The rooms are pretty tiny, on the whole, but you'll be surrounded by cafés and restaurants. For quieter nights, request a room not facing bustling Columbus Avenue.

▶ *The famous City Lights bookstore (see p100) is just up the street.*

Washington Square Inn

1660 Stockton Street, between Union & Filbert Streets, CA 94133 (1-415 981 4220, www.wsisf. com). Bus 10, 12, 30, 39, 41, 45, 91. **Map** p313 M3. Close to one of San Francisco's prettiest urban parks, in a quiet part of North Beach, this convivial little inn is beautifully decorated with large gilt mirrors, pots of exotic orchids and lots of character. Each of the smallish rooms is furnished with antiques and luxurious fabrics. While all have dedicated bathrooms, a couple are across the hall from the room. The service is excellent: guests are provided with tea, wine and hors d'oeuvres every afternoon. The rates also include Wi-Fi and a decent continental breakfast – though you'd be foolish to forgo getting in line early for the outstanding breakfasts at Mama's across the square.

Budget

San Remo Hotel

2237 Mason Street, at Bay Street, CA 94133 (1-415 776 8688, www.sanremohotel.com). Bus 30, 39, 47, 91/cable car Powell-Mason. **Map** p312 L2.

It's difficult to imagine this meticulously restored Italianate Edwardian serving as a boarding house for dockworkers displaced by the Great Fire. Although guest rooms are on the small side and the spotless shower rooms are shared (there's also one bath), you'd be hard-pressed to find a finer hotel in

San Francisco at this price. Features include brass or iron-framed beds, pinewood furniture, and Oriental-style rugs. Be forewarned that some rooms face interior hallways: if you value fresh air, book an exterior room. For a splurge, book the Penthouse Room, a freestanding rooftop shack with en-suite bathroom and knockout views. There are no TVs and no elevator – plan to climb stairs.

FISHERMAN'S WHARF

There are two big-chain favourites of tour groups and meeting planners in the area: the lively, brightly renovated 529-room **Sheraton Fisherman's Wharf** (2500 Mason Street, CA 94133, 1-877 271 2018, 1-415 362 5500, www. sheratonatthewharf.com) and the 313-room, family-friendly **Hyatt Fisherman's Wharf** (555 North Point Street, CA 94133, 1-888 591 1234, 1-415 563 1234, www.fishermanswharf. hyatt.com).

Expensive

Argonaut Hotel

495 Jefferson Street, at Hyde Street, CA 94109 (1-415 563 0800, www.argonauthotel.com). Streetcar F/bus 19, 30, 47, 91/cable car Powell-Hyde. **Map** p312 K2.

The top hotel at Fisherman's Wharf occupies a vast former Del Monte cannery, built in 1907 of giant timbers and red brick salvaged from the 1906 earthquake. Located directly opposite Hyde Street Pier, the property celebrates the city's seafaring past, evidenced in the blue and yellow maritime decor and the abundant nautical props. The enormous lobby adjoins a Parks Service visitor centre, with glorious displays of model yachts, lighthouse lenses and a recreation of the Gold Rush-era San Francisco waterfront. Rooms are fittingly decorated in a nautical theme, with anchor prints, porthole-shaped mirrors and plush indigo carpet. Breakfast is served in the Blue Mermaid on the ground floor. At 10.30am on Saturdays and Sundays, National Park Service rangers lead free tours of the park and wharf, beginning in the hotel's lobby.

The Mission & the Castro

THE MISSION

Moderate

Inn San Francisco

943 S Van Ness Avenue, between 20th & 21st Streets, CA 94110 (1-415 641 0188, www.innsf. com). BART to 24th Street Mission/bus 12, 14, 49. **Map** p316 K11.

ESSENTIAL INFORMATION

RALSTON'S PALACE

The rise, fall and rise of a landmark hotel.

One of San Francisco's most famous hotels, the **Palace** (*see p277*) was the vision of financier William Ralston, whose meteoric rise and tragic fall are as steeped in San Francisco lore as the hotel itself. Ralston began work on the hotel in 1873, part of his grand vision to make San Francisco a world-class metropolis. Two years later, just days before his dream was to become reality, Ralston was found floating in the Bay. William Sharon, one of his partners, had created a run on the Bank of California, which Ralston had co-founded in 1864, by selling massive portions of his holdings. As depositors panicked and attempted to withdraw their money, it was found that Ralston had been using the bank's capital to fund his private investments. Early on the morning of 27 August 1875, Ralston resigned and went to take his daily swim off North Beach; his body was recovered later that day.

Barely five weeks later, on 2 October 1875, the Bank of California reopened its doors. On the same day, right on schedule despite its owner's death, the Palace Hotel welcomed the first members of the public as the largest and most lavish hotel in the country, offering modern innovations that included electric call buttons in each room, plumbing and private toilets, and the first hydraulic elevators in the West.

The hotel survived the 1906 earthquake, but not the fire that followed. When the blaze threatened to destroy Market Street, firemen tapped the Palace's massive reservoir system to fight the flames. But after the hotel's emergency tanks were exhausted, the 'Grande Dame of the West' was left to burn and had to be demolished.

A very different Palace soon rose in its place. American illustrator Maxfield Parrish was commissioned to paint a mural for the hotel's 1909 reopening; the result was the 7ftx16ft *Pied Piper of Hamelin*, which still hangs behind the bar in Maxfield's, the hotel's watering hole. On the opposite wall are photos of the Palace's many famous guests, who have included Thomas Edison, Winston Churchill, Charlie Chaplin, Oscar Wilde and President Ulysses S Grant. In fact, the Palace was the site of perhaps the most mysterious presidential death in American history: Warren G Harding passed away in the Presidential Suite in August 1923, though no one has been able to say for sure how he died.

The hotel also suffered the effects of the Loma Prieta earthquake in 1989. While the damage wasn't extensive, the owners took the opportunity to close it for restoration. Today, the dining rooms and public spaces are breathtaking, with a spectacular 80,000 panes of stained glass in the Garden Court's ceiling dome and a covered swimming pool that is by far the finest in the city. Free tours of the hotel are offered on Saturday mornings through San Francisco City Guides (www. sfcityguides.org).

ESSENTIAL INFORMATION

The friendly staff at this 1872 Italianate Victorian inn encourage you to relax in the beautifully restored sitting rooms. You can also take advantage of the garden hot tub or the panoramic city views from the rooftop if your antiques-bedecked room starts to feel a bit too cosy. All but two of the rooms have private bathrooms; thick rugs and carpets help to muffle the noise common to older hotels. However, if you're here to check out the huge number of bars and restaurants in the Mission, then you probably won't be going to bed early. The ample breakfast buffet is served until 11am, allowing late sleepers a chance to restore themselves.

Parker House
520 Church Street, between 17th & 18th Streets, CA 94114 (1-888 520 7275, www.parkerguesthouse. com). Metro to Castro or Church & 18th Street/ bus 22, 33. **Map** *p316 J10.*
A couple of blocks from the heart of the Castro, this smartly renovated Victorian (with an Edwardian annex) caters to gay and lesbian travellers, but everyone's welcome. Most rooms have private bathrooms, and all feature homely, contemporary decor. There are slight variations in amenities (dataports, desk sizes, shower versus bath), so let the staff know if you have special requests when booking. The English gardens provide respite from the bustling street scene on sunny days. Continental breakfast, internet access and a wine social are included in the rates.

The Haight & Around

HAIGHT-ASHBURY
Moderate

Stanyan Park Hotel
750 Stanyan Street, at Waller Street, CA 94117 (1-415 751 1000, www.stanyanpark.com). Metro to Carl & Cole/bus 6, 33, 37, 43, 66, 71. **Map** *p315 E9.*
This beautifully maintained, three-storey Victorian building on the edge of Golden Gate Park has been accommodating travellers in fine style since 1904; it's even listed on the National Register of Historic Places. The handsome rooms (size and views vary) are decorated with Victorian antiques and period furnishings. Large groups may be attracted to the six big suites with full kitchens, dining rooms and living spaces – great for extended stays. Rates include free Wi-Fi, breakfast and afternoon tea.

THE WESTERN ADDITION
Moderate

Queen Anne Hotel
1590 Sutter Street, at Octavia Street, CA 94109 (1-800 227 3970, 1-415 441 2828, www.queen anne.com). Bus 2, 3, 38, 47, 49, 90. **Map** *p312 J6.*

Queen Anne Hotel.

One of the more successful Old-World hotel operations in San Francisco, the Queen Anne is, as its name suggests, housed in an extremely handsome Victorian property. Having begun life as a finishing school for the city's posh young debs (the headmistress, Mary Lake, is rumoured to haunt her former office, now Room 410), it was converted into a hotel in the 1980s. Each of the individually decorated rooms contains Victorian antiques, and the lobby area is a splendid space. Continental breakfast, afternoon tea and sherry, and a weekday-morning downtown car service are all included in the rate, and guests also receive a discount on day passes to the posh Cathedral Hill Plaza Athletic Club two blocks away.

Budget

Metro Hotel
319 Divisadero Street, between Oak & Page Streets, CA 94117 (1-415 861 5364, www.metrohotelsf. com). Bus 6, 21, 24, 71. **Map** *p315 G8.*
The 24-room Metro is cheap, convenient and a good base for exploring neighbourhoods off the tourist track. The decor is bare-bones, the walls are a little thin and the street-side rooms are noisy at night. Still, at these prices, complaining seems a little churlish. Request a room overlooking the back garden.

ESSENTIAL INFORMATION

Pacific Heights & the Marina

PACIFIC HEIGHTS

Expensive

Hotel Drisco
2901 Pacific Avenue, at Broderick Street, CA 94115 (1-415 346 2880, www.hoteldrisco.com). Bus 3, 24. **Map** p311 F5.
The Hotel Drisco has been in business for more than a century, but the contemporary-classic rooms only pay gentle homage to its history. (A few rooms have private but detached bathrooms down a hall.) Freebies include a morning town car service to the Financial District (weekdays), a breakfast buffet, wine and cheese in the evenings, and a pass to the Presidio YMCA.

Moderate

Jackson Court
2198 Jackson Street, at Buchanan Street, CA 94115 (1-415 929 7670, www.jacksoncourt.com). Bus 1, 3, 10, 22, 24. **Map** p312 H4.

This fantastic neighbourhood B&B is still, happily, flying under most visitors' radar. Located on a calm residential stretch of tony Pacific Heights, Jackson Court is built into a beautiful 19th-century brownstone mansion and is as quiet as a church. Each of the eight rooms and two suites is furnished with a soothing combination of antiques and contemporary pieces; all have private bathrooms and some have working fireplaces. Rates include continental breakfast and afternoon tea.

Laurel Inn
444 Presidio Avenue, between California & Sacramento Streets, CA 94115 (1-415 567 8467, www.jdvhotels.com). Bus 1, 2, 3, 43. **Map** p311 F5.
A motor inn renovated in midcentury modern style, this gem packs plenty of hip into a modest shell. The rooms are chic, with great bathroom amenities and modern accessories; some also have kitchenettes and city views. Located well off the downtown path, the Laurel nonetheless has easy bus transport options just out front. The lobby level is home to the popular Swank Cocktail Club (*see p119*), which brings in the scenesters on weekend nights. Service is excellent, continental breakfast is included, and there are great restaurants close at hand.

COW HOLLOW
Moderate

Hotel Del Sol

3100 Webster Street, at Greenwich Street, CA 94123 (1-415 921 5520, www.jdvhotels.com). Bus 22, 28, 30, 41, 43, 45, 91. **Map** p311 H3.

This former 1950s motel was made over with a splashy tropical palette and hip decor that separates it from the many no-tell motels along the Lombard strip. A (very rare) outdoor pool gives it another edge. The 47 rooms and ten suites (three with kitchenettes, two with fireplaces) are decorated with bright crayon colours; cool details include clock radios that wake guests to the sound of rain or waves. The family suite has bunkbeds, toys, books and games. Complimentary coffee, tea and muffins are served by the pool each morning, and the free parking is a valuable commodity in these parts.

Union Street Inn

2229 Union Street, between Fillmore & Steiner Streets, CA 94123 (1-415 346 0424,
www.unionstreetinn.com). Bus 22, 28, 41, 43, 45, 91. **Map** p311 G4.

Rooms at this B&B are furnished in traditional style, with canopied or brass beds, feather duvets and fresh flowers. All have private bathrooms, some of them with Jacuzzi tubs. The English Garden room has a private deck, while the Carriage House behind the inn has its own garden. An extended continental breakfast can be taken in the parlour, in your room or on a terrace overlooking the hotel garden. Evening wine and hors d'oeuvres are included in the price.

THE MARINA &
THE WATERFRONT
Moderate

Inn at the Presidio

42 Moraga Avenue, at Funston Avenue, CA 94129 (1-415 800 7356, www.innatthepresidio.com). Bus 43. **Map** p310 D4.

This mellow alternative to downtown hotels is run by the National Park Service in the Presidio overlooking the Golden Gate Promenade. The red-brick inn was

Hotel Del Sol.

originally built in 1903 to house bachelor officers, and in 2010 was converted to a boutique B&B. Seventeen of the 22 rooms are 530sq ft one-bedroom suites, but even standard rooms are gigantic. All are tastefully turned out, with distressed leather furniture and white-on-white damask sheets. Some ground-floor rooms open straight on to a rocking-chair veranda. Outside is a wonderfully atmospheric fire pit, views of the Golden Gate Bridge and 24 miles of hiking trails. The obvious drawback is the out-of-the-way location, but free daytime shuttles get you there in 30 minutes. Trust us – waking up in this glorious national park more than compensates.

Budget

Marina Inn

3110 Octavia Street, at Lombard Street, CA 94123 (1-800 274 1420, 1-415 928 1000, www. marinainn.com). Bus 28, 30, 91. **Map** *p312 H3.*
Spread over four floors of this quiet Victorian-style inn (it actually dates to 1924), rooms are all furnished with floral wallpaper, pine fittings and four-poster beds. Continental breakfast is included.

Sunset & Richmond
Budget

Seal Rock Inn

545 Point Lobos Avenue, at 48th Avenue, Richmond, CA 94121 (1-415 752 8000, www. sealrockinn.com). Bus 38.
San Francisco doesn't really do beach motels, but this 1960s motor lodge comes pretty close. Most of the large, spotless rooms have at least partial ocean views, and at night you can fall asleep to the sound of distant foghorns. Furnishings won't win any awards, but most of the third-floor rooms have wood-burning fireplaces (in this foggy part of town, these book up early). Family-sized units include a folding vinyl wall for a bit of privacy, and all accommodation includes a mini-fridge and coffee maker, or a kitchenette. Seal Rock is across from the Cliff House, perched on the edge of the Pacific, and has free covered parking, a patio and, for the thick of skin, a heated outdoor pool.

Hostels
Adelaide Hostel

5 Isadora Duncan Lane, off Taylor Street, between Post & Geary Streets, Tenderloin, CA 94102 (1-415 359 1915, www.adelaidehostel.com). Bus 2, 3, 27, 31, 38/cable car Powell-Hyde or Powell-Mason. **Map** *p312 L5.*
Until 2003, the Adelaide was a friendly, old-fashioned pension, but the owners expanded the 18 rooms to add six en-suites and two 12-bed dormitories. Accommodation starts at a mere $38 – including continental breakfast and internet access.

HI-San Francisco Downtown

312 Mason Street, at O'Farrell Street, Union Square & Around, CA 94102 (1-888 464 4872, 1-415 788 5604, www.sfhostels.com). BART & Metro to Powell/bus 2, 3, 4, 30, 38, 76 & Market Street routes/cable car Powell-Hyde or Powell-Mason. **Map** *p313 M6.*
Make your reservation at least five weeks in advance during high season to stay at this popular 260-bed hostel. It prides itself on its privacy and security, with guests accommodated in small single-sex rooms; some larger rooms also have their own bathroom. Beds for walk-ins are available on a first-come, first-served basis; bring ID or you'll be turned away. Rates include breakfast and Wi-Fi.

Hostelling International runs two other hostels in SF. The 75-room City Center hostel (685 Ellis Street, between Larkin & Hyde Streets, Tenderloin, 1-415 474 5721) has been refurbished to a good standard, while the Fisherman's Wharf location (Building 240, Fort Mason, at Bay & Franklin Streets, Marina, 1-415 771 7277) offers a wide variety of rooms (some private), free parking and great views of the Bay.

ESSENTIAL INFORMATION

Getting Around

ESSENTIAL INFORMATION

ARRIVING & LEAVING

By air

San Francisco International Airport (SFO)
1-650 821 8211, 1-800 435 9736, www.flysfo.com.
SFO lies 14 miles south of the city, near US101. If you're staying downtown, take the train from the **BART** station in the International terminal (accessible from all terminals via SFO's free Airtrain). The journey to town costs $8.65 and takes 30mins; trains leave SFO from 4am to 11.50pm. BART is a far better bet than the three **SamTrans bus routes** – the KX, the 292, the 140, the 398 and the 24-hour 397 – that serve SFO (fares vary from $2 to $5); the buses can take ages to make the journey from the airport to the city.

Shuttle vans, which hold eight to 12 people and offer door-to-door service, are a more direct option. Shuttles operate on a walk-up basis at the airport, though you must book for your return journey. Firms include **SuperShuttle** (1-800 258 3826, www.supershuttle.com) and **American Airporter Shuttle** (1-415 202 0733, www. americanairporter.com); the airport's website has a full list. The fare into San Francisco will be around $16; ask about discounted rates for two or more travellers in the same party. Vans leave regularly from the upper level of the terminal: follow the red 'passenger van' signs outside the baggage-claim area.

Taxis run to and from SFO, though they're pricey: expect to pay around $50 plus tip, though you might be able to haggle a flat rate. For a limousine, use the toll-free white courtesy phones located in the terminal to summon a car (walk-up service isn't permitted). The fare will likely be at least $60 plus tip.

You can also use your mobile phone to request web-based car service **Uber** or **Lyft** (and brave the wrath of taxis). Uber cars are only authorised on the departure level.

Mineta San Jose International Airport (SJC)
1-408 392 3600/www.flysanjose.com.
SJC is the airport of choice for many Silicon Valley travellers. However, those without cars but with San Francisco lodgings face a lengthy and/or pricey journey to the city. Without a car, the best way to get to San Francisco from SJC is by train. Ride the **Airport Flyer bus** (20mins) from the airport to Santa Clara station, then take the **Caltrain** service to San Francisco station (4th & King Streets, $9.25, 90mins). Door-to-door shuttle vans, available on a walk-up basis, are quicker, but cost up to $90. A **taxi** will set you back $130 plus tip.

Oakland International Airport (OAK)
1-510 563 3300, www.flyoakland.com.
The ride into San Francisco from Oakland Airport is simple by train. The **AirBART** bus shuttle links the airport to the Coliseum/Oakland Airport **BART** station; the ride costs $6 and takes 15-20mins. From the station, take the next Daly City or Millbrae train to San Francisco ($4.05; about 25mins to downtown). Note: this is not a safe option for lone passengers at night. Instead, take one of the myriad **shuttle vans**, available on a walk-up basis, or a very expensive taxi/limo ride.

Major airlines

Air Canada *1-888 247 2262, www.aircanada.com.*
American Airlines *1-800 433 7300, www.aa.com.*
British Airways *1-800 247 9297, www.britishairways.com.*
Delta *domestic 1-800 221 1212, international 1-800 241 4141, www.delta.com.*
Southwest *1-800 435 9792, www.southwest.com.*
United Airlines *domestic 1-800 864 8331, international 1-800 538 2929, www.united.com.*
US Airways *1-800 428 4322, www.usairways.com.*
Virgin Atlantic *1-800 862 8621, www.virginatlantic.com.*
Virgin America *1-877 359 8474, www.virginamerica.com.*

By train

Until the **Transbay Transit Center** (www.transbaycenter.org) is completed, the nearest **Amtrak** station for national rail services is in Emeryville, in the East Bay (5885 Horton Street, www.amtrak.com). Amtrak's **Thruway bus service** connects the station to several central San Francisco stops in about an hour. Designed by Pelli Clarke Pelli Architects and scheduled to open in late 2017, the so-called 'Grand Central Terminal of the West' will feature a 1,400ft-long rooftop park, shops and restaurants.

By bus

National bus services, run by **Greyhound**, arrive and depart from the temporary terminal at 200 Folsom Street, between Beale & Main Streets, SoMa (1-415 495 1569, www.greyhound.com) until the new Transbay Transit Center opens.

PUBLIC TRANSPORT

San Francisco's mass-transit network is comprehensive and efficient. Buses, Metro – operating both underground and at street level – and cable cars are run by the **San Francisco Municipal Railway**, aka **Muni** (www.sfmta. com, 1-415 701-2311 or 311 within San Francisco), while the **Bay Area Rapid Transit rail network**, aka **BART** (1-415 989 2278, www.bart. gov), connects San Francisco to Oakland, Berkeley and beyond. Maps and timetables are available online, and free leaflets available at stations offer details on popular routes and services. However, Muni's system-wide Street & Transit Map ($3) is always a sound investment, available from bookshops, drugstores and the **SFVIC** (*see p297*). Further details on Bay Area transit, including route guidance, can be found at www. transit.511.org, or by calling 511 from a local phone.

Fares & tickets

If you plan to travel often in the Bay Area, the **Clipper card** may help: the reusable ticket is valid on all major transit networks, including Muni, BART and Caltrain. Tag the Clipper card when you start your journey (and, on BART, when you exit). The cost of the ride will be deducted, and any remaining value can be used on your next trip. When the card runs low, add funds at machines around the transit network. Clipper cards are available online and at shops displaying the Clipper logo; for more information, see www.clippercard.com.

Alternatively, the **Passport**, valid for unlimited travel on all Muni vehicles (but not BART trains), is aimed at tourists. Passports are valid for one day ($17), three days ($26) and seven days ($35), and are sold at the the **SFVIC** (*see p297*) or the cable car ticket booths, both downtown at Powell and Market, Ghirardelli Square at Hyde and Beach Streets, and in Fisherman's Wharf at Bay and Taylor Streets, Montgomery metro station, the TIX booth in Union Square, the SFMTA Customer Service Centre and SFO.

Monthly Muni passes are valid from the first of the month until three days into the following month. The **A Pass** ($83) is also valid on the eight BART stations within the city of San Francisco, but not beyond (so you'll have to pay extra to get to Oakland, Berkeley and SFO). The **M Pass** ($70) is valid only on Muni. Monthly passes are available at the locations listed above, with the exception of TIX.

BART

Bay Area Rapid Transit is a network of five high-speed rail lines serving San Francisco, Daly City, Millbrae and SFO Airport, and the East Bay. It's modern and efficient, run by computers at Oakland's Lake Merritt station, with announcements, trains, ticket dispensers, exit and entry gates all automated. BART is of minor use for getting around San Francisco – it only has eight stops in the city – four on Market Street, two on Mission Street and two further south – but it's the best way to get to Berkeley and Oakland and a convenient way to get to the airport from Downtown.

Fares vary by destination, from $1.85 to $11.25. Machines at each station dispense reusable tickets encoded with the amount of money you entered (cash and credit cards are both valid). Your fare will be deducted from this total when you end your journey, and any remaining value will be valid for future trips. You can add value to the card at all ticket machines.

Stations are marked with blue and white signs at street level. Trains run from 4am on weekdays, 6am on Saturday and 8am on Sunday, and shut down around midnight. For further information see www.bart.gov.

Buses

Muni's orange and white buses are the top mode of public transport in SF. Relatively cheap, they can get you to within a block or two of almost anywhere in town. Bus stops are marked by a large white rectangle on a street with a red kerb; a yellow marking on a telephone or lamppost; a bus shelter; and/or a brown and orange sign listing buses that serve that route.

A single journey on a Muni bus is $2.25; seniors, under-18s and the disabled pay $1 while under-5s travel free. Exact change is required. Free transfers, which let passengers connect with a second Muni bus or streetcar route at no extra charge, are valid for 90 minutes after the original fare was paid. (The transfer tokens serve as your ticket/receipt; always ask for one when you board.)

Buses run 5am-1am during the week, 6am-1am on Saturdays and 8am-1am on Sundays. From 1am to 5am, a skeleton crew runs the **Owl**, eight lines on which buses run every half-hour.

Cable cars

Cable cars move at top speeds of 9.5mph on three lines: **California** (California Street, from the Financial District to Van Ness Avenue), **Powell-Mason** and **Powell-Hyde** (both from Market Street to Fisherman's Wharf). Lines operate from 6am to midnight daily. If you don't have a Muni pass, buy a $7 one-way ticket from the conductor. Transfers are not valid. The stops are marked by pole-mounted brown signs with a cable car symbol; routes are marked on Muni bus maps.

Ferries

Ferries are used mainly by commuters during peak hours, but they double as an inexpensive tourist excursion across the Bay to Sausalito, Tiburon or Larkspur. There are also ferries from San Francisco to Alcatraz and Angel Island in San Francisco Bay.

Blue & Gold Fleet (1-415 705 8200, www.blueandgoldfleet.com) runs boats to Sausalito, Tiburon, and Angel Island from Pier 41 at Fisherman's Wharf. Commuter services to Alameda, Oakland (both $6.70 one way), and Vallejo ($13.40) leave from the Ferry Building on the Embarcadero. The competing **Golden Gate Transit Ferry Service** (1-415 455 2000, www.goldengate.org), meanwhile, runs services from the Ferry Building to Sausalito and Larkspur ($11.25 and $10.50, respectively).

Metro/streetcars

Muni Metro streetcars are relatively quick and efficient. Five lines (J, K, L, M and N) run under Market Street downtown and above ground

ESSENTIAL INFORMATION

MAJOR BUS ROUTES

San Francisco's bus network is comprehensive but complicated, especially for newcomers to the city. The Muni maps are very useful, but for quick reference, here are some key routes.

5, **6**, **7**, **9**, **21** These five routes run down Market Street from the Financial District to Civic Center; for ease of use, we've used the shorthand '**Market Street routes**' for them in our downtown listings. Route **5** continues through the Western Addition to the northern edge of Golden Gate Park; routes **6** and **7** head into the Haight, with the 6 then running into the Sunset and the 7 taking the southern edge of Golden Gate Park; route **9** runs south down Potrero Avenue in the Mission and all the way to the edge of the city; and route **21** cuts through the Hayes Valley to the northeast corner of Golden Gate Park.
14 Runs the length of Mission Street; good for riding between downtown neighbourhoods and the Mission.
38 Apart from a stretch in central San Francisco, where the one-way system means it's forced east down O'Farrell Street, this route runs the length of Geary Street/Boulevard.
45 After stopping at SBC Park, SFMOMA, Union Square, Chinatown and North Beach, this useful route then heads west along Union Street through Cow Hollow into the Presidio.
49 Links Fort Mason, Polk Gulch, the Tenderloin, Civic Center and the Mission along Van Ness Avenue, before heading further south.

elsewhere, while the F line runs vintage streetcars on Market Street and along the Embarcadero as far as Fisherman's Wharf. The newest addition T runs along the bay front and an ambitious project is now building an extension to Chinatown. Fares are the same as on Muni buses, and transfers are valid.

Along Market, the Metro makes the same stops as BART; past the Civic Center, routes branch out towards the Mission, the Castro, Sunset and beyond. Above ground, streetcars make frequent stops. Lines run 5am-1am Mon-Sat; 8am-1am Sun. Buses replace K, L, M, N and T for an irregular night Owl service.

Taxis & car services

Due to San Francisco's compact size, taxi travel is relatively cheap. The base fare is $3.10, with an additional charge of 45¢ per one-fifth of a mile ($2.25 a mile); there's a $2 surcharge for all rides starting at SFO. The problem is that there simply aren't enough cabs, especially during morning and evening rush hours and sometimes late at night. If you're downtown, your best bet is to head for one of the bigger hotels; or, if you're shopping or out to dinner, to ask the shop or restaurant to call a cab. In addition to the car services below, you can download one of the digital apps to your mobile phone, and request your ride online. **Uber, Lyft, Sidecar** and **Flywheel** all operate in the Bay Area. Cars usually arrive within minutes; prices vary based on distance and demand.

City Wide Dispatch
1-415 920 0700.
Luxor *1-415 282 4141, www.luxorcab.com.*
National *1-415 648 4444.*
Veteran's *1-415 552 1300.*
Yellow *1-415 333 3333, www.yellowcabsf.com.*

Outside San Francisco

The **Caltrain** commuter line (1-800 660 4287, www.caltrain.com) connects San Francisco with San Jose and ultimately Gilroy. Fares are calculated by the number of zones through which the train travels; fares range from $2.50 to $12.50 one way; discounts, eight-ride tickets, and daily and monthly passes are all available.

Several companies run bus services around the rest of the Bay Area. **AC Transit** (www.actransit.org)

runs buses trans-bay and to Alameda and Contra Costa Counties; buses A to Z go across the Bay Bridge to Berkeley and Oakland. **Golden Gate Transit** (1-415 455 2000, www.goldengate.org) serves Marin and Sonoma Counties from Sausalito to Santa Rosa. And **SamTrans** (1-800 660 4287, www.samtrans.org) looks after San Mateo County, with a service to downtown San Francisco.

DRIVING

Two words: avoid it. Traffic is no worse than in the average US city, but the hills are hellish and the parking is horrendous. There's very little street parking, and private garages can charge as much as $15 to $30 a day.

However, if you must drive, be aware of a few things. The speed limit is 25mph; seatbelts are compulsory. Texting or talking on cell phones (unless you're hands-free) is also prohibited, and if you're caught, you'll pay a hefty fine.

Cable cars always have the right of way. When parking on hills, set the handbrake and 'kerb' the front wheels (towards the kerb if facing downhill, away if facing uphill). Always park in the direction of the traffic, and never block driveways. Don't park at kerbs coloured white (passenger drop-off zones), blue (drivers with disabilities only), yellow (loading and unloading commercial vehicles only) or red (bus stops or fire hydrants). Green kerbs allow only ten-minute parking. And if you venture across the water, make sure you have enough cash to pay the toll ($7.25 for the Golden Gate Bridge and $4 to $6 for the Bay Bridge), levied on the return trip.

For information on the latest highway conditions, call the 24-hour **CalTrans Highway Information Service** on 511 within the city, or check online at www.dot.ca.gov.

Parking

There are garages around town, but you'll pay for the privilege of parking in them. Inquire about discounted (or 'validated') rates, but always ask your hotel: few have their own lots, but many have an arrangement with a nearby garage.

Vehicle hire

Most car-hire agencies are at or near the airport, though some have satellite locations downtown. Book well ahead if you're planning to visit

during a holiday weekend. Every firm requires a credit card and matching driver's licence; few will rent to under-25s. Prices won't include tax, liability insurance or collision damage waiver (CDW); US residents may be covered on their home policy, but foreign residents will need to buy insurance.

Alamo *US: 1-877 222 9076, www.alamo.com. UK: 0800 028 2390, www.alamo.co.uk.*
Avis *US: 1-800 331 1212, www.avis.com. UK: 0844 581 0147, www.avis.co.uk.*
Budget *US: 1-800 527 0700, www.budget.com. UK: 0844 544 3470, www.budget.co.uk.*
Dollar *US: 1-800 800 3665, www.dollar.com. UK: 020 3468 7685, www.dollar.co.uk.*
Enterprise *US: 1-800 261 7331, www.enterprise.com. UK: 0800 800 227, www.enterprise.co.uk.*
Hertz *US: 1-800 654 3131, www.hertz.com. UK: 0870 844 8844, www.hertz.co.uk.*
National *US: 1-877 222 9058, www.nationalcar.com.*
Thrifty *US: 1-877 283 0898, www.thrifty.com. UK: 0203 468 7686, www.thrifty.co.uk.*

CYCLING

San Francisco is a real cycling city. A grid of major cycle routes across the town is marked by oval-shaped bike-and-bridge markers. North–south routes use odd numbers, east–west routes even; full-colour signs indicate primary cross-town routes; neighbourhood routes appear in green and white. For maps, bicycle laws, parking, and transit information, the **Bicycling Resource Guide** (http://bicycling.511.org) and the **San Francisco Bicycle Coalition** (www.sfbike.org) are terrific resources. Daunted by the hills? Pick up the *San Francisco Bike Map & Walking Guide*, which indicates the gradients of the city's streets. There are also two scenic cycle routes: one from Golden Gate Park south to Lake Merced, the other heading north from the southern end of Golden Gate Bridge into Marin County.

You can take bicycles on BART free of charge (except in rush hour). Bike racks on the front of certain Muni buses take up to two bikes. On Caltrain, cyclists can take their bikes on cars that display yellow bike symbols. You can also stow bikes in lockers at Caltrain stations.

Resources A-Z

ADDRESSES

Addresses follow the standard US format. The room and/or suite number usually appears after the street address, followed on the next line by the city name and the zip code.

AGE RESTRICTIONS

Buying/drinking alcohol 21
Driving 16
Sex 18
Smoking 18

BUSINESS

Conventions

Big conventions are held at the **Moscone Center** (747 Howard Street, between 3rd & 4th Streets, SoMa, 1-415 974 4000, www. moscone.com), situated on two SoMa blocks. The busiest times are usually February-March (when the city hosts the MacWorld Expo), May and September.

Courier services

DHL 1-800 225 5345, www.dhl.com.
Federal Express 1-800 463 3339, www.fedex.com.
UPS 1-800 742 5877, www.ups.com.

Office services

FedEx Office 369 Pine Street, at Montgomery Street, Financial District (1-415 834 1053, www. fedex.com/us/office). BART & Metro to Montgomery/bus 1, 2, 3, 9, 10, 12, 31, 38, 41 & Market Street routes/ cable car California. **Open** 7.30am-9pm Mon-Fri; 10am-6pm Sat; noon-6pm Sun. **Map** p313 N5.
Other locations throughout the city.

The UPS Store 268 Bush Street, between Montgomery & Sansome Streets, Financial District (1-415 765 1515, theupsstorelocal.com). BART & Metro to Montgomery/bus 1, 2, 3, 9, 10, 12, 31, 38, 41 & Market Street routes/cable car California. **Open** 7.30am-6.30pm Mon-Fri; 9am-3pm Sun. **Map** p313 N5.

CONSULATES

Australian Consulate-General
Suite 1800, 575 Market Street, at Sansome Street, CA 94105 (1-415 644 3620, www.usa.embassy.gov.au/ whwh/SanFranCG.html). BART & Metro to Montgomery/bus 2, 3, 10, 12, 14, 30, 31, 38, 45, 91 & Market Street routes. **Map** p313 N5.
British Consulate-General
Suite 850, 1 Sansome Street, at Market Street, CA 94104 (1-415 617 1300, www.britainusa.com/sf). BART & Metro to Montgomery/bus 2, 3, 10, 12, 14, 30, 31, 38, 45, 91 & Market Street routes. **Map** p313 N5.
Consulate-General of Canada
Suite 1288, 580 California Street, at Kearny Street, CA 94104 (1-415 834 3180, www.can-am.gc.ca/san-francisco). Bus 1, 3, 10, 12, 30, 31, 38, 45, 91/cable car California. **Map** p312 N4.
Consulate-General of Ireland
Suite 3350, 100 Pine Street, at Front Street, CA 94111 (1-415 392 4214, www.consulateofirelandsan francisco.org). BART & Metro to Embarcadero/bus 1, 3, 9, 10, 12, 14, 21, 31, 38, 41 & Market Street routes. **Map** p313 N4.

CONSUMER

Attorney General: Public Inquiry Unit 1-800 952 5225, http://oag.ca. gov/consumers.
Call to complain about consumer law enforcement or any other agency.

Better Business Bureau 1-866 411 2221/1-510 844 2000, http:// goldengate.bbb.org.
The BBB provides information on the reliability of a company and a list of companies with good business records. It's also the place to call to file a complaint about a company.

CUSTOMS

US Customs allows foreigners to bring in $100 worth of gifts (the limit is $800 for returning Americans) without paying duty. One carton of 200 cigarettes (or 100 cigars) and one litre of liquor (spirits) are allowed. Plants, meat and fresh produce of any kind cannot be brought into the country. You will have to fill out a form if you are carrying more than $10,000 in currency. You will be handed a white form on your inbound flight to fill in, confirming that you haven't exceeded any of these allowances.

If you need to bring prescription drugs into the US, make sure the container is clearly marked, and bring your doctor's statement or a prescription. Marijuana, cocaine and most opiate derivatives, along with a number of other drugs and chemicals, are not permitted: the possession is punishable by a stiff fine and/or imprisonment. Check in with the **US Customs and Border Protection Service** (www.cbp.gov) before you arrive if you're unsure.

HM Revenue & Customs allows returning visitors to the UK to bring £390 worth of 'gifts, souvenirs and other goods' into the country duty-free, along with the usual duty-free goods.

DISABLED

Despite its topography, San Francisco is disabled-friendly; California is the national leader in providing facilities.

ESSENTIAL INFORMATION

All public buildings are required by law to be wheelchair-accessible, though not all are compliant – wheelchair-users can contact the **Independent Living Resource Center** (1-415 543 6222, www.ilrcsf. org) for assistance. Most city buses can 'kneel' to make access easier; the majority of city street corners have ramped kerbs; and most restaurants and hotels can accommodate wheelchairs. Privileges include free parking in designated (blue) areas and in most metered spaces; display a blue and white 'parking placard' for both.

ELECTRICITY

US electricity voltage is 110-120V 60-cycle AC. Except for dual-voltage, flat-pin plug shavers, foreign appliances will usually need an adaptor.

EMERGENCIES

Ambulance, fire or police *911.*
Coast Guard *1-415 399 3530.*
Poison Control Center *1-800 222 1222, www.calpoison.org.*

GAY & LESBIAN

For gay and lesbian resources, *see pp203-211.*

HEALTH & MEDICAL

Accident & emergency

Medical treatment can be pricey, so international visitors should ensure it's covered by their travel insurance before departure. Call the emergency number on your insurance policy before seeking treatment and you'll be directed to a hospital that deals with your insurance company. There are 24hr emergency rooms at the locations listed below.

California Pacific Medical Center *3700 California Street (1-415 600 6000, visit www.cpmc.org). Bus 1, 2, 33.* **Map** p316 H9.
Other locations throughout the city.
St Francis Memorial Hospital *900 Hyde Street, between Bush & Pine Streets, Nob Hill (1-415 353 6000). Bus 1, 2, 3, 19, 27, 38.* **Map** p312 K5.
San Francisco General Hospital *1001 Potrero Avenue, between 22nd & 23rd Streets, Potrero Hill (1-415 206 8000). Bus 9, 10, 27, 33, 48, 90.* **Map** p317 M12.
UCSF Medical Center *505 Parnassus Avenue, between 3rd & Hillway Avenues, Sunset (1-415 476 1000). Metro to UCSF/bus 6, 43, 66.* **Map** p314 D10.

Clinics

HealthRight360 *558 Clayton Street, at Haight Street, Haight-Ashbury (1-415 746 1940, www. healthright360.org). Metro to Cole & Carl/bus 6, 33, 37, 43, 66, 71.* **Open** by appointment; call for details. **Map** p315 E9.
Health care, including a variety of speciality clinics, is provided to the uninsured on a sliding-scale basis; most patients pay little or nothing.

Contraception & abortion

Planned Parenthood *1650 Valencia Street, at Mission Street, Mission (1-415 821 1282, www. plannedparenthood.org). BART to 24th Street/bus 12, 14, 27, 36, 49.* **Open** 8.30am-8pm Mon, Tue, Thur; 8.30am-5pm Wed, Fri; 8.30am-4.30pm Sun. **Map** p312 K6.
In addition to contraception, Planned Parenthood provides low-cost general health-care services, HIV testing and gynaecological exams; with the exception of the morning-after pill, all are by appointment only.

Dentists

1-800 Dentist *1-800 336 8478, www.1800dentist.com.* **Open** 24hrs daily.
Provides dental referrals.
University of the Pacific School of Dentistry *2155 Webster Street, at Sacramento Street, Pacific Heights (1-415 929 6501, http://dental. pacific.edu). Bus 1, 3, 12, 22.* **Open** 8am-5pm Mon-Fri. **Map** p311 H5.
Supervised dentists-in-training provide a low-cost service.

HIV & AIDS

AIDS-HIV Nightline *1-415 434 2437/1-800 628 9240.* **Open** 5pm-5am daily.
Hotline offering emotional support.
California AIDS Foundation *1-800 367 2437.* **Open** 9am-4pm Mon-Fri.
Information and advice.

Opticians

City Optix *2154 Chestnut Street, between Pierce & Steiner Streets, Marina (1-415 921 1444, www. cityoptix.net). Bus 30.* **Open** 10am-6pm Mon-Wed, Fri, Sat; 10am-8pm Thur; noon-5pm Sun. **Map** p311 G3.

Note that the optometrist is not in on Mondays or Sundays.

Pharmacies

The following locations of pharmacy chain **Walgreens** (www.walgreens. com) are open 24 hours: 3201 Divisadero Street, Marina (1-415 931 6417); 498 Castro Street, at 18th Street, Castro (1-415 861 3136).

HELPLINES

All numbers are open 24 hours.

Alcoholics Anonymous *1-415 674 1821, www.aa.org.*
Drug Crisis Information *1-415 362 3400, hearing-impaired 1-415 781 2224.*
Narcotics Anonymous *1-415 621 8600, www.na.org.*
San Francisco General Hospital Psychiatric Helpline *1-415 206 8125.*
Trauma Recovery Center *(rape counselling) 1-415 347 3000.*
Suicide Prevention *1-415 781 0500/1-800 784 2433, www. sfsuicide.org.*
Talk Line Family Support *1-415 441 5437, www.sfcapc.org.*
Women Against Rape Crisis Hotline *1-415 647 7273.*

INSURANCE

Non-nationals and US citizens should have travel and medical insurance before travelling. For a list of San Francisco urgent-care facilities, *see left.*

INTERNET

In-room Wi-Fi and shared computer terminals are commonplace in hotels. A number of cafés and even a few bars across the city offer free wireless access, and the city has a handful of wireless hotspots; the best known is in Union Square. If you don't have a laptop, head to the Main Library *(see p64)*, which has several free-to-use terminals. For more on getting online in the city, see www.bawug.org or www.wififreespot.com/ca.html.

LEFT LUGGAGE

Larger hotels should allow you to leave bags on your arrival/departure day, while at SFO, you can store everything from bags to bicycles at the Airport Travel Agency (1-650 877 0422, 7am-11pm daily), on the Departures level of the International Terminal. The **California**

Welcome Center at Pier 39 (Building B, Level 2, 1-415 981 1280) offers luggage storage between 9am and 7pm at a cost of $5 per bag.

LEGAL HELP

Lawyer Referral Service
1-415 989 1616, www.sfbar.org.
Open 8.30am-5.30pm Mon-Fri.
Callers are referred to attorneys and mediators to deal with all legal problems.

LIBRARIES

For **San Francisco Main Library,** *see p64.*

LOST PROPERTY

Property Control *850 Bryant Street, between 6th & 7th Streets, SoMa (1-415 553 1377). Bus 12, 19, 27, 47.* **Open** 8.30am-4.30pm Mon-Fri. **Map** p317 M8.
Make a police report – then hope.

Airports

For items lost en route, contact the specific airline. If you leave a bag at the airport, it may get destroyed, but it's worth calling the numbers listed below.

San Francisco International Airport *Terminal 1, 1-650 821 7014.* **Open** 8am-8pm Mon-Fri.
Mineta San Jose International Airport *Terminal A, Baggage Claim, 1-408 277 5419.* **Open** 8am-5pm Mon-Fri.
Oakland International Airport *1-510 563 3982.* **Open** 9.30am-noon Mon-Fri.

Public transport

Muni *1-415 923 6372.*
BART *1-510 464 7090.*
AC Transit *1-510 891 4706.*
Golden Gate Transit *1-415 257 4476.*
SamTrans *1-800 660 4287.*

MONEY

The US dollar ($) is divided into 100 cents (¢). Coin denominations run from the copper penny (1¢) to the silver nickel (5¢), dime (10¢), quarter (25¢) and less-common half-dollar (50¢). There are also two $1 coins: the silver Susan B Anthony and the gold Sacagawea. Notes or 'bills' are all the same green colour and size; they come in denominations of $1, $5, $10, $20, $50 and $100. The $20 and $50 have recently been redesigned with features that make them hard to forge, including, for the first time, some subtle colours other than green and black. Old-style bills remain legal currency.

ATMs

There are ATMs throughout the city: in banks, stores and even bars. ATMs accept Visa, MasterCard and American Express, as well as other cards, but almost all charge a usage fee.

Banks & bureaux de change

The easiest way to change money is simply use the ATM machines. Your bank will give you the current rate of exchange and the fee is usually no more than you would pay in commission anywhere else anyway. Most banks are open from 9am to 6pm Monday to Friday and from 9am to 3pm on Saturday. Photo ID is required to cash travellers' cheques. Many banks don't exchange foreign currency, so arrive with some US dollars. If you arrive after 6pm, change money at the airport. If you want to cash travellers' cheques at a shop, note that some require a minimum purchase. You can also obtain cash with a credit card from certain banks, including all branches of Wells Fargo, but be prepared to pay interest rates that vary daily.

American Express Travel Services *455 Market Street, at 1st Street, Financial District (1-415 536 2600, www.americanexpress. com/travel).* BART & Metro to Montgomery/bus 1, 2, 3, 9, 10, 12, 14, 31, 38, 41 & Market Street routes. **Open** 9am-5.30pm Mon-Fri; 10am-2pm Sat. **Map** p313 N5.
AmEx will change travellers' cheques and money, and also offers (for AmEx cardholders only) poste restante.

Credit cards

Bring at least one major credit card: they are accepted – often required – at nearly all hotels, restaurants and shops. The cards most accepted in the US are American Express, Diners Club, Discover, MasterCard and Visa. Call the following numbers to report lost or stolen cards:

American Express *Cards 1-800 992 3404. Travellers' cheques 1-800 221 7282.*
Discover *1-800 347 2683.*
MasterCard *1-800 622 7747.*
Visa *Cards 1-800 847 2911. Travellers' cheques 1-800 227 6811.*

POLICE

In an emergency only, dial **911**.
If you need to report a crime, the stations below are in central areas.

Central Station *766 Vallejo Street, between Stockton & Powell Streets, North Beach (1-415 315 2400). Bus 10, 12, 30, 39, 41, 45, 91/cable car Powell-Mason.* **Map** p313 M3.
Southern Station *850 Bryant Street, between 6th & 7th Streets, SoMa (1-415 553 1373). Bus 9X, 12, 19, 27, 47.* **Map** p317 M8.

POSTAL SERVICES

Post offices are usually open 9am-5.30pm Monday to Friday, 9am to 2pm Saturday. All are closed on Sunday. Call 1-800 275 8777 for information on your nearest branch. Stamps can be bought at any post office and also at some hotels, vending machines and ATMs. Stamps for postcards within the US cost 44¢; for Europe, the charge is 98¢. For couriers and shippers, *see p293.*

Poste Restante *Main Post Office, 101 Hyde Street, at Golden Gate Avenue, Civic Center (1-800 275 8777). BART & Metro to Civic Center/bus 5, 6, 19, 21, 31, 71.* **Open** 10am-2pm Mon-Sat.
Map p316 L7.
If you need to receive mail in SF and you're not sure where you'll be staying, have the envelope addressed with your name, c/o General Delivery, San Francisco, CA 94102, USA. Mail is only kept for ten days from receipt, and you must present some photo ID to retrieve it.

RELIGION

Calvary Presbyterian *2515 Fillmore Street, at Washington Street, Pacific Heights (1-415 346 3832, www.calvarypresbyterian.org). Bus 1, 3, 10, 22, 24.* **Map** p309 E3.
Cathedral of St Mary of the Assumption *1111 Gough Street, at Geary Boulevard, Western Addition (1-415 567 2020, www.stmaryc athedralsf.org). Bus 2, 3, 31, 38, 47, 49, 90.* **Map** p312 J6. Catholic.
Glide *330 Ellis Street, at Taylor Street, Tenderloin (1-415 674 6000, www.glide.org). Bus 27, 31, 38/cable car Powell-Hyde & Powell-Mason.* **Map** p312 L6. Methodist.
Grace Cathedral *1100 California Street, at Taylor Street, Nob Hill (1-415 749 6300, www.grace cathedral.org). Bus 1, 2, 3, 27/cable car California.* **Map** p312 L5. Episcopalian.

Masjid Darussalam (Islamic Society of San Francisco) *20 Jones Street, at Market Street, Tenderloin (1-415 863 7997, http://islamsf.com). BART & Metro to Civic Center/ streetcar F/bus 5, 31 & Market Street routes.* **Map** p316 L7.

St Paul's Lutheran Church *950 McAllister Street, between Buchanan & Laguna Streets, Western Addition (1-415 673 8088). Bus 5, 21, 22, 31.* **Map** p312 J6.

Temple Emanu-El *2 Lake Street, at Arguello Boulevard, Presidio Heights (1-415 751 2535, www. emanuelsf.org). Bus 1, 2, 33.* **Map** p310 D6. Judaism.

Zen Center *300 Page Street, at Laguna Street, Lower Haight (1-415 863 3136, www.sfzc.org). Bus 6, 21, 71.* **Map** p316 J8. Buddhist.

SAFETY & SECURITY

Crime is a reality in all big cities, but San Franciscans generally feel secure in their town. There is really just one basic rule of thumb you need to follow: use your common sense. If a neighbourhood doesn't feel safe to you, it probably isn't. Only a few areas warrant caution during daylight hours and are of particular concern at night. These include the Tenderloin (north and east of Civic Center); SoMa (near the Mission/6th Street corner); Mission Street between 13th and 18th Streets; and the Hunter's Point neighbourhood near the old shipyard. Golden Gate Park should be avoided at night. Many tourist areas, most notably around Union Square, are sprinkled with homeless people who beg for change but are usually harmless. If you're unlucky enough to be mugged, your best bet is to give your attackers whatever they want, then call the police from the nearest pay phone by dialling 911. (Don't forget to get the reference number on the claim report for insurance purposes and to get travellers' cheque refunds.) If you are the victim of a sexual assault and wish to make a report, call the police, who will escort you to the hospital for treatment. For helplines that serve victims of rape or other crimes, *see p294*.

SMOKING

Smokers may rank as the only group of people who are not especially welcome in San Francisco. Smoking is banned in all public places, including banks, sporting arenas, theatres, offices, the lobbies of buildings, shops, restaurants, bars, and any and every form of public transport. There are many small hotels and B&Bs that don't allow you to light up anywhere inside. On the other hand, a select few bars cheerfully ignore the law.

STUDYING

To study in the Bay Area (or, for that matter, anywhere in the United States), exchange students should apply for a J-1 visa, while full-time students enrolled in a degree programme must apply for an F-1 visa. Both are valid for the duration of the course and for a limited period thereafter. Foreign students need an International Student Identity Card (ISIC) as proof of student status. This can be bought from your local travel agent or student travel office.

TAX

Sales tax of 9.5 per cent is added on to the label price in shops within city limits, and 9.5 to 9.75 per cent in surrounding cities. Hotels charge a 14 per cent room tax and the same percentage on hotel parking.

TELEPHONES

The phone system is reliable and, for local calls, cheap. Long-distance, particularly overseas, calls are best paid for with a rechargeable, pre-paid phonecard ($6-$35) available from vending machines and many shops.

In an **emergency**, dial 911. All calls are free (including those from pay and mobile phones).

For the **operator**, dial 0. If you're not used to US phones, then note that the ringing tone is long; the engaged tone, or 'busy signal', consists of much shorter, higher-pitched beeps.

Collect calls are also known as reverse-charge calls. To make one, dial 0 followed by the number, or dial AT&T's 1-800 225 5288, Sprint's 1-800 663 3463, or the aptly named 1-800-Collect's 1-800 265 5328.

For **directory assistance**, dial 411 or 1 + area code + 555 1212. Doing so may cost nothing, depending on the pay phone you are using; carrier fees may apply. Long-distance directory assistance may also incur long-distance charges. Toll-free numbers generally start with 1-800, 1-888 or 1-877, while pricey pay-per-call lines (usually phone-sex numbers) start with 1-900. For a directory of toll-free numbers, dial 1-800 555 1212.

For **international calls**, dial 011 + country code (Australia 61; New Zealand 64; UK 44), then the number (omitting any initial zero).

Area codes

Even if you are dialling within your area code, you must dial 1 + area code + phone number.

San Francisco & Marin County 415, 628
Oakland & Berkeley 510
The peninsula cities 650
San Jose 408
Napa, Sonoma & Mendocino Counties 707

Public phones

Public pay phones are few and far between these days. If you can find one, they only accept nickels, dimes and quarters, but check for a dial tone before you start feeding in your change.

Local calls usually cost 50¢, though some companies operate pay phones that charge exorbitant prices, The rate also rises steeply as the distance between callers increases (an operator or recorded message will tell you how much to add).

Mobile phones

San Francisco, like most of the continental US, operates on the 1900 GSM frequency. Travellers from Europe with tri-band phones will be able to connect to one or more of the networks here with no problems, assuming their service provider at home has an arrangement with a local network; always check before travelling. Rates may be hefty and you'll probably be charged for receiving as well as making calls. European travellers with dual-band phones, however, will need to rent a handset upon arrival; **TripTel** (1-650 821 8000, www.triptel.com), located in the international arrivals terminal at SFO Airport offers phone rental and sells prepaid SIM cards, which you can use in an appropriate handset. The counter is open daily 8.30am-9.30pm but there's a drop-off box if you're flying home after operating hours.

TIME & DATES

San Francisco is on Pacific Time, which is three hours behind Eastern Time (New York) and seven hours behind Greenwich Mean Time (UK). Daylight Savings Time, which overlaps the entirety of British Summer Time, runs from the first Sunday in March, when the clocks are rolled ahead one hour, to the last Sunday in November. Going from the West Coast to East Coast, Pacific Time is one hour behind Mountain

Time and two hours behind Central Time, three hours behind Eastern Time. In the US, dates are written in the order month, day, year, so 2/5/16 is 5 February 2016.

TIPPING

Unlike in Europe, tipping is a way of life in the US: many locals in service industries rely on gratuities as part of their income, so you should tip accordingly. In restaurants, you should tip at least 15 per cent of the total bill and usually nearer 20 per cent; most restaurants will add this to the bill automatically for a table of six or more. In bars, bank on tipping around a buck a drink, especially if you want to hang around for a while. If you look after the bartender, they'll look after you; tipping pocket change may leave you dry for a while. In general, tip bellhops and baggage handlers $1-$2 a bag; tip cab drivers, hairdressers and food delivery people 15-20 per cent of the total tab; tip valets $2-$3; and tip counter staff 50¢ to 10 per cent of the order, depending on its size.

TOILETS

Restrooms can be found in prime tourist areas such as Fisherman's Wharf and Golden Gate Park, as well as in shopping malls. If you're caught short, don't hesitate to enter a restaurant or a bar and ask to use its facilities. In keeping with its cosmopolitan standing, San Francisco has installed 25 of the French-designed, self-cleaning JCDecaux lavatories throughout the high-traffic areas of the city. Keep an eye out for these forest-green commodes (they're usually plastered with high-profile advertising). Admission is free for 20min, after that, you may be fined for indecent

exposure, because the door pings open automatically. Do be aware that some people use the toilets for purposes other than that for which they were designed.

TOURIST INFORMATION

San Francisco Visitor Information Center *Lower level of Hallidie Plaza, 900 Market Street, at Powell Street (1-415 391 2000, www.sanfrancisco. travel).* BART & Metro to Powell/bus 27, 31, 38, 45 & Market Street routes/ cable car Powell-Hyde or Powell-Mason. **Open** 9am-5pm Mon-Fri; 9am-3pm Sat, Sun. **Map** p313 M6. Located downtown, this is the visitor centre of the efficient and helpful San Francisco Convention & Visitor Bureau. You won't find any parking, but you will find tons of free maps, brochures, coupons and advice. The number above gives access to a 24hr recorded message listing daily events and activities; you can also use it to request free information about hotels, restaurants and shopping in the city.

VISAS & IMMIGRATION

Currently, 37 countries participate in the Visa Waiver Program (VWP; www.cbp.gov/esta) including Australia, Ireland, New Zealand and the UK. Citizens of these countries do not need a visa for stays in the US shorter than 90 days (business or pleasure) as long as they have a machine-readable passport (e-passport) valid for the full 90-day period, a return ticket, and authorisation to travel through the ESTA (Electronic System for Travel Authorization) scheme. Visitors must fill in the ESTA form at least 24 hours before travelling (72 hours is recommended) and pay a $14 fee; the form can be found at https://esta.cbp.dhs.gov/esta).

If you do not qualify for entry under the VWP, you will need a visa; leave plenty of time to check before travelling.

Immigration

Your airline will give all visitors an immigration form to be presented to an official when you land. Fill it in clearly and be prepared to give an address at which you are staying (a hotel is fine).

Upon arrival in the US, you may have to wait an hour or, if you're unlucky, considerably longer, in Immigration, where, owing to tightened security, you can expect slow-moving queues. You may be expected to explain your visit; be polite and prepared. All visitors to the US are now photographed and electronically fingerprinted on arrival on every trip.

WHEN TO GO

San Francisco may be in California, but its climate, like its politics, is all its own. When planning a trip, don't anticipate the normal seasons, climatically, at least. Spring and autumn are relatively predictable, with warm days and cool nights. During the summer, however, days are often foggy and chilly, but the nights are usually mild. In general, temperatures rarely stray above 80°F (27°C) or below 45°F (7°C), though in this age of climate change and global warming, San Francisco has seen more over-85°F days in a single year than it usually sees in a decade. San Francisco is small, but the weather varies wildly between neighbourhoods. The city's western terrain is flat, and so fog often covers Golden Gate Park and the Sunset and Richmond areas. However, the fog is often too heavy to climb further east, so the areas east of Twin Peaks – the Mission, the Castro, Noe Valley, Potrero Hill – are often sunny. Add in the wind that whips in to Fisherman's Wharf, and you may experience four seasons in one day.

Public holidays

New Year's Day 1 Jan
Martin Luther King Jr Day 3rd Mon in Jan
President's Day 3rd Mon in Feb
Memorial Day last Mon in May
Independence Day 4 July
Labor Day 1st Mon in Sept
Columbus Day 2nd Mon in Oct
Veterans' Day 11 Nov
Thanksgiving Day 4th Thur in Nov
Christmas Day 25 Dec.

LOCAL CLIMATE

Average temperatures and monthly rainfall in San Francisco.

	High (°C/°F)	Low (°C/°F)	Rainfall (mm/in)
Jan	13 / 56	8 / 46	114 / 4.5
Feb	15 / 60	9 / 48	71 / 2.8
Mar	16 / 61	9 / 49	66 / 2.6
Apr	17 / 63	10 / 50	38 / 1.5
May	17 / 64	10 / 51	10 /0.4
June	19 / 66	11 / 53	5 / 0.2
July	19 / 66	12 / 54	2.5 / 0.1
Aug	19 / 66	12 / 54	2.5 / 0.1
Sept	21 / 70	13 / 56	5 / 0.2
Oct	20 / 69	13 / 55	28 / 1.1
Nov	18 / 64	10/51	64 / 2.5
Dec	14 / 57	8 / 47	89 / 3.5

ESSENTIAL INFORMATION

Further Reference

BOOKS

Fiction & poetry

Isabel Allende *Daughters of Fortune*
Delightfully written piece about one young woman's search for love during the Gold Rush.
James Dalessandro *1906: A Novel*
A fictionalised, though grippingly researched, account of San Francisco's catastrophic year of earthquake and fire.
Dave Eggers *A Heartbreaking Work of Staggering Genius*
A beautiful memoir of moving to San Francisco and raising a younger brother.
Allen Ginsberg *Howl and Other Poems*
Grab your chance to read the rant that caused all the fuss back in the 1950s.
Glen David Gold *Carter Beats the Devil*
A sleight-of-hand comedy thriller set in 1920s San Francisco.
Dashiell Hammett *The Maltese Falcon*
One of the greatest detective writers and one of the world's best detective novels (later filmed with Humphrey Bogart), set in a dark and dangerous San Francisco.
Jack Kerouac *On the Road; The Subterraneans; Desolation Angels; The Dharma Bums*
Famous for a reason: bittersweet tales of drugs and sex in San Francisco and around the world, from the best-known beatnik of them all.
Jack London *Tales of the Fish Patrol; John Barleycorn*
Early works from London, set in the writer's native city. For his musings on the Sonoma Valley, pick up *Valley of the Moon*.
Armistead Maupin *Tales of the City* (6 volumes)
This witty soap opera, later a successful TV series, follows the lives and loves of a group of San Francisco friends starting in the 1970s.
Frank Norris *McTeague*
Working-class life and loss set in unromanticised Barbary Coast days. A cult classic of the 1890s.
Domenic Stansberry *The Last Days of Il Duce*
A fearsome, authentic piece of noir fiction, set in North Beach.

John Steinbeck *The Grapes of Wrath*
Grim tales of Northern California in the Great Depression by the master of American fiction.
Amy Tan *The Joy Luck Club*
A moving story of the lives and loves of two generations of Chinese-American women living in San Francisco.
Alfredo Vea *Gods Go Begging*
A San Francisco murder trial has ties to the Vietnam War.
Tom Wolfe *The Electric Kool-Aid Acid Test; The Pump House Gang*
Alternative lifestyles in trippy, hippy 1960s California.

Non-fiction

Walton Bean *California: An Interpretive History*
An anecdotal account of California's shady past.
Herb Caen *Baghdad by the Bay*
Local gossip and lightly poetic insight from the much-missed *Chronicle* columnist.
Carolyn Cassady *Off the Road: My Years with Cassady, Kerouac and Ginsberg*
Not enlightened feminism, but an interesting alternative examination of the beats.
Joan Didion *Slouching Towards Bethlehem; The White Album*
Brilliant essays examining California in the past couple of decades by one of America's most respected authors.
Timothy W Drescher *San Francisco Bay Area Murals*
A well-resourced book with plenty of maps and 140 photos.
Lawrence Ferlinghetti & Nancy J Peters *Literary San Francisco*
The city's literary pedigree examined by the founder of City Lights.
Robert Greenfield *Dark Star: An Oral Biography of Jerry Garcia*
The life and (high) times of the Grateful Dead's late frontman.
Emmett Grogan *Ringolevio: A Life Played for Keeps*
Part-memoir, part-social history, part-fable, *Ringolevio* traces the story of Grogan, one of the founders of the Diggers, from New York to 1960s Haight-Ashbury.
Michael Lewis *Moneyball: The Art of Winning an Unfair Game*
Oakland A's GM Billy Beane may go down as one of the most influential baseball executives of the last

half-century. This vital book profiles Beane and his team.
Beth Lisick *Everybody into the Pool*
A tremendously enjoyable and occasionally laugh-out-loud funny collection of essays from a suburbanite who became a chronicler of Bay Area subculture.
Malcolm Margolin *The Ohlone Way*
How the Bay Area's original inhabitants lived, researched from oral histories.
John Miller (ed) *San Francisco Stories: Great Writers on the City*
Contributions by Herb Caen, Anne Lamott, Amy Tan, Ishmael Reed and many others.
Ray Mungo *San Francisco Confidential*
A gossipy look behind the city's closed doors.
John Plunkett & Barbara Traub (eds) *Burning Man*
Photo-heavy manual to the annual insanity that is the Burning Man Festival.
Marc Reisner *Cadillac Desert: A Dangerous State*
The role of water in California's history and future; a projection of apocalypse founded on shifting tectonics and hairtrigger irrigation.
Nathaniel Rich *San Francisco Noir*
San Francisco's cinematic history gets re-examined in this beautifully written piece, which falls somewhere between guidebook, cultural criticism and academic tract.
Richard Schwartz *Berkeley 1900*
An in-depth account of the origins of complex and controversial Berkeley.
Joel Selvin *San Francisco: The Magical History*
A tour of the sights and sounds of the city's pop music history by the *Chronicle*'s music critic.
Randy Shilts *And the Band Played On*
Shilts's crucial work is still the most important account of the AIDS epidemic in San Francisco.
Gertrude Stein *The Making of Americans*
This autobiographical work includes an account of Stein's early childhood in Oakland.
Tom Stienstra & Ann Marie Brown *California Hiking*
An outstanding guide to over 1,000 hikes all over the state (Stienstra is the outdoors columnist for the

San Francisco Chronicle). Other books in the excellent Fogohorn Outdoors series on California cover camping, hiking, biking and fishing.

Robert Louis Stevenson
An Inland Voyage; The Silverado Squatters
Autobiographical narratives describing the journey from Europe to western America.

Bonnie Wach *San Francisco As You Like It*
City tours to suit pretty much all personalities and moods, from Ivy League shoppers to cheapskate fitness-freak vegetarians.

FILM

Birdman of Alcatraz (1961)
The movie is hopelessly overlong and laughably inaccurate, but, thanks largely to Burt Lancaster's likeable title turn, it's a decent film regardless.

Bullitt (1968)
This Steve McQueen action flick boasts the all-time greatest San Francisco car chase.

Chan is Missing (1982)
Two cab drivers search for a man who stole their life savings in this movie, which gives an authentic, insider's look at Chinatown.

The Conversation (1974)
Gene Hackman's loner surveillance expert gets in a little deeper than he planned in Coppola's classic movie. The opening scene, shot in Union Square, is a cinematic tour de force.

Crumb (1994)
An award-winning film about the comic book master and misanthrope Robert Crumb.

Dark Passage (1947)
This classic thriller starts in Marin County, where Bogart escapes from San Quentin Prison, and ends up in Lauren Bacall's San Francisco apartment.

Dirty Harry (1971)
Do you feel lucky? The first in a series starring Clint Eastwood.

The Graduate (1967)
Dustin Hoffman at his best, with shots of Berkeley as well as a cool wrong-direction shot on the Bay Bridge.

Harold and Maude (1971)
Bay Area scenery abounds in this bittersweet cult classic about an unbalanced boy who falls in love with an elderly woman.

Jimmy Plays Berkeley (1970)
Stirring footage of the town in its radical days, plus Hendrix at his very best.

The Maltese Falcon (1941)
Hammett's classic made into a glorious 1940s thriller, full of great street scenes.

Milk (2008)
Gus Van Sant's brilliant chronicle of Harvey Milk, California's first openly gay elected official.

Mrs Doubtfire (1993)
Relentlessly hammy Robin Williams plays a divorcee posing as a nanny to be near his kids.

San Francisco (1936)
Ignore the first 90 minutes of moralising and sit back to enjoy the Great Quake.

So I Married an Axe Murderer (1993)
This San Francisco-set romantic comedy features Mike Myers giving an immensely funny send-up of 1950s beat culture.

Vertigo (1958)
A veteran cop becomes obsessed with a mysterious blonde. A die-cast San Francisco classic.

The Voyage Home: Star Trek IV (1986)
The gang come to SF to to save some whales in this original-cast movie, the best of the series.

The Wedding Planner (2000)
This update of the San Francisco-set screwball comedy is a bit clunky, but J-Lo is immaculately cast.

The Wild Parrots of Telegraph Hill (2000)
A delightful documentary about Mark Bittner and the North Beach birds who love him dearly.

Big Eyes (2014)
The riveting tale of artist Margaret Keane and her big-eyed waifs paints a nostalgic portrait of 1950s beatnik North Beach.

Big Hero 6 (2014)
While technically not filmed in the city, this animated Disney feature renders a marvellous, imaginary mashup of San Francisco and Tokyo called San Fransokyo.

MUSIC

Big Brother and the Holding Company *Cheap Thrills* (1968)
Classic Janis Joplin, housed in a classic Robert Crumb sleeve. Tracks include 'Ball and Chain' and 'Piece of My Heart'.

Chris Isaak *Heart Shaped World* (1989)
What a 'Wicked Game' to be so good-looking, with a voice like that.

Creedence Clearwater Revival *Willie and the Poor Boys* (1969)
Classic Southern rock with a San Francisco touch.

The Dead Kennedys *Fresh Fruit for Rotting Vegetables* (1980)

Excellent, angry San Francisco punk band.

Erase Errata *At Crystal Palace* (2003)
Angular, uplifting rock from the queens of the underground.

Gold Chains *Young Miss America* (2003)
Bay Area hip hop, 21st-century style.

The Grateful Dead *Dick's Picks Vol.4* (1996)
Jerry Garcia and the boys in their 1970 prime, playing at the Fillmore East.

Jefferson Airplane *Surrealistic Pillow* (1967)
Folk, blues and psychedelia. Singer Grace Slick helps define the San Francisco Sound.

Joshua Redman *Wish* (1993)
Quality jazz from the Bay Area tenor saxophonist.

Primus *Pork Soda* (1993)
Wryly intelligent punk-funk in the Zappa tradition.

Sly and the Family Stone *Stand!* (1969)
Funk-rock masters. If you haven't heard this, you haven't really heard the 1960s.

WEBSITES

www.timeout.com/ san-francisco
Our inspiring online guide to San Francisco includes the latest local events and trends, current movie listings and the best restaurants, bars and shops, all rated and reviewed by *Time Out* critics.

www.sanfrancisco.travel
The official San Francisco tourist board site is packed with information on the town.

http://sfgov.org The city and county of San Francisco's site is a gateway to everything from parks to Wi-Fi, plus there's a section specifically aimed at visitors.

www.sanfrancisco memories.com
Wonderful photographs of the city in days gone by.

www.sfgate.com
The *San Francisco Chronicle* online – at least what's not behind the paywall.

www.sfweekly.com
Local news, features and blogs from the alt weekly.

www.streetcar.org
The past and present of San Francisco's classic F Line streetcars.

http://transit.511.org
A useful resource for information on all forms of Bay Area public transport and traffic.

Index

INDEX

INDEX

De Young Museum.

INDEX

Golden Gate Bridge from the Presidio
Golf Course.

Chinatown.

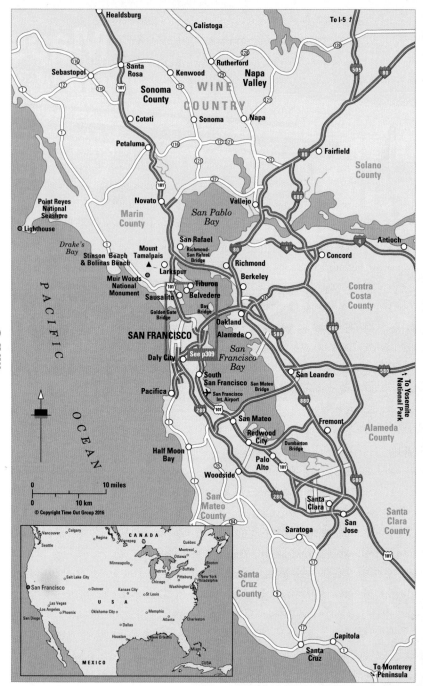

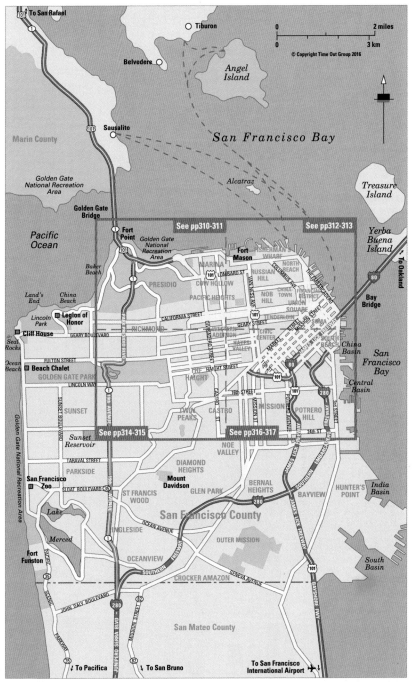

MAPS

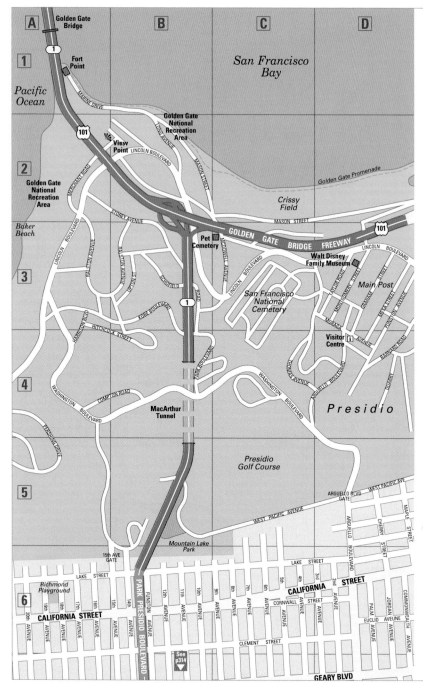

MAPS

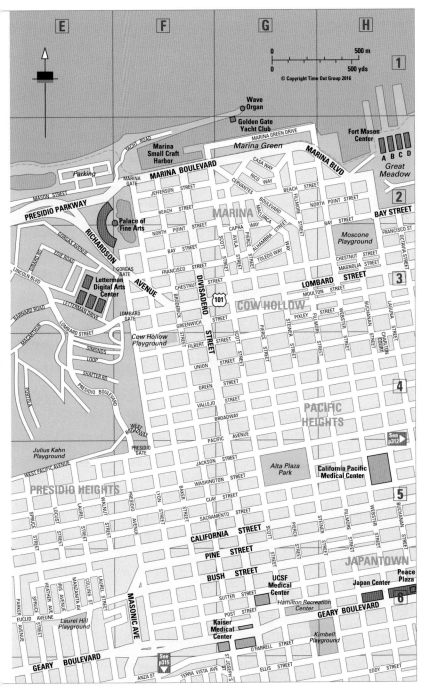

MAPS

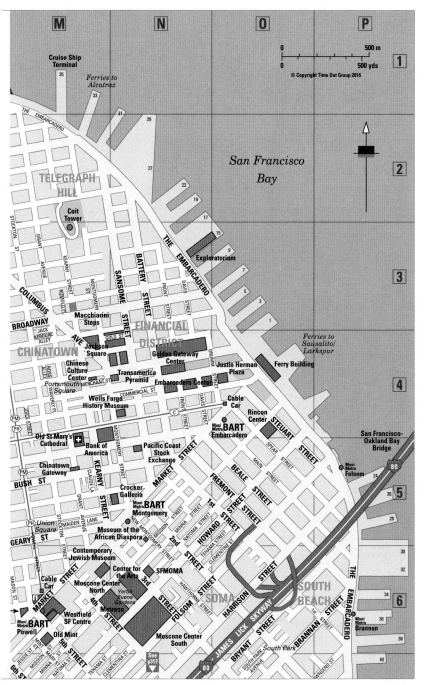

MAPS

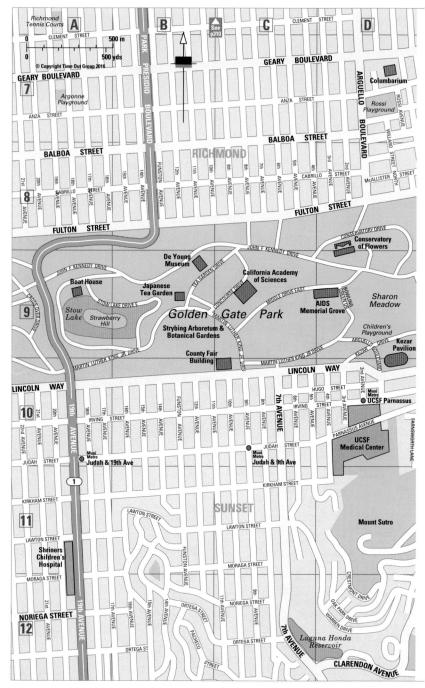

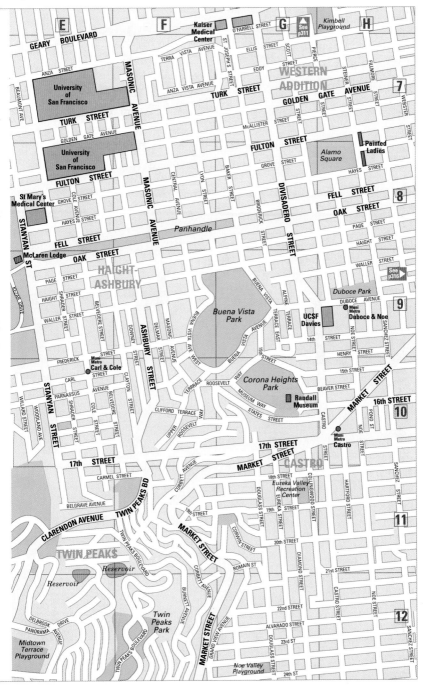

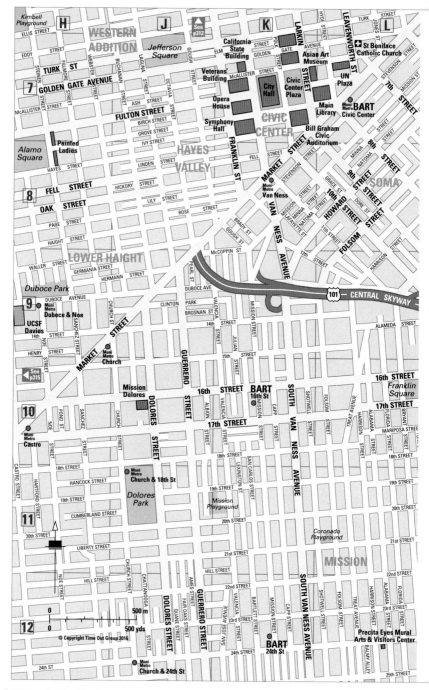

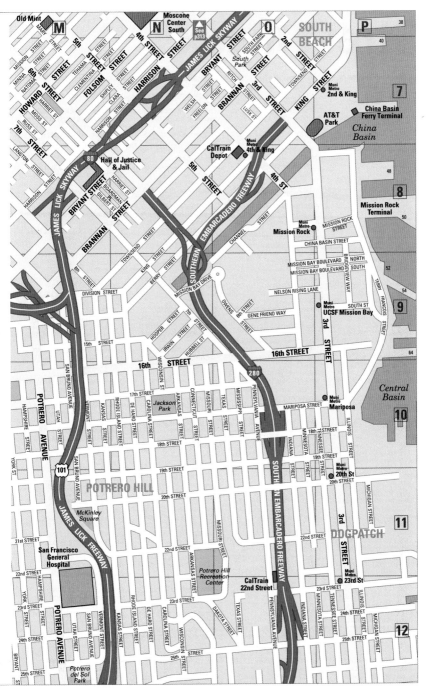

Street Index

STREET INDEX

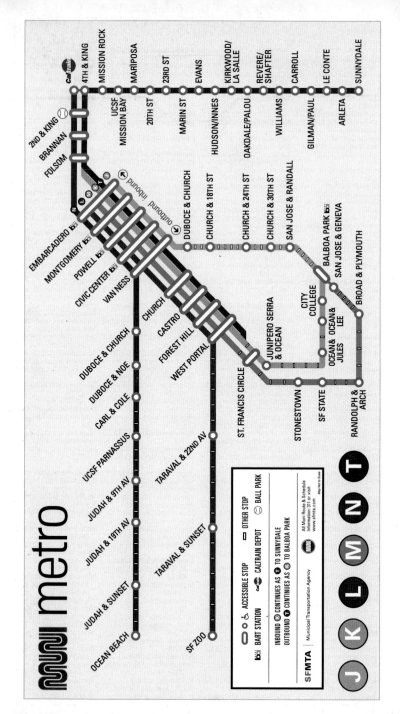